Inculturation

and

Healing

Coping-Healing in South African Christianity

Stuart C. Bate O.M.I.

Cluster Publications
1995

This is a book in the Monograph Series of Cluster Publications.

ISBN 1-875053-01-8

First published in 1995.

Published by Cluster Publications
P.O. Box 2400
Pietermaritzburg
3200
Republic of South Africa

Contents

ABBREVIATIONS

AG	*Ad Gentes Divinitus* (Decree on the Church's Missionary Activity. Vatican II)
AIC	African Independent church.
ANC	African National Congress
CCL	Code of Canon Law.
CD	*Christus Dominus* (Decree on the Pastoral Office of Bishops in the Church (Vatican II)
CT	*Catechesi Tradendae* (Apostolic Exhortation of Pope John Paul II, October 16 1979.
EN	*Evangelii Nuntiandi* (Apostolic Exhortation of Pope Paul VI, December 8 1975).
ETSA	"Evangelisation Today in South Africa" Report to the SACBC 1976.
GS	*Gaudium et Spes* (Pastoral Constitution on the Church in the Modern World. Vatican II).
ICT	Institute of Contextual Theology
JB	Jerusalem Bible
Lausanne	The Lausanne Covenant (Statement of the International Congress on World Evangelization meeting in Lausanne, Switzerland 1974)
Lima	World Council of Churches statement on "Baptism, Eucharist and Ministry" adopted in 1982
Lineamenta	Synod of Bishops: Special Assembly for Africa, *Lineamenta.* Vatican City 1990.
LG	*Lumen Gentium* (Dogmatic Constitution on the Church. Vatican II)
NGK	*Nederduitse Gereformeerde Kerk* (Dutch Reformed Church).
PG	*Patrologia Graeca* (J.P. Migne)
PL	*Patrologia Latina* (J.P. Migne)
RM	*Redemptoris Missio.* Encyclical Letter of Pope John Paul II, December 7 1990.

RSV	Revised Standard Version
SA	*Slavorum Apostoli.* Encyclical Letter of Pope John Paul II, 2 June 1985.
SACBC	Southern African Catholic Bishops Conference.
SACC	South African Council of Churches.
SC	*Sources Chrétiennes*
WARC	World Assembly of Reformed Churches.
WCC	World Council of Churches.
UR	*Unitatis Redintegratio* (Decree on Ecumenism. Vatican II).

Acknowledgements

The work of producing a book is actually a communal affair even when the name of one person only may appear as the author. This work is no different. There are many people to thank for their contributions. To my parents I say, thanks for your patience and your efforts to understand a son who turned out very different to your expectations. During the time of the preparation of this work I have been a member of St. Joseph's Oblate Scholasticate community at Cedara in Natal. To the Superior Fr. Michael Foley and to all my brothers there I say thanks for your encouragement, support and prayers during these three years. Thanks also to all the people who participated with patience in the interviews, discussions and healing services attended during this time. The help of Fr. Zaba Mbanjwa in the interview with "Mrs T" is particularly appreciated.

This book is based upon a doctoral dissertation submitted to the University of South Africa. It has been a pleasure to work with Prof. Willem Saayman whose availability, support and friendship kept me going when it all seemed too much. For all his work in typing the many drafts and redrafts, thanks also to Michael Ndlovu.

This book is published with the aid of the Institute of Missiology Missio. I wish to thank the Institute for their generous help and assistance in making the publication possible.

In first and last place, though I give thanks to God for my vocation and for the paths of healing along which he has led me.

Cedara, March 1995.

PART I

INTRODUCING THE PHENOMENON

Chapter 1

Method in Contextual Missiology

1.1 The Healing Ministry

Between 1980 and 1990 in South Africa, the number of Christians belonging to mainline churches such as Anglican, Methodist, Catholic and Dutch Reformed Church declined by 25 percent from 12.1 million to 9.1 million.[1] During the same period the number of Christians belonging to those churches offering religious and faith healing increased by 23% from 5.6 million to 6.9 million. These figures come from the census of 1980 and that of 1990 and whilst they need more careful interpretation than given here, they do reflect a major change in the nature of South African Christianity. Clearly there has been a phenomenal growth in the number of churches and organisations which offer a "healing ministry" to people in South Africa and this growth is found amongst all the various cultural groupings which make up the country. In fact, the growth of the Coping-healing churches is probably one of the most visible phenomena in South African Christianity today (Bate 1991:57-58).

It is also a controversial ministry. Claim and counter claim regarding the nature of the "healing" which goes on in the "healing ministry" has led to a polarisation amongst Christians. On the one hand, many people genuinely claim to have been healed through this ministry. Many conversions to Christ have also occurred. On the other hand, some people claim they have been hurt by the traumatic experiences they have undergone - especially when there was no healing. Some committed Christians consider the whole process of faith healing to be emotional and psychological manipulation and a money making racket. This is especially seen to be the case in the "healing churches" which have emerged recently.

In looking at this phenomenon we hope to throw some light on this controversy and to find a way of resolving some of the conflict. In order to facilitate this process we will refer to the phenomenon as the "Coping-healing phenomenon" by which we mean all that is involved in healing through prayer, faith and other "spiritual" means. The churches which centre themselves on this ministry we will refer to as "Coping-healing churches". The addition of the word "coping" renders the topic more neutral since finding ways and means of coping with reality may be experienced subjectively as healing but may not necessarily be that. Adopting this terminology allows us to centre our enquiry around the question: "to what extent is the Coping-healing phenomenon a manifestation of the Church's healing ministry?"

Prescinding from the fact that a similar trend is noticeable elsewhere in the world, the question arises as to why this ministry should have such a general and obvious appeal in South Africa? The analysis of this question forms another dimension of the content of this study.

1.2 Inculturation

The questions we have posed are theological questions. They call us to develop an adequate theological response. Such a response may be made in terms of understanding and articulating the nature and scope of the Church's mission in this situation. We contend that the inculturation model offers the best way of developing such an understanding and of creating a meaningful articulation of mission.

The term inculturation has not been widely used in South Africa. Here, theologians have preferred to speak of the contextualisation of the gospel or of contextual theology.[2] However, at this point in our history, it seems that the theological key of inculturation has an important contribution to make to the South African discourse. Three reasons can be given for this assertion. Firstly, inculturation leads to a reappropriation of culture in the South African context. Secondly, it tackles the issue of unity and plurality within the Church[3] which is so essential in an ecclesial reality which comprises so many separate churches. Finally it situates the contextual manifestations within a historical framework thus opening them to the future.

As the disaster of fragmentation and separation, which was the apartheid policy, begins to crumble and it slowly dawns on South Africans that they share a common land, a common nation and a common heritage, the reappropriation of culture becomes of major importance. The term "culture" was abused by the apartheid ideologues who constructed the myth of separate nations with separate cultures in separate areas who nevertheless had to participate in a single socio-economic and socio-political entity as though culture was somehow divorced from these latter two fundamental realities (De Haas 1989:1,5).

South African anthropologists have shown that much of the fixing of the so-called cultural identity of the various so-called "National Groups": Zulu, Xhosa, Sotho, Venda and so on was a reality imposed by the pre-apartheid colonial administration rather than a reflection of the actual state of the cultural reality of the black people of sub-saharan Africa (De Haas 1989:2). Such a fixing was done in terms of an understanding of culture as *ethnos*, an understanding originating in the "Romantic School" of German philosophy. *Ethnos* refers to a type of shared bio-genetic identity and culture within this framework becomes an innate feature of a particular group who share blood relations: an ethnic group (:5; cf. *infra* 9.3.1).

This understanding of culture is not accepted by anthropologists today yet it continues to inform the self understanding of the majority of the population both Black and White. The reality of culture is, however, so important in the lives of people that an adequate understanding of it is essential. Consequently, the reappropriation of this notion is now imperative. In our South African context, this is particularly so since the more commonly accepted notion of culture as historically transmitted shared patterns of understanding, provides a means whereby South Africans can be united through culture rather than being divided by it (cf. Geertz 1973:89). We hope to show that the reappropriation of culture in the South African context leads to the fact that a common culture is already existent and indeed still emerging. How this process is occurring will be the topic of chapter nine of this work.

A recognition of the emergence of cultural unity will do much to help both in grounding the growth towards unity between the churches as well as in the emergence of unity within the fragmented groupings of people which make up the one community of faith.[4]

Unity and Plurality

The aim of contextual theology is to attempt to abstract a horizon[5] of understanding within a horizon of a common experience of faith shared by a community of faith in order to articulate the presence of God within the experience. It is within the horizon of understanding that the Spirit's guiding principle, which is calling that people onwards in its journey towards the Kingdom of God, is discerned. Thereby, the community is empowered to praxis. From this we can see that contextual theology is called also to transcend its horizon, for its experience can only be rendered intelligible (the epistemological moment) and its journey in faith rendered coherent (the praxis) when the context and the text are understood in terms of the One Spirit who calls all (Rom 12; 1 Cor 12) and the One God who is called to be all in all (1 Cor 15) as well as the one People of God to which all contexts and groups belong (cf. Eph 4,4-5).

South African theology often suffers from a weakness in this regard. The experience of faith in this country has been one of division and fragmentation. There are some five thousand separate Christian churches (Villa-Vicencio 1988:31), more than anywhere else in the world. The great Protestant missionary endeavour in South Africa with its emphasis on faith, the Scripture and the personal experience of God's presence, as well as the prophetic witness of faith has sowed a depth of faith in the country which has resulted in many people, both Black and White, being practising Christians and the influence of the Church in society being relatively high. This religiosity actually forms part of the common culture which exists or which is emerging within the country.

However, the great weakness of this movement has been the lack of focus on a lived unity amongst all: a manifestation of the one Church of Christ in the lived experience of people. And further, the need that this manifestation be articulated in structures of community rather than just acknowledged as a transcendental virtue or metaphysical reality which is incomplete on earth. This weakness has been recognised in other parts of the world and has led Richard John Neuhaus (1987:285) to speak of a "Catholic Moment" which is emerging in world Christianity and which requires a "renewed demonstration of unity in diversity".

This situation is exacerbated in South Africa where fragmentation within the Church has been reinforced by the predominating "values" of separation and division which form part of South African cultural understandings. The rediscovery of the universal and transcendental dimensions of contextual theology does not imply a return to a search for universal theological norms and absolutes which can be implemented in each and every context. Rather it is the rediscovery of the essential solidarity of all peoples with God's people understood as the Church (LG 9) since all are in the end God's people created and redeemed by Him. In this way the community of faith is called to reflect the essential solidarity of the whole human race. Now the concept of inculturation has, from the outset, been concerned with this issue since the question of the unity of faith in a plurality of expression is central to recent Catholic thinking.[6] Consequently, it is suggested that the reflection already done in this field can make a contribution to the missiological discourse in this country.

Affirming Theology as History

Bernard Lonergan (1971:178) has shown that the particular object of history is to reflect on the plethora of meanings and understandings present in a time in order to grasp "what was going forward in particular groups and at particular places and times" and in this way, to determine "how God disposed the matter . . . through particular human agents". This vision of the presence of God's Spirit inspiring, leading, calling and empowering people throughout history as he leads his people on their journey to the promised land, is central to an adequate understanding of the nature of the Church (cf. Küng 1967:5).

We have indicated elsewhere (Bate 1991:97) that the inculturation model, especially as developed by Arij Roest Crollius, lends itself more easily to the interpretation of phenomena through history than does the contextualisation model. This results from the predominantly static nature of the root concepts of text and context. By contrast, the concept of culture on which the inculturation model is based, is historical by its very definition (Roest Crollius 1986a:53,58). Inculturation as a theological model can thus help in the reappropriation of the history and tradition of the community of faith in South Africa. This is an important point since there is a tendency today to wish to make a radical break with the past as we now move on to the "New South Africa". We hope to show that such a radical break is paradoxically only possible as we reappropriate the history and tradition of the country. Facile assertions that "apartheid is dead" and we must "forget the past" need to be exposed as false and impossible since they deny the reality of what it means to be a human community. The reappropriation of our history and tradition in terms of the gospel and our faith as well as a confession of sin, guilt and reparation are a necessary part of the journey we are called to travel. A journey which is as historical as we are historical.

1.3 Inculturation and The Healing Ministry

From the ouset we assert that the healing ministry in the Church - as indeed similar healing movements outside it - can be best understood by means of a cultural analysis of the South African context. We hope to show that a correct cultural analysis of this context will reveal that there exists - albeit in an embryonic and fragmentary way - a common South African culture which transcends the various ethnic cultural groupings and understandings which are currently understood as making up the South African society. However, part of this culture is rooted in human understandings based on human and Christian "disvalues" rather than on human and Christian values. This means that although one can perceive a type of common South African culture much of it is also a sick culture. Consequently it is in need of healing and healing becomes the major mode through which South African society and culture can become human. The Coping-healing phenomenon is providing a response to the manifestation of these needs.

This is reflected in a particular way within the community of faith: the Church. A local Church emerges within a particular community sharing a common culture so that the people within the culture are evangelised and live their faith within the cultural understandings. The model of inculturation attempts to explain how this process occurs. It is only such an inculturated local Church which can challenge the deficiencies of the culture so that it may be a transforming influence within that culture. This transformation role can be understood in terms of the healing of the culture which the local Church is called to evangelise "to the roots" (EN 20). Consequently, the process of inculturation actually becomes a process of healing or rather the healing ministry should become the major manifestation of the inculturation process.

1.4 Inculturation as Theological Key

An analysis of culture as the key to understanding the sickness-healing process leads naturally to the appropriation of inculturation as theological key for the interpretation of the phenomenon. In presenting our own understanding of inculturation, we will base ourselves on the early work of Roest Crollius (1978) since we believe that this model can more easily speak to African experience and understanding.[7] Of particular importance is the third stage of Roest Crollius's model which he calls the "transformation stage". In this stage, the local Church has a "more active role in transforming this culture" (:733). The culture becomes a challenge to the local community of faith since from within the horizon of the culture it becomes aware of those aspects of the culture which do not correspond with the gospel. Its identity as community of faith within that culture then calls it to strive for the transformation of those non-Christian elements.

1.5 Methodological Presuppositions

This work is an exercise in "contextual theology". By contextual theology, we mean the attempt to reflect upon the experience of faith which is lived in a particular context (see n.2). We take as our starting point for the understanding of theology the definition of St. Anselm: "*fides quaerens intellectum*" (cur Deus Homo 1.II, c.11). It is faith which is searching for understanding and in particular, the lived experience of that faith within the community. To say that the community's experience is necessarily lived within a particular context is seemingly to state the obvious. But this reality has been frequently overlooked as being essential to the analysis of faith. Similarly, that the experience of faith is essentially a communitarian one, seems also to be a statement of the obvious. Nevertheless it does need to be stressed that contextual theology is by its very nature communitarian and that a work such as our own here can only represent the crystallisation of an experience of faith lived in community. By situating this work on inculturation within a methodology of contextual theology understood in the way we have outlined, we intend to widen the concept of "context" to include the type of cultural analysis we wish to do. We have already noted earlier, that the value of inculturation is that it deals with the question of history and lived community as local Church in a way that contextual theology has not adequately done in South Africa.[8]

The Understanding of Church

The question of the communitarian dimension of the experience of faith and of contextual theology leads directly to the question of Church. Jesus founded only one Church (Mt 16:18) and the credal confession of belief in One, Holy, Catholic and Apostolic Church is common to many Christian denominations.

The South African reality of over five thousand separate churches stands in stark contrast to the will of Jesus (Jn 17:21) and to a correct understanding of the notion of the Church (cf. LG 8; WCC 1991:84). This fragmentation seems to be a reflection of the praxis of separateness which forms part of the fibre of the country, rather than of the will of God. There seems to have been an overemphasis on the diversity of the gifts of the Spirit at the expense of the reality of the Oneness of the source of those gifts (cf. 1 Cor 12). We will hope to show how the struggle to respond to this fragmentation forms part of the healing process of inculturation which is being called for at this time. However, before that, we feel that it is necessary at the outset to adopt an understanding of Church that will promote this process. Accordingly, we take as our point of departure the understanding of the Church as the "community of faith". By this we mean "all who have been justified by faith in baptism [and who] are [thus] incorporated into Christ . . . [and who] therefore have a right to be called Christian" (UR 3). It is the communal articulation of this faith which manifests the Church and thus the Church is manifest as the community of faith (cf. LG 8). In South Africa, the various communities have been isolated as a result of historical divisions and the ideological conditioning of saparatedness. But today we see a new movement towards a coming together in commonality of purpose. This, too, is a manifestation of being Church. By this we mean the emergence of a family of churches which are slowly coming to see their interdependence as a process of mutual openness occurs.[9]

The Guiding Anthropology

At the centre of culture, as of the Church, as indeed of the enterprise of theology, stand human persons. Consequently it is necessary to elucidate the vision of humanity which can inform our understanding of these three realities. Our anthropology is clearly a Christian one which views the human person as the object of God's love who, after the creation, "saw all that he had made and indeed it was very good" (Gn 1,30). This is the same humanity which God so loved "that he gave his only Son so that whoever believes in him should not perish but have eternal life" (Jn. 3,16). This optimistic anthropology reflects the understanding as outlined in *Gaudium et Spes* (12-39). Humankind is fundamentally good since the human person is created in God's image (GS 12). This image is not destroyed by sin but distorted so that the current existential situation within humankind is one of division within and between human beings (GS 13). It is the healing of this division and the restoration of the fullness of creation that the incarnation, life, suffering, death and resurrection of Jesus achieves, so that new life is available even now to those who are justified by faith and live in the Spirit. This presents us with an eminently positive view of the human person redeemed in Christ and called to be fully alive without denying the reality of evil and sin and the daily struggle against them.

We hold a vision which affirms the locus of human life as the world and the project of God as the restoration of God's Kingdom within the world. Human persons are Being-in-the-world and Being-with-others-in-the-world. Each person becomes himself or herself through the process of self realisation in the world together with others. This process of co-creation is what is meant by culture and is at the root of our affirmation that people are cultural beings. In this world, human persons are called to be oriented towards the goal of salvation understood as the coming of God's Kingdom. It is a goal which is not reached in isolation but, rather,in participation with God who becomes human in order to provide a way of life which is Being-together-with-God (cf. Roest Crollius 1980:258-266).

The Kingdom is not yet fulfilled but it is manifest to the extent that the community of faith witnesses its faith and lives out the truth of that witness. To the extent that Christ is present, incarnate, crucified and resurrected in the world and in history, the Kingdom is present amongst us (Fuellenbach 1987:71-5). This is human persons fully alive and if there is an emphasis we make in our anthropology it can be summed up in the famous quote of St. Irenaeus "gloria enim Dei vivens homo" (Adv. Her. Lib. 4, 20, 7; SC 100, 648). It is the community of human persons fully alive who participate in God's Kingdom even today and evangelisation and mission imply the witness and proclamation of this truth (EN 33-35).

1.6 The Theological Method

The mission of the Church is rooted in God's mission for the salvation of his people and flows from the "fountain-like love" of God the Father (AG 2). The identification and expression of the Church's mission in a particular context always reveals itself as a dialectic which begins from the concrete situation in which the Church finds itself and which moves through its attempts to orientate that situation in terms of the vision or "*telos*" of the Kingdom, and by means of the construction of a channel through which the love of God can flow. Theological method which serves mission has to reflect this process and this is why we use a method which begins from the experience or current praxis of the community of faith and returns to this praxis in order to propose the next step forward. Many theologians are using such a method in one form or another and its use has formed one of the hallmarks of Catholic theology since Vatican II. The roots of this method clearly go back further than that, though, and Gutierrez (1973:6) has pointed out how Augustine's City of God is " based on a true analysis of the signs of the times and the demands with which they challenge the Christian community". Nevertheless in the twentieth century this method has re-emerged at centre stage in Catholic theology primarily due to Joseph Cardijn and his YCW movement who introduced it as "See, Judge, Act" in the early 1930's (Cardijn 1955:83,86-87).

We will focus on the work of three theologians in developing our own methodology: Clodovis Boff, Bernard Lonergan and Jesús Andrés Vela. All three theologians follow the basic dynamic of developing a method in theology which runs from life back to life. However each of them provide insights which help us to understand different dimensions of the process. Lonergan's (1971:7,9) well known "transcendental method" emphasises the importance of intentionality in theological method. Here we are particularly concerned with the process from perception, through intelligibility and reason to responsibility. These four operations with their differing intentionalities will form the basis of our own analysis of the Coping-healing phenomenon in the Church and Lonergan's theological approach also provides the basis of our own method in this work. Boff's (1987) investigation into the epistemological foundations of liberation theology also provides us with a theoretical framework within which we can develop our own methodology. His emphasis is on a theology of liberation as a "political theology". The notion of politics amongst many liberation theologians, including Boff, is often misinterpreted. The point is that this theology is concerned with the transformation of the world in accordance with God's will. "The hermeneutics of the Kingdom of God", observed Schillebeeckx, "consist in making the world a better place" (in Gutierrez 1973:13). Politics is the name that is given to this process. So Boff's (1987:xxv) theology is a "theology of the political". This point is important as we will go on to show that the inculturation process which is occurring now in South Africa and of which the Coping-healing phenomenon is a major manifestation, forms part of the political process of transformation to which the country is being called. This political process can be understood theologically as a praxis in which Christians are involved. Having said this, we also wish to affirm that Boff's (1987:xvi) aim is in fact to determine the correct understanding of theology in the liberation process so that it is not reduced to mere political, social and cultural activity.

For Boff (1987:xxi), praxis is the locus of theology, the place where theology takes place. It is theology's "point of departure, its milieu and its finality". Praxis refers to the "*complexus of practices* orientated to the transformation of society, the making of history" (:6). It is within this *complexus* that we find the practices of the community of faith in the Coping-healing phenomenon. The analysis of these practices provides the material theoretical "object" for our reflection. This reflection leads to a process of discernment understood as a hermeneutic mediation searching for truth and value which relates to that context. The process of discernment leads to the next step in the praxis: a practical mediation of faith (cf. Boff 1987:xxiv-xxv). It is through the action in context: the praxis, that a new set of circumstances emerges: a new context, which forms the basis for the subsequent socio-analytic mediation. Gustavo Gutierrez (1973:8), in his classic work, has the same process in mind when he refers to "*the very life of the Church* as a *locus theologicus*". In emphasising this point he notes that the "pastoral activity of the Church does not flow as a conclusion from theological premises. Theology does not produce pastoral activity; rather it reflects upon it" (:11).

Vela (1984:142) provides insights regarding how the pastoral action of the Church forms the locus of theological process. He notes that the task of "pastoral theology" is not merely to apply the conclusions of dogmatic theology to particular situations but rather to develop a theology which leads to pastoral action based on a theological reflection rooted in a "situated praxis" [*praxis "situada"*] (:141). Otherwise, theology runs the risk of becoming ideology. The reality of the context must be understood by adopting the epistemology and methodology of the human sciences in order to develop a "scientific understanding" [*realidad conocida "cientificamente"*] (:146) of the social reality. Both the social and cultural dimensions of the reality must be taken into account since both factors affect the reality of the situation.[10] In our own work we take the notion of mediating a phenomenon through the epistemological lens of the human sciences one step further. A major portion of this work will be the attempt to understand the Coping-healing phenomenon from the perspective of several epistemological lenses including philosophy and theology.

We have dwelt on this point at some length since it indicates a methodology which we consider essential in any contextual missiology. It is a methodology which takes the context seriously by attempting to use human wisdom as expressed in the human sciences in the attempt to understand a phenomenon. In this way the theological reflection is less open to the ideologising referred to by Vela.

1.7 The Importance of a Phenomenological Approach

Any study needs to clarify at the outset what its object will be. This question turns out to be more complex than would appear at first sight and Boff (1987) devotes the first four chapters of his book to clarifying some of the issues involved. He is at great pains to indicate the ideological parameters which surround the identification of this object and his comments regarding the empirical method are particularly important in this regard (:20-24). In our study of the Coping-healing phenomenon in the Church we will not adopt a so-called empirical method using questionnaires, interviews and so on. The usefulness of such an approach is not denied but it is precisely because this method is often given more credit for "objectivity" and "truth" than it perhaps deserves that we wish to use another approach. We opt for a phenomenological approach which considers a phenomenon as it manifests itself and as it is received and interpreted by an active subject.

The value of the phenomenological approach is seen in its willingness to take into account the two dimensions of subject and object without lapsing into an introspective subjectivism or the illusion of positivist empirical objectivity (Spiegelberg 1982:687-690). Both subject and phenomenon are somehow influenced by their own context both diachronically and synchronically. Consequently the object of the study is already mediated as it is manifested. This does not mean that phenomena and their meaning are reduced to mere subjectivistic interpretation for the phenomenological approach has its own methodology.[11] In adopting this approach we will consider the Coping-healing phenomenon in South Africa as it is appearing and manifesting itself to the community of faith here and as it is being received by someone who is a White Priest rooted in the Roman Catholic Church and the South African context.

1.8 The Analysis of the Phenomenon

The analysis of the Coping-healing phenomenon in South Africa will first concentrate on rendering intelligible the diverse phenomena which make it up. Here the search is for understanding and this step leads to what Lonergan (1971:9) calls the "intellectual level on which we inquire, come to understand, express what we have understood". Here, we are trying to discover what the phenomenon really is or as Boff (1987:xxv) has it, determine the material theoretical object of our study. This study of the Coping-healing phenomenon, articulated in the Coping-healing practices of Christians, will be achieved by a series of theoretical mediations. In this way we wish to observe the phenomena through a series of analytical spectacles, as it were, in order to see it from different points of view and widen our understanding of it.

In this section of the study, which comprises part II of this work, we will filter the phenomenon through the lenses of medicine, psychology, anthropology, sociology, philosophy and theology. In this step, we will be trying to understand how these disciplines have examined and interpreted the phenomenon.

Following Lonergan, we move from the "intellectual level", with its intentionality of intelligibility in the search for understanding, to the "rational level" where we are concerned to pass judgement on the truth or falsity of our intelligible understandings. Thenceforth we go on to consider the "responsible level" where our search will be for the "good" in terms of faith values, thus indicating the direction for action. Lonergan (1971:235) refers to the "dialectic functional speciality" in which the aim is to resolve the conflicts which emerge from the various interpretations which have been proposed. Clearly the resolution which occurs will depend on the standpoint of the one making the judgement and in particular on the religious values which determine that standpoint.[12] These two tasks will be our concern in part III where after presenting a phenomenological description of the Coping-healing phenomenon based on the results of our epistemological mediations, we will go on to develop a theological model which can respond to what we have discovered. We will see how the concept of culture is central to this theological model and in chapter nine we will attempt to reappropriate the concept of culture in a way that can inform theological models in South Africa. The theological model we will develop based on a reappropriated understanding of culture is the inculturation model and in developing it we hope to show how this model is a powerful missiological tool in indicating the direction the Church's mission should take in responding to boundary phenomena occurring in the area between the Church and the world. The notion of paradigm shifts in theology will also be important in this section.[13]

From this we hope to be able to propose our main conclusion which says that in the South African context at present, inculturation is largely concerned with healing and that the Coping-healing phenomenon is the strongest sign of this truth. By this we mean that "Inculturation" and "Healing" are linked copulatively through the two terms common to them both: "culture" and "mission". Our final chapter will briefly summarise the main conclusions.

Should our schema seem too logical and systematic, it is necessary at this point to acknowledge Boff's (1987:214) comments regarding the "ongoing dynamic character of the relationship between theory and praxis". Whilst a work such as this can only be done in a theoretical key (:209) this does not imply the prioritisation of ideas and theories which then have to be put into practice. The two are in dialectical relationship - Boff's "major key" (:209) - and it is the "mutual overlap that provides the possibility of both a theory of praxis and a praxis of theory" (:211). Thus we acknowledge, throughout this work, the way in which the pastoral practices we consider, the Coping-healing ministry in South Africa, as well as the history, tradition and experience of the author, a Roman Catholic priest with eight years pastoral experience in a semi-rural Natal setting in both English speaking and Zulu speaking contexts, inform the theoretical part of this work.

By the same token, we acknowledge the validity of our intention which is to make a logical and rigorous analysis leading to objective transcendental judgments concerning the nature of this praxis and leading to fields and projects for action. The ability of the community of faith to reflect in this way and of its theologians to intuit, focus and express this reflection is explicitly affirmed.

Chapter 2

The Coping-Healing Ministry in South Africa

2.1 Introduction

In the fields of missiology, practical theology and pastoral theology, one is always concerned with what is going on along the boundary where the life of the "community of faith" encounters the presence of the Holy Spirit sent to guide it on the next step of the journey in the world. That is why approaches to these disciplines which focus on either a "scientific" understanding of social reality or the application of conclusions of dogmatic theology are usually limited (cf. Vela 1984:141,144). Both approaches tend to become highly theoretical and run the risk of being easily "ideologized".

Jesus Andrés Vela (1984:146) has shown that the starting point for pastoral theological reflection is the pastoral action of the Christian community. Only by focusing on the life of the community as it manifests itself in its action and by controlling our reflection by frequent recourse back to that action to test the reflections, can we hope to provide a theology which will help the community move into the future along the way that the Spirit is guiding it. This movement is, by definition, the mission of that community and thus this type of theology is a missiology.

The pastoral action we concern ourselves with here is the Coping-healing ministry of the Church as it is manifesting itself in South Africa at this time. The task of this chapter will be to present this phenomenon as it manifests itself to us: a phenomenological investigation of the Coping-healing ministry. The phenomenon will be investigated from two perspectives: firstly we will look at those involved in this ministry to see what they are doing and secondly, we will attempt to listen to them in order to hear what they say they are doing when they are healing and what they say happens when they are healed. By "those involved in this ministry" we understand both the ministers as well as those receiving healing. We will attempt to see and hear both groups. Thus our first task will be to present the Coping-healing phenomenon as it has been witnessed both by ourselves as well as by other researchers in this field. After that, we hope to undertake a preliminary ordering of this ministry in terms of what those people involved experience as happening when the ministry is exercised.

We will concentrate on the so-called "Coping-healing churches". By this we mean those churches which have emerged recently and which emphasise the healing ministry as one of the major dimensions of their total ministry. However, at the end of the chapter we will also present some experiences of how the phenomenon is growing in some of the larger "mainline" churches.[1]

2.2 What Others Say: Coping-Healing as Observed by Researchers

In this section we wish to describe a variety of experiences of the Coping-healing ministry as they have been observed by researchers who were present. We have divided these experiences into two major groupings: "healing services" in the various churches, and the healing ministry as an interpersonal encounter between healer and patient usually in some form of consultation. In general we begin with our own experiences and observations and this will be followed by examples from the extant literature on the subject. Generally, we have limited the research to the Natal region and in particular the Durban/Pietermaritzburg axis. But other research has been included when it appears to fill a lacuna and if it is judged to fairly represent what is also happening in this region.

2.2.1 Services in the "Coping-Healing Churches"

The major form of exposure that most people have to some form of healing ministry is when they attend a "healing service". Some churches have "healing" as part of every service whereas others have special "healing services" from time to time. Special services such as at the beachfront and in "Tent Crusades" also only occur from time to time.

A Typical Zionist Healing Service

Experience of several Zionist "healing services" has shown us that whilst there are certain commonalities within these services, there is also quite a lot of leeway for the various healers to "improvise" depending on the "spirit of the moment". The all night service tends to follow a particular structural pattern which is not rigidly adhered to depending on the "work" to be done. Kiernan (1990:76) has describes this pattern as:

1) Introductory greeting and explanation of the work to be done. Welcoming of people, especially visitors.
2) Prayer
3) Preaching
4) Healing

The service described here followed this pattern. It took place in the Inanda area of Durban in June 1991. About twenty five people were gathered in a largish rectangular building (approx. 6x4 meters) on the homestead *(umuzi)* of the minister of the church. Since 9.30 p.m. there has been singing interspersed with some spontaneous prayers by the people present. At about 10.30 p.m. as we arrive, the service is officially opened by the greetings and welcoming of guests. It is a Saturday night.

The minister *(umfundisi)* leads the service but the bishop of this particular circuit of the church is also present and enters into the service now and then to take charge of a prayer or to read a text and preach on it. It seems that this is the regular place of worship of this bishop when he is not visiting other churches on his circuit, even though this is not his place but the home and church of the minister. Both are workers: the bishop is a factory worker and the minister is a truck driver. The younger man was ordained by this bishop but seems to be the richer of the two. So an interesting arrangement of control and power seems to have emerged to the satisfaction and harmony of all.

Inside the church building there is a wooden pillar situated more or less in the centre and holding up the roof centre beam. From time to time, the people dance around this in a procedure which seems to be determined by one of the "deacons" present who leads most of the singing and dancing of the group. At the one end of the church, opposite the door, is a small altar where the Bible is kept and candles are lit. The bishop, myself and two other men are seated on the left of this altar in conformity with Zulu tradition. The women are on the other side. Those with higher status are generally closer to the altar.

At around 2.30 a.m. the minister introduces the change of key which leads into the "healing service" when he rises to conclude the preaching/witnessing/singing cycle. As one of the songs comes to an end, he stands and raises his hands. The singing gradually stops and he asks for mats *(amacansi)* to be brought forward and laid before him. He explains to the people that we are now going to heal the sick. I was asked to be the one who would first "lay hands" on those who are sick. Almost immediately, a young woman comes forward and kneels on one of the mats. I go forward and lay hands upon her, praying for her in a soft voice that the Lord might heal her. By this time, several people have knelt down in a line and I move from one to the other laying on hands and praying. I am followed by the other ministers present, one of whom is a visitor like us, but from a nearby Zionist church. The bishop, however, remains seated and does not participate. Each of the other ministers lays hands and prays for the person but in loud voices calling on the evil spirits and demons to go from her. By this time I have sat down and as I watch I see that each minister is concentrating on a different sick person from the group which has come forward. This part of the service now becomes more animated as a one-to-one style of healing between minister (healer) and sick person begins to emerge. Prayers and commands to chase the demons and evil spirits away, now become more pronounced, louder, more emotional and develop an ejaculatory style. They are accompanied by a whole series of actions. Some people are spun around many times as a prelude to the healing process and there is a good deal of touching of the various parts of the body as well as slapping of the shoulders, back, arms and base of the head. Several ministers hold the hands or forearms of a person and pull them in a kind of extending exercise. I asked one of the ministers present what this was for and he said that this was a way of freeing the person from the "*imimoya emibi*" (evil spirits) which might still be present inside. This process, which he referred to as "*ukwelula amathambo*" (to stretch out the bones) of the person, was a way to help to free the evil spirit that might be trapped or hiding in the person by a kind of drawing it out.

The healing process was quite a long one and as it progressed it became quite chaotic with different healers healing different people. Some of the sick people moved from healer to healer and some healers moved from sick person to sick person. People (either healers or sick) would sit down if they felt they had had enough. The whole process was accompanied by singing and drumming which created a frenetic, charged atmosphere within the room. I was also influenced by this atmosphere and the prevailing experience was being assailed by so many stimuli that I felt totally involved in what was happening in that room as if nothing existed outside it. Gradually the number of people in the centre diminished as people sat down, and when the last healer had finished with the last person, this part of the service came to an end. There was no pressure from the minister in charge to cut the prayers short and we waited until everyone had finished. About ten people went through the healing process. The bishop took no part in it whilst the minister was involved for a while and then sat down. The visiting Zionist minister seemed to be the principal healer together with one of the deacons and two other women. The "healing" part of the service" lasted almost two hours.[2]

Coping-Healing in the "Miracle Tent Crusade"

The setting is a large tent set up in a field near the Durban beachfront. Advance publicity has exhorted people to "hear world travelled evangelists" and to "come believing . . . go receiving". Advertising pamphlets claim that "the deaf hear", that "wheelchairs are vacated in a mass prayer for healing", and that a young man who was only able to walk with crutches was "after prayer ... able to walk properly".[3] The service follows the normal ritual observed in many of these churches:

1) Singing and building up of enthusiasm.
2) Prayer and offering.
3) Scripture and Sermon.
4) "Altar call" to give your life to Jesus.[4]
5) "Healing service".

The sermon has been an exhortation for people to believe in the power of Jesus to heal and a call to give their lives to Him. It has condemned doctors, lawyers, academics and "rational people" who refuse to believe or who put their trust in reason. It has called the people to "expect a miracle in their life tonight" for Jesus says "Whatever you ask for in my name, I will do it." (cf. Jn 14, 13-14).[5]

After the sermon the preacher calls the people to come forward and give their lives to Jesus. Many do and he leads them through a confession of faith. Then, the people are asked to do one more thing. "We want to give you something to help you." They are asked to go into a side tent where counsellors are available to speak to them. They file off into the side tent and the congregation begins to sing led by the choir. After a few songs, when everyone has returned, the main minister, Fred Roberts, takes over the microphone. The "healing service" is about to start. He exhorts the people to "lose sight of sickness! lose sight of the person next to you! Focus yourself on Jesus! Worship Him!" As the music plays softly he continues:

- He's the saviour of my soul! He's the healer of my body!
- The Holy Spirit is here tonight to heal your body. To raise you from your wheelchair. To dispel your angina and arthritis;

  to heal those kidneys!
  to heal those lungs!
  to heal that angina!
  to heal that weak heart!
  to heal that stomach of yours!
  to set you free from that ulcer!
  to make you well!
  to heal you completely tonight!

- He's our healer divine! I want you to reach out in faith!

He continues:

- There's someone here tonight who has problems with their eyes. Your eyes are always running, matter is coming out; your sight is getting worse.
- There are people here tonight suffering from migraine headaches. Forgive the people you have things against. Just let forgiveness flow. Forgive those who have hurt you. That man who has gout in his foot, ask God to forgive you tonight. Forgive the person who has hurt you. Forgive in Jesus' name.
- Now lift your hands everyone. Let's thank the Lord for his healing power flowing here tonight.

He addresses the evil spirits:

- I take dominion of every sickness. Every demon of sickness, I rebuke you in the name of Jesus Christ!
- Every spirit of infirmity I command you to leave this tent!
- Spirits of infirmity I bind you!
- Spirits of crippling arthritis I bind you!
- Arthritis leave!
- You, migraine, go from the bodies that are suffering tonight!
- Migraine headaches go! Leave in the name of Jesus Christ!
- You spirits of wickedness, you spirits of evil oppression, you infirm devils causing people to be cripples, I charge you in the name of Jesus Christ, leave those bodies now!!

He speaks to the people:

- Raise your hands and let Him touch your body!
- As you sense God's healing power working on you just get out of your place and make your way down here quickly! Just get out of your place, throw down those crutches and begin to walk - quickly!
- The spirit of God is healing you. Make your way down here quickly.

The people come forward in large numbers. Some are supported by others holding them, comforting them and praying for them. At the front others have already fallen down: "slain in the Spirit" as they call it. The minister points to one of them in front of him and asks what is wrong with this lady. They tell him that she had a pain in the chest. "And is it gone?" he asks. "It is gone", they tell him. "Check out some of those people over there", he says, pointing to a group standing close by, "I think God has already touched them."

Now he invites all those in front of him to come up on the stage so that he can pray for them one by one. They line up and are brought to him one by one. Here is an example of one of the interchanges:

- What's wrong with you?
- Epilepsy.
- I believe tonight is the end of your epilepsy. Do you believe that?
- Yes
- Say after me "in the name of Jesus Christ I denounce you, devil, you foul devil. I command you to go from me".

She repeats this and he shouts:

- In the name of Jesus Christ go from her.

He pushes her on the forehead and she, surprised, falls back. She is caught by the assistants standing besides her. She gets up and the minister says:

- Anoint her head! Fill her in the Holy Ghost!

She starts to shake as he presses his hand on her head. She begins to utter sounds:

- Uhu, uhu, uhu uhu . . .!

He says:

- Just go ahead and speak with the language the Holy Spirit gives you.

She utters the same sounds louder and faster and then falls to the ground.

The next person describes her problem as pain all over. He says: "It is gone in Jesus' name!" and pushes her on the head. She just falls down. He moves onto the next one. People come with all kinds of problems: A child needing a kidney transplant; a woman with arthritis; a woman with blindness in one eye; a youth with a hearing loss in one ear; someone with gout; another with a back problem; another with epilepsy. Some claim to have been cured there and then. A woman claims she was blind in one eye and now she can see. But as she goes away she doesn't seem too excited about what should be a miracle in her life. Another is able to touch his toes whereas before he had back problems. A young teenager comes forward and says he was deaf in one ear and now "I can hear properly". Two badly crippled men are brought last of all. They are prayed for and left lying on the stage almost till the end of the proceedings. There has been no miracle for them. They are led away after their ordeal.

Healing and Purification at the Sea

The scene is Durban beachfront just before dawn. It is still dark and the sea is still undisturbed by early morning bathers and surfers. This is the time of the Zionist "baptism" ceremonies and as I arrive, a small group of worshippers is just concluding its morning ritual. They leave and I am alone for ten minutes or so before another group makes its way down the steep sand bank to the water's edge in front of me. There are around thirty of them: men and women as well as teenage boys and girls. Females outnumber males by about two to one. They remove their outer garments and put on the familiar Zionist uniforms. Each uniform is different yet the predominating colours of green, blue and white lend a superficial sameness to them all and identify this group as a Zionist group. One of the older women sits apart from the group, quite close to me, and one by one, a few of the younger women come close to her and kneel before her. They bring their problems, anxieties and sins to her and she offers advice and then she prays over them.

The group then assembles together and lights four candles which are placed in the sand in the form of a square (cf. Oosthuizen 1989b:182). These candles burn throughout the time the group is at the water's edge. They begin to sing and a drum beats. The song is quite chaotic and raggedly performed with only some people entering fully into it. The people face the sea but the leader faces them with his back to the sea. He prays asking a blessing on his group and the work they are about to do. Then he turns around and walks to the water's edge. He prays with outstretched hands over the water driving the spirits of the sea away and asking the Holy Spirit to come over the sea and sanctify it (as he later explained to me). He then enters the water until the waves are breaking over his waist. Now the people come to him one by one and he takes hold of them by the arms and pulls them into the water so that they lose their footing and go under the water. Then he begins to slap them on the back and arms which, he tells me, is to get rid of the evil spirits, and then again he pulls them into the water so that it covers them completely. They emerge coughing and spluttering from the water and as they come onto dry land they are staggering and disoriented. Many lie recovering at the water's edge. One woman lies close to where I am sitting, recuperating after the ordeal. All of a sudden she lets out a loud long wail and her body begins to writhe in the sand. Then she becomes quiet, lies there for a few more minutes and then gets up, removes her uniform and quietly begins to dress.

All of the people present go through the sea experience, which they called "baptising". Even the small children and babies, who screamed through the whole process, are taken into the water although the minister is very gentle and careful with them. Finally he takes the whole bundle of white sticks *(izikhali)* which have been tied together and stuck into the sand during this whole time. He washes the whole lot, together, in the sea. By now, some of the people have drifted off but as the minister emerges from the sea, he calls the group together to conclude the service. Firstly, they sing a song: "Amen, Alleluia", led by the drummer and he says a brief prayer. By now, everyone has changed into clean new clothes and they leave after their purification, healing and renewal ceremony.

A "Healing Service" in a Mainline Church

It is a Tuesday evening in one of the mainline churches in the Durban area. The parishioners have been informed that there will be a "healing service" and to bring the sick along. About seventy people have come along. The form of the service is simple: after an opening hymn, the guest minister greets the people and explains the purpose which is to pray for healing of the sick. After a brief ritualised confession of sin there is a prayer asking God to forgive the sins of those present and to bless the assembly. Two Bible readings follow: James 5:13-20 and the healing of the blind man in chapter nine of John's gospel. The congregation is predominantly White and in his homily the preacher emphasises the sickness which is brought on through the stress and anxiety of living in a changing society. He refers to the high rate of suicides, divorces, violence and killing in the country and the pain and suffering arising from problems such as alcoholism, gambling and broken families. After the sermon some perfumed oil is brought and prayed over. The minister invites all those who need healing to come forward to be anointed and have hands laid on them. Almost the whole congregation comes forward and several ministers anoint those present and lay hands on them praying silently over them. The people return to their seats and after a closing prayer and blessing, the service, which has lasted about one hour, concludes.

At the end of the service, the guest minister invites all those who have special problems, sicknesses and needs and who wish to be prayed for privately, to remain behind. About thirty people, almost half, do so. After the service he returns to the sanctuary area of the church and the people come to him one by one. They tell him of their problems worries and needs. The problems are many including drunkenness, wife beating, lost children, terminal cancer, and homosexuality. The minister listens to each one and says a prayer with the person sometimes holding their hands, sometimes with his hands on their shoulders or on their head as a blessing. Some are overcome and in tears. Most go away apparently with at least some release and feeling of joy.

2.2.2 "Healing Services" as Described in the Literature

The above services were ones at which I was present. However at this point it would seem necessary to present an indication of the way in which other researchers have observed this phenomenon. Because of the importance of letting the phenomenon manifest itself to us in accordance with the stated objectives of this chapter, wherever it is possible, we have tried to present the services, verbatim, as they are reported by these researchers rather than to synthesise and interpret their data.

Description of Zionist "healing services" can be found in the work of several authors. Sundkler's seminal work (1948, 1961) devotes the whole of chapter six to healing and in it he describes a daytime service in the "Christian Zion Sabbath Apostolic Church" (1961:183-187) in which the emphasis is on casting out demons and "prophesying" the source of the illness in terms of demon possession:

> Everything so far, however, has only been a preparation for the real business that follows, the *healing service*. The prophet announces: "The sick, come forward!" One man and eight women, three of them carrying children on their backs, move to the centre of the room. Enoch approaches the little group of patients, while the others walk in a procession round the healer and the patients, singing and shouting. The prophet shuts his eyes and begins to pray. He seizes one old woman by her arms and begins to shake her violently, beating her with his fists on arms and shoulders and shouting "Depart, thou demon (*phuma dimone*)!" He now "prophesies" to the patient: "You are possessed by a demon, like a snake which first entered your womb and then went into the stomach and then to the head causing a terrible headache." The old woman admits with an "Ehhe" (yes) that his prophetic diagnosis is correct in every detail. Enoch hands over the woman to the drummer who by feeling her with his hands all over her body apparently attempts to press the blessings of the Spirit into her being. Still another prayer-woman takes charge of the old patient, praying for her in the same drastic way as the prophet and the drummer. Enoch the while busies himself with the other patients, sometimes chiding them with his brass rod while crying: *"Phuma dimone!"*. [Sundkler 1961:186-187]

Berglund (1973:23-26) describes a "healing service" which occurred in 1969 in Northern Natal. In this service the sick woman is called "to speak the things that you carry in your heart" (:23).

> She begins by describing her illness. She has experienced sharp pains in her head, chest and shoulders, in the upper regions of her stomach and in her sides below the rib-bones. She proceeds to describe, with great emphasis and giving specific details, how she has been involved in a quarrel with a neighbour about goats which had trespassed into the neighbour's gardens. The dispute had grown and now involved considerable hatred and ill feelings. Her suspicion was that the neighbour was the cause of her physical ailments. She very clearly associated her personal ill health with the anger which had developed between her and her neighbour...she proceeded to relate her experience of loneliness and forlornness, describing how friends avoided her for fear of anger. With the decrease of association with friends and relatives went increase in her personal sufferings, both physical and mental. "So today I have come to this place of speaking out and salvation. I have come to be cleansed (lit. baptised) from all these evils. Yes, these are all the demons of which I have experience . . ."
>
> [Berglund 1973:23-24]

She is followed by four others and when the "confessions" are over the "prophet" rises and begins to

> chant and [starts] walking clockwise around the sick in a circle. He soon increases the tempo to a trot. The congregation members, one after the other, join him in running around them, each singing as loud as the voice would allow. The drummer beat his instrument both vigorously and with great feeling.
>
> [Berglund 1973:24]

Berglund goes on to describe with great colour how the liturgy becomes more and more emotional, dramatic and even violent as the sick woman is pummelled, stripped to the waist, slapped and shaken whilst the prophet screams at the demons to come out of her finally beating her "vigorously over the back" with his holy sticks stopping only when she stopped crying and became silent and seemingly unconscious. Then:

> when water . . . was poured over her and ash placed on some wounds on her back (caused by the prophet . . .) she sat up, drank a quantity of water . . . collected her clothing and sat down with her back against the hut. Perfectly relaxed and enveloped in an undescribable atmosphere of calm and peace, she reacted neither to the prophet's healing . . . of the remaining patients nor the congregation's participation.
>
> [Berglund 1973:26]

This experience of Berglund illustrates the degree of involvement, drama and actual physical and emotional energy which is expended in some Zionist "healing services".

Berglund's one time confrère at the Lutheran Theological College in Mapumulo, H.J. Becken (1972:217-218) describes a much calmer "healing service" which occurred in the church of Hezekiya Ndlovu at Mount Hlonga in northern Natal. Here the sick approach the healer who merely lays hands on them and prays a blessing over them sometimes touching the sick body part. A similarly calm service is described by Becken (1975) in a later article. In the healing part of this Sunday service at the "Nazareth Church", Babanango, northern Natal, the people "stand in a circle along the walls of the hut leaving a space open in the centre, where now the suffering people who desire intercession enter one by one" (Becken 1975:236). The congregation sings to drumbeat while the leader lays hands on them followed by four other healers who assist him. No miraculous healing is reported but the sick have brought their suffering before the Lord.

The Services described by Kiernan seem to fall between these two extremes. Kiernan (1990:93-102) describes, in a more general way, the process of what goes on in a Zionist "healing service".

Again there is a healing circle made up by "designated healers" who dance ("trot") around in a circle. The sick person steps into this circle and then:

> Individual healers step from the circle, place their hands on the patient's head or shoulders, or on the region affected, and pray vigorously and ecstatically over him or her (patients are predominantly female). Quite often, the touch of the hands is supplemented by pressure from the healer's staff laid on the afflicted part of the sick person. Whether hands or staff are employed, two distinct types of action are involved: forceful pressure and brushing off. [Kiernan 1990:95]

The healer's staff is also employed to touch the sick body part. The spontaneous and often wild singing and drumming make the noise "deafening". In this same service a divination occurs. Kiernan describes it as follows:

> A woman dressed as a Zionist approached "Mt," the leading prophet, during the healing session, and was conferring privately with him when one of the junior prophets began to loudly harangue her. He declared that she was very frightened and that she even had dreams at night. The same thing that caused the dreams was affecting her all over her body afflicting her with pain. The woman replied that it was an affair of the home. She had previously been living with her husband's people at Inchanga but she had since moved to another place in the same district and this was an uncultivated piece of ground. She cultivated this land and made something of it: the result was hatred towards her and gossip about her among her affines who wondered why she had not been as industrious while she lived with them. This causes her to be cursed (*thakathi'd*) and her body was afflicted. She still lived at Inchanga.
>
> At this point "Mt" interrupted to say "there is something belonging to you that is lost. I don't know what it is, but it is lost and you are worried." She replied that it was her Zionist headdress that was lost at her father's kraal. The junior prophet prescribed the cure; she must continue to attend the meeting for the sick or worse will befall her. Also near to her present residence at Inchanga there is a valley with a stream. She was to go there after fresh rains, draw water and boil it before drinking it.
> [Kiernan 1990:96-97]

Charles Williams (1982) in what seems to have been the most exhaustive and systematic study to date of healing in Zulu Zionism, participated in forty Zionist "healing services" in the greater Durban area during 1981. His description of the process in two of these services confirms the experience of other writers: the healing circle, drums, slapping and pummelling of those to be healed with cries of "*phuma demoni!*" (get out, demon!) and other ejaculatory prayers

(Williams 1982:138-141). The all night service is described in more detail. It seems to have three moments to it. In a first calm moment, there is laying on of hands and praying over the sick people. Three healers pray over each sick person in turn. Then the mood changes and becomes more emotionally charged.

> The first [healer], who is also the presiding minister at the service, puts his right hand on the left shoulder of his patient. As he does this he closes his eyes and looks away from the patient while holding his left hand on his hip. His posture and facial expression indicates that he is being communicated with and he appears to be listening to some inner voice. Then the healer bends over the patient, and, while cupping her neck in his hands, he shouts into her ear. It is impossible to hear what he shouts because two drums are being played simultaneously and the congregation has increased the intensity and tempo of its singing and dancing. The healer then slaps the patient very hard on her back; and he presses his palms against her chest. The patient appears to stumble and she veers away from the healer. The first healer is followed by two other healers who like him, wade through the gathered candidates for healing. Their healing styles are similar to his, and they seem, like him, to be guided by some inner voice or vision.
>
> Before the first healer had touched all of the patients, a marked change in the service is signalled by the manifestations of various congregants becoming possessed. The singing has increased and congregants, who at first walked slowly around the candidates now have begun to move much faster. The first healer, as though provoked by this change of tempo, slaps some candidates harder and harder, in doing so he also appears to veer out of control. As one woman sputters and jumps up and down, he spins her around. Later he explains that he did this to her so that a good spirit would get into her . . .
>
> As the momentum for the healing circle builds, prophets appear to be caught by the spirit. One prophet begins to jump and whistle in short staccato bursts. Others gyrate in their own orbits, within the circle of congregants that continues to move. This period of healing continues for well over an hour and seems to have only fatigue as a reason for ending.
>
> However, there is only a brief silence before several prophecies are uttered, some fast and furiously, as though they are the means of releasing pent-up feelings, but also seemingly to show that they come from a source that lies beyond the control of the healers.
>
> In his first prophecy the healer tells the woman that she is experiencing pain in her lower abdomen which he says signals future difficulty in bearing children; he also says that she is experiencing pains in her neck indicating that the ancestors are unhappy with her, and she should make a sacrifice (*ilhati*) [sic] using four white fowls and four white candles, and that she must get a white robe. The woman answers that she is thankful for the prophecy, and that some of the things which he has prophesied are true. Hearing this prophecy, one woman comes over and presses her hands against the lower part of the patient's abdomen.
>
> A man in the congregation, who is wearing a red robe with white stars and crescents stitched to it, is told that he is being attacked by evil spirits. The prophet tells him that he should go into the sea and be baptized. The reason for the attack is explained to the man as his failure to make a sacrifice (*ilhati*) [sic] to the ancestors. Because this has

> not been done, the red robe which he is wearing offers him no protection against evil spirits. The prophet tells the man that he must use Jeye's [sic] fluid and paraffin to throw away the evil that is keeping him from coming to church. If he doesn't do these things, the prophet says there's going to be a split in his family. The ancestors are also getting on his shoulders because they do not want him to get married and so he should do what they say.
>
> In response to this prophecy, the man says that what he has been told is true. He says that he feels confused. He says that others have told him that he is being bewitched, and he has dreamed about these things. The man ends by saying that he is going to buy things which the healer has told him to get.
>
> [Williams 1982:139-140]

In a most interesting article, G.C. Oosthuizen (1989b) has studied the "baptismal"/purification rites of Zionists on the Durban beachfront. Although his comparative style makes it difficult to isolate the phenomenon as such, a perusal of his work makes it possible to indicate the following events as being typical of these services:

(i) "The bishop or baptizer walks into the sea with outstretched arms . . . He (or she) challenges the demons, monsters and evil spirits of the sea" (Oosthuizen 1989b:146).

(ii) The group often dances in a circle and people are often spun around before baptism (:146;175).

(iii) There is normally fasting before the baptism (:148). The leaders often fast for up to five days, those being baptised for a shorter time like three days (:165).

(iv) A three fold immersion of new members with a trinitarian formula has been reported. (:165)

(v) Burning candles are used, one for each person to be baptised/purified, and these are placed in a circle on the beach before the baptism (:173). These candles, when they are coloured, often represent ancestral spirits (:182).

(vi) The reasons people go for baptism/purification include:

- washing away of sins (:180)
- to get new life (:181)
- to get power (:181)
- to get the "spirit" (:181)
- to free people from evil spirits (:182-3)
- to give the sick power (:183)
- to heal (:187)
- to restore and strengthen relationships (:184)

J.C. Rounds (1979:180) describes a "healing service" in the Apostolic Faith Mission which is a church formed at the time of the Pentecostal Revival and

Holiness movements in the early part of the 20th Century. The service has many similarities to the services described above and is interesting as it describes a "root" of them since the "healing services" described above can all be said to have some roots in these movements. The service is much calmer than the Zionist services described above but most of the same elements are present. There is singing and handclapping throughout the service. The dancing is limited to a "shuffling of the feet". The healers use touch in healing: "They grip the supplicant firmly on the head and shoulders, pressing and shaking all the time, shouting exclamations and barely comprehensible bits of prayer, often lapsing into glossolalia" (:180).

Morran and Schlemmer (1984) describe the form of a "healing service" at Christian City in Durban:

> After the altar call comes the healing line. This takes different forms: sometimes the people are healed in their seats and told to come forward only if they have already been healed, sometimes specific complaints are called for, for example anybody who has asthma or a sore shoulder. Once people are lined up in front of the stage the annointed [sic] healer lays hands on each person individually, rebuking the illness and commanding it to leave in the name of Jesus. At this point, many people fall over backwards and are caught by catchers and laid on the floor. This experience is referred to as being slain in the spirit. [Morran & Schlemmer 1984:119]

Matthews (1988:26) emphasises the importance Pastor Theo Wolmarans gives to the teaching of the Bible on healing. Wolmarans affirms that "there was absolute certainty that Jesus had the power and authority to heal people that night and in that place. All that was needed was their belief in his ability to do that and come forward for the laying on of hands."

> Factors worth noting were the participation of the congregation in creating the kind of atmosphere reminiscent of the faith and expectancy of the bystanders in the days of Jesus' healing ministry. Equally noteworthy, was the ever-deepening experience of worship and communion with God, evoking deep emotional participation and response. The consequence was a reduction of all defences and fears and negative preconceptions in the hearts and minds of those to be healed, and a developing within them of an ever increasing sense of expectancy and immediacy.
>
> When the moment seemed most ready and appropriate the pastor called forward those desiring healing. Having previously emphasised with tremendous confidence the power and presence of Jesus, and the promises given within Scripture by use of repetition reminiscent of the suggestive techniques that Weatherhead (1951) describes so positively of Jesus - the pastor then laid his hands on each person. Frequently, he made physical contact with that part of the body that needed the healing and then in a tone of absolute confidence and expectancy, he commanded the healing to follow. Numerous patients fell to the ground in a state of semi-unconsciousness. Others responded immediately to declare their healing. At times the pastor imitated the actions of Jesus in touching the ear or mouth or eyes in ways that reflected the events of Jesus' healing ministry on earth.
>
> The community remained involved and the healed persons were invited to speak of their experiences immediately after the healing within the congregation and across the microphones. In that way the community's own sense of expectancy and confi-

> dence was enriched and the new, perhaps tentative experiences of the patients were reinforced and affirmed publicly. [Matthews 1988:26-27]

Oosthuizen (1975) has studied the healing ministry in those Pentecostal churches which have focused their mission on South Africans of Indian origin in the Durban Area. In his work, he shows how the Coping-healing ministry of these churches has played a major role in drawing people to them. The work of Pastor Rowlands and his followers and imitators has led to a significant "Pentecostal penetration" of this group of people and especially the Hindus amongst them. Hindus make up about 68% of the total so-called "Indian" group in this area (Oosthuizen 1975:6). The culture and religious background of these people leads to a tendency to demonise sickness and ill health (:309). Thus healing is strongly linked to exorcism. The laying on of hands is considered a powerful healing form by people within these churches:

> Laying on of hands is considered necessary by the largest majority but most important is "being touched by His supernatural hands." "I performed the Hindu rites but still remained ill but when I attended a revival service. [sic] I felt how the illness disappeared when the pastor laid his hands on me". The Bible is used as evidence for this practice. [Oosthuizen 1975:312]

The case of a Pentecostal minister, quoted by Oosthuizen, provides an insight into some other methods used in these churches:

> The Rev. H.S. has more adult followers than he has Sunday school children and one of the reasons which accounts for this is his emphasis on healing and exorcism so that adults are continuously drawn to this church. The author attended some of his healing services; the healers' own explanations will be reflected here.
>
> Believers are anointed with oil - a drop on the head - and hands are layed [sic] upon the sick believer according to the injunctions of James 5:16. Sometimes a mass prayer is said for all the sick in the church and the sick are told "to touch Him, the Great Physician."
>
> Rev. H.S. also anoints special handkerchiefs with Acts 19:11,12 printed on them. These are small pieces of cloth which are cut and sent out to people "even overseas" such as to India and America. "People write for them. God brought special miracles through the handkerchief of Paul."
>
> Non-believers are approached differently by Rev. S. They are first instructed about Jesus. "The Healer is brought to them first." Non-believers are not anointed with oil, but hands are layed [sic] upon them after instruction. "I use as texts Acts 16:31, 1 John 1:9, Proverbs 28:13." Hands are then layed [sic] upon them by Rev. S. who then prays for their healing and says: "God Bless you; find peace within God".
>
> Usually Rev. H.S. fasts before he attempts a healing campaign. He has already fasted 21 days continuously remaining without food day and night. [Oosthuizen 1975:315]

The examples presented in this section show both the variety and the extent of penetration of "healing services" amongst Christians in this region. These services would appear to derive from the Pentecostal movement of the early part of this century. The basic form of the healing ministry of this movement is, in fact, readily discernible: the conviction that God heals people today through faith; the necessity of praying for healing and the use of the biblical method of the laying on of hands were all somehow present throughout the various services we have described. Nevertheless, this basic form has been passed through religious and cultural filters and has emerged translated into the various types of services we have presented above.

The "healing service" is a community exercise which attempts to move a group of people through a series of transformations which is then experienced as "healing". We now go on to consider the Coping-healing phenomenon in its interpersonal mode as we consider the encounter of healer and patient in the ministry of consultation, counselling and personal prayer.

2.2.3 The One-to-One Encounter Between Healer and Sick Person

The many examples quoted above indicate that there is a varied, numerous, and apparently effective ministry of "healing services" going on at this time in South Africa. Services are, however, not the only place where healing occurs. The interpersonal dimension of this ministry is one of its major manifestations. It expresses itself in the one-to-one encounter between healer and sick person and in the visiting of the sick by prayer groups and other ministers.

The interpersonal healing ministry is very evident in the African Independent churches where a whole practice of consultation, diagnosis, prophecy and healing has grown up. In the Neopentecostal, Western culture, churches this ministry is usually referred to as counselling. But often the reality of what is done is quite similar to what the AIC's do even though the form, including the symbol system and language and terminology of its encounter and expression, are different. We seem to be seeing what is basically the same kind of ministry expressed within the parameters of different cultural paradigms.[6]

Within the African Independent churches, a whole ministry of healing through consultation has developed. All the major authors refer to this fact but perhaps West (1975) and Williams (1982) have reported on this in most depth.[7] The case studies of Mkhize (1989) and Hodgson (1983) also present us with valuable in depth studies on the nature of the healer. Edwards (1985) Cheetham and Griffiths (1982, 1989) and others analyze the phenomenon from the psycho-medical perspective and these will be discussed in the next chapter where we attempt to analyze and understand the phenomena from that point of view.

Our own experience in this field is limited to one or two contacts with *abathandazi* (prayer people) and *abaprofethi* (prophets). Consequently we will rely heavily on the secondary literature. Whilst attempting to limit our focus to the Natal area, especially the Durban/Pietermaritzburg axis, the work of West although focused on Johannesburg seems to reflect the situation in our area and is included because of its importance.

Mrs T is usually referred to by people as a prayer woman *(umthandazi)* but she calls herself a prophet *(umprofethi)* and most of the people of her own church, the Zion Christian Catholic Church of God in South Africa, agree with her. She says that her job as a healer, which is part time as she also works in Pietermaritzburg, involves healing by praying and dispensing "holy water", *(isiwasho)*. Originally she was a practising Methodist but after her marriage to another Methodist, she suffered two miscarriages and was told by the doctor that she would never bear children. So she went to consult a prophetess of the church she now belongs to and was told that she could be easily helped. The prophetess gave her holy water, salt, and a red and green cord to tie around her waist. Her third pregnancy was normal and her doctor subsequently told her that there was nothing wrong with her and she could bear children normally. From this, she began to believe in the power of prayer to heal and in fact discovered that she was also able to pray for people and they were cured. As a result of all these experiences, she left the Methodist church and joined the church of the prophetess who had healed her. In time, she too was eventually admitted as a prayer woman or faith healer *(umthandazi)*.

She believes that it was the Holy Spirit who led her along this journey and that it is not she, but the Holy Spirit, who cures those who come to her for help. This Holy Spirit, she says, is a force *(amandla)* which directs her, and all Zionist healers, in their work. She says that many of the people who come to her are not members of Zionist churches but of mainline churches and that they often come at night in order not to be seen by other members of their congregations. Other prayer women we spoke to confirmed this practice amongst mainline Christians.

Martin West (1975:96-104) refers to two types of Christian healers: faith healers and prophets, describing their calling and work, which are similar, in many respects, to those of Mrs T. As an example of a faith healer he cites the following:

> The Revd M.M. was already adult, and a prominent lay member of a mission church, before he realised that he had healing gifts. He had no history of illness, but had a vision while asleep in which his shades called him to be a healer, and said that they would help. M. ignored this as he did not believe that he could be a healer, and continued to think nothing of his vision for about a year. He then started having visions of a similar sort again, and felt increasing pressure on him. Finally he had a vision that the next day a girl would come to his house with stomach-ache, and that he should recite the Lord's Prayer over her. He said that he forgot about this until on the following day a young girl did come to the house en route to a doctor as she was suffering from a stomach-ache. M. said that he then greatly surprised members of his family by praying for the girl. She returned the following day to say that he had cured her, and from then on M. started to heal, using the ancestors to help him. He uses prayer, laying on of hands and holy water in his healing, but does not wear elaborate robes. To be more free to do his healing he left his mission church and subsequently founded his own, Independent church. His powers developed as he continued, and he needed no training. [West 1975:96]

Whilst some people are faith healers *(abathandazi)* and others call themselves prophets *(abaprofethi)* there is no clear demarcation between the two

(West 1975:46). My own research has shown that the tendency is for the prophet to have a slightly higher status. West gives various examples of prophets of which the following is typical:

> Mrs. S.M. also started having dreams from an early age - about 20. She was ill for a very long time with symptoms including a distended stomach, general pains over her body and bad headaches. Western doctors were unable to help her, and she eventually went to a prophet in Soweto, who was able to give her some relief. At that time she was a member of the Presbyterian Church of Africa, an Ethiopian type church, and shortly afterwards she married and joined the Methodist church of her husband. Later they both left the Methodist church and joined the Presbyterian Church of Africa. Mrs S.M. found that her condition deteriorated after marriage. Again western doctors were unable to help, and she was 'sick but walking' for some time. She had operations and numerous injections without success, and then in 1960 she finally consulted another prophet, who healed her and told her that she would not recover permanently until she herself became a prophet. This she agreed to do, and she went through a series of rituals including purification by immersion in a river and through use of emetics, offerings to the shades and to God, and of course the usual observation of the healer at work and sessions of interpretation of dreams. Thus Mrs S.M. became a prophet, and began seeing things in church 'like a bioscope'. This was unacceptable to the Presbyterian Church of Africa, and she was asked to leave. She and her husband, who was an elder in the church, then formed their own healing church with their first congregation members being patients who had been healed by Mrs S.M. A prominent feature of this church is healing through giving holy water.
>
> Like the other prophets described above, Mrs S.M. feels that illness can be sent by God as punishment for sin as well as being caused by the Devil or by evil spirits. When she heals she wears a cape and also uses a healing stick, prayer , holy water and various other substances. She is assisted in her work by her shades, who intercede on her behalf with God. As her powers come from God through the shades, they are superior to those of evil spirits which do not come from God. Unlike sangomas, she can only heal through the power of God - 'I trust God. *Madlozi* (the shades) can't be strong with God, God is strong with *madlozi*. I can only help when I trust in God.'
>
> [West 1975:103-104]

H.B. Mkhize (1989:283-289) presents an interesting case study of an *umthandazi* in which many of the prayer woman's own difficulties, illnesses and fears are related. She cures people both by visiting them and through consultation. She sees God as the major source of her power but acknowledges the influence of her ancestors as well (:289). Her vocation has come through dreams (:287-288) as well as through her membership of a holy congregation. She heals through prayer and touch but sometimes uses particular substances, such as Vaseline, water and salt, when she feels that people's faith is weak (:289).

Martin West (1975:104-113) has reported on the consultation procedure of one of the faith healers over a four month period. A wide range of sicknesses are reported on. They comprise sickness expressed in terms of physical symptoms as well as more emotional, relational or generic symptoms such as bad luck, money problems, work troubles, family troubles and so on. The consultation procedure is quite simple as West relates:

> Mrs M. R. interviews her patients at a small table on which is placed her healing-stick, a Bible, a candle and a glass of water (the latter is not always present). She herself will be wearing a cape, the colour of which is normally determined by what she sees to be the guidance of the Holy Spirit, although on occasions she will select a colour she herself deems to be appropriate. After interviewing a patient she is guided by the Spirit as to which of her remedies she should use in that particular case . . . It should be noted that in all consultations the patient was prayed for, and this includes laying of hands and blessing with a healing-stick. Water is important in a number of the remedies, but most importani as holy water; holy-water is prayed for by the prophet and then given to the patient to drink in a glass. Sea water is also administered in this way, and is believed to be a particularly potent remedy. The importance of holy water in healing can be seen by the fact that it was given to patients in 79 per cent of consultations. [West 1975:107]

Other remedies include baths, ash, enemas, and even holy wool made into cords which are tied around the body. Advice is always given and the consultation is often an opportunity for people to "talk about their problems and get advice" (1975:108-109).

Charles Williams gives an interesting overview of the consultation process and we quote him here at some length.

> Healing that is conducted by consultation between a Zionist healer and a patient is usually more direct and specific than healing at Zionist services, although clearly it is no less a ritual process. Consultative healing also includes a specific set of ingredients that differ from healing conducted during Zionist services. The first of these is waiting. This is done in the healer's home, whether she is present or not, and usually in the company of other patients. Often patients bring food with them in anticipation that the wait will be a long one. The mood is relaxed and informal, and the healer and her assistant (*thwasa*) come and go during the waiting period. Patients don't complain about the long wait, and this is partially understandable because long periods of waiting are associated with status in Zulu society, so that the healer's status may be elevated as much in her patient's eyes as in her own by the long waits she requires of them. [Williams 1982:142]

He describes some typical consultations as follows:

> When a patient's turn has come the person is motioned to a grass mat in front of the table. There the patient kneels quietly while the healer asks about the symptoms of the illness. Always there is a period of questioning before the healer physically touches the patient. For initial consultations the healer may give the patient two candles to light, then she puts her hands on the patient's shoulders, closes her eyes, and prays that a vision will come about this illness and how it should be treated. This is done for only a few moments, after which the candles are extinguished, and the healer tells the patient what she has been told by the vision. Not every patient who comes to consult with the healer is prophesied over using lighted candles because many patients are returning as they have been told to do, to receive additional supplies of *isiwasho*, or to receive cords that have been prepared by the healer. One patient who came for a consultation brought his own cords and candles with him. These cords were passed over the candle flames, put on his head, and stretched and snapped in the air by the healer before she returned them to him to put on.
>
> I observed the healing consultations of male as well as female Zionist healers, and there was essentially no difference between the two. During one period of consultation

> three young mothers separately knelt before the healer after the service had ended and asked him to pray over their children. Very carefully he held the head of each child, and as he did so he asked each mother to explain what her child was suffering from. The mothers responded in low voices, but even before he received this information the healer had his eyes closed and began his ritual chant of healing. "Yah . . . eh . . . Yah . . . Yebo . . . Amen . . . ah, ehhe . . . Ameni, Alleluia." To the first mother he said that her baby still had a twisted umbilical cord and this was causing the baby's hard tummy and pain. It would be necessary, he said to slaughter two chickens to relieve the baby of this ache. Another baby he diagnosed as suffering because the child was conceived out of wedlock, and as yet no compensation had been made to the bride's relatives. The ancestral spirits were therefore taking out their vengeance upon the child. The third child was suffering from a damaged brain because the mother's labor had come too early. The healer said that while the mother had gone to hospital to be treated for her condition, she had gone too late, and this had led to the baby's illness. For this baby he prescribed that she be taken to the river seven times and have a green cord tied around her middle. [Williams 1982:143-145]

Sundkler, Becken and others have also reported on the existence of healing centres in Natal where people are encouraged to stay with the healer until they are well. Sundkler (1961:233) reports the case of Beselina who stayed at the prophet Sibiya's kraal for nine months recovering from tuberculosis. Becken (1972:218) relates his visit to Hezekiah Ndlovu's healing home where he found twenty patients living at his kraal. Ndlovu's healing ministry with these patients is "mainly by prayer; once or twice I bring them for cleansing down to the Tugela river; and then, of course, I give them *isiwasho*, pure water, over which I had prayed." Becken also relates the following experience which occurred at Ndlovu's kraal:

> We met a Lutheran woman in this place who was visiting her son, aged approximately twelve years. She told us that she brought her beloved Mfanafuthi to the Healer because he was suffering from chest trouble and spitting blood. The Healer told her that for healing her son would need a sojourn of one year's duration in his healing home. For this whole period he charged her the moderate fee of four Rand which included board and lodging provided by the congregation. The mother was quite satisfied with the improved health of her son and hoped that he would soon be able to return home and to attend school again. Meeting her son, we asked him to tell us something of what is going on in the healing home, and he told us:
>
>> No I am a Christian, I was baptized in the Lutheran Church with the name Johannes. I have lived here with Pastor Ndlovu for a whole year in order to be prayed for because I had chest trouble. We are many here in the homestead of Ndlovu, but I did not join the Zionists. Every morning we are cleansed by the pastor, however he occasionally skips a day. We vomit in the morning into a dish after which we eat *imicuku* [a kind of maize porridge] and we drink blessed water. After breakfast we go out to tend his goats until afternoon. Having brought back the flock we will enjoy sports and games. Later in the evening we have a good meal, potatoes or meat, in summer time also sour milk. Being a Christian, I pray every evening on my own before retiring to rest. On certain days, the pastor goes down with us to the Tugela river, we are immersed thrice in the running water and he blesses us. After coming back to shore, he lays his hands on our heads to bless us, still there near the river. [Becken 1972:219]

Williams also notes the existence and importance of residential healing homes and centres and indicates that it is a phenomenon which is rapidly growing:

> One aspect of consultative healing which is becoming increasingly common among the Zionists is the boarding of patients by Zionist healers at the latter's homestead so these patients may be treated and observed over extended periods of time. When such arrangements are made the healer's homestead is referred to as a hospital (*esigodlweni*) [sic]. The patients who stay at the esigodlweni vary in age and in the nature of their ailments. At one Zionist hospital I visited most of the patients were young teenagers or adults who had been either brought to stay with the healer or who were being boarded there by a relative who had tried both Zulu and Western medical practitioners and found them to be unsuccessful.
>
> The hospital I visited partially functioned as a commune, for its members were expected to participate fully in all the household chores, such as cooking, fetching water, and gardening once they were reasonably able to do so. Such routines gave the patients a renewed sense of their worth and undoubtedly fulfilled psychological as well as physical needs. In interviewing several patients at one healer's home, It was clear that a variety of illness had brought the patients to the healer. The illnesses reported included: epilepsy, mental confusion, anaemia, a bruised or sprained leg, alcoholism, and a sore leg. Many of these patients had stayed with the healer over a four month period while some remained for only a week or two before they left because they considered themselves cured or, which was the rarer procedure, until they were sent home by the healer.
>
> The diagnoses offered for several of the patients reflected the healer's belief that the patient had contracted an illness through contact with a polluted environment. One healer told me that before she would allow one of her young male patients to return to his home it would be necessary for her to first go and purify the homestead. The family of the young man agreed with the healer's assessment and requested the healer's assistance in "taking out" medicines which were suspected as the source of misfortune among the family members including the man who stayed with the healer.
>
> [Williams 1982:145-6]

My own research indicates that the practice of the sick staying at the home of the healer or Church leader for varying lengths of time is quite common where space permits. Nor is such a practice confined to the African Independent churches. I was able to meet with two ministers of mainline churches who also offer a ministry of this kind. In the one case, the minister, who has a large Church in the Durban area, discovered by accident that people who came to him for help were healed by his prayers. He conducts a regular prayer service for healing in his church each week and people come to see him for individual consultations. The day we visited there were about 20 people waiting to see him. His method is to let them speak and listen to their problems and then to offer advice and pray for them. Several people were staying with him in a building next to the church which had been given over to the sick. They stayed there for periods of up to a month at a time, participating in the prayers and services of the church and consulting with the minister each day or so.

Both these mainline church ministers were extremely reluctant to speak to me about the work they were doing. The second minister, after an initial contact, declined to be interviewed as he had experienced difficulties in the past with his church in regard to his healing ministry. He felt that the work he was doing, quietly helping people, was more important than exposing the issue for discussion and the inevitable controversy which seemed to surround it.

In these churches, which include the Pentecostal, Neo-pentecostal and those mainline churches offering healing, consultation takes two main forms: prayer and counselling. Theron (1986:159-170) reports on eleven cases of people who claim to have been healed by prayer or some form of healing ministry. The cases come from various Christian denominations operating within a largely Western cultural paradigm.

In the case of Martin Barnard, the healing was effected by his own minister in the privacy of his own study after Barnard had confessed a sin to the Lord and the minister had prayed for him (Theron 1986:159). Barnard had suffered severe back pain for about twelve years and had participated in many "healing services" all of which proved ineffective. Only after confessing his sin in the silence of his own heart did the pain disappear. It eventually returned but then disappeared for good after some women prayed for him (:160).

Theron (1986:182) also reports the case of a woman with severe psoriasis who discovered during a counselling session "that she was in a state of spiritual pain . . . Her counsellor not only prayed for her and for her disease but showed her a different approach. For the first time she was helped to identify her sin by name, to confess it and be forgiven." Her condition gradually improved after this encounter.

South African literature on this ministry is almost non-existent and yet the ministry of counselling and of personal prayer is probably the most common and mundane form of healing. In a survey we carried out in three mainline churches in the Durban/ Pietermaritzburg region many ministers indicated counselling and private prayer as a major form of their healing ministry. Within the mainline churches, the procedure seems to be that people see their minister at times of stress and the counselling process helps them to deal with that stress. This is a ministry that has been going on for a long time. What is new is that many people are now referring to this process as a healing one. Prayer is normally part of it.

2.3 What They Say: Coping-Healing Articulated from Within

The observation, from without, of the healing ministry as it is encountered by researchers and writers (including this one) reveals one dimension of the phenomenon. A further dimension is revealed when we listen to people within the ministry, both as ministers and the ministered to, articulating what is going on and what the phenomenon of healing is for them. Clearly these two dimensions, the "etic" and the "emic", are linked and our previous section has also included perceptions articulated from within the phenomenon. Nevertheless, the attempt to allow the phenomenon of the Coping-healing ministry to speak to us from within, by listening to how those participating in it understand it, provides a type of preliminary ordering of this phenomenon.

2.3.1 The Healers

In a very general sense, we need to take account of the fact that those practising the Coping-healing ministry and those being healed report their experience as such. It is healing. In all the services I attended both in English and in Zulu, a direct call was made to God, to Jesus or to the Holy Spirit to heal the person from sickness. In many cases some response to this call, experienced as healing, was reported. This may seem to be a statement of the obvious but nevertheless we emphasise the fact that people perceive themselves to be actually involved in a healing ministry despite some contrary observations, opinions, perceptions and tests of those outside it. In what follows, we hope to listen to some of the ministers involved in the Coping-healing ministry to hear what they understand themselves to be doing when they heal.

Cliff De Gersigny is founder of Dove Ministries in Kloof near Durban. An offshoot of the Catholic Church it still retains some links with that church through the Catholic Charismatic Renewal movement in Durban. De Gersigny describes a method of healing which he uses himself in a consultation situation (De Gersigny n.d.).[8] The method is attributed to the American Evangelist, John Wimber and has five steps to it.[9] It requires at least fifteen minutes and at least two ministers should be involved. We paraphrase De Gersigny's tape as follows:

> First Step : The Interview.
>
> Here the task is to allow the person to present their problem as it appears to them. We listen to the problem. We are creating confidence and "preparing the person for their release of faith".
>
> Second Step: The Diagnosis or the Discernment.
>
> Having listened to the problem, the aim now is to discern the root cause of the problem: sin, emotional, demonic, psychosomatic, a curse etc. This is a discernment of the spirits and leads to a decision regarding the type of prayer needed.
>
> Third Step : Prayer Selection.
>
> After making the correct diagnosis, we now try to find the correct prayer for this person: a prayer of petition; a prayer to heal emotional wounds or to take away sin; a command made to the sickness, to the germ, cancer etc.: "I rebuke the malignant cells." One may use whatever words one likes.
>
> Fourth Step: Prayer Engagement.
>
> You have to take time, ask questions and be patient. Pray with the eyes open, watch for signs of what the person/spirit is doing: shaking, trembling, falling to the ground, crying, laughing, screaming and so on. If we are praying in the realm of the spirit we are concerned with unconfessed sin, unbelief, repentance and forgiveness. If we are praying in the realm of the soul, we are more concerned with things like bitterness,

> guilt, hatred, bad memories, rejection, alcohol, drugs, sexual deviation, emotional hurts and so on. If you are on the right track it manifests itself. If we are praying in the realm of the body then it is important to lay hands, touch the affected part and pray for physical healing. If we are praying for the deliverance from demons, then it is important to pray together with another person. Never do this ministry alone. Command the demon to leave and then replace the spirit with God's Spirit or seven more evil spirits will come in.
>
> Fifth Step: After Prayer (Post Prayer) Direction.
>
> Here we wish to give directions to a person concerning how to maintain their healing. We tell them: "Get right with God, and accept and believe your healing and stay right with God. Change your lifestyle, prayer life, diet, relationships and so on".

De Gersigny (n.d.) relates several healing experiences in which he has been involved: He claims to have seen a finger grow on a person within thirty seconds after he prayed for the person: "We just saw this finger multiplying. I watched it grow from nothing. At the end of thirty seconds he had two fingers which were the same size and within twenty four hours all the muscle had come back and everything was normal". He tells of a woman from Sasolburg whose short polio-affected arm grew five inches in a few minutes, after he had prayed for her and encouraged her to confess the unconfessed sin which was still within her. "As she confessed that sin God began to work...and we suddenly became aware that the arm had grown . . . Her picture was on the front page of the paper the next day" (De Gersigny n.d.). He says: "We have to understand that salvation and healing is the ordinary will of God. Healing for body, soul and spirit."

The two examples quoted would be categorised as miracles by De Gersigny since there is a direct quick intervention by God. Healing *per se* is seen as a more gradual process. Ray McCauley agrees with this understanding:

> There is a great difference between the working of a miracle and a healing. The working of a miracle is a supernatural intervention in the ordinary course of nature. For example, if a person has brain damage or they do not have the correct number of brain cells it is no use praying for healing. What is needed is a miracle, a supernatural intervention in the course of nature so that God places new brain cells there. For instance if I have an eye missing a miracle is required to form a new eye. I personally have not seen many miracles, although I have seen thousands of healings, but I believe that in the last days we will see more miracles through the lay people, through the housewives, through the students, through children, through businessmen, through those who make themselves available for the power of God to flow through them.
>
> We had a situation where one of our members, during a home group meeting, fell under the power of God. As she did so, she gashed her head wide open on the corner of a table. The blood was flowing freely, although the lady herself was not aware of the injury but continued to pray in tongues. My wife and I, with others, carried her to the bathroom. I thought to myself, 'Lord, I don't know what has happened here because I know that when your power flows no-one will be hurt.' So I took a cloth and wiped away the blood, saying as I did so, 'In Jesus name be healed.' As I spoke the wound totally disappeared. There was no trace of even a scar. [McCauley 1988:46]

What exactly is spiritual healing for these practitioners? McCauley explains how he understands it and what sets it apart from other, more natural types of healing:

> Gifts of healings are for the supernatural healing of disease without natural means of any sort. This is termed the gifts of healings because there are different administrations and diversities. We believe in doctors, we believe in hospitals and are not against them in any way at all but we must understand that the gifts of healings are totally supernatural. [McCauley 1988:48]

McCauley points out that healing does not always occur and in fact the opposite can happen as a result of Satan's work especially when one is a beginner in the ministry.

> When I started preaching on divine healing, I was about the only person who did not get sick by the following week! Jesus taught His disciples (Mark 4) that the devil comes immediately to steal the Word, because once you get the Word down in your spirit, then he can't steal it. But when you get the revelation of divine healing in your spirit, and you start to meditate and rejoice in what is yours, saying 'Hallelujah, by His stripes I'm healed, He bore my sicknesses, therefore I am healed', suddenly the flu attacks you worse than ever before. That is the time to confess the Word even more. [McCauley 1985:45]

McCauley also stresses the point that the internal disposition or motivation of the ones being prayed for is also important and affects whether they are healed or not.

> I asked the Lord a little while ago why we get 350 people saved during a healing campaign and the next week we can only find three or four of them. The Lord told me that most of those people come to God as a last resort, like a lucky dip packet, to try and get healed and they think that by coming up for the altar call to get saved, they will get God to move in their lives. They do not really want to get born again, they are just coming forward, because they think if they do, God will heal them. A lot of people will try everything else first and, at last, when there is nothing else left they will try God, but only as a last resort. Now I am not saying that God does not want to heal you, He does. But you must get your priorities right: do not come before God with ulterior motives in your heart. If you come to be born again, you should have a desire in your heart to be born again and to serve God. Do not come to be born again because actually you do not want to, but you need God's healing power in your life. [McCauley 1985:210]

There are two essential steps in the healing ministry for these practitioners: To preach the word and to believe. Reinhard Bonnke (1989:84) is forceful on the first of these steps: "He doesn't heal unless you preach the healing." He continues:

> We proclaim Jesus Christ the Healer. For us our model is the Lord who proclaimed liberty and showed what liberty was by healing the sick . . . Some have thought healing was an incidental result, a mere attachment to the gospel. Never! It is an ingredient of the message . . . Christ is the Healer and his healing extends in every direction towards soul, body, mind and circumstances. Healing includes the authority to cast out demons. Demons may sometimes be directly behind sickness and depression. Not every sickness or weakness is demonic. [Bonnke 1989:90-91]

McCauley (1985:49) agrees with this but also emphasises the second step, the importance of faith in healing: "You can hear scriptures of healing, deliverance and salvation from the Word of God but if you do not mix them with faith they will not help you at all" (:98). He gives an example of this process in action:

> One night, when Sandy Brown was preaching, a drug addict was brought in. During the sermon we heard a big noise and we saw a man on the floor. It was the drug addict. God had knocked him clean off his feet . . . when he got up he shouted 'I am delivered and set free. I am healed, I am free.' [McCauley 1985:180]

Another important aspect of the understanding of these ministers is that they see themselves doing the will of God whose voice they hear commanding them. Bonnke's first healing indicates how they perceive this process.

> I was about fifteen years of age when God first put His hands on mine and used me in a special way. I was in my pastor father's church prayer meeting in northern Germany. We were all kneeling when the power of God came over me and I felt as if as if my hands were filled with electricity. I clearly heard the Lord tell me, in my heart, 'Arise and lay your hands upon Sister C.' I nearly fainted thinking of the consequences, for my father was a very strict man. How could I just get up and put my hands on that lady? But when I hesitated, the Lord seemed to turn up the voltage, and I felt as if I were dying. Slowly, I lifted my head and peered around for Sister C. I kept down and crept to her so I would not be detected. Then I put my hands on her head. At that moment I felt the power of God go through my hands into her. Father had seen me, however, and his face showed he was not pleased. He went straight to her and said, 'What did Reinhard do to you?' She replied, 'Oh! When Reinhard laid his hands on me, it was as if electricity flowed through my body - and I am healed!' By going to her as God commanded, I learned this lesson: 'Open the window . . .' When Joash had done that, the next command could be given. [Bonnke 1989:144][10]

Rodney Seago founder and pastor of the huge "City of Life" complex in Pinetown relates an experience of the healing ministry in action. The person concerned was a neighbour with whom he had previously had an argument and had asked the man for forgiveness. He continues the story:

> Some years later, after I had returned from Bible College and was assistant pastor in my home church, I received a phone call from this man's wife requesting me to come and pray for her husband who had a tumour on the brain. He was in excruciating pain. I then had the joy of leading him to receive the Lord Jesus Christ as his Lord and Saviour. I also laid hands on him and prayed for his healing. A few days later they phoned to report that the violent headaches had ceased and the doctors could find no trace of the tumour. God had performed a miracle! [Seago n.d:22]

Seago emphasises three elements here: first, the man's acceptance of Jesus as his Lord and Saviour; second, Seago lays hands on him and third, he prays for the healing. A similar emphasis is seen in the ministry of Pastor Frank Victor of Ebenezer Temple, Chatsworth, where the congregation and minister are all of an Indian cultural background. Again, the emphasis is on the faith of the person being prayed for, the laying of hands and praying in the "Name of Jesus". A further element emphasised here is the "claiming" of the healing

(Oosthuizen 1975:318). For Pastor Victor, yet another element comes into play when one is dealing with demon possession: this is the necessity of "rebuking" the evil spirit (:318).

Within the African Independent churches, the elements are sin, the devil and demons as the cause of sickness and the prophet as the agent of the Spirit of God in healing the sick. Mrs M.R. a prophet-healer interviewed by Martin West understands her ministry as follows:

> People become sick because they have sinned, but also through the actions of the devil and *amademone* . . . The prophet has the power through the Holy Spirit to see what is happening, why it is happening and what remedies should be employed. Of her consultations with patients Mrs M.R. says *'uMoya* leads me to do it - sometimes I am led by dreams, but specially it is the Holy Spirit'. [West 1975:100]

H.J. Becken asked J. G. Shembe of the Shembe Church to explain how he understood healing. Shembe's explanation also emphasises faith in Jesus as well as the mysterious power of God to heal especially through the sign of the laying on of hands:

> We cannot explain it. We believe that anyone can lay hands on a sick person who is a Christian and that person would get healed, provided that the person laying hands has enough faith in God, faith in Jesus Christ. The whole idea of healing comes from the teachings of Jesus Christ: Go ye in all the world and preach the Gospel, lay hands on the sick; if they will believe, they will be healed. When people start explaining these faith healings and so on scientifically, I do not believe it; it is impossible. We do it blindly. It is a matter of faith. I believe that anyone with enough faith in Jesus Christ is in fact a healer on [sic] other people, may be a child or maybe an old person, it makes no difference. But once we start saying that I know what I am doing, there is no faith in it, and there is no Christ in it. [Becken 1989:236]

Felicity Edwards has worked with a Xhosa Prophet healer in the Grahamstown area and attempts to articulate his understanding of what he is doing when he heals (Edwards 1989b:331-345). Central to his healing ministry is to be in a state of "living consciousness" (*isazela esiphilileyo*). Edwards quotes the healer as follows:

> This kind of consciousness, he says, "is always together with the Spirit of God" . . . "In living consciousness . . . one prays and one is connected with God. When one sins one breaks off this living consciousness. When one confesses his sins his living consciousness revives" . . . "The sickness of a person is in his consciousness. All the diseases that trouble him are in his consciousness" . . . "When consciousness is healed," he says, "the body heals." [Edwards 1989b:331-4]

The first part of the healing process is to prophesy or diagnose the cause of the sickness. Edwards describes this process as follows:

> In every case Mr Ntshobodi prays that the Spirit of God will help him, will tell him what is wrong, and what to do to help and heal the patient . . . Prophecy may be what we would call precognitive; it may be in dreams or visions or it may be what Mr Ntshobodi calls "seeing in the Spirit." He frequently dreams before a patient comes to see him of who is coming and of what is wrong. The dream may be repeated and may need interpretation. Or, while awake he may have what he calls a vision. "I am sitting

> here in my chair," he says (this being in a room which does not overlook the road) "and I see a man being brought up the street in a donkey cart . . ." and so on. Or, in the healing service itself it may happen that he "sees in the Spirit," as he calls it. This may be almost a literal seeing, but it is seeing which is knowing. It may begin by his seeing a light surrounding a particular person in the congregation. He then prays intensely and knows interiorly, through the Spirit, what is wrong with the person. He will check it out with the person, saying to him alone, while the congregation is singing loudly, so that confidentiality is maintained, "The Spirit says you are having marriage problems (or whatever), Is this right?" And the person will say, Yes." . . . A third way of diagnosis is by direct intuition. "Sometimes", Mr Ntshobodi says, " I just know what is wrong, but only if I pray to God to enlighten me." Or, "I know what is wrong the moment I start praying." [Edwards 1989b:337-338]

The "healing service" follows the normal procedure as described elsewhere. The healer explains what is happening as the atmosphere becomes more charged:

> His hands or his whole body may vibrate and he may visibly shake. He describes a very intensely concentrated form of awareness, sometimes such that he is unconscious of his surroundings. He also reports that he experiences energy like that of an electric current being transferred from his body through his hands to the patient . . . Frequently here Mr Ntshobodi gives the patient specially prayed-for water to drink . . . Giving water is particularly important; Mr Ntshobodi refers to "Jesus having started his way as a living sacrifice in water" (the baptism), and in Genesis we are told that the spirit of God settled on the waters. "So, [sic] he says "whenever we are invoking the Spirit of God, water must be there." [Edwards 1989b:341-342]

The patient is often spun around and the healing finishes by dancing in a circle around the sick person. The healer explains this as follows: "when Abraham offered a sacrifice to God he took some stones and built an altar in a round form" (Edwards 1989b:342). Edwards continues, paraphrasing the healer's explanation:

> He explains that whilst they are going around in a circle they are surrendering the sick person, and at the same time they are "finding the consciousness of the person." He says explicitly that "they connect with the consciousness of the person being healed." [Edwards 1989b:342]

The parallels between De Gersigny's method and that of Ntshobodi are striking if one is able to look beyond some of the differing cultural expressions present in each healing process. In fact from all the cases presented above one is able to identify a number of parallel and common elements:

1) The sense of being in the realm of the supernatural.
2) The sick persons are allowed to express their sickness in some form or another for example by speaking or by agreeing with a diagnosis or through some form of gesture like dance or other bodily movements.
3) There is a diagnosis, prophecy or discernment of the disease through recourse to God's power.
4) Sin, demons, feelings, relationships and emotions are all involved in sickness.

5) The importance of preaching the word of God and of acknowledging his power through faith.
6) There is a prayer for healing which is usually accompanied by some form of bodily gesture or action: laying of hands, spinning and dancing in a circle and so on. Laying of hands is specially important.
7) The use of materials and objects such as holy water, oil, cords, cloths, Vaseline, Jeyes Fluid, candles and so on which are used by healers especially, but not exclusively, within the African cultural paradigm.

The understanding that healers have of the process has revealed many common elements within the Coping-healing phenomenon. It has also indicated a prevailing sense of mystery which pervades it. To conclude this section, we now listen to those people who seek out Christian spiritual healing to hear how they understand their own experience.

2.3.2 Experiences and Interpretations of Those Asking for Healing

The Coping-healing phenomenon is growing so rapidly because it responds to a need which people have. It is therefore important to listen to those who ask for healing to hear what it is they are seeking and in particular, what it is they experience when they are "healed". We again consider the phenomenon from the two major cultural perspectives which have run throughout our observations.

Most people attending the Zionist services I went to, referred to themselves as having been sick and having been healed either at the service or by one of the prayer people or prophets. The sicknesses people referred to when speaking to me were often quite vague: "I was sick and I was healed"; "I had pains all over and they prayed for me and the pains went away"; "I had family problems and they prayed for me and the problems were solved". I do not claim to have undertaken a rigorous programme of research here, but rather I report on impressions gained from talking to people at the services attended, usually after the conclusion during the meal which often follows the all night services. From these impressions, it seems to me that the healing being received by people was always real for them and generally expressed in terms of an increase in "life" or "well-being".[11]

The kinds of sickness that people bring for healing are extremely diverse and do not always correspond to what those operating within a Western cultural paradigm would call sickness. Martin West (1975:106) has made a list of complaints that people brought to Mrs M.R., a prayer-healer, in their quest for healing. A total of 361 separate consultations were surveyed. He divides this list into two classes: class A are physical symptoms ranging from stomach ache, headache, through to body pains, pimples and so on. Class B are complaints which are less physical such as bad luck, family problems, nightmares, love problems and so on. It is also important to note that the division is made by West and that people within this cultural paradigm are far less likely to separate these two types of illness.[12]

In an interesting little article, V. Msomi (1967) reports on a series of interviews he conducted with people from various churches who said that they had been healed. We quote several of these:

A Member of Apostolic Zion Church.

> I was sick and the members of my family sent me to the prophet Mbatha. He is now Archbishop. He prayed for me. They gave me Ash-Water, 'Iziwasho'. I was immediately healed. I chose the Lord there. [Msomi 1967:69]

Ohlangeni Z.C.C.

> I got sick. I had isitshopo [sic]. My feet and legs were swollen and were very painful. I was treated by a well known inyanga. In spite of all his endeavours there was no help. My condition was critical. Some people advised me to go to UMkhokheli[13] CHRISTINAH. When I came to her she prayed for me thus:-
>
> [. . .] [Zulu text omitted]
>
> Almighty God I pray for this Thy Child: Grant to him while he is within these *gates* healing. Give me power so that as I pray for this water the *power* in the Water be your power.
>
> She gave me some ash-water to warm (thoba) my feet and legs. The swollen legs became normal. Suddenly the pain was gone. I was healed. I arranged for umsebenzana - thanksgiving party. The congregation was present at my home. Ngaketha iNkosi [tr. I chose the Lord] I had seen with my own eyes *SALVATION*.
>
> [Msomi 1967:69-70]

Amanazaretha Church.

> At home we were all full members of the American Board. My father was sick and he could not get help anywhere. So he went to Kwa-Banya - Vryheid. Inceku prayed for him. He was healed. My sister who was sick was prayed for there. She was also healed. They both became Amanaza [Nazareth Church members]. I got sick and I was healed at the same place. During the healing service the Inceku had a piece of cloth which he uses. He started praying thus: "Moya kaNkulunkulu Nampa abantu bakho abagulayo Umoya wakho ongcwele mawehlele kubo ubasindise" [tr. Spirit of God, here are your sick people. May your Holy Spirit descend upon them and save (or heal) them.] All the people screamed. He hit us with the cloth. He continued to pray. "Kufa okukulaba abantu phuma akusiye owakho lomuntu okaNkulunkulu" [sic] [tr. death which is in these people come out. This person is of God and not yours] I vomited. I was healed immediately. I saw INSINDISO [salvation] with my own eyes so I became uMnazaretha [member of the Nazareth Church]. [Msomi 1967:71]

Msomi also relates a case of someone who was not healed and yet received advice and was converted:

Apostolic Zion Church:

> My husband died not long after our marriage. I became sick soon after his death. My mother in-law [sic] was a full member of Abaphostoli [Apostolic Church]. She advised me to go to them to be prayed for. I was taken to the home of Umkhokheli. This Umkhokheli had a gift of Ukuboniswa- UKUPROFETHA [seeing and prophesying]. She prayed for me. She gave me water boiled with ash. I drank this water 'ISIWASHO.' I used it as phelaza [vomiting]. Umkhokheli laid hands on me. I was *not* healed. In the

> course of my stay with umkhokheli I chose the Lord. Umkhokheli advised me that I could go to a European Doctor as a last resort. I had a disease that was difficult to heal. It is allowed on special occasions to go to European Doctors. When you return you will be purified in Church. You are sprinkled with Holy Water. [Msomi 1967:68]

Becken reports on the case of Mrs Bertina Luthuli who was healed by J. G. Shembe in the 1960's:

> I know this father (J. G. Shembe) well, I witness to his great deeds. I was ill in Zululand. He came and entered the house in which I lay ill and he interceded for me. When he left, he enquired from me: "Does your strength not yet return?" I replied: "No, not even a bit." Then he said: "I see that it does not yet come and that you progress very slowly." When he had left, he came to me in a vision while I was sleeping and, dreaming, I saw him entering the room while I was on my bed. I saw him like coming from a baptism; he handed to me the stick which he usually carries if he intends to baptize. I grasped it. He said (in my dream) that I should not let loose. I kept it, trembling. Then a door opened there near my head, because there he went out taking my disease away. On the next morning, I walked around the whole courtyard. Thus from this day onwards, I was always of good health. [Becken 1989:233-234]

The experience of healing is similarly very real amongst those people who look for it in the Neopentecostal churches. People I have spoken to have claimed to be healed from a wide rage of diseases, especially arthritis, deafness, back problems and migraines. Their experiences, as they are being prayed for, are often remarkably similar. When prayed for in a "healing service", many feel something: "power", "shivers throughout my body" or "heat" and the affliction seems to disappear. The next day it has often returned but less than before and then it gradually, over a period of days or weeks, completely disappears.

Among the people I spoke to, one of the most interesting was a Charismatic Christian who believed in healing on an intellectual level but had never experienced it personally. She related the following experience to me:

> I was in excruciating pain from a dislodged vertebra and a slipped and a ruptured disk. I could only sleep in a sitting position, and had to be pulled out of bed in the morning. I was told that the only possibility was a Spinal Fusion operation. Then I heard about a doctor in Stanger who healed through prayer and the laying on of hands and I was encouraged to go.
>
> I visited him and he examined me as he was also a medical doctor. He confirmed the diagnosis of the other doctor but then he said that he could heal me by the power of faith in the Lord Jesus Christ. I agreed to this and he laid hands on me and prayed for me in tongues. As he prayed I felt these sharp shivers and tingles in my back and heat there. When he finished praying he asked me to stand up and touch my toes. I had not been able to do this for years but I gingerly tried and found I was able to do it. As I stood up, I found there was no pain and from then on I was able to sleep horizontally. When I went back to my doctor in Durban he said my spine had slipped back in and the disks appeared normal. I have since had no trouble with it.

Theron (1986:159-160) reports a similar, if more severe, case of back pain disappearing after prayer. He quotes a further ten cases of people who have experienced healing through prayer. We cite two of these as examples:

a) Bonny's Healing

Bonny's healing was 'the most fantastic experience of my life'. She had been suffering from fibrositis for eleven years. Her father had to massage her shoulder, which often seemed to have contracted into a hard knot. The doctor was not much concerned but said something about a possible acid deposit. To her the pain was an urgent reality with which she had to live from her Std 6 year onwards.

At the end of 1984 she attended a service at her church where the emphasis was on healing. As far as faith is concerned, she feels that the service helped her to grow in faith until she was ready to go forward for prayer. She certainly also relied on the faith of the person who led the service - particularly with regard to her legs, one of which was shorter than the other. When the leader prayed for her briefly, the effect was much more striking than she had anticipated. She became aware of deep sadness and guilt and began to cry her heart out. The person praying for her instantly realised that more was at stake than physical healing and encouraged her to reject all that had been embittering her life, to cast it out of her body - in practical terms, to cough it out. She tells how she felt something leaving her body. 'It was like bonds being untied. It was like toothpaste being squeezed out of a tube'. She felt that the Lord had healed her totally in more than one area of her life. Amongst other effects, the physical pain disappeared instantly and totally. She realised then that the pain, heartache and fibrositis had been a part of her life ever since the death of her grandfather. A manipulative grandmother had been blaming her for something that happened on the evening before his death. Only during the healing process did she become aware that there had been a connection between the grandfather's death and her illness. It was a very great day when she was healed of physical pain and spiritual guilt. [Theron 1986:167-168]

b) Mrs Minnaar.

When Mrs Minnaar had X-rays taken in preparation for an operation on a broken nose, the plates showed a spot which was described as an erosive tumour. At the next Sunday service she was specially laid hands on, prayed for and anointed with oil. Only a few people really knew what was wrong. More X-Rays were taken the next day, first at a clinic and later by the same radiologist. The spot was gone. At first the radiologist thought he had made a mistake. She explained the situation. Her sinuses had also cleared up in the process - something which another doctor had described as an impossibility in her case. [Theron 1986:169]

Although the South African literature is scanty on witnesses of people who have been healed, several overseas authors have catalogued a series of testimonies from those who have been healed. One of the best known of these is Catherine Kuhlman, whose two books: "I Believe in Miracles " and "God Can Do It Again" contain an enormous number of such testimonies (Kuhlman 1962, 1969). By way of example, however, we have decided to cite a few examples from the testimonies received by Andy Arbuthnot at the London Healing Mission. These also seem to mirror some of the examples and experiences of people in South Africa.

R told us: 'Four weeks ago you prayed over me for healing of migraine that I'd been having for more than ten years, and praise the Lord with me, that very day I was completely healed!'. [Arbuthnot 1989:151]

> S a friend telephoned recently because she had not long to live with cancer. The doctors are now flabbergasted because the cancer has died instead of her; and although the healing is not quite finished in her bloodstream, the tumour itself has died. [Arbuthnot 1989:151]

> B [said that h]er hearing has been healed, having been bad since birth. Doctors had said it could never be improved. [Arbuthnot 1989:155]

These witnesses certainly indicate that amongst the people who seek healing through prayer, there is a perception that such healing is available and that indeed, some of them perceive themselves to be healed. The numbers of people who claim healing are quite significant and their witness acts as an incentive for others to seek healing. At the same time, not all are healed and the criteria for healing are not easily verifiable nor repeatable. This has led to the issue becoming controversial and caused some people to question the whole business.

2.4 When There is No Healing

By no means all the people who come for healing actually receive it. Many people I have spoken to report that they go up for healing at the services and even consult healers but no healing occurs. One person said in front of all the people at a service that he had had his hearing restored in one deaf ear, but when I spoke to him later he said that it was in fact still the same but in the emotion of the moment he had felt that his hearing had been restored.

Several people have left the Neopentecostal churches disillusioned because they did not receive healing. Often they are blamed for this fact, being told that their faith was too weak. The SABC TV presented a feature on this in June 1983 (SABC 1983). Several people who had not been healed complained that they were often made to feel worse when they didn't receive healing and that the experience of having their hopes dashed was a traumatic one. Many were critical of the exaggerated promises made by faith healers. Many mainline church ministers also indicate that they have to counsel people who have not received healing in Neopentecostal churches. Authors such as Stumpf (1985, 1986), Rose (1968) and Levin (1985) are even more critical, contending that miracle healings are totally unsubstantiated and that most of what goes on in Coping-healing churches is fraudulent.

2.5 The Response of the Mainline Churches

For the sake of completion, we felt that it was necessary to enquire whether the growth of the Coping-healing churches had had an impact within the so-called mainline churches.

We have already indicated that it is possible to find healers and a healing ministry within the mainline churches although this is often a discreetly done ministry, especially amongst blacks, because of perceived difficulties with ecclesiastical authorities. Nevertheless, we felt that there had been a general increase in awareness and involvement in the healing ministry within mainline churches and we wished to test this feeling. Accordingly, a questionnaire was drawn up and distributed to ministers and priests in charge of congregations of three mainline churches in the Durban/Pietermaritzburg area.[14]

Our survey shows that besides being aware of an increased perceived need for healing, the mainline churches have also responded by setting up a varied series of ministries to respond to that need. Several ministers of the mainline churches were most enthusiastic about this ministry and some even advocated collaboration with the Neopentecostal churches. Others were more circumspect and reported that much of their ministry revolves around counselling people who had been hurt by these churches: people who had not been helped and had suffered the trauma of being accused of weakness in faith and commitment. Other respondents were positively antipathetic to the whole business considering it to have nothing to do with Christianity and accusing it of being a money making racket.

It should be noted that several of the respondents indicated counselling as one of the healing ministries they were involved in. Some understood this to be seeing people and listening to the various personal problems they have and trying to help them deal with these. Others reported on the considerable time they had to spend counselling people who had "been hurt" by their negative experience in the Coping-healing churches. Others understood counselling as listening to peoples problems and then praying with them. Counselling in most of these forms has traditionally been part of the work of the clergy. What is interesting here is the fact that this traditional role of the minister is now being seen by some of them as a "healing ministry".

In general, then, we can conclude that the increase in the Coping-healing ministry, whilst perhaps more spectacular in those churches which focus on it almost exclusively, is not limited to them. The traditional churches seem to be opening themselves partially to this ministry and so one can detect a movement throughout the whole of the community which calls itself Christian in this part of the world.

2.6 Conclusion to Our Observations

We have attempted in this long chapter to present the phenomena associated with the Coping-healing ministry especially as it is manifesting itself in the new, Independent, Neopentecostal and Indigenous churches mainly in the Durban/Pietermaritzburg area of Natal. The approach has been to describe what is happening from the perspective of a participant-observer, including this author and others who have written on the subject. Then we have attempted to allow those involved in these ministries, both on the giving and receiving side, to articulate what is going on and what they understand themselves to be participating in. Finally we have attempted to indicate something of the penetration of this ministry within traditional or mainline churches.

Our study indicates a varied, enthusiastic and effective ministry operating in all the areas of the Christian Church that were investigated. The ministry is attracting large numbers of people because it is responding to a perceived need people have for it. There are enough experiences of what people perceive as healing for testimonies to be made which attract other people and so the ministry has grown. It is now making some inroads into the more traditional or mainline churches. The ministry is found among all sectors of the population in the multicultural Durban/Pietermaritzburg area of Natal and it tends to express itself within the cultural paradigm of each group.

Our next step will be to change the standpoint of our observation to that of others who find themselves within the horizon of the Coping-healing phenomenon and who attempt to render it intelligible within their own perspective. This step will be a hermeneutic mediation. In taking it we wish to see how the phenomenon of the healing ministry is seen and understood from psycho-medical, cultural-anthropological, socio-economic, philosophical and theological perspectives. This will be the task in our next part.

PART II

MEDIATING THE COPING-HEALING PHENOMENON

The Necessity of Multidisciplinary Mediation

The plethora of experiences, practices, beliefs and testimonies in the previous chapter, impress upon us the complexity of the phenomenon which is the churches' Coping-healing ministry. Nor have we considered all of its dimensions since we have ignored the more traditional healing ministry of the Church as expressed in hospitals, clinics, primary health care, hospital visitation, counselling as well as the more traditional expressions of the Sacrament of the sick. In limiting ourselves to the more recent emergence of a Coping-healing ministry in some way rooted in the Pentecostal Tradition and observing the manifestation of this ministry as it has grown in the South African context, we observe an explosion of different modes, understandings and assertions - a claimed new outpouring of the Spirit which was not part of the Church's former tradition. The more we attempt to observe and grasp the phenomenon in its fullness, the more it seems to elude us. As the veracity of one set of claims and experiences is convincingly made, along comes counter claim and experience to confound us. Clearly the phenomenon is complex and it manifests itself in different forms depending on the standpoint of the observer.

In order to make some sense of all of this, we are called to look more intently and attempt to see our phenomenon more deeply before we can attempt a phenomenological description. "Seeing more deeply", is the aim of this section as we attempt to render the phenomenon more intelligible to us by varying the perspective. This process corresponds to what happens on Lonergan's (1971:9) "intellectual" level "on which we inquire, come to understand, express what we have understood, work out the presupposition and implication of our expression". Important in this respect is the question of standpoint, for the frame of reference of the beholder to a large extent provides the "epistemological lens" through which the phenomenon passes before it is seen. It is thus seen, on this deeper level, in terms of the categories of understanding which make up a particular framework of reference.

The phenomenon of healing has been observed and understood from many standpoints. We have attempted to reduce these to five major perspectives: the psycho-medical, the anthropological, the socio-economic, the philosophical and the theological. When the phenomenon is studied from a particular standpoint and an attempt is made to render it intelligible within the categories of that standpoint, we refer to this process as a "mediation". By this we mean that the phenomenon is mediated by the frame of reference or epistemological categories of the observer who is psychologist, anthropologist, philosopher, sociologist, theologian (or a combination of more than one of these). What is seen and what is reported is done so in terms of the particular frame of reference concerned. Saying this is not saying much since we all mediate phenomena. The fullness of phenomena is never available to us and all that we observe is mediated. The importance of contextual theologies and the study of the so-called *paradigm shift* in epistemology is the attempt to highlight the reality of this process and thus to move away from the absolutisation of intellectual positions. The words of Clifford Geertz[1] are relevant here:

> . . . we need to replace the "stratigraphic" conception of relations between the various aspects of human existence with a synthetic one; that is, one in which biological, psychological, sociological, and cultural factors can be treated as variables within unitary systems of analysis. The establishment of a common language in social sciences is not a matter of mere coordination of terminologies or, worse yet, of coining artificial new ones; nor is it a matter of imposing a single set of categories upon the area as a whole. It is a matter of integrating different types of theories and concepts in such a way that one can formulate meaningful propositions embodying findings now sequestered in separate fields of study. [Geertz 1973:44]

Chapter 3

The Psycho-Medical Mediation: Coping-Healing as a Psycho-Medical Phenomenon

3.1 Introduction

The professions of medicine and psychology have, of late, begun to acknowledge the complexity of the healing/curing process and the existence of a wide range of factors operating in the field of the sickness, illness, cure and health paradigm. What follows is an overview of how psychologists, medical doctors and others in the psycho-medical field are attempting to grasp the elements and structure of this emerging reality.

Current views within the medical profession affirm a crisis regarding the notions of sickness and health. Many doctors feel that they are often diagnosing symptoms and prescribing drugs to effect short term cures for some diseases without getting either to the source of the illness within the person or to a way of bringing the patient to a more lasting state of health.

> To summarize one aspect of the current medical care crisis, it may be said that discontinuity of medical practice and consumer demand result from emphasis on *curing* of disease, ie., the diagnosis of diseased organs and intrusive microbes, and prescriptions of pharmaceutical or other medical regimens, while patients wish *healing* of illness. [Boucher n.d.:15]

In an attempt to redress this problem an initial attempt was made to understand and respond to illness behaviour in terms of a "psychological model" which responds to that illness not covered by the more conventional medical model of diseases. In the "psychological model" those not seeking or responding to normal medical treatment of disease are indicating the existence of "irrational factors" or psychological elements within the individual (Boucher n.d.:10).

It seems that we can posit both a medical paradigm which recognises the person as chemistry, mechanics and emotional drives as well as a psychological paradigm which approaches the individual person as a *complexus* of thoughts, meanings, feelings, consciousness and subconsciousness, together with behavioural mechanisms. The science of psychosomatics has risen up as these two paradigms have been incorporated into a greater whole where the reciprocal influence of psyche and soma, is studied (Jackson 1981:36). Jackson (:64) understands this as "the relation of mind, emotion, thought and feeling to the physical well-being of man" and he emphasises the importance of achieving "intropsychic balance" (:66) within the individual. In fact certain types of diseases can be directly linked to emotional causative factors so that

> persistent anger and frustration is apt to lead to a stomach ulcer, while fear and anxiety may be the forerunners of heart disease. Persistent irritation tends towards dermatitis, and unresolved grief to ulcerative colitis. So the understanding grows of the relation of emotion to bodily states. [Jackson 1981:79]

The role of unconscious factors is also of prime importance within the psychological model and these can cause even spectacular physical symptoms such as blindness and deafness. The physical symptoms result from an unconscious motivation often resulting from some earlier trauma which has been repressed. Thus the blindness is caused by a fear of "seeing something" and deafness by an unwillingness to "hear something". The something in both cases is linked to the repressed traumatic experience. These "hysterical syndromes" are well known to the psychiatric profession and can often lead to striking non-medical cures.

> As one physician reports, he told a blind patient that in order to see, 'he must not only open his eyes but he must also use his brains and look'. The patient failed to respond to this suggestion, so the physician then approached him through a lower level of consciousness. 'The following day his condition was unchanged, and I decided to try some psychotherapy on him. He was very easily placed in a hypnotic state and then told that at the count of ten he would be able to see. At the count of ten he did not fail me, and has enjoyed normal vision since that moment.' But then, interestingly, the physician continues with this judgment. 'This form of therapy which fills the entire bag of tricks of the Christian Scientist and chiropractor and other cultists, might well be put to more frequent use by ourselves, and would be if we recognised more often the psychogenic nature of many conditions. [Jackson 1981:84-85]

Psychology teaches us that whilst people do not normally consciously wish themselves to be sick, unconscious factors can sometimes play a stronger role and the conflict between the conscious and unconscious can lead to physical symptoms of illness. Stress situations such as war and even school examinations can also lead those under pressure to manifest symptoms as simple as the common cold and as dramatic as blindness and lameness. Psychologists refer to this well documented phenomenon as "Conversion Hysteria" (Jackson 1981:69), "Hysterical Psychosis" (Wessels 1989:100) or "Conversion Disorder" (Nair 1985:153).

Psychological studies have clearly shown the operation of psychological factors in the etiology of certain diseases. Boucher reports studies on duodenal and peptic ulcers, multiple sclerosis, asthma and heart disease.[2] Jackson (1981:41-

42,157) reports studies on diabetes, addictions to alcohol and tobacco, rheumatoid arthritis, asthma, heart disease, skin irritations, congestion of the respiratory tract and spastic colon.[3] These studies indicate that all these conditions may have a psychological component in their etiology.

Jackson (1981:66-67) emphasises the notion of balance within the person as the key to life and health. The various emotional, physical as well as conscious and unconscious mental processes lead to a setting up of pressures and forces within the organism. Both illness and healing are attempts to maintain this balance. On the physical level an adaptive process of *homeostasis* is constantly at work and medication or surgical intervention is usually aimed at assisting or even initiating this process. On the psychological level a state of intropsychic balance is the goal within the human person.

3.2 Psycho-Medical Studies on the Coping-Healing Phenomenon in South Africa

3.2.1 The Limitations of Psycho-Medical Studies

Psychological and medical studies on the Christian Coping-healing phenomenon tend, almost exclusively, to show two typical characteristics both of which impose limitations on their conclusions. In the first place, the studies are almost entirely focused on healing on the African Independent churches and so a psychological and/or medical account of Coping-healing in the Neopentecostal churches is almost entirely lacking. The second characteristic of these studies is the universal tendency to situate this ministry/phenomenon within the structure and characteristics of "indigenous" and "cultural" healing systems. Thus it is often difficult to know whether any specificity can be attributed to Christian healing since the question is not usually asked. What follows below needs to be understood within these two limitations.

3.2.2 Studies on the Diagnosis of Illness by AIC Healers

S.D. Edwards et al (1985) report on a case study on the treatment of a case of *umeqo* (cf. fig. 3.2) by a "Faith Healer" (zulu: *umthandazi*) and by Western psychiatric methods. After a paralysis on her left side, "Mrs Z" was taken to an *umthandazi*, a full Minister in the Zionist Church:

> According to Mrs.Z, the Faith Healer burnt *impepho* - a herb to invoke the ancestors - and prayed. He was then able to divine the affliction as *umeqo* sorcery and from his description of the *umthakathi* or sorcerer, Mrs Z was able to make out that it was her husband's brother's third wife, who according to the Faith Healer was jealous of Mrs Z, who was haughty and proud, and had sons, which the *umthakathi* did not have. The Faith Healer made small incisions at the joints of Mrs Z's left shoulder, arm and leg and rubbed black powdered medicines (*insizi*) in to relax the muscles in order that they might twitch again, with advice to keep on rubbing the affected parts with (*isiwasho*) (holy water) of which he gave her a litre. *Izinyamazane* was also prescribed to be burnt and inhaled to strengthen Mrs Z. Mrs Z continued with the tradi-

> tional course of treatment for a week without abatement of her symptoms, so did not return for her appointment with the Faith Healer, but was admitted to Stanger Hospital. [Edwards et al 1985:66]

At the hospital Mrs Z's condition was diagnosed as psychogenic and conversion hysterical as a result of stress within the family situation. The treatment was hypnotherapy with cultural counselling. Under hypnosis she was able to walk again and suggestions were given to her in this state which enabled her also to walk in the waking state. The case shows that whilst the *umthandazi* had been able to diagnose the sickness as being of a relational nature, he had not been able to cure it and the patient had looked for help elsewhere. This approach to health care in terms of efficacy, where people try various avenues until they are healed, seems quite common.

Felicity Edwards (1989a) has investigated a case of healing within a Zionist church in the Eastern Cape. The patient was sick at home and had lost consciousness after a disturbed night. The prophet healer, Mr N., was called and diagnosed a case of *amafufunyane*[4] after praying for him when he heard sounds in another language coming from his stomach. After commanding the spirit to leave the person and after going through a Zionist healing service some days later, the patient made a good recovery and was able to resume his job. Edwards (:217) attempts to explain the *amafufunyane* spirit possession in terms of disturbed interpersonal relations and stress build-up resulting from living with a constant state of animosity. Animosity resulting from jealousy of a person who has good fortune or success can also result in this type of illness. The disease is a socially acceptable one and so is a way of dealing with the stress. Edwards also reports a second type of *amafufunyane* spirit possession, again resulting from stress, where people find themselves "in a situation with which he or she is psychologically and personally unable to cope . . ." (:218).

Western psychiatrists interpret *amafufunyane* spirit possession as "brief reactive psychosis" for which the prognosis is good if it is treated properly, i.e., if the stress factors are removed and the symptoms cured. Edwards isolates six different types of *amafufunyane* possession and concludes that the term refers mainly to a

> constellation of stress related phenomena associated with socio-cultural transition . . . and is evidence . . . of one of the ways in which humankind deals with conditions in which the threshold of psychological tolerance has been overstepped. [Edwards 1989a:222-3]

Clearly the Zionist church is providing, in its healing ministry, a socially acceptable way of dealing with the stress and the symptoms.

Researching within a Zulu cultural milieu, Wessels (1989:108) asked ten faith healers from African Indigenous churches (cf. ch.2 n.1) what reasons people have for consulting them. Figure 3.1 shows the results of his inquiry:

Trouble with Spouse	93%
Work Troubles	87%
Problems with Pregnancy	80%
Trouble at home	73%
Bad luck	73%
Poisoning/evil agent	73%
Talking in sleep	73%
Barrenness	67%
Nightmares/visions	67%
Holy Spirit troubles	47%
Money problems	47%
Madness	47%

Fig. 3.1 Reasons for Consulting Faith Healers (Source Wessels 1989:108)

In the same study, Wessels investigates the proficiency of faith healers to diagnose and treat fifteen predominantly psychiatric conditions which are well known within the Zulu traditional world-view. Figure 3.2 gives the conditions both in Zulu and Western psychiatric terminology:

Zulu understanding	Western Psychology
uhlanya	Schizophrenia
isidalwa	Mental Retardation and/or Physical deformity
isithutwane	Epilepsy
indiki/ufufunyane/izizwe	Brief reactive psychoses Hysterical Psychosis
idliso	Psycho-somatic G I Tract disorder
iqondo	Uro-genital disease
uvalo	Anxiety disorders
umeqo	oedema and paralysis of legs
ukuthwasa	Atypical psychosis or severe anxiety disorder
ukudlula	Obsessive-Compulsive disorder/kleptomania
abaphansi basifulathele	Depression(minor or major)
umnyama	Depression (minor or major)
umhayizo	Hysteria

Fig. 3.2 Fifteen Illness Categories Expressed Within the Western Psychological and Zulu World-views (Source Wessels 1989:96-105 - Figure abstracted from the text)

Wessels (1989:108) concludes that the faith healers he has studied have a good ability to recognise these disorders, although not quite so good as traditional diviners, and that "they fulfil an extremely useful function in assisting with the handling of day-to-day problems of living in the African community."

The Independent church movement as such is said to provide a vehicle which enhances the mental health of those it attracts. Thus Motala (1989:197) states that "[t]he independent church movement seems to be a Black response to an alien world of urban values, that could lead to an integration of personality." Dube (1989:133) emphasises the importance of the concern shown for the person and the person's total well being in Zionist healing. Oosthuizen (1989a:87) refers to the value of creating a psychologically supportive space within which people feel comfortable, at home and cared for and where the emphasis is on re-integration. He contrasts this with the dissociative experience of hospitalisation which usually means "individualisation in distress".

3.2.3 Studies in AIC Healing Methods

A large number of techniques and methods are used by Zionist healers. Dube (1989:127) mentions the importance of touch in the Zionist healing process. The affected parts of the body are touched, stroked and even beaten during the various healing processes. The psychological value of touch in the curing/healing process has been clearly established and is well documented. Wessels (1989:107) indicates nine preferred treatment methods used by the faith healers he studied. Prayer is only the third most important method as fig. 3.3 indicates.

	%Times Mentioned	First Mentioned
Vomiting	34	11
Holy Water	21	0
Prayer	15	2
Inhalation	14	1
Steaming	12	0
Western Medicine	11	1
Enema	6	0
Ropes	5	0
Purging	4	0

Fig. 3.3 AIC Treatment Methods (Source: Wessels 1989:107)

We have already noted Felicity Edwards' (1989) study of healing in terms of consciousness (*isazela*) as expounded by a Zionist prophet healer she worked with. The healer explains himself as follows: "A person is consciousness . . . It is consciousness that moves the body because the body is controlled by consciousness . . . The sickness of a person is in his consciousness . . . when consciousness is healed . . . the body is healed" (Edwards 1989b:333-4). In the healing process the healer says there is a transference of the sickness from the patient to himself as he enters into the consciousness of the person. The link between this and the therapeutic psychiatric relationship is quite striking as is the concept of transference which is also part of the healing process in psychiatry. Sundkler (1961:228-230;154) also points out the existence of psycho-analytic transference present within the atmosphere of mystery and expectation at the "healing services" of Shembe. Central to this notion is the building up of relationship between the healer and the patient and the fact that the dimension of relatedness is much greater and much more emphasized within the African situation than in normal Western psychotherapy where "therapist and patient experience themselves as existing separately from one another and the usual therapeutic modalities take place with the presupposition of that separateness and that externality" (Edwards 1989b:343). Edwards compares this process with the work of psychologist Alvin Mahrer of Canada who speaks of and practises the experience of an "intentional merging" of healer and patient in order to share the patient's experience. Within this process a transference of sensations occur and the therapist is able to effect healing.

Vera Bührmann (1989:34) a Jungian analytical psychologist, sees the growth of African Independent churches and the healing ministry within them as "an intuitive integration of religion as a psychic instinct and the acknowledged spiritual realities of the African people". Following Jung, she recognises the "religious" and its framework as a "psychological instinct on a par with the sex and power instinct" (:33) and the healing process within Independent churches as a psychological healing process within a particular cultural framework.

3.3 Responses of Psychology and Medicine to Faith Healing and Miraculous Cures

The confusion within the medical profession regarding faith healing and miraculous cures is illustrated by the wide diversity of views on the topic. Botha summarises these views as follows:

> We have those believing that spontaneous healing is a result of the body's capacity to heal beyond medical expertise. Others feel that no real healing without some form of therapeutic intervention, ranging from a wound dressing to organ transplantation, is possible. We meet also those who have become less critical because of a specific experience, and finally those who practise the art of medicine combined with prayer.
>
> [Botha 1986:190-191]

3.3.1 Medics Against the Notion of Faith Healing

The attitude of those who deny religious and miraculous cures in particular can be summed up by the views of Des Stumpf, a medical doctor and committed Christian. In a letter to the South African Medical Journal he writes:

> As a committed Christian, I have made an in-depth theological, sociological and medical investigation into the Pentecostal and Charismatic movements and their preoccupation with and heavy emphasis upon so-called 'miraculous' healings. Regrettably I have not witnessed a single genuine miracle, nor confirmed that one has oc-

curred at the hands of these people. [Stumpf 1985:574]

Stumpf does not deny that healing does sometimes occur in these gatherings, however, he insists that "[s]o called 'miracles' are found only in the psychosomatic and not in the organic area" (Stumpf 1986:217). Stumpf's letter in the South African Medical Journal elicited a reply from S. Levin (1985:796) who himself had made a similar enquiry into miracle cures in 1966 also without witnessing a miracle cure. In the same letter Levin (:796) cites the study of the psychiatrist L. Rose (1968) who failed to find a "single substantiated miracle cure" in a study of thousands of "faith cured folk" over a period of 15 years.

Anderson (1986:177) also affirms "a strong element of magical powers and quackery in much that is deemed to be faith healing". And Ikin points out that one of the reasons why the medical profession distrusts "healing missions" is that whilst the emotional arousal may be what is required to help some people deal with their problems, this same arousal may cause a compounding of problems amongst others:

> This is one reason why after a healing mission in which many may have been cured there is often a great increase of mental instability in others, and the doctors find their hands full of those who had only just kept their mental balance prior to such reinforcement, but who had been swept away by the emotional effect of the mission. This is one of the reasons why the medical profession tends to distrust healing missions. Doctors come up against the harm they do amongst the emotionally unstable, whereas those who have found help do not come to them, so that they do not see those who have genuinely responded spiritually. [Ikin 1955:54]

Leslie Weatherhead (1951:201-203) in his classic work, says that there are often temporary cures of individuals as they feel some "power" entering in them as a result of the emotion of the moment. As the emotion wears off, the condition usually returns. Weatherhead (:204-208) posits six major objections to healing missions in general. These are summarised below:

1) *The Power of Suggestion is too dangerously used.*
   The emotion charged atmosphere and the claims made in the mission set this power in motion. The missions tend to attract "hysterics of all types",and rather than curing the hysteria it is just displaced in another area so that the "great sinner" now becomes a "great saint" but remains as removed from reality as before.[5]

2) *The publicity surrounding healing missions exacerbates the dangers.*

3) *A mistaken notion of faith is promulgated where faith and suggestibility are too closely linked.*
   The problem of no healing resulting from a lack of faith puts severe psychological burdens on those who are not cured.

4) *There is no New Testament authority for such healing missions*

especially regarding the notion of faith used.

5) *Many people coming to healing missions are in an unhealthy emotional state.*
   They are hoping for a cure when other means have failed. The danger is that God is being used as a means to human ends.

6) *Most people are not cured.*
   The fact of bringing so many people who are sick together and raising their hopes only to dash them when there are no cures is to leave people disillusioned and worse off than when they started. Thus on a pro-rata basis, whilst some may be cured, the majority are actually harmed.

3.3.2 Medics With More Positive Attitudes to Faith Healing

When the focus is shifted away from the strictly organic and the excesses criticised above, many medics, usually as a result of personal experience, have a much more open attitude to the healing ministry. Such views can be summed up in the approach of Paul Brand (Brand & Yancey 1983:15) "a committed Christian involved in the field of medicine for four decades [who] . . . view[s] the upsurge of enthusiasm over healing with mixed emotion." His major problem with the extreme faith healing perspective is that

> it seems to ask me to put absolute faith in something that does not ordinarily prove true in life. God neither protects Christians with a shield of health nor provides a quick dependable solution to all suffering . . . It is obvious from common observation that God does not *always* intervene in physical healing . . . Why does he heal some and not others? [Brand & Yancey 1983:16]

From his own research and experience Brand comes to the following conclusion:

> What most people think when you say the word "divine healing" - a supernatural intervention that reverses natural laws governing our bodies - is extremely rare indeed. God does not normally interact directly at the organic level, and, in fact, it would not affect my faith in the least if he chose never to reverse those natural laws. [Brand & Yancey 1983:18]

However, he then goes on to widen the notion of healing to the psychosomatic and points out that most supernatural healings occur in particular types of diseases: "neurasthenia, bursitis, arthritis, lameness, deafness, allergies, migraine headaches" (Brand & Yancey 1983:19). He follows the opinion of many scientists and physicians in attributing such healings to the power of the mind and suggestion. He goes on to illustrate the power of the mind to influence the body through some documented studies (:19). These are summarised below:

1) The mind can control pain either by mental discipline (eg Hindu fakirs) or by methods, such as acupuncture, which distract the nervous system with other sensations.
2) The placebo effect also illustrates the ability of faith in the effect of the

pill to cure or relieve symptoms.

3) Under hypnosis some people can be made to lose the sense of pain so much that they can be operated on without anaesthetic.

4) Research on biofeedback indicates that people can train themselves to control involuntary bodily processes such as blood pressure, heart rate and even hand temperature.

These and other examples cited by Brand indicate how science is only now becoming vaguely aware of the power of the mind and of suggestion to control the body. The role of emotion, feelings and stress also operate on this level. He claims that many so-called spiritual cures can be demonstrated to be achieved through the operation of these psychosomatic mechanisms (Brand & Yancey 1983:19).

Other writers are more ready to claim that a spiritual dimension of healing does exist and that they have witnessed its effects. J.D. Anderson (1986:179) of the University of the Orange Free State affirms that "healing by prayer does work and there are many cases on record where people have been helped or even been cured of apparently incurable diseases." He gives two examples from his own experiences (:179-180). Jim Glennon (1984:107) also presents the personal testimony of a medical practitioner who incorporated the healing ministry of prayer into his own work in paediatrics. Within a period of nine months after beginning this, he began to get the impression that

> patients were recovering faster than when other people treated them; there were less complications of illness and treatment . . . It was in the intensive care unit that the effect was most noticeable, because of the rapidity of improvement and decline of many neonatal disorders. In I.C.U. I found that rarely did 'disasters' and deaths occur while I was on duty compared to their rather more common occurrence when others were on duty. [Glennon 1984:107-108]

John Knight (1982:140) a medical practitioner in Australia, is another sceptic who has changed his views as a result of his own experiences. He writes "Doctors do not believe in miracles. I don't either. Or I didn't until my patient was cured of her shoulder disability". The case concerns a woman who had suffered with severe arthritis of the arm for many years and was unable to raise it more than 45 degrees from her body. She had tried all kinds of cures without success. She was cured on national television by the laying of hands of a faith healer whom she had never met. Dr. Knight was asked by the television company to bring a patient to the show. The woman with arthritis was his patient. He writes:

> The faith healer . . . said that he was unable to "cure" anybody, but divine power mediated through his hands might help the lady. A few moments later he laid his hands on the woman's disabled shoulder, called for special power in a loud voice, perspired profusely - his face was very wet - then told my patient to raise her healed arm into the air.
>
> Which she immediately did!

> No pain, no lack of movement, no hesitation! The effect was electric. The studio gasped in disbelief. So did my patient, who had not raised her arm to full overhead height in years.
>
> Today, three years later, the joint is still free from pain, supple, mobile, flexible as ever. She has not required any medication for her disorder, for it no longer exists. [Knight 1982:140]

Des Proctor, a committed Christian and medical doctor from Port Elizabeth was prompted by the "rather harsh" attitude of Stumpf to faith healing to respond in the South African Medical Journal as follows:

> Unlike Drs Beck and Stumpf, I have on many occasions personally witnessed genuine inexplicable miracle cures, instantaneous as well as delayed. Healing does not have to be instantaneous to be a miracle. In fact, in a broad sense, any form of healing, operative or otherwise, is a miracle, because it is under God's control. God created the natural laws of science. Man has only discovered some of them. No phenomenon can supersede God's laws. Our Lord reveals to us so much of these laws at a time according to His perfect plan, and with time our knowledge increases . . . Let us expose or condemn imposters and bogus 'faith-healers', but be careful not to discredit the power of prayer. [Proctor 1985:784]

Proctor raises an issue which concerns many researchers. Is faith healing a manifestation of natural laws that we do not yet understand fully, or have not yet discovered or, rather, is it a manifestation of a supernatural direct intervention of God which suspends the natural or rather transforms the natural by the power of the supernatural?

3.3.3 Poorly Understood Psycho-Physical Factors Relating to Healing

A number of authors posit the existence of natural psychic forces which are operating in the field of healing and which play a role in the healing process. Some people have a greater ability than others to mobilise and to control these forces and these people often become gifted healers. Anderson (1986:177) insists that besides the psychological influences on somatic illness and somatic influences on the psyche, there is a third dimension, the spiritual, which must be considered. "We cannot make this third element of our life disappear because we do not believe in it" (1986:177). He suggests that faith healing is just one of the normal means available to us from God "to be used in conjunction with God's other instruments of healing" (1986:181). Jackson (1981:22-23) refers to the Wainwright seminars which have brought together "psychiatrists, doctors of internal medicine, surgeons, representatives of the healing arts in other countries along with psychologists, clergymen and practitioners of spiritual therapy". Participants in the Wainwright seminars affirm the existence of such healing forces.

> Those who have participated in these seminars have affirmed that there is a healing force medically verified but not medically explained that it is at work in and through the persons of certain gifted healers. Dr. Robert Laidlaw, Chief of Psychiatric Services at Roosevelt Hospital in New York, reported that this healing force is character-

> ised by a deeply penetrating and intense form of heat. He also claimed that the type of person who possesses these gifts is invariably a spiritually dedicated and outgoing type of personality. [Jackson 1981:23]

Jackson (1981:72) also cites the research of Weinberger, a physicist who has been able to measure "radiation passing from the hands of a praying clergyman into the body of a person being prayed for". Bernard Grad, a Biochemist and medical researcher at McGill Medical School has also conducted experiments on this force. Grad worked with a man who claimed to have had success in healing people by the laying on of hands. An experiment was devised using mice which had had goitres developed in them. The aim was to see if there was any difference in healing produced by the healer laying hands on them. The mice were divided into three groups. The faith healer laid hands on the first group for fifteen minutes, twice a day for forty days. The second group received a heat treatment to reproduce the amount of heat that the healer's hands would normally produce in that time. The third group was not given any treatment. Grad's (1970:20) results showed that the group which received laying of hands fared far better than the other groups.

Another experiment carried out by Grad concerned the rate of healing of wounds in mice. He was able to show that LH (Laying of Hands) by the faith healer

> did accelerate significantly the rate of wound healing in mice as compared with animals which received no LH at all, or were treated by LH by persons who made no claims to a gift of healing. Here also, evidence was obtained that body heat could not be invoked as the cause of the accelerated healing. [Grad 1970:21]

A further experiment (Grad 1970:21-22) showed that the same healer had a marked ability to influence the growth rate of barley seeds. Grad's research leads him to the conclusion: "That healing by LH [Laying of Hands] is a reality supported by the experiments cited in this paper . . . [T]here are persons with the power to heal who do much to alleviate suffering quietly and selflessly" (Grad 1970:25-26).

Renée Haynes (1981:22-23) also affirms the existence of some energy operating through the healer. She calls this form of healing psychic healing and describes it as follows:

> The term psychic healing can then be used for a phenomenon which looks as if it were based on the transmission of some form of energy as yet unknown from healer to patient. In many instances this may be analogous to the force at work in psychokinesis; in fact one might call the whole process psychokinetic healing.
> [Haynes 1981:22-23]

Psychiatrist Daniel Benor (1991:5-16) refers to this form of healing as "Psi healing" and defines it as "the intentional influence of one or more people on one or more other living organisms without intervention through physical or chemical means" (:5). He suggests that it can operate through the laying on of hands or through mental influence alone and that distance appears to have little or no effect on it. His research has "identified 140 controlled trials of psi-healing" and of these sixty one (44%) indicate significant evidence of the phenomenon (:6). He also cites a study of 149 experiments on psycho-kinetic phenomena by Braud (1989) in which fifty three percent yield significant results. For Benor (1991:11) this effect is a natural one which has not yet been detected by science.

Clearly our scientific understanding of these phenomena and their meaning is only in its infancy. Much research in the medical and psychological fields needs to be done. At present the evidence seems to indicate the presence of some phenomenon operating which can have a healing effect on people. However, its exact nature as natural, neurological, emotional, psychological, epistemological or some combination of these is yet to be determined.

3.3.4 Demon Possession and Psychology

Much of the Coping-healing ministry we presented in the previous chapter appears to work within the epistemological framework of "demons". Sickness is seen as resulting from demon possession and healing is seen as casting the demons out. A study of epistemological frameworks is made in our philosophical mediation but here we will focus on the psychological dimension of demons, demon possession and the like.

Hollenweger (1972) devotes a full chapter to the issue of demons in his classic work and concludes that most "possession" by demons can actually be explained "within the framework of modern psychiatric knowledge" (:380). Nevertheless, he argues that an "inexplicable remnant" does not lend itself to such an explication. This does not necessarily point to the existence of demons but rather to a lacuna in our ability to explain reality (:381). Despite this, effective healing depends on the ability of the healer to set up a psycho-therapeutic relationship with the sick person. Such a relationship is one which is prepared to enter into dialogue with the person in his or her own existential context. This may mean accepting the reality of the demon at least for the sick person. Hollenweger (1972:381-382) cites the case of "Pastor Blumhardt" who enters into a person's sickness by accepting the reality of the demon in the life of the person. Hollenweger's partially psychological interpretation of the healing suggests that by dialogue-ing with the demon (or psychosis) and "becoming in part subject to it . . . by entering into the situation of the psychosis, Blumhardt finally overcame it."

For Bührmann (1986a:92) the possession is merely an outward manifestation of something deeper and neurotic sickness is developed in order to correct psychic balance. Demons, ancestors and dreams are ways of getting in touch with the deeper recesses of the unconscious. She claims that healing or effective therapy will not be achieved without a change in personality and attitudes. In Western culture, psychotherapy puts the emphasis on understanding the dream whereas in religious healing, which accepts the world-view of demon possession, the healing is effected by destroying the demon through the use of a greater power. In African culture, demons and other symbols are effectively acted out and ritualised without recourse to the conscious, leading to perceived emotional and psychological benefits for the participants.

3.3.5 Religious Development and Psychological Illness

Ikin (1955:60-66) draws attention to the important fact that faulty religious development is sometimes the source of many illnesses as a result of guilt feelings and unreasonable fears. A religion which becomes an escape from life rather than the unifying factor of life becomes destructive of the person and those around. Those who carry around with them an infantile underdeveloped faith are often carrying around a similarly immature psycho-emotional development (:65).

3.4 Psychological and Medical Studies on "Indigenous Healing" in South Africa

3.4.1 "Indigenous Healing" as Psychotherapy

The South African medical and psychological professions have tended to focus their research on "indigenous healing" in South Africa. This usually refers to that healing done within an African cultural paradigm. Christian religious faith healing is usually seen as but one aspect of current indigenous healing practices. Consequently, from the perspective of this mediation it is useful to look at studies on indigenous healing in general - which are much more numerous - in order to abstract results and conclusions which would be seen by these authors as generally applying to the Coping-healing phenomenon we are studying.

Vera Bührmann, is convinced of the centrality of the psychological dimension of African traditional practices. Indeed, in her celebrated work, *Living in Two Worlds* (1986a:13-14) she points out that her aim is precisely to demonstrate that Xhosa traditional healing techniques are "not 'magical' in the usual sense of the word but based on sound principles of depth psychology, especially as formulated by Carl Gustav Jung and his followers."

The South African psychologist T.L. Holdstock (1979) refers to the current proven effectiveness of indigenous healing techniques within South Africa. In his short article he emphasises the following values in the indigenous healing process:

1) Within the therapeutic relationship of healer to patient, effectiveness is enhanced when both share the same cultural system (Holdstock 1979:119).
2) It is holistic in nature which is in keeping with recent developments in psychology (:120).
3) The healer has a high prestige amongst the community which leads to an increase in trust levels enhancing the condition for the possibility of

a cure (:120).

4) Modern advances in brain research indicate "the importance of the non verbal consciousness of the right hemisphere and areas buried deep inside the brain...Perhaps the indigenous healers are the clearest proponents of right hemisphere dominance" (:120).

5) "In the only study of its kind in South Africa, Robbertze [sic] (1976) of the University of Pretoria rated the therapeutic efficacy of indigenous healers as being superior to that of psychiatrists, psychotherapists or medical doctors in the treatment of certain conditions" (:120).

6) It is much more readily available to black people since there are healers of all types in the black areas of the country and most charge relatively small amounts for their services (:121).

Holdstock argues for the recognition of indigenous healers and for some kind of incorporation within a more comprehensive health service. He presents an impressive list of South African psychologists and psychiatrists who have expressed similar sentiments.

Wessels (1984) points out that the kind of conditions which indigenous healers are effective in treating are the "culture bound" syndromes.[6] He acknowledges that there are many of these and that it is necessary to distinguish between them and those more severe psychological conditions which would not usually respond to the treatment of indigenous healing. Ikin (1955) speaking within the context of Western religious healing also emphasises the same point.

> This brings out a factor of great importance, the necessity for recognising diseases of psychogenic origin, that is to say diseases which arise through the inability of the persons concerned to adapt themselves satisfactorily to life. Cure by Unction or the laying of hands in these cases, while it may, and frequently does, give startling and dramatic results, may leave the sufferer spiritually in an even worse case, believing himself or herself so specially blessed by God that the egoism so frequently at the base of this type of disorder, is strengthened, instead of cured. The *point cannot be over-stressed at present.* The danger of loss of mental balance following the application of so-called spiritual healing is very real. There must be *intelligent insight* into the mental, moral and spiritual state of the patient, if spiritual healing is to be effective in the real sense of restoring true health of *spirit* in right relation to the Divine in which our human spirits are rooted. [Ikin 1955:59]

Mkhwanazi (1989:278-279; 1986:110-111) shows how much of the activity of the Zulu traditional healer is, in fact, psycho-therapeutic. Following Frank (1961), she highlights six common features of all psychotherapeutic processes as follows:

-an emotionally charged, confiding relationship.

-a therapeutic rationale accepted by client and therapist.

-provision for new information.

-strengthening of the clients expectation of help.

-provision of success experience.

-facilitation of the emotional arousal.

The focus of her research is on establishing the relationship between the degree of empathy and warmth in the *sangoma* (healer) and the positive improvement of the client. Whilst her results tend to show that such a causal relationship does exist, they were not conclusive and in fact were suggestive of other factors enhancing effectiveness. She describes these as "cultural", linked both to a shared world-view as well as to expectancy attitudes in the client and his/her level of trust and belief in the power of the healer (Mkhwanazi 1986:111-112).

Cheetham and Griffiths (1989:310) also highlight Frank's common elements of psychotherapy practices throughout the world in reference to the work of traditional healers. For them, "success experiences" for both psychotherapist and traditional healer "are largely provided through the relief of anxiety". Transference, suggestion or regression are suggested as the means by which emotional arousal occurs and it is the expectation or trust of the patient in the healer and his or her context which facilitates this process.

Mkhwanazi (1989) and Bührmann (1986b) emphasise the importance of *naming* the condition from which the patient is suffering. The naming process has the effect of moving the sickness from the realm of the unknown, and thus unpredictable, to the known and thus more hopefully manageable. Bührmann (1986a:16) speaking within the context of Western therapy, elicits the following principle: "By giving external and concrete form to fantasy and dream images they become meaningful and less threatening." Mkhwanazi suggests that the naming process whereby the sickness is labelled during the divining process: "is one of the most important components of all forms of psychotherapy and may, in and of itself, be effective in alleviating many of the client's problems. The very act of naming is, therefore, therapeutic" (Mkhwanazi 1989:265). Clearly these comments which refer to traditional healers can also be applied to healing in African Independent churches. We would also contend that at least some healing in the Neopentecostal churches fulfils these criteria of indigenous healing as psychotherapy. The comments of Mkhwanazi as well as Cheetham and Griffiths would seem to be applicable as would some of Holdstock's values. The caveat of Ikin seems to be specifically directed to the Neopentecostal type churches in Britain and the U.S. and so would apply equally to those churches in South Africa.

3.4.2 Symbols and Rituals in Healing

Bührmann and Mkhwanazi deal in some depth with the importance of ritual in healing. Mkhwanazi links the essence of the healing ritual to the naming process illustrated above. She suggests that healing rituals move through three separate stages:

(i) The illness is labelled with an appropriate and sanctioned cultural category;

> (ii) The label is ritually manipulated or, to put it another way, culturally transferred;
>
> (iii) A new label, such as cured or well, is applied and sanctioned as meaningful symbolic form that may be independent of behavioral or social change.
>
> [Mkhwanazi 1989:265-266]

Unfortunately she does not clarify what the second step entails but nevertheless sees in this transformation process the centrality of the manipulation of cultural symbols, a dimension of healing which is considered in our anthropological mediation.

Bührmann (1986a:13) illustrates the essential difference between Western and African forms of therapy as the fact that "preliterate people in therapy *act out* what Western people *talk about*". She suggests that ritual and ceremony allow people to bypass ego control mechanisms and thus to get in touch "with superpersonal forms" (:96). Bührmann also emphasises the importance of the symbolic which is the normal means of communication between unconscious and consciousness which is most clearly experienced by Westerners in dreams. The symbolic allows us to communicate with these deeper levels of the psyche and for Bührmann, this process is easier within cultures that are to a larger extent in touch with these symbols. The Xhosa people she worked with are said to belong to such a culture. "During healing ceremonies these symbols are touched and can transform the patient bringing health and vitality to many a sick and troubled person" (:22). The issue of symbols and rituals in healing is dealt with more fully in the next chapter.

Perhaps we should note here that the view of traditional healers as psychotherapists whilst a useful one could also be seen as reductionist. It does not take into account, for example, the vast amount of knowledge many have regarding the medicinal effects of herbs. Nor does it consider cultural factors in the healing process as we shall also see in the anthropological mediation. Nevertheless, South African psychologists and medical researchers have seen the value of healing offered by traditional and faith healers working within a traditional African cultural context. Unfortunately very little local research is available on faith healers working within a Western cultural paradigm. In order to look at this area, we widen our focus to include Western researchers in general who have studied healers working within a Western cultural paradigm with which South African Western culture is linked.

3.5 Psycho-Medical Understandings of Illness and Healing in General

3.5.1 What is Illness?

We close this chapter by trying to indicate the major paradigms of understanding operating within the psycho-medical field regarding illness and healing in general in order to see how phenomena such as the Coping-healing ministry outlined in the previous chapter can fit in. We start by asking the question:

What is illness? And this simple question is the source of great complexity in the replies. Cheetham and Rzadkowolski indicate this complexity as follows:

> The literature of the past 10 years manifests a dispute over the concepts of 'mental health' and 'mental illness'. Furthermore, there is no universal consensus as to the concept of physical illness, which is variably defined in terms of suffering, aetiology, a pathological lesion or demonstrable physiological change, or finally, the need for treatment. [Cheetham & Rzadkowolski 1980:321]

They go on to say that it is in the field of mental illness where the dispute is greatest, possibly as a result of more objective criteria being available to measure physical illness. "The field of mental health and mental hygiene has become permeated with value judgements and moral and ethical statements, hidden behind a facade of science" (Cheetham & Rzadkowolski 1980:321). Understandings vary from a totally biological approach where mental health and sickness is explained in terms of physical biological systems through to a totally cultural approach where mental sickness is "only what is perceived as such in a culture" (:322). Most understandings, however, are a mixture of both approaches and Cheetham and Rzadkowolski opt for an "eclectic holistic approach" and in particular a "general systems theory" understood as follows:

> If the human organism is viewed as composed of a number of hierarchically organized subsystems (particles, molecules, cells, organs) and itself belonging to larger systems (family, group, organization, society, nation, ecological environment), with each system relating reciprocally to the others, health will be understood as a dynamic balance of the systems and illness as a disequilibrium. If this is acceptable, the dichotomies mentioned above will cease to exist.
> [Cheetham & Rzadkowolski 1980:322]

Many authors point out the difference between the "medical model" in which the focus is on curing the disease and the "healing" model where the focus is on healing the illness (Kleinman & Sung 1979:7-8 cf. Boucher n.d.:15). Boucher notes that the preoccupation of the medical system with the former, especially in its organisation, is often opposed to the perception of the patient who wishes to be healed from illness and this dichotomy leads to people searching for alternative forms of healing. Curing the disease is what the Western medical system preoccupies itself with and cures are both physical (surgical and other interventions) and chemical (drugs and other chemical cures such as herbs). Healing the illness is the preserve of traditional healing practices and of the religious healer although many of them also claim to cure physical sickness. This division is also reflected to some extent in Ngubane's (1977:23-24) well known distinction between "*Umkhuhlane*" and "*Ukufa kwabantu*" (ch.2 n.2) where the former refers to illness as a biological factor whereas the latter is seen as "disease of the African peoples" and are called such "because the philosophy of causality is based on African culture" (:24).

Turning now to the more psychological dimensions of illness, we begin by highlighting the place of the well known "conversion disorder" or "conversion hysteria". The disorder was known to the ancient Greeks but was given its first psychological etiology by Freud. These disorders typically occur in situations of stress or conflict (Nair 1984:153). Conversion disorder results in the manifestation of a wide variety of organic symptoms such as blindness, deafness, various types of lameness and paralysis as well as a number of visceral symptom such as a choking, breathing difficulties and so on (Whittaker 1966:208). Nair (1985:154) points out that the current theory regarding the cause of this disorder is "that of a fixation in psychosexual development in the oedipal complex". He notes that with the development of a "more open acceptance of sexuality in Western culture "(:154) the disorder seems to be disappearing in Western society. However it is still observed in the "less sophisticated and less educated especially in the underdeveloped countries" (:154).

Edwards (1985:49-60) affirms the incidence of this disorder in his work with Zulu patients at King Edward VIII hospital in Durban and reports the following:

> The results are similar to those of other studies of hysterical reactions with regard to the high incidence in females, the younger age groups, less sophisticated cultural settings, and frequency of occurrence of hysterical or somatoform symptoms.
>
> [Edwards 1985:55-56]

Some of the symptoms manifest in the patients examined are reflected in fig. 3.4. There is clearly some correspondence between these symptoms and many of those from which people are healed by faith healing.

O1 Akinesia (typically 'unable to walk')	22
Seizures	13
Paralysis	11
Aphonia	10
Dyskinesia	7
Abdominal pains	6
Vomiting	4
Tremors	2
Total Number of Symptoms reported	80
(Total Sample 63 patients)	

Fig. 3.4 Conversion Disorder Symptoms - times reported (Source: Edwards 1985:56)

Psycho-medical understandings of illness and healing, then, can be described in terms of three basic paradigms. The medical paradigm looks at curing organic disease. The psychological paradigm accepts that organic symptoms can result from psychological factors and can be cured by psychological mechanisms. Finally, a more exotic, holistic model is posited which attempts to place sickness and healing within a systems approach.

3.5.2 Understanding Religious Healing

With regard to religious healing[7] and psycho-medical understandings of this phenomenon, we begin with Hollenweger's (1972:370-373) assessment of healing through prayer. Firstly he notes that "miracles are ambiguous and not specifically Christian" (:371). There are too many examples for the phenomenon to be dismissed and he describes them as, so far, "inexplicable events". He notes that it is unscientific to speak of these events as "breaking the laws of nature" since science deals with experience and as our experience of nature changes, so science must adapt to this. Healing through prayer is seen as significant and perhaps its importance has been underestimated since its effectiveness cannot be denied. However it should not be seen as an alternative to the practice of medicine (:371-372).

Harold Vanderpool (1977:255-259) asks the question "Is Religion Therapeutically Significant?" and draws the conclusion that it is indeed so for two fundamental reasons. The first relates to cultural and philosophical world-view factors in that

> religion - inevitably allied with philosophy - supplies an over-arching conceptual understanding of the world in which medicine is practised. Religion, that is, often supplies a set of "ultimate explanations" for the existence and meaning of illness and curing. It addresses itself to whether sickness is natural or unnaturally intrusive, an unmitigated evil or partial good, a result of impartial or personal causes, an enemy that is to be actively eradicated or an entity that should be passively accepted. It often informs powerfully the values and social images of medical practitioners and influences the sanctioning or prohibiting of certain human activities, e.g., diet, sexuality, drug-taking, and so on. [Vanderpool 1977:255-259]

The second reason relates to the practice of a healing ministry within the Church which is clearly healing many people of perceived illness. Vanderpool sees both a curing and a caring dimension to this ministry and suggests that two major factors play a role in "curative religious healing" that are often absent from medical curative programs:

> These involve, first, intensely subjective personal interaction and, second, an extraordinary degree of group support. These factors are notably different from the scientific model of the physician-patient relationship as one characterized by objectivity and individualized interaction. [Vanderpool 1977:258-259]

He suggests that these factors are similar to those operating within many other "non-Christian healing rites" (:259). Clinical psychologist Clifford Kew, (1961:31-32) presents six therapeutic dimensions of typical church "healing services":

1) "They create an atmosphere of serenity and faith and an awareness of God which satisfies some of their conscious and unconscious needs" (:31).
2) They help people to relax their defences so that they can express their emotions.
3) They create an atmosphere of group concern so that people experience being surrounded by concerned, caring others.

4) An attitude of faith in a positive outcome on the part of the sick person and love on the part of the healer contribute to an effective therapeutic relationship.

5) Prayer is "the most powerful form of energy that one can generate" (:32).

6) "The healing service helps one to identify out of proximity and participation in the group, with something outside of himself and with a Higher Power" (:32).

He also points to the "similarities between the techniques of psychoanalysis and certain religious healings indicating the operation of mechanisms such as increased suggestibility, transference, emotional change and acceptance of new beliefs and thought" (Vanderpool 1977:32-33). Botha (1986) addresses this same issue in his short article and suggests that the following factors play an important role in the healing process:

1) *The attitude of the patient.*
All healing, including medical and surgical, is facilitated by attitudes of compliance, motivation and faith and retarded by anxiety and guilt feelings (:182-83).

2) *Most healing is spontaneous and occurs without any outside human intervention.*
Much research is being done into the area of spontaneous healing and Botha quotes evidence of healing without outside intervention in many sicknesses which are normally considered to require some form of intervention (:184).[8]

3) *People continue to seek other forms of healing when traditional forms of medicine fail.*
This is especially the case when their experience of hospital and doctors has been a negative one especially as a result of "ineffective doctor patient relationship" (:187).

4) *Sickness is sometimes a consequence of psychological and emotional factors*
Some people even consciously manufacture symptoms for their own personal reasons (:187-188).

5) *Inexplicable healings do occur.*
We are as yet unable to say how and why this is so. More research is needed. Nevertheless the medical profession should not appropriate to itself all competence in the field of healing (:190).

Jung's view of the importance of the transcendent function as the major unifying determinant in the life of a person is emphasised by Bührmann (1989:33) as a major contributing factor in the growth of the African Independent churches and, by extension, to other churches fulfilling this role. Religion is a psychological instinct on a par with the sex and power instincts and provides a unifying factor in the disparateness of a person's life. Concerning Black traditional healers in South Africa, Bührmann (1986b) indicates that some of the important factors operating in the healing process are as follows:

1) *The personality and attitude of the healer (:108).*
   The healer needs to have an attitude of respect and confidence, the ability to exert a "strong 'suggestive' influence on the patient".
2) *Confession and Catharsis (:109).*
   These two aspects exercise the effect of destroying the isolation of the person by revealing himself or herself to another and of restoring relationship as well as the emotional gain experienced in "emptying oneself of evil and allowing goodness to enter".
3) *Ritual (:110).*
   This provides an entry into the non rational areas of the psyche. It is seen as an "artificial means of bringing the healing powers of the unconscious into play".
4) *Dance (:110-112).*
   Dance is interpreted as working together with ritual and confession to produce a "therapeutic unit" (:110). The form of dance in a circle creates a symbol of unity and wholeness: an expression of the universal mandala symbol. In this way the experience of containment, security and belonging is enhanced in the participants with corresponding therapeutic gain.
5) *Role of Culture (:113).*
   Uniformity of culture enhances the communication process and greatly increases the efficacy of healers working with people suffering from the effects of acculturation. This is particularly the case with "spirit healers" in the African Independent churches.

3.5.3 The Relationship between Faith and the Power of Suggestion

Techniques such as the "positive thinking" of Dr. Norman Vincent Peale and the principle of repetitious creative affirmation found in Christian Science highlight the value of suggestion in promoting well being. The basic premise here seems to be that conscious patterns of thought can reach and modify the lower reaches of consciousness and that it is possible, in this way, to programme ourselves to health by positive thoughts. Such ideas are very popular today and form much of the psychological dimension of the modern health movement (Jackson 1981:141-142).

Clearly the effectiveness of the power of suggestion depends on the receptivity of the receiver. In an interesting study by Gibbons and Jarnette (1972:152-156) the relationship between perceived religious experience and hypnotic susceptibility was examined amongst a group of 185 university students. A standard psychological test was administered to determine hypnotic susceptibility.

Those students who scored very high and very low on the test were then further examined through a follow up questionnaire relating to their religious beliefs and experience. The results indicated that "whilst there was no significant relationship between hypnotic susceptibility and frequency of church attendance . . . those who were in the high susceptible group reported *without exception*, that their conversion was primarily an *experiential* phenomenon" (authors' emphasis) (:154). The authors conclude as follows:

> The present data support the conclusion that the existential phenomena which comprise the experience of conversion and salvation - and, by extension, perhaps other types of transcendental experiences - are in reality "hypnotic" phenomena, which occur without a formal induction in response to implicit or explicit suggestions conveyed by the speaker, the setting, or the attendant ceremony. Because of individual variations in suggestibility, however, the ability to experience such phenomena as objectively real events may not be within the range of all who may desire to do so. *It may be limited to that minority of the population which is capable of experiencing "deep trance" phenomena in hypnosis*. (authors' emphasis)
>
> [Gibbons and Jarnette 1972:155]

Turning to the role of faith in healing, Jackson (1981:23) cites Frank's work at John Hopkins Medical school which indicates that faith does indeed play a pivotal role in healing. Such medically defined faith is divided by Frank into four components: expectancy, suggestion, personality structure and status (:25). Expectancy refers to the essential attitude of the patient who expects that a cure will occur. Many placebo effects in medicine rely on this factor (:25-26). Suggestion works in a synergistic way with expectancy and enhances it. Research has indicated that the positive reinforcement and suggestion of well-being has a marked effect on the healing process (:28). The research of Frank and others has indicated that certain personality structures are more open to suggestion and expectancy attitudes and thus to healing through faith. The optimum personality profile is one "oriented about external factors" rather than one who is "oriented about his own inner sense of balance". This is further defined as one who is "accepting, responsive and less rigid" as opposed to those who are "rigid, aggressive and suspicious". Jackson (:29) summarises this personality type as the "traditionally religious person, with a capacity for faith, a mood of expectancy and hope and an ability to relate one's self to others in a strong and life-modifying relationship".

The fourth dimension of faith considered by Frank is "status" and by this he refers to "one's attitude towards one's self in relation to other persons" (Jackson 1981:29). If the disease produces a particular status in the emotional life of the person then a cure will only be effected if a compensating emotional experience occurs which provides a greater status in the life of the sick person. It is as if the disease itself is having a perceived, positive emotional effect on the person and will only be traded for a greater emotional reward.

Jackson (1981:83-84) ascribes three ingredients to faith itself: beliefs on the mental level; convictions on the emotional level; and organic acting out on the physical level. When the role of faith on healing is considered, then all three of these levels are involved but to differing extents from person to person. In this way either the mental or emotional may play a greater or lesser role in influencing the physical. Weatherhead (1951:470) also emphasised these factors in his earlier work. He notes that the following factors can have a strong causative influence on illness: emotional condition especially worry and fear; unconscious emotional conflicts which manifest themselves as physical disease; feelings such as guilt, hate, resentment and envy. He also concurs that attitude of mind is itself a powerful healer even in sickness which is totally physiogenic. Central to the healing process is the movement to integration in which personality as body, mind and spirit is restored to "perfect functioning in its relevant environment" (:466).

3.5.4 The Importance of the Role of the Leader

Sundkler (1961:237) was the first to point out how "Faith healing among the Zulu is intimately bound up with the personality of the prophet" and psychologists such as Fuller Torrey (1972) have pointed to this as one of the universal components of psychotherapy (in Cheetham & Griffiths 1989:309). Hollenweger (1972:382) stresses the point that healing actually occurs when the healer abandons a ministry of merely instructing and consoling the sick person and actually enters into a dialogue with the sick person on the sickness "setting the faculties of experience free to receive a new experience" (:382). In this dialogue the "area of consciousness" is enlarged and it is this process which heals. One has to enter into the psychosis in order to cure it. This has similarities to the approach of Ntshobodi discussed by Edwards (1989b) and to the healing work done by Canadian psychotherapist Mahrer discussed in the same article. Clearly empathy, as a process of entering into the sickness and its parameters in order to help the patient re-experience its etiology and thus be freed from it, plays a role in some healing processes. Nevertheless, Boucher (n.d.:222) reports that the role of the healer is not always determinant and that in her research healings occurred "also in the absence of belief in the healer's personal power . . . Indeed successful healings occurred in two cases where the client was in active conflict with the healer and doubted her efficacy".

3.5.5 The Importance of Psychological Transference in Healing

Sundkler's (1961:154) refers to the operation of this mechanism in his description of a "healing service" for 250 barren women at Ekuphakameni. For Sundkler, the transference was a manifestation of Shembe's ability to "establish a bond of fellowship and dependence which easily surpassed in intensity all other leader-follower relations which I have witnessed in these churches" (:154).

F.S.Edwards (1989b:343-344) also points out how the Zionist healer she studied was able to assume the transferred symptoms onto himself whilst maintaining his own wholeness and identity "in the trans personal level". It is the taking onto himself of the transferred symptoms which effects the healing in this case.

3.5.6 The Role of Consciousness and Re-experiencing in the Healing Process

The role of consciousness as a healing force was also emphasised by F.S. Edwards (1989b) in her work with the Zionist healer Ntshobodi. His understanding of consciousness is a little different to that of Western psychologists since it also includes a level of "consciousness" of which the person is not aware: what Western psychologists would call the subconscious or unconscious. Healing occurs in the consciousness for Ntshobodi and involves a coming to awareness (:334).

Jackson also refers to this dimension, articulating the healing achieved through the "re-experiencing" of events and memories of the person's life. He explains this as follows:

> The processes of re-experiencing are varied and complicated. Much of what is involved in psychoanalytic procedure is the releasing of accumulated emotional energy in deeper levels of consciousness by the process of cathexis, a bringing to the conscious level of the submerged source of the accumulated emotion.
>
> [Jackson 1981:150]

The re-experiencing of memories can be a powerful healing tool and was the subject of a popular book by two Jesuit Priests, Matthew and Dennis Linn (1978).

3.5.7 Altered States of Consciousness

Boucher (n.d.:224) reports that healing rituals often induce an "Altered State of Consciousness" (ASC). The techniques used by the healer together with suggestion, may also have the same effect (:236) She contests that

> Cognitive states are profoundly affected in the ASC. This is the result of brain chemistry and communication. The central nervous system responds to stress, e.g., by alteration of previous patterns of response . . . In healing, the ASC cancels the illness perception, leaving the client open to positive suggestion in affirmation.
>
> [Boucher n.d.:236-237]

She suggests that the role of the ASC has been undervalued in much of what occurs in traditional and religious healing. They have positive emotional effects and allow a person to cope with situations of stress (Boucher n.d.:241). Easthope (1986:133) agrees that such a state is effective in providing the condition whereby a change in identity can occur through which a person reconstructs himself or herself in terms of positive rather than negative factors and symbols.

3.5.8 The Role of Balance in Health

Several authors suggest that the human system adapts to change and stress by attempting to maintain a balance either somatically or psychologically and that sickness is often a manifestation of the attempt to maintain that balance. Jackson (1981:37) notes that "[m]uch so-called physical illness [is] the physical symptom of loss of inner balance and maladjustment to living". Intropsychic balance is disturbed as a result of defensive and aggressive reactions, external events and circumstances which are not known or understood (:154). Jackson

(:66-67) cites the work of Le Shan (1977) who has shown how restoration of intropsychic balance can have a positive effect on cancer remission. Jackson (:199 ch.4 n.3) also quotes the opinion of Dr.Norman Shealey, a neurosurgeon, who suggests that "prayer may yet be discovered to be the most effective resource for fighting cancer through recreating the inner climate that activates the body's own immunological resources to resist the development of neoplasts".

3.6 Conclusion

It is only since the work of Kiev in 1964 that the medical and psychiatric professions have begun to recognise, in a positive way, the work of healing being done by traditional and religious healers and only since the 1970's that commonalities were recognised between traditional and scientific healing systems (Rappaport and Rappaport 1981:774). Our research in this section has shown that a lively debate still rages within the psychological and medical professions regarding the status and mechanism of religious and traditional healing. Whilst it is almost certainly true that accounts of some religious healings are, for one reason or another, exaggerated, we do feel that enough scientific evidence has been presented here to conclude that extraordinary healing powers, which are little understood scientifically, are manifest in some people. Equally we conclude that these are not restricted to a Christian or even religious context. Religious healers are able to build up experience in dealing with cases, especially those consulted on a client basis. Both their intuitive ability and their experience enables them to both diagnose and heal in both the medical and psychotherapeutic fields. It is also clear that religious ceremonies do have the ability to effect psychological and psychosomatic states. Experience shows that these effects can have positive as well as negative outcomes. The perceived positive outcomes are usually understood as healing.

One of the important factors which has been constantly emerging during this section in the role of culture and cultural factors both in illness and healing. It is to a deeper examination of these factors that we now turn in our anthropological mediation of the Coping-healing phenomenon.

Chapter 4

The Anthropological Mediation: Culture's Central Role in Coping-Healing

4.1 Introduction

Description of the healing practices of non-Western cultures has been part of the work of anthropologists since the beginning of the discipline. The early Western ethnocentric nature of the discipline has meant that it is only in recent times that anthropology has begun to incorporate Christian healing into its area of interest. Even so, the focus has tended to be on so-called "syncretistic" movements where Christianity is expressed in non-Western cultural modes such as the African Indigenous (Independent) churches. Of late, the more unusual Christian expressions, even within Western culture, have been the topic of some anthropological studies, especially the Pentecostal and Neopentecostal churches with their emphasis on healing. In this chapter we present and analyze some of these studies. At the outset, however, it would seem useful to indicate the parameters within which we intend to work since both "anthropology" and "healing ministry", the two foci of this section, are not easy to grasp clearly.

With regard to anthropology, we need to note that the boundaries of the discipline are extremely fuzzy and overlap both into sociology and psychology. This is particularly so when one studies "healing" and so as a consequence some of the research presented here has actually been done within these related fields. We also note the emergence of "medical anthropology", whose authors will be widely quoted, as the attempt to relate and interpret various cultural expressions and understandings of sickness and health, disease and curing. We take the category of "culture" as the central organising key of anthropology and in doing so take a standpoint within the discipline. For our understanding of culture we accept for the moment[1], Geertz's well known description:

> It denotes an historically transmitted pattern of meanings embodied in symbols, a system of inherited conceptions expressed in symbolic forms by means of which men communicate, perpetuate, and develop their knowledge about and attitudes toward life.
>
> [Geertz 1973:89]

In accepting both this definition and the centrality of the cultural category we recognise that religious healing and, specifically, the Christian healing ministry, is going to be interpreted and understood in terms of cultural categories (cf. Chidester 1989:21-23). This is the purpose of this mediation. An important consequence is that anthropologists see religious healing including the Christian Coping-healing phenomenon, within the category of cultural healing, often expressed as "folk healing". This is often contrasted to Western medicine, interpreted as curing disease (Boucher n.d.:15). An important corollary to this is that the conclusions from studies of cultural healing can often be applied to the Christian Coping-healing phenomenon. Because of the paucity of direct anthropological research on the Coping-healing phenomenon in Neopentecostal churches in particular, we intend to make use of this corollary in our own reflections.

The discipline of anthropology has generated three main schools: "functionalism", "structuralism" and "semiotics", although most anthropologists use insights from all three. The functionalists study culture and practices from the view point of the function of the culture and practices within a society. Functionalist interpretations of the Coping-healing phenomenon tend to emphasize its role in restoring disturbed relationships within the society and creating harmony within the group through the elimination of disturbing elements (cf. Kleinman 1980:82; Douglas 1970a; Easthope 1986:122-123). Semiotic interpretations of the Coping-healing phenomenon search to identify and understand the symbols which are operating within the healing process. Healing within this model is seen as the manipulation of these symbols leading to a transformation within the consciousness of the person in which the "world" is seen and understood in a new, more positive, way. The link between culture and consciousness in this model is crucial (cf. Moerman 1979; Landy 1977; Geertz 1973). Structuralist understanding of healing attempt to show how cultural expressions are manifestations of a deeper human, transcultural reality which is part of the make-up of the human person, and that various cultural healing processes affect mechanisms within this transcultural reality (cf. Dow 1986:56; Glick 1977:69-70). Structuralist interpretations often recognise that the symbols operating in the healing process are culturally conditioned but that the process which occurs is a universal one. Structuralist interpretations often come close to psychology when they suggest that the fundamental change in healing is a change in identity for the sick person (Easthope 1986:125). The best synthesis of the symbolic and structuralist interpretations comes from Dow (1986) who suggests that:

> It is widely accepted that religious healing, Shamanism, and Western psychotherapy invoke similar psychological processes (Opler 1936; Lederer 1959; Frank 1961; Tseng and McDermott 1981). They seem to be versions of the same thing, but what is that thing of which they are all versions? Moerman (1979) has called it "symbolic healing," and that is what it will be called here. Labeling, however, leaves unanswered the question of its universal structure. What is the common structure that can describe and explain the organization of all forms of symbolic healing regardless of the culture in which they occur? [Dow 1986:56]

He goes on to indicate a four step process which, he contests, is common to all types of healing. Dow's approach raises several important issues which have been the focus of anthropological studies into healing. Firstly it is important to recognise that both illness and health have a large cultural component. Kleinman (1980:78) goes so far as to say that "illness is always a cultural construct". Secondly, anthropologists point out the importance of a shared world-view between healer and sick person as the essential background or framework within which any healing can occur. Thirdly, it is necessary to recognise the role of symbols within the healing process: both how they are created and how they are manipulated. Moerman (1979:66) suggests that the construction of healing symbols ***is*** healing whereas Kleinman (1980:372) suggests that the symbols are manipulated (often ritually) and reconstructed in the therapeutic process. Fourthly, the transcultural structural dimension needs to be studied and verified as a human process operating in all forms of cultural healing.

These four issues will describe the major framework of our anthropological mediation and subsequent analysis. However before entering into that, it is necessary to consider some anthropological studies of the Coping-healing phenomenon, both in South Africa and beyond in order to see how this phenomenon is situated within cultural healing in general.

4.2 Anthropological Studies of the Coping-Healing Phenomenon

4.2.1 Studies of the Coping-Healing Phenomenon in South Africa

Non-Zionist Healing

In chapter two we described the Coping-healing ministry in several types of churches in South Africa. Unfortunately, however, when it comes to anthropological studies, the focus is almost entirely restricted to the African Independent (Indigenous) churches and especially the "Zionist" churches. Clearly these are numerically by far the largest group. Nevertheless, ethnocentric Western factors operating in researchers may also be playing a role by tending to restrict the focus to non-Western healing. In this section we wish to indicate some of the studies on non-Zionist healing which can inform our anthropological mediation.

Studies on the healing ministry of non-Zionist churches amongst anthropologists in South Africa are limited to some anthropological considerations by Oosthuizen (1975) in his book on the Pentecostal penetration amongst South Africans of Indian origin as well as the largely sociological study of Morran and Schlemmer (1984) into "new churches" in the Durban Area. These authors do not focus specifically on the healing ministry of the churches they study but rather integrate this as one part of a whole process they study. This process is tied up with the change of identity a person undergoes in joining and submitting him or herself to the "subculture" of the new church (Morran & Schlemmer

1984:4,185-6; Oosthuizen 1975:327,337,340). Thus whilst Morran and Schlemmer (1984:4-5) point out that healing was the initial focus of the ministry of these churches, they have now become broader in scope "emphasizing all the gifts of the Holy Spirit". Members' lives become centred on the church which takes up the majority of their time and they tend to socialize with people who have been "born again" (:134). In this way a subculture with its own symbols and structures is built up and members of these churches live their lives largely within this subculture. Morran and Schlemmer (:135) report that "[g]enerally a picture emerged . . . that their social and personal lives had indeed dramatically changed".

Oosthuizen (1975:340-341) also emphasizes the importance of the new subculture to which Indian Pentecostals belong. He suggests that the symbols, myths and rites of Hindu culture are inadequate to most of the needs of people experiencing rapid social change and life within Western culture. Pentecostalism offers a new set of symbols within which people can find meaning as well as the means and mechanisms necessary for coping with life.

> Pentecostalism develops a sub-culture and its teachings are rationalised in a special scheme of values but this culture is not merely the result of social, economic, political or intellectual deprivation but has a deep religious dimension in which the lasting values are carried forward. Through their sub-culture and Christian activities Pentecostals in general meet the world and its problems much more effectively than traditional Christians. [Oosthuizen 1975:327]

However, entry into this subculture and integrity within it demand a change in identity. The identity change on entry is referred to as conversion whereas the maintenance of integrity within the subculture is achieved through the rites and experience of healing and purification from sin. Healing can also occur in the conversion phase as many testify that their conversion resulted from having been healed (Oosthuizen 1975:337; 325-6; 344-345). This link between healing and identity is an important one and is considered at length later.

Zionist Healing

Martin West (1975:190-192) was one of the first to attempt to develop an anthropological analysis of the African Independent churches. Working in the Soweto area, he sees these churches as attempting to provide a "this-worldly" framework within which certain perceived needs of people (members) may be met. In developing the key to this analysis, he adopts the approach of Peel (1968) who sees traditional African religious systems as "this worldly" as opposed to the "other worldly" emphasis "of, for example, Christianity as conveyed by some missionaries" (West 1975:191). Added to this, West uses the key of "power" as explaining the function of religion. Religion provides access to power for the control of life.

The healing ministry of these churches is seen as the manifestation of a "this-worldly" power which reinforces people's sense of control over their lives. Such reinforcement is necessary since the social environment in which they live is largely one of perceived powerlessness. The prevalent experiences of powerlessness are in "*deprivation* the felt lack of desired economic or social goods, and . . . *anomie*, the absence of stable social relations and authority as a result of abrupt social change" (West 1975:193). This interpretation of West seems to correspond to Oosthuizen's notion of the creation of a "subculture" within Indian Pentecostalism, as a response to acculturation effects and the perceived powerlessness of traditional religion to help people adjust to the new society.

West (1975:194) echoes Sundkler's (1961:302) reflection on African Independent churches when he calls them "'adaptive structures' in city life in South Africa". West notes that the membership of these churches is largely made up of first generation town dwellers, suggesting that acculturative factors play a large role and that this role may disappear in the second and third generation (:196). The issue of protection against a hostile environment is important here and healing is often administered both as a cure for current illness *as well as* for supernatural protection (:197). Kiernan (1990:78-79) also emphasizes this point showing how the Zionist meeting is a cutting off from the real world in order to be purified, healed, transformed and prepared through protection symbols for re-entry into it. (cf. Dube 1989:114-115, 130-131).

Concerning protection, Williams (1982:157) sees this "defensive approach" to treating illness as the principal means of identifying it. The world is seen as a dangerous place and entry into the Zionist meeting room is a liminal experience of leaving that world and entering into another. So people leave their shoes at the entrance, the doors and windows are closed and the curtains are drawn during the healing ritual (cf. Kiernan 1991:79). Similarly, at the beach purification ceremonies, people change their dress during the ceremony. They come to the water's edge in their ordinary clothes, then change into the Zionist dress. After the ceremony they put on new clean clothes (cf. Oosthuizen 1989b:166-168). Further to this, Williams also emphasises that norms for protection against the cause of the sickness are part of every Zionist healing procedure:

> In every treatment prescribed by a Zionist healer, the patient is told to wear something, or to buy an item of clothing that will, when worn, protect the patient from future attacks by evil spirits. This protective approach is significant for two reasons. On the one hand, it illustrates the Zionist belief that illnesses are caused by the intentional endangering or polluting of specific physical environments or social contexts in which people routinely live and move. On the other hand, by emphasizing the defensive side of treatment Zionists healers socialize their patients into modes of thought that promote the public displaying of Zionist symbols as one aspect of treatment. Thus the message that is communicated by a Zionist patient who wears certain colored robes and cords is not simply that he or she has been treated by the Zionists, but equally important is the fact that the individual has also been socialized into and has adopted a belief system in which there are a variety of symbols and rituals which are a necessary part of the healing. [Williams 1982:157]

Kiernan (1990:77ff.) has shown how Zionist ritual healing must be seen within the framework of the "work" that is done during the whole service. This "work" is a process which "constitutes, transforms and molds" (:78) the participants.

> They are brought in from outside and their membership recognized, from acting as separate individuals they perform in unison; under the lash of universalist exhortation they move towards fellowship and community; finally, they work upon wayward and troubled individuals with the aim of attaching them more securely to the collectivity. [Kiernan 1990:78]

Within the functionalist paradigm operated by Kiernan, the meeting is explained as follows:

> One way of viewing the progress of a Zionist meeting is to see it as a development from a statement of Purpose (the intended outcome of the work) to the separating out of Function (the special activities within the work which are appropriate to a distinct rank or status) and from there to the assertion of Powers (the contribution of gifted individuals irrespective of consideration of rank). These phases follow upon a primary enabling stage in which a group of individuals is constituted a collectivity.
> [Kiernan 1990:77]

The healing ritual is seen by Kiernan as the work of a "healing and caring community" (1990:93). It is the work of the community within which various "powers" are to be manifest. "These powers remain in most of the initiated and healing members of the congregation" (:93). The use of the circle in dance and its symbol of wholeness is significant here. The sick person indicates his affliction by stepping into it. The cathartic dimension of healing is enhanced by the ritual, its abandon and the encouragement given to participants to let themselves go. Kiernan (:101) expresses this sickness as "a) tension is expressed; b) tension is exaggerated and released; c) tension is resolved, only to give way to the first stage again". However, he considers this explanation inadequate since the process, for him, is a planned and controlled one in which tension is "carefully nurtured" and enthusiasm "organised" in order to achieve the goal of reconstituting the purified and healed group whilst reinforcing the relationships and bonds between members themselves and especially between member and the leader.

The collective dimension of Zionist healing is also affirmed by Dube (1989:134). The illness of an individual has an effect on the whole group since "a person's 'messenger' is prone to being handicapped by other people's illness." Illness is described as a "weight" on the whole group. The whole group is thus responsible and involved in the healing process but more than that, the group provides a framework of recognition, affirmation and status: symbols producing well-being to those whose situation in society is such that they do not normally experience these values. The African concept of health as life, plays an important role in healing. Dube (:131-132) stresses that Zionist healing must be seen within the cultural framework of this symbol. "In African thinking, life is a whole and a person becomes an embodiment of the community. Zionists are in search of wholeness of life." A healthy person is one who has life (*umuntu onempilo*). This implies being in harmony with the whole environment which comprises the family, the clan, the ancestors and the community as a whole

(Bate 1991:59). Indeed the whole notion of being a person implies being-in-community. "A person is a person through other persons" is a well known proverb in many African languages (:59). Setiloane (1975:31) expresses "person" as a "dynamic concept" using the analogy of a magnetic field. The social *complexus* is a field of relationships and any disturbance in this relationship has consequences on all within it and is interpreted as a lack of life or sickness (cf. Ngubane 1977:27-28). Consequently an important dimension of the diagnosis of sickness is the indication of the causes of the sickness and especially who is responsible. Western healing techniques are seen as defective in this regard since only a remedy is given without sharing the causes of the sickness (Williams 1982:154; cf. West 1975:118-121). The cause of the sickness is usually another person, living or ancestor, and part of the cure is to respond to this person either through a protection or through the restoration of the disturbed harmony the sickness reflects (Williams 1982:157).

Besides these functionalist interpretations of healing, several authors indicate the importance of symbolic factors in the Zionist healing ministry. Sundkler (1961:164-166) originally showed the integrating role played by symbols within African Independent churches although he did not link this to healing. Williams (1982:158) sees the Zionist approach to healing as an orientation of "both patients and healers towards a new framework of thought which places treatment within a ritual and symbolic framework." This framework provides a means through which a process of communication can occur between the healer and the sick person. This communication is one of power and the symbols are the carriers of this power. "As my study progressed it was clear that 'power', its manifestations and its transformations, became the pivotal theme in most Zionist rituals" (:214). Thus physical and emotional power, through dance, music and ritual, can be transformed into spiritual and psychological power which is available for charismatic healing (:214-217). It is the communication of these symbols of power which effect the healing. The symbols of power can be charismatic, dynamic and spontaneous as in visions received by prophets and the techniques of healers used in the healing ritual (:150). They can also be physical through touching, beating, spinning and the use of staffs (*izikhali*) (:152). They can also be of a less transient nature serving to recall experiences to consciousness such as candles, water, robes and cords (:150). The symbols employed have been built up in an eclectic way drawing from various backgrounds both Christian and traditional. In this way, Williams (:230) considers Zionism to be syncretistic even though he notes that some powerful symbols are actually common to both Christianity and Zulu tradition and gives the example of water. It is these common symbols which become the more effective symbols within Zionism and through them a holistic religious healing system has been developed.

> It is largely because of its capacity to adapt its resources to the changing needs of its members and to range beyond simply a solely Zulu historical approach to medicine that Zionism has succeeded as a medical as well as a religious system. For in reality

> Zionism functions for those who convert to its constellation of beliefs and activities, or even for those who only sample some of its healing resources, as a system of interdependent parts. These parts are comprised of [sic] religious, social, medical, recreational, and even economic components - all of which complement each other in various ways. For those Zionists, who feel alienated in the stress-producing environments in which they now live and work, Zionism provides relief and security. Through its services and opportunities for social interaction, Zionism is fulfilling many of the emotional, cultural, social and religious needs of its members. It can be said, then, that even though Zionism ostensibly functions as a religious system, there is an underlying system of holistic medicine which is fostered by Zionism and reinforced by its symbols, allocations of time and resources, designations of personnel in healing roles, and the official sanctioning of techniques and forms of treatment.
>
> [Williams 1982:222-223]

It is most informative to note the extent of commonality in the interpretations of Morran and Schlemmer (1984), Oosthuizen (1975) and Williams (1982) regarding the various healing churches that they have studied in the Natal area. All these authors recognise alienation from prevailing cultural and social conditions as etiological factors in sickness, stress or fear and thus as motivating factors in people's move into the Coping-healing churches. The different churches they study all seem to provide a subcultural and symbolic framework within which people can experience relief from stress, affirmative healing, purification and well-being and also where they can develop a mechanism for coping with the alienating culture or society in which they live their daily lives. Structural, symbolic and functional factors seem to play a role in the healing process and it is to a discussion of how these mechanisms are seen to operate that we now turn.

4.2.2 General Anthropological Interpretations of Coping-Healing

The British sociologist, James Beechford (cited in Jones 1985:77-79) suggests that times of intensive social and cultural change give rise to a response which involves a "turning inward" in order to develop a socio-cultural frame of reference with which people can feel safe and well. This movement to interiority operates on both the individual and community level and involves psychological and social factors. New Religious movements, the holistic movement, Charismatic (or Neopentecostal) churches and African Independent churches are given as examples of this phenomenon.

R. Kenneth Jones (1985:113) invokes the common hypothesis that "religion is seen as a coping device to enable individuals to manage the exigencies of life" and that those who belong to the more extreme religious sects, as a result of sudden conversion, are likely to have some kind of predisposing psychological illness. Indeed he suggests that research has indicated the predisposed personality type as the simple, extroverted, neurotic and guilt ridden person.

Easthope (1986:111-112) interprets "faith healing" as a "form of 'primitive' psychotherapy" and his research suggests that a mechanism similar to the placebo effect is operating when religious healing takes place. The therapeutic relationship between patient and healer and the social context within which the healing occurs are seen to be the most important factors influencing effectiveness. However, Dow (1986:57), whilst admitting some parallels between psychotherapy and faith healing, recognises that the psychotherapy model is not sufficient to explain faith healing and shamanism in general. He sees these latter as "a type of symbolic healing that involves the ritual manipulation of supernatural forces" (:57).

Sometimes, faith healers are able to heal people rapidly - instantaneously in some "healing services" - and the intimacy of relationship and sharing present in psychotherapy is rarely present in faith healing. Dow (1986:62) suggests that this rapidity of cure is related to the experience of conversion in which the sick person totally changes his or her symbols of understanding and frame of reference and undergoes a "rapid resolution of paradox and a rapid acceptance of a particularized mythic world" (:62). He says that the healer is able to manipulate the emotions of the patient by attaching them to "transactional symbols in this particularised mythic world" (:66). In manipulating these symbols in the healing process, the healer is able to manipulate the emotions. The experience of catharsis is obviously important here and whilst Dow does not go as far as Girard (1977:287) in suggesting that "catharsis is the base of all religious healing", he is of the opinion that "Catharsis is a name for what may be several different types of emotional transactions and needs much more investigation" (Dow 1986:58; cf. Jules-Rosette 1981:134-6). Jules Rosette (1981), investigating faith healers in the urban Zambian context, suggests, following Turner (1957), that the use of symbols in the healing process operates as follows:

> Each step in the therapeutic process is expressed symbolically in terms of the curative system. The definition of the illness (i.e. its content) is established through diagnosis at the crisis point. That is, the illness is culturally coded with reference to a symbolic system and to the social actors involved. Symptoms do not have an *absolute* etiology, even with a single therapeutic system. [Jules-Rosette 1981:131]

Easthope (1986:67-69) examines the symbolic nature of places of healing and in particular shrines. He considers the example of Lourdes and suggests, that Lourdes is a symbol of power since it reflects disorder in two ways. Firstly it is situated in a "wild" area and has a "'natural' grotto" as its focus and, secondly, the *Domaine* and the pilgrimage represent movements away from the normal way of life. Consequently going to and being at Lourdes is a "liminal" experience in which "the world of God breaks through into the ordinary mundane world of man . . . It is a channel for God's grace" (:68). Passing through the Lourdes experience allows a disordered person to step out of life and go through a process of personal re-ordering through the power of God available in the symbol. The new "healed" person may then move back into the ordinary world (:69-70).

4.3 Anthropological Categories of Healing

Anthropologists try to describe and understand phenomena within the categories of understanding available to them in their discipline. Such is also the case with healing. It is helpful to identify these categories in order to recognise the perspective of the anthropological understanding. Once again we will need to widen the focus from "religious healing" to a more general one. We have already noted that anthropologists usually categorize religious healing within the framework of cultural healing as opposed to medical curing. Religious healing falls into the healing category as opposed to the curing category and is referred to as "Cultural Healing" (Kleinman 1980:82), "Folk Healing" (Simons and Hughes 1985) and "Symbolic Healing" (Moerman 1979; Dow 1986). In this section we explore four major themes which anthropologists have studied with regard to such healing in an attempt to cast some anthropological light on the religious healing ministry. These themes are:

(i) The role of culture in sickness and healing.

(ii) The role of a shared world-view in the healing process.

(iii) The role of symbols in healing.

(iv) Transcultural or structural factors in healing.

4.3.1 Culture, Sickness and Healing

Whilst it is true that research has shown that many diseases affect people without regard to culture, economic status, or other social, geographical and historical factors, it has also become clear to anthropologists that the question of sickness and health has a strong, often determinant cultural component. This component influences the etiology, understanding, diagnosis, and remedy as well as the form and content of the curing and healing process (Landy 1977:1-9). This fact was recognised by early anthropologists such as Tylor and Fraser but the prevailing mode of thought then was that these were "primitive" factors which would be eliminated during the process of "civilisation" when the people they were observing would learn the real truth about sickness and disease, curing and healing. The British anthropologist W.H.R. Rivers (1926) was the first to attempt to draw up a theoretical model which showed that so-called "primitive" medical systems had their own internal logic and "were not to be dismissed lightly as bizarre, esoteric, illogical and irrational" (in Landy 1977:4). Indeed Rivers showed that, for example, disease causation within all cultures, including Western culture, could be categorised within a single framework of three major classes: those relating to natural, human or supernatural causes. Rivers' work was, unfortunately, largely ignored and it is only since the 1960's that medical anthropology has become an important field for research.

Medical anthropology takes as its frame of reference, the cultural context of disease and illness, curing and healing. Richard Lieban (1977:13-15) points out that there are two interrelated ways in which culture influences disease. Firstly, culture is to do with the way that people perceive themselves and understand the world around them: the way they communicate within that world. Consequently, the way in which sickness is identified, understood and dealt with, and the way in which health is interpreted and achieved must, by definition, have a cultural component. Secondly, however, Lieban suggests that culture can itself (as a result of the above factors) be directly pathogenic:

> Indications are that the stressful reactions of individuals who are convinced that they are the victims of sorcery, witchcraft, or axiomatic punishment for violations of taboos can lead to their illness and death (Cannon 1942, Lester 1972). In such cases, culture is pathogenic. [Lieban 1977:15]

In an attempt to respond to these factors, Western writers have developed the couplets "disease and curing", "illness and health". Kleinman describes the relationship between disease and illness as follows:

> A key axiom in medical anthropology is the dichotomy between two aspects of sickness: disease and illness. *Disease* refers to a malfunctioning of biological and/or psychological processes, while the term *illness* refers to the psychosocial experience and meaning of perceived disease . . . Illness involves processes of attention, perception, affective response, cognition, and valuation directed at the disease and its manifestations (i.e., symptoms, role impairment, etc.). But also included in the idea of illness are communication and interpersonal interaction, particularly within the context of the family and social network. Viewed from this perspective, illness is the shaping of disease into behaviour and experience. It is created by personal, social, and cultural reactions to disease. Constructing illness from disease is a central function of health care systems (a coping function) and the first stage of healing. [Kleinman 1980:72]

Now cultural factors influence both disease and illness since these are both "explanatory concepts rather than entities themselves. They can be understood only within defined contexts of meaning and social relationships" (Kleinman 1980:73). This is particularly clear with regard to symptoms since the symptoms themselves are part of the process of the perception of the disease and thus are influenced by personal and family beliefs and experiences which are always mediated through a cultural framework. In his classic work, Kiev (1964:455-456) pointed out how culture influences the patterning of sick roles in a society and how illness itself has different social significances within different cultures. Thus illness may be seen as a sanction or punishment for wrongdoing which Lieban (1977:24) sees as "a feature of Judeo-Christian beliefs concerning the consequences of sin". This viewpoint is clearly at work in some of the Neopentecostal churches we have studied. Illness is also seen as a form of deviance and this is particularly so in Western culture. This culture has a particular interest in limiting illness because of the value ascribed to work and production. Consequently illness is frowned upon and the sick are motivated to return as quickly as possible to functioning health. In other cultures illness is seen as possession by supernatural forms (cf. Oosthuizen 1989a:76; Wessels 1985:55). In some cases such possession has just to be accepted and the role of such a possessed person is functional and accepted with the culture. "*Thwasa*" experiences and the resultant acceptance of a calling to and training as an *isangoma (igqira)*[2] would be an example of this (cf. Bührmann 1986a:36-39).

In determining sickness, people use the beliefs and values they have within their framework of experience and understanding. That these are culturally mediated has already been stressed. As cultural change occurs so sicknesses and their cure also change. Part of the phenomenon of the emergence of indigenous Christian healing churches is a manifestation of this fact (cf. Lieban 1977:20). If sickness and healing are so closely linked then one would expect to find sickness specific to different cultures. This turns out to be the case and many authors attest to the existence of culture bound sicknesses: sicknesses specific to a particular culture and not found outside it. (Simon & Hughes 1985; Yap 1977, Kleinman 1980; Wessels 1985; Edwards *et al* 1982). Simons and Hughes (1985) have collected studies of these sicknesses which they call "folk illnesses" from around the world. The collection includes such exotic illnesses as "The Cannibal Compulsion Taxon", "The Fright Illness Taxon" and the "Sudden Mass Assault Taxon" ("Amok"). At the end of their book they list almost 200 different "culture bound" syndromes from around the world - a by no means exhaustive list.

Coming to the South African context, Edwards *et al* (1982) describe fifteen Zulu culture bound psychiatric syndromes which fit into the category, referred to by Ngubane (1977) as "*ukufa kwabantu*". For Edwards (1982:86) the culture bound syndromes "reflect culturally flavoured versions of problems in living that are common to all people in all cultures". Wessels (1985) also describes several of these syndromes and indicates that these are psychiatric conditions which are experienced in terms of the cultural framework of the people exhibiting them. Wessels suggests that these syndromes can be treated by Western techniques but that

> Western therapeutic approaches should emphasize knowledge of the culture of the patient and incorporation of that knowledge in the assessment and holistic management of the patient . . . [since] Western trained doctors do not have a monopoly on knowledge, we should co-operate with and learn from traditional healers. Only in this way can our patients be treated effectively. [Wessels 1985:63]

Wessels (1985:26) also suggests that the attempt to classify these disorders within Western systems such as DSMIII[3] is difficult since such a classification is Western culture bound. It is for this reason that Simon and Hughes adopt the more general term "folk illness".

Since Western culture provides the framework of this discussion, ethnocentric considerations may cause us to overlook such "Western Culture-bound sicknesses". Fortunately some authors have attempted to redress this bias. Yap (1977) has attempted to indicate some of the culture bound syndromes of Western culture as follows:

> Atypical culture-bound variations of psychogenic reactions in European and American countries include homosexual-panic; depression . . . mass excitement, sometimes

> accompanied by fainting of female adolescents at the sight of popular male idols; and perhaps also school-phobia and anorexia nervosa. [Yap 1977:344]

Simons (1985:25) makes other suggestions regarding Western culture bound syndromes such as "American obesity" and "petism": "isolated elderly Americans and Britons who live surrounded by great menageries of dogs and cats". Another candidate suggested by Hughes (1985:11) is the "Type A" personality.[4] Olivier (1988) suggests that family murder, where one adult member of the family takes the life of all the others and then commits suicide, has become a "socio-psychological phenomenon" in South Africa. She indicates some possible causal factors of this situation.

Dubos points out that biological diseases can also be shown to have cultural, social and geographical etiologies.

> While all human beings can develop cancers, the incidence of various types of this disease exhibits spectacular differences from one country and one social group to another. Lung cancer is the most common cause of cancer deaths among men in the United States, England, Wales and several other Western countries, but it is much less frequent in Iceland. In contrast, stomach cancer accounts for 50 percent of cancers among men in Iceland and Japan but for only 10 percent in the United States and for even less in Indonesia. Liver cancer causes half of all cancer deaths amongst the Bantus in Africa but less than 4 percent in Europe and North America. Breast cancer is over 8 times more common among women in Israel than among women in Japan. Cancer of the cervix accounts for half of all cancer deaths among Hindu women. [Dubos 1977:37-38]

These differences are ascribed by Dubos (1977:38) to environmental, social, economic and geographic variation. Alland (1977:42-43) and Wellin (1977:54-57) show how biological diseases such as sickle cell anaemia, malaria, kwashiorkor, venereal diseases and others have a cultural component to them. Simons (1985:26-31) affirms, however, that there is a complex intermingling of psychological, social, cultural and biological factors which gives rise to these syndromes and that it is usually simplistic to point to any of these as central. Citing Lehrman's (1970) work he suggests that a better approach is to recognise that all behaviour is "100% determined by the biology of the behaving organism . . . However the same instance of behaviour is also 100% determined by the organism's experiential history" (Simons 1985:28). Thus culture specific syndromes occur only if a certain neurophysiological event occurs and only if one is a member of a society which shares a belief in such a disease. Kleinman (1980:75-76) describes one of the mechanisms by which culture can affect sickness. The illness begins as the person perceives something as being wrong. These early symptoms are given a label and this label is always culturally conditioned. A vague feeling of unwell-ness may be variously labelled as "sickness", "depression", "misfortune", "guilt from sin", "possession by a spirit", "witchcraft" or some other label. These labels can then condition both the direction of the experience of the sickness as well as the means of a treatment which will satisfactorily respond to it and thus heal the person. Clearly the weight given to the label by the culture will also influence the accompanying stress levels thus helping relieve or exacerbate the sickness. Hallowell (1977:136) shows that it is for this reason that diagnosis as divination is so important in cultural or folk healing, since the isolation, indication and confirmation of the cause lessens the anxiety associated with the condition and thus reduces stress levels. For Hallowell (:136) therapy in such cases comprises "anxiety reducing devices".

Cultural Dimensions of Health Care Frameworks

Anthropologists such as Freidson (1970), Hallowell (1977) and Kleinman (1980) show that healing in all societies and cultures operates within a therapeutic framework of health: a system of perceived states of sickness and health and procedures of moving between them. Kleinman (1980:34) emphasises that all healing procedures must be related together as a whole and seen within the particular context, world-view and frame of reference that they operate. It is the shared belief in this system which effects much of the healing. The health care system is created by two inter-related elements: a collective common view or understanding of health and sickness, together with a shared pattern of usage (Kleinman 1980:39). These beliefs and behaviours are governed by cultural factors (:26).

Cheetham and Griffiths (1982:954-956) compare the African and Western therapeutic techniques and show that Western psychotherapeutic techniques are inappropriate to Black patients in South Africa and largely ineffective. From this they conclude to the cultural dependence of psychotherapy as practised in the West (:956). Jelliffe and Jelliffe (1977:331) come to a similar conclusion on a more general level, contrasting Western and non-Western approaches to therapy. They conclude that the "allopathic" (reactive) nature of Western therapy renders it ineffective in some illnesses. "Some methods of healing and techniques of social support in bio-traditional cultures are often more effective in some conditions in which linear Westernism has been shown to have only partial value" (:331). Kleinman berates the "ingrained ethnocentricism and scientism that dominates the modern medical and psychiatric professions . . . [resulting in] a disastrous bias [which] has diminished the significance of all social science inputs into medicine and psychiatry" (1980:32). The criteria people utilise in choosing between health care alternatives are described by Kleinman (1980:80) as reducing to two basic factors: the ascribing of values to the illness and the judgment of the sick person regarding the effectiveness of the treatment. The operation of the second factor is clearly seen when considering the Coping-healing phenomenon in the churches, for often, people have tried other forms of treatment before coming to the "healing service" or consulting the faith healer. This is particularly so in those who are not members of the Coping-healing church in question. The first factor is also important since part of the role of the religious healer is to indicate the sickness and its cause, thus providing a framework of reference within which the sick person can understand the disease. The type of disease affects the type of cure. This explains why religious healers are always attempting to show the spiritual or religious significance of the sickness and, by implication, the need for a spiritual or religious cure.

4.3.2 The Role of Symbols in the Coping-Healing Process

Anthropologists who follow the semiotic school consider the role of symbols to be central to the healing process. Symbols within this school are seen as articulated carriers of meaning (cf. Geertz 1973). Thus the understanding attributed to the term is extremely wide. Within the context of healing, Moerman (1979:60) describes these symbols as "healing metaphors" and for him they are essential to the healing process. They operate within a "metaphorical structure", a system of healing, which is by definition culturally specific.

> I will argue that the metaphorical structure, the system of meaning, of a healing discipline is decisive in its effectiveness, as important as any other "actual", "physical", [or] "pharmacological" elements . . . In both the personalistic and naturalistic medical systems, there is a clear symbolic metaphorical component. This is not to say that herbal medicines do not have significant specific medical effects; they certainly do. What I am arguing is that the symbolic component of treatment is significant as well, that it is these healing metaphors which provide the symbolic substance of general medical treatment. [Moerman 1979:66]

Moerman goes on to indicate that the healing process occurs through the construction of healing symbols by the patient. This construction happens through interaction with the healer or during the healing ritual. He affirms that: "The construction of the healing symbols ***is*** healing" (1979:66). In quite a telling comment he suggests that many modern Western medical techniques do not work for the assumed reasons: pharmacological and surgical, but as a result of the effects of the operation of symbolic healing in the patient (Moerman 1979:62-64).

Dow (1986:63-64) also emphasises the important role of symbols and myths as communication devices between different levels of the human person: biological, conscious and social. He notes that the healing symbol works on two levels: the general and the specific. The general symbol or myth exists within the symbolic framework of the culture as an accepted sign of health, healing or power. It is a culture-specific symbol, a cultural myth. Jesus is such a symbol amongst Christians, ancestors amongst the Yoruba [or Zulu] and so forth (:63). The construction of particularised symbols for the sick person from these general myths or symbols in the healing process is done by "letting Jesus come into your life", or "speaking in tongues" or discovering the identity of the ancestor and so forth. Dow (1986:63) refers to these symbols as "transactional symbols" and they are available for use in symbolic healing.

Jules-Rosette (1981:144-145) specifies some of the dominant therapeutic symbols operating in Africa as "witches", "*mashave* spirits", "manic water spirits" and "demon possession". The healing process in African Independent churches is the casting out of these demons. Oosthuizen (1989b:146) highlights the importance of the circle symbol used in dance both in all night Zionist services and as a prelude to baptism and Bührmann (1986a:58) indicates the link between this and the universal mandala symbol of Jung. Dube (1989:121-123) points out how the important water symbol present in both pre-Christian Zulu culture and Christianity is used as a symbol of cleansing, health and purity in Zionist churches, through holy water for drinking or washing *(iziwasho)* and so on. Kiernan (1990, 1991) has made an extensive study of Zionist signs and symbols suggesting the importance of instruments (1990:104-120), colours (1991) and clothing (1990:112; 1991) in Zionist healing processes. Dube (1989:122) suggests that the role of these specific items is to bring about a specific relationship between the person and the environment which allows the powers of sickness to be controlled.

Dow (1986:56) outlines the process of symbolic healing in four steps. Whilst the symbols are different from group to group, he suggests that the process is always the same and can be called the "universal structure of symbolic healing". His structure is as follows:

1) The experiences of healers and healed are generalised with culture-specific symbols in cultural myth.
2) A suffering patient comes to a healer who persuades the patient that the problem can be defined in terms of the myth.
3) The healer attaches the patient's emotions to transactional symbols particularized from the general myth.
4) The healer manipulates the transactional symbols to help the patient transact his or her own emotions.

The mechanisms by which the transactional symbols are manipulated by the healer are highly culture specific and thus frequently unintelligible to outsiders (Dow 1986:65). They include: laying on of hands, casting out demons, identifying sorcerers, drinking holy water, vomiting and so on. Many of the etic studies of religious healing in South Africa have spent time indicating, and attempting to understand, these symbols (Kiernan 1991; Williams 1982; Oosthuizen 1989b:145; Sundkler 1961; Dube 1989:121). According to Dow the central aim of the symbolic healing process is the transaction of emotions. "Emotions are the generalized media that link the self and somatic system . . . [they] have an integrative control function. They summarise complex processes at a lower level in a single message to a higher level" (Dow 1986:64). This is perhaps the weakest area of his argument, as, with it he comes firmly down into the psychological camp indicating that healing is merely an emotion transfer process and is a personal affair. Whilst he indicates the importance of the restoration of social relationships as healing, he only sees the value of this to the extent that it impinges upon the individual emotional state.

Mary Douglas (1970a:302-308) in a review article on Turner's (1957;1962;1967;1968) four volumes on Ndembu, highlights his important contribution in emphasising the "relationship of the symbolic to the social order, showing how each gives form to the other in a dynamic intermingling of meanings" (Douglas 1970a:303). The context within which the symbols are generated is an important dimension since it reflects a whole complex of realities, physical, ecological and social in nature. Douglas highlights Turner's special contribution to the understanding of the healing ministry as the recognition that:

> the healer is not working on the psyche of the patient, in terms of a private set of fears, but on those of the friends and kinsmen at his bedside in terms of their widest social concerns. His business is with how they internalise the values of their society. Useless for him to propose heroic sacrifice if it is not already validated; useless to open new perspectives of hitherto unimagined love and harmony which leave his audience unconvinced. If his therapy works it is because the symbols are creative instruments of a particular social structure. [Douglas 1970a:307]

A healing procedure which does not create an environment within which the person can continue to be healed will ultimately be ineffective. That is why many Coping-healing churches provide a social and cultural framework, such as the Zionist band or the Neopentecostal congregation and prayer group, which the sick person is encouraged to join and make his or her home. It is also why healers are often so powerful in setting up rules for behaviour and morality within the culture or community that they operate. The healer needs to persuade the patient to accept a particular understanding of the problem and then heals it from this perspective. This is a means of entry by the patient into the healer's world and value system.

> Typically, a patient comes to the folk healer with a complaint or request that is already formulated. Nevertheless, this complaint has to be reformulated within the healer's interpretive system. Divination is a process of inquiry that requires a question to be asked to a specialist who generally operates an oracle or other mechanical objects. Its position in the therapeutic process is structurally comparable with that of Apostolic prophecy . . . The point of crisis in the folk healing system is reached when the patient accepts the specialist's definition of the situation. Conflicts in the work or home setting may be diagnosed as the negative products of witchcraft. The acquisition of a protective charm is the first stage in redressive action. The charm must be prepared by the folk healer and used only in specified ways by the patient. The final curative act is the application of the charm. A patient may , however, complain that the charm has not been effective. Then an alternative charm or a curative rite may be administered. [Jules-Rosette 1991:132-133]

In this way the healer brings the patients into a new way of seeing and understanding the world: a world-view within which they can be healed and also continue to be healthy. The question of world-view occurs at the meeting point of culture and philosophy: the epistemological dimension of culture. We will treat the question of world view more fully in chapter six but we also consider the issue here because of the important role a shared world-view plays in how anthropologists understand the healing process.

4.3.3 The Role of a Shared World-View in Coping-Healing

In the survey of the literature of religious and folk healing presented here, one of the essential conditions for healing noted by psychologists, medics and anthropologists is the importance of a shared world-view between the healer and the patient. For the psychologists, this is essential for the development of the therapeutic relationship and the patient's growth in faith and trust in the healer or the healing ritual. As we have already noted, it is this relationship and the faith of the sick person in the ability of the healer which elicits the healing (Bührmann 1986a:92-93; Mkhwanazi 1989:276-277; Cheetham & Griffiths 1989:309-311). For the anthropologists, the emphasis is more on the ability of the symbol to communicate to the sick person and the concomitant enhancement of the healer's ability to manipulate the symbol to effect the healing. Horton (1971:96) believes that the weakness of nineteenth century Protestant missionary Christianity as brought to Africa was that, as a result of the growth of modern science, it "had dropped all pretence of providing a theory of how the world really worked or a recipe for controlling the course of its affairs". Such a Christianity was very limiting for a people with a cosmology in which the spiritual plays a determinant role in daily life. Hence the search in African Christianity for a "this-worldly" religion ("explanation-prediction-control" to use Horton's clumsy but more descriptive terminology). This was also the reason for the

> tremendous appetite for certain kinds of Western cosmological literature and testimony [as they] seek confirmation of their beliefs, not only from the writings of Western faith healing sects, but also from those of the Rosicrucians, the Spiritualists, the Theosophists, and other such followers of Western occultism. [Horton 1971:105]

Oosthuizen (1968) in an early work of his, also affirms the importance of the spiritual in African cosmology perceived as "force" and "life". This spiritual dimension is seen to permeate all things and is available to people in different degrees so that some are more alive, well or stronger than others.

> In traditional African philosophy, things (*bintu*) are forces or 'beings', although not endowed with reason and life. When a traditional African maintains that he is becoming stronger, he does not refer in the first instance to his physical nature but to his nature, his personality, his status . . . Man's being thus increases, and what he has in a material sense is part of his being, part of himself . . . The idea of eternal life in heaven, and 'there and then', is unacceptable in the face of the 'here and now'. It is for this very reason that Western culture, with its material benefits, has made a greater impression than Christianity . . . It is most difficult in such a situation to associate God's love with sickness, poverty and suffering. Shropshire says that 'he has a desire to possess, and be *en rapport* with this abundant life and, indeed, much of his time is given to a cult of health, for he fears famine, plague, pestilence, death and sickness. Time and again the healing aspect is specially emphasised, in order to prove the truth of the Gospel message. The consequence of salvation is freedom from these things . . . All the questions about death, sickness, poverty, and social conditions indicate how seriously the message is taken in all its aspects. The old religion had to do with the whole life, not just the soul; with the supernatural divine presence in all spheres of life through the presence of the ancestors. The Greek dichotomy between body and soul means nothing to the African. [Oosthuizen 1968:88-89]

Moving now to a Western cultural context, Robert Fishman (1980) has made a study of "Spiritualist Healing" within an urban spiritualist organisation in western New York. He shows how "healing is dependent on a continued belief in the spiritual world in which the importance of developing and maintaining a belief in the ability to transcend the earth plane cannot be overstressed" (:219). People coming for healing or joining this church are called to accept a belief system which is not widely accepted within the normal cultural framework in which they live. The new belief system is esoteric, yet healing only occurs if it is accepted by the sick person. In the "Western" part of South Africa, such a situation has been noted both in the "new" (Neopentecostal) Coping-healing churches (Morran & Schlemmer 1984) and the Pentecostal Churches (Oosthuizen 1975) both of which provide a belief system which is esoteric to the prevailing cultural belief system in which people are living.

We note here an important distinction between Western faith healing sects which are usually antithetic to Western culture and African faith healing movements which have belief systems which are synthetic of African traditional culture and the urban township culture in which they operate. This distinction indicates a major difference between the two groupings and is often a source of much consternation to Africans who discover this fact and with it the realisation that the part of Western culture they are in agreement with is far from the conventional wisdom of the West (Horton 1971:107).

Finally Wellin (1977:49-50) shows the important link between world-view, theories of disease causation, and medical practice. He summarises Rivers' work on "Native medicine as part of culture" (:49) indicating the three enduring theoretical contributions as

> first, that primitive medical *practices* follow from and make sense in terms of underlying medical *beliefs*, and, secondly, that both are best conceived not as quaint folklorisms but as integral *parts of culture* . . . Further, native medical practice and belief, taken together, constitute a "social institution...[to be studied in terms of the same] . . . principles or methods found to be of value in the study of social institutions in general" (Rivers 1926:61). [Wellin 1977:49]

4.3.4 Trans-Cultural Considerations

Whilst the focus of this chapter has been to indicate the role of culture in healing, it is nevertheless significant that many anthropologists consider it necessary to go beyond this to identify a general human substrate of condition, experience and process of which the cultural is a particular contextualised expression. Much of this work derives from the French schools of Emil Durkheim in sociology and, more importantly, Claude Levi-Strauss in anthropology. Here the aim is to discover generalisations regarding sickness and healing which apply across all cultures as well as to search for universal categories and criteria which can be applied to all healing systems. Following this approach, Dow (1986:56) affirms that "religious healing, shamanism and Western psychotherapy . . . seem to be versions of the same thing . . . 'symbolic healing'". He further suggests that one can develop a universal structure for symbolic healing and we have already presented this structure. Following the linguistic structuralist philosopher, Chomsky, he affirms that this "universal structure of symbolic healing" comes from a deeper universal structure which is part of the human condition: "a result of the way that human communication has been biologically organised by evolution" (:66).

Kleinman (1980) deals with this issue by making the clinical study of illness as a human experience the focus of his study. He writes:

> As a clinician I have found myself frequently disappointed by anthropological and cross-cultural studies of health care, because these studies often are so remote from or irrelevant to the chief interests of a clinician: the exigent and difficult reality of illness as a human experience and the core relationships and tasks of clinical care. Most anthropological and cross-cultural research on health care, even research by health scientists, has had little or nothing to say about these clinical issues. On the other hand, I entered medicine and remain in it because of my fascination with such matters; they are the chief interests behind my cross-cultural work and this book. But I do not think I have imposed an *a priori* clinical category on cross-cultural materials. Instead, I wish to advance the notion that clinical categories are intrinsic to all cultures and that their analysis and cross-cultural comparison are essential for understanding "medical systems". [Kleinman 1980:xii]

Kleinman (1980:50) develops a model of health care which, he suggests, can be applied in all situations. The model has three overlapping parts: the popular, the professional and the folk sectors. The popular sector comprises "a matrix containing several levels: individual, family, social network and community beliefs and activities" (:50). Most illness is dealt with here without recourse to outside experts. The professional sector comprises the organised healing professions within a sector. These are consulted when the popular sector is ineffective. The folk sector comprises the non-professional, non-bureaucratic healing sources and is a mixture of many different components: religious, naturalistic, counter cultural and so forth. The illnesses taken to this sector are considered outside the competency of the professional sector.

Kleinman also identifies five core functions of all cultural (including religious) healing and care systems. These are clinical tasks which any healing system has to perform. These are :

1. The cultural construction of *illness* as psycho-social experience.
2. The establishment of *general* criteria to guide the health care seeking process and to evaluate treatment approaches that exist prior to and independent of individual episodes of sickness.
3. The management of *particular* illness episodes through communicative operations such as labelling and explaining.
4. Healing activities per se, which include all types of therapeutic interventions, from drugs and surgery to psychotherapy, supportive care, and healing rituals.
5. The management of therapeutic outcomes, including cure, treatment failure, recurrence, chronic illness, impairment, and death.

[Kleinman 1980:71-72]

Whilst the models of Kleinman and Dow are illuminating and do point to the reality of an underlying human condition to which the experiences of sickness and healing are responses, their analyses are also somewhat disappointing for two reasons. Firstly, the underlying human structure is described in only a little more detail than the bland assertion that people get sick, realise it and then get better either with or apart from others. As Wellin rightly points out, the common point of departure in medical anthropology over the years has comprised

> three empirical generalizations - (1) the universality of disease as part of the human condition, (2) the fact that all human groups develop methods and roles for coping with disease, and (3) the fact that all human groups develop beliefs and perceptions for cognizing disease. [Wellin 1977:57]

Secondly, both Kleinman and Dow focus on the individual as the human unit and so are fundamentally psychological approaches. The issue of societal or cultural sickness is not adequately considered and this dimension is surely fundamental to the fact of the existence of many of the healing churches in the South African context as we shall see in our next section on socio-economic understandings of this ministry.

4.4 Conclusion: How Cultural Factors Operate in Coping-Healing

After considering the more theoretical anthropological understandings of healing in general, we conclude this chapter on the anthropological mediation by moving to more practical considerations. We focus on how anthropologists see cultural factors operating in the Coping-healing phenomenon.

4.4.1 The Correlation of Cultural and Physiological Factors

Firstly we note that anthropologists show that cultural factors do influence physiological states. Moerman (1979:61-62) considers three areas of biomedical research which have affirmed the influence of "mental, symbolic or cultural phenomena on [the] physiological state: psychosomatic illness, biofeedback and host pathogen interaction". With respect to psychosomatic illness, he presents a large body of research evidence to show how cultural, psychological and sociological phenomena can "be shown to correlate with a variety of physiological symptoms". In the more esoteric field of "biofeedback" he presents research which has shown that the mind can be focused to directly influence even so-called "involuntary actions" such as heart rate, blood pressure, body temperature, alpha rhythms and so on. With regard to "host pathogen interaction" he also presents recent research which indicates how emotions, psychological and social factors can influence the immunological system of the body. He posits the hypothalamus as the centre of the mediation between psycho-social and cultural factor on the onc hand and the physiological on the other.

> Hence there seems to be a complex interacting web of factors - pathogen, carcinogen, immunological system and mental or emotional state - which determines the course

> of disease. The hypothalamus is the most likely link between conscious and immune systems. [Moerman 1979:62]

Moerman (1979:59) also believes that "healers decisively mediate culture and nature; they are enacting *cultural physiology.*" By this he means that healers are able to indicate, articulate and manipulate the symbols of healing and health which exist within a culture and that this process has an effect on all dimensions of the person's being (psychological, somatic, etc.) so that healing is perceived and experienced by the sick person. These symbols are always culturally determined since symbols are precisely expressions of culture. Moerman refers to these symbols of health and the healing process as "healing metaphors". It is these healing metaphors which enable and guide the healing process within the particular person's experience.

> What I am saying is that the symbolic component of treatment is significant as well, that it is these healing metaphors which provide the symbolic substance of general mechanical treatment. [Moerman 1979:60]

It is the symbols which manifest the cultural understandings of healing. Paradoxically, it is in modern Western culture with its Cartesian dualism where the mechanism of this process is so difficult to accept. The understanding of body, mind and spirit as separate symbols of the human person makes the notion of communication between them so difficult. Religious (spiritual) healing is only a "problem" for Westerners. Symbols such as "laying of hands", "tongues", "falling down or being slain in the spirit" and even reflexology, homeopathy, chiropractic and so on are only effective for those who allow themselves to accept the symbol as a healing one. A certain suspension of belief is required for the Westerner which is not so necessary for the non-Westerner. This is often why Coping-healing churches within Western culture are so anti-science, anti-medicine and anti-academic (reflected in the sermon refered to in 2.2.1). In African culture and Black urban township culture in South Africa, such symbols are much more readily accepted and thus more easily effective. Hammond-Tooke (1989:50) refers to the important symbol of harmony in African healing and illustrates its functioning through the values of reverence and respect especially for the elderly and ancestors. He emphasizes the centrality of the ancestors in the Zulu healing process (:49). Symbols such as water (*iziwasho*), staffs (*izikhali*), clothing (*izembatho*) are all effective in the healing process as authors such as Kiernan (1990:104-120) point out. These symbols evoke a healing response in the persons using them and in this way effect the healing.

4.4.2 Cultural Healing as Coming to Understanding

Kleinman (1980:365) suggests that the mechanism of cultural healing works by "providing behavioral and explanatory (experiential) models . . . that are the opposite of those maladaptive and malfunctioning ones previously held by . . . patients". This involves two main factors:

1) On the epistemological level, a switching of model or metaphor from the nega-

tively valued anxiety laden one that the sick person arrives with to the positively valued, adaptive one of the healer and/or his cult or group which provides the possibility of personal mastery over anxious feelings.

2) On the behavioural level, the learning of techniques and behaviours which reduce the anxiety. These can be as diverse as taking medicine, dance, speaking in tongues, or talking and sharing with others.

Kleinman (1980:365-367) also shows that the group itself enhances this process in several ways. It provides an opportunity for social learning of successful behaviour through contact with other cult members and the opportunity of being with cured, seemingly happy, calm people. It also provides opportunities for esteem as the person joins and gains status within the social hierarchy of the group, and, finally, it provides a "therapeutic milieu": an environment within which a person can feel at ease and well (:366, 369-370).

4.4.3 Coping-Healing as the Transformation of Identity

Easthope (1986:116-124) describes the healing process as a transformation of identity in the person as a result of a transformation or change in the socialisation process. The healing process involves the reconstruction of a person's identity in terms of the more positive symbols of the new social or religious grouping in which that person is healed. A new process of socialisation into this "world" occurs and this is experienced as healing. For Easthope this type of healing involves a culture change. Identity change is always a transcendental process since it involves giving up one's identity so that a new identity may emerge (Easthope 1986:133). Boucher (n.d. 243-244) emphasises the importance of "Altered States of Consciousness" in empowering this process and the fact that much of healing ritual is concerned with providing the context within which such "Altered States of Consciousness" can occur. The experience of catharsis and emotion transference is clearly linked with this process.

4.4.4 Culture and the Coping-Healing Churches

Coming finally to the question of the cultural nature of the Coping-healing churches, it would seem that this is a non-question as far as anthropologists are concerned. We have already showed that they consider religious healing to be part of cultural or folk healing. With regard to the Zionists, Dube (1989:111-136) brings together a large body of research evidence to indicate how Zionists heal within an "African understanding of the cosmos" (:119). "African ideas about health are basic to the understanding of the healing work of Zion" (:111). Acculturative factors resulting from the increasing Westernisation and urbanisation of Blacks in South Africa have been emphasised by West (1975) and Kiernan (1990) who show that healing in these churches is an urban Black cultural response expressed in the acculturated keys of both African and Western categories which have together informed the new urban Black cultural paradigm. Sickness comes as a result of new cultural factors and healing as an integration of these within a new whole.

Moving to the Pentecostal and Neopentecostal churches, the comments of Hollenweger (1972:490) are interesting. In his unstructured allusions to the cultural dimension of these churches he suggests that: "Pentecostal teaching can be understood as the rationalised scheme of values of a particular sub-culture" and concludes that a central feature of this subculture "presumably lies in the experience of being taken into a fellowship which involves a change in one's whole way of life, and which develops a scheme of values which is easier to comprehend and communicate . . ." (:491). The correspondence between this and the analyses of both Kleinman and Easthope hardly needs comment.

The cultural analysis of religious experience and in particular of the Coping-healing phenomenon is clearly crucial. This survey of current anthropological research has indicated the importance of cultural factors within this ministry. The necessity of widening the field to all cultural healing in order to draw useful conclusions has however highlighted the necessity of further anthropological research focusing specifically on the Coping-healing ministry. Cultural and social factors are strongly linked as this section has indicated. However, the focus of the disciplines of anthropology and sociology are different and we now move on to consider the Coping-healing phenomenon from a sociological perspective.

Chapter 5

The Sociological Mediation: Socio-Political Dimensions of Coping-Healing

5.1 Introduction

The healing ministry of the churches is a social phenomenon which brings together those wounded, diseased, disordered and taken ill, those they believe can heal them and a community of support which shares a common understanding that the healing can be effected. The illness and the healing occur within a social framework and so it is only natural to assume that social factors will impinge upon both realities. Our study of the Coping-healing phenomenon thus in some way implies a study of society. One of the clearest statements that one can make about society today is the fact that it is undergoing rapid change. This change is described variously as "modernisation", "urbanisation", "Westernisation", "industrialisation" and so on. The process of change affects the more traditional, closed societies down to the roots so that change itself becomes the most important reality of the society. Clifford Geertz (1973:148) using an example from Java, suggests that both people's perception of the society to which they belong, as well as their daily life within it, is undergoing fundamental transformation:

> much of Javanese social change is perhaps most aptly characterised as a shift from a situation in which the primary integrative ties between individuals (or between families) are phrased in terms of geographical proximity to one in which they are phrased in terms of ideological like-mindedness. [Geertz 1973:148]

He goes on to describe how this fact influences the rituals of the people he studies. Changes occur on the level of meaning where old rituals take on changed or even new significance and where the rituals themselves are changed or rejected as a result of new beliefs and behaviour.

The Coping-healing churches we have been studying and the Coping-healing phenomenon as it manifests itself within them, seem to be further examples of the process described by Geertz. In order then to continue our "observation" of them it is necessary to look at this phenomenon from a social perspective. Since "social" is one of these catch-all words, which could include all the perspectives studied in this section, we limit it here to the specifically socio-economic and political dimensions of its meaning. We wish to ask questions regarding the relationship between economic matters, socio-political matters and the Coping-healing phenomenon we have presented in chapter two. The notion that such a relationship might exist is not new. J.C.Rounds (1982:77) cites eighteen sources indicating the presence of such social factors as inequality, racism, deprivation, oppression, colonialism and White power as "causes accounting for the rise of religious movements". The function of such groups is seen in their ability to be "insulating social groups which protect and assist their members in their confrontation with foreign environments" (:77). Within the South African context, Sundkler (1948:169) had earlier indicated the effect of the "politico-social environment" on the emergence, cohesion and stability of African Independent churches. Sundkler (:169) identifies three important social factors which influence the emergence of these churches:

1) Increasing political and economic deprivation of Africans especially since the 1913 Land Act.
2) Increasing division between white and black where "the early close relations and the practice of common worship has been increasingly superseded by social distance".
3) The experience of Africans of living in a society in which leadership roles are denied them.

In this "sociological mediation", there is an emphasis on the social factors surrounding the emergence and development of the churches as such rather than social factors surrounding their healing ministry in general. We do this for two reasons. Firstly, the amount of literature focusing on the social dimensions of the healing ministries is quite restrictive. We widen the focus in order to identify all the socio-economic factors which impinge on these churches since many of these indirectly affect the Coping-healing phenomenon. Secondly, the Coping-healing phenomenon is what identifies these churches and "healing" is, in fact, what happens so that someone can become a "person" in the understanding that these churches give to this term: "born again", baptised, healed, filled with life, purified and so on. As a real person they can then take up their place and live in the new "society", which is what the particular church represents.

Morran and Schlemmer (1984:21ff.) present seven "broad overlapping theories" as being relevant to the development of "charismatic fundamentalist and conservative religious movements" such as the "new churches" they study amongst Westerners (predominantly white) in the Durban area. Some of these theories such as "conversion theories", "personality theories" and "meaning and belonging theories" have already been discussed. Here we consider the specifically social theories that Morran and Schlemmer present. There are three of them (1984:21): 1) Social disorganisation theories; 2) Deprivation theories and 3) Theories concerning authoritarian and political conservatism.

Social disorganisation theories indicate that the more "economic and social unrest" there is in society, the more certain kinds of religious groups increase membership. Deprivation theories concern the effect of economic, social, ethical, physical and psychological deprivation on the rate at which people join sects and new religious movements. Theories concerning authoritarian and political conservatism illustrate the fact that in times of social stress, politically conservative and authoritarian organisations, especially churches, tend to increase their appeal. This is either because they allow people to live and affirm the values they have been socialised into, which the social stress is challenging, or because they provide a haven of security for those who are confused by the changes.

We will also consider the social function of the Coping-healing churches and their impact on society in general. This gives rise to the whole question of society's view of healing and the question of the control of the therapeutic process within society. Finally, we will consider the question of the implicit political role of the Coping-healing phenomenon as it is expressing itself in the South African context.

Our starting point, however, will once more be the experience of illness and disease in society. Many authors have noted the socio-economic etiology of some illness and disease and others emphasise the fact of illness as a socio-economic or even political construct. It is to these issues that we first turn as we begin to mediate our phenomenon sociologically.

5.2 Social Etiologies of Illness and Disease

Faith Katherine Boucher (n.d.:10-12) has summarised the main developments in our understanding of the relationship between social environment and illness. She emphasises four major areas of this relationship:

(i) The role of society in determining health and illness and in proscribing the "sick role" (:10);

(ii) The role of social factors such as high population density and the "quality of social interactions and position with the group" (:11).

(iii) Organic effects of the social and physical environment (:12).

(iv) The effect of the "stability of the social environment" upon stress factors in disease (:12).

We suggest that her four areas can be combined with those of Morran and Schlemmer to posit three major social etiologies of illness and disease which we would outline as: 1) Sickness as social deprivation; 2) Sickness as social deviation and 3) Sickness as the response to social disorganisation.

Social deprivation theories show how people get sick as a result of economic, political and other social forms of deprivation. This deprivation is a denial of humanity and can operate on the physical, mental, spiritual, cultural and social levels. It gives rise to sickness either directly or through some of the mechanisms discussed in the psychological and anthropological mediations. Social deviation theories of sickness revolve around the fact that it is society and its authority which determines the nature of sickness and acceptable responses to it. Sickness here is seen as a behaviour which is deviant to the society's norms. In these theories, it is society which also often attributes etiology, responsibility and therapy. Social disorganisation theories apply in societies which find themselves in change, turmoil and crisis. In such societies, the prevailing norms are often challenged and ineffective. Illness is seen as a response to the stress provoked by the crisis. Healing is often the search for organisation around a more effective set of societal norms. Such healing involves a conversion process to the new set of norms.

5.2.1 Sickness and Social Deprivation

Newmann (1977:319-326) in a study of ecology and nutritional stress concludes that geographical and ecological factors such as climate combine together with socio-economic factors such as productivity and output to influence mortality and disease. Disease and poor nutrition are often linked and the ability of a society to provide adequate nourishment for its people is clearly linked to its wealth. Disease is also clearly linked to social conditions such as overpopulation and the provision of clean water and other infrastructure. Much of the work of the World Health Organisation is concerned with the provision of physical, social conditions which promote health. Hypertension is seen as a sign of stress in the individual which may then lead to a wide variety of sicknesses. Seedat and Meer (1984) have investigated the role of psychosocial factors in the development of hypertension amongst "urban Indian, White, Zulu and rural Zulu subjects" (:92). Results showed that hypertension could be ranked from highest to lowest as indicated in fig 5.1.

The study shows that urbanisation amongst Zulus has had a major impact. Hypertension was "low in the rural Zulu and very high in the urban Zulu". Deprivation factors were considered central here:

> members of a closely integrated self subsistent rural community, sharing a common life style, suffer no deprivation because there is no deprivation to suffer, that is, there is no inequality in the distributions of available resources. But members of that same consumption in an urban slum suffer from a sense of acute deprivation because of the fact and the consciousness of their discrimination. [Seedat & Meer 1984:97]

Urban Zulu females	27	% of the total sample
Urban Zulu males	23	%
White males	22	%
Indian females	16,7	%
White females	13	%
Indian males	11,2	%
Rural Zulu females	10	%
Rural Zulu males	8,7	%

Fig. 5.1 Incidence of Hypertension amongst Racial Groups in the Natal area. (Source: abstracted from article of Seedat & Meer 1984)

Perceived alienation from society is also seen to be an important causative factor in sickness. In their study, Seedat and Meer (1984:98) note that whilst all the subordinated race groups in South Africa would be expected to experience this, the effect is less for Indians and rural Blacks who find support in "the social structures they create for themselves":

> Thus, while alienated from the official system, they enjoy different levels of integration in the 'folk' systems. The Indians are integrated, the continuing strength of the Indian family, and the religious systems of Hinduism and Islam, are very important. The Coloureds and Blacks are by contrast poorly integrated, the Blacks primarily because of the effects of the migrant labour system, the Coloureds because of their marginal relationship with the Whites with whom they share a common culture but not a common society. [Seedat & Meer 1984:98]

Amongst White males, the high rate of hypertension was related to "the heavy responsibilities of administering the country in every sphere, political, economic, academic, military, sport under conditions of growing hostility and insecurity" (Seedat & Meer 1984:98). The results also revealed that "the hypertensives were generally more dissatisfied with their living and working conditions, had more worries and had poorer relatives at home, work and in the neighbourhood" (:101). It would seem reasonable to suppose that the group of people on the look-out for healing would have quite a preponderance of people like these amongst them.

Dube (1989:114) suggests that "urban settlements are characterised by suspicion, mistrust and even lack of cooperation among neighbours." He calls such an environment "hostile" and suggests that Africans in such a situation experience that "the demands of the industrial world leave the environment full of ritual impurity caused by mystical agencies and failure to observe taboos . . . This situation . . . affects the people's view of health" (:120-121). These factors are interpreted within a framework of mystical and spirit causation resulting in states of ill health. Such illness is always present since illness removed from people in non-legitimate ways remains to "pollute the environment. Since human life conforms to cosmic rhythms, people will inhale this pollution as it intensifies in response to the changing seasons " (:114).

5.2.2 Sickness and Social Disorganisation

Many of Seedat and Meer's results can also be explained in terms of social disorganisation theories. It is the people who find themselves in stable, centred social groupings who score low in hypertension. those who are in some form of social transition or alienating experience score much higher. Clearly such hypertension will manifest itself in various types of sickness. Social disorganisation results in the previous perceptions and understandings of sickness and disease being unable to cope with new experiences of unwell-ness. Consequently the old sickness-healing paradigm has to be modified or discarded. In this vein, Hammond-Tooke (1989:54) suggests that the process of social change has led to the introduction of new spirit forms within the African cosmology. He suggests the "spirits of affliction" (*amandiki, amandawe*) and the Holy Spirit (*umoya*) as examples of this process. These spirits can possess people, giving rise to some of the newer forms of sickness experienced in their new social circumstances (:57; 64). He suggests that the understanding of the Holy Spirit as power and the link between power and "moya-theology" is an expression of, or reaction to, the powerlessness of Blacks in South Africa (:62).

Amongst those frequenting the Neopentecostal churches, a different set of understandings (or of demons) has emerged. The demons are communism and atheism which are at the root of the social unrest. They operate together with their two main facilitators: liberalism in morality and the academic fraternity. The way of countering these demons is through the ceaseless propagation of the message of "God, country, capitalism and anti-communism to the masses" (Gifford 1988:4).

5.2.3 Sickness and Social Deviance

Sociological understandings of illness which revolve around the question of illness as a form of social deviance describe illness as occurring when persons are no longer able to fulfil their social responsibilities in the normal way. Using studies based on Parsons (1951) and other medicalisation theorists (Zola 1972; Freidson 1970) Schoffeleers (1991) presents the thesis that sickness is a form of social deviancy. Societies develop therapeutic structures and systems to provide legitimate, accepted ways of helping a person identify the illness and return to active social responsibility. In this way, Schoffeleers asserts, "the sick role can be made into a convenient tool to maintain the *status quo*, and . . . doctors, being the gatekeepers who regulate access to that role, become, thereby, agents of social control" (:13).

Feierman (1985:93-105) has studied the important role that political and economic decision makers in society have in determining the nature, quantity and distribution of disease in a society. Decisions regarding the extent of investments in "sanitation, education, health care, and family support" (:93) determine the kind of diseases which will be controlled and those which will not. Feierman's focus is Africa and he shows how decisions made by power holders in the political and economic spheres are shaped by their own interests and do not necessarily benefit the whole of society. Feierman's study also shows that many diseases which are often considered to have natural causes can in fact be shown to have socio-economic etiologies. Yet the responsibility for such sickness is laid upon the individual rather than the economic and political power structures of big business and government. In the South African context he studies the question of migrant labour and indicates how the system is oriented towards maximising the economic benefit of the worker to the industry whilst minimising the social responsibility of the industry to the health consequences, both short term and long term, in the workers (:93-96). He then poses the question: "Does this mean there is no hope of improving health in South Africa without a total transformation of the labor system?" (:104). His answer is as follows:

> Perhaps in one sense this is so. Certainly a broad definition of occupational health concerned with the families of workers, with those living next to factories, and with the long term effects of carcinogens, is incompatible with an economy heavily dependent on migrant labor. Centralised health planning, by itself, is not likely to create significant change. The possibilities for change become clear only by examining the relation of the healing occupations to power, and to democratically-based movements for change. [Feierman 1985:104-105]

Jean Leger (1989) provides a survey of the major trends of occupational diseases within the mining industry and highlights the "attempts by the state, in particular the mines inspectorate, to contain conflict over safety and health issues and to protect the interests of employers" (:1). He concludes that the new legislation being presented emphasising privatisation in safety and health monitoring results in the fact that "management prerogatives have been bolstered in a new framework of managerial regulation" (:45). These authors are attempting to show how the question of illness, its identification and the means society adopts for its control, is clarified through an analysis of power interests within the society.

5.3 Social Etiologies of Coping-Healing Churches

5.3.1 Deprivation Theories

Deprivation theories represent the oldest sociological attempts to understand the growth of sects and New Religious Movements. Early research in the United States showed that sects grew most rapidly amongst the economically deprived sector of the population who "transcend their feelings of deprivation by acquiring feelings of religious privilege which the status of sect member accords them" (Morran & Schlemmer 1984:25). Regarding the African Indigenous churches, we have already cited the works of Sundkler (1961) and Rounds (1979) pointing to the fact that social, economic and political deprivation are some of the factors leading to the emergence of these churches. Zulu (1986) attempts to specify these factors and their role in detail. He affirms that:

> economic and political dominance by the white group have resulted in complete control over the country's resources, both political and economic, and have also yielded a cultural hegemony for the white group and relative subservience for the Africans. It is this political and cultural subservience which, in religious terms has given birth to a myriad of separatist churches as men, in search of God, try to redefine both themselves and their existential situation. [Zulu 1986:151]

Following and developing Barrett's (1968) analysis of reasons for the emergence of these churches in Africa, Zulu agrees that the fact of a large proportion of Whites in the country with both political and cultural power has evoked two main responses in the African majority:

> i) they either found strength in organizing and consolidating the black majority against white rejection (black consciousness and black theology fall into this specific category) or
>
> ii) they retreated into their own separatist churches where they felt they could redefine their existential situation. [Zulu 1986:152]

Regarding the effect of the Black-White economic gap, he affirms that this plays an important role especially when there is a gap between people's economic expectation and their economic capability. Such a situation gives rise to frustration which may be expressed through religious independency. Dube (1989:30) affirms that "Zionist healing measures are effective in a community which finds itself disadvantaged". The reason for this is that these measures impinge upon all dimensions of the person's life including the social and give him or her a way of responding and coping with them. Socio-economic deprivation is life deprivation and "Zionists are in search of wholeness of life "(:132). Within the church they experience life-enhancing activities expressed as healing, and that is why they go.

Stephen Sales (1972) has attempted to discover a relationship between economic conditions and the membership of authoritarian churches in the United States. In a historical study of church records between 1920 and 1939, a period of "extreme variations in economic conditions" (:422), he measured the rate of conversion to a series of authoritarian churches and correlated this with an estimate of per capita income in the country. As wealth increased conversion rates increased to non-authoritarian churches (Congregational, Presbyterian and Northern Baptist). A wealth decrease, in economic bad times, was positively correlated with an increase in conversion to more authoritarian churches (Seventh day Adventist, Mormon, Roman Catholic) (:424-425). In a more specific study in the Seattle area during the 1960's, converts to the Seattle United Presbyterian Church (non authoritarian) and the Roman Catholic Church (authoritarian) were correlated with government studies of economic condition in the area during the period under review. The results again indicated a positive correlation of movement to the authoritarian type church during periods of economic difficulties (Sales 1972:426-427).

In the Durban area, however, the Neopentecostal churches are winning converts from more affluent sectors of society. Morran and Schlemmer (1984) point out that economic deprivation does play a role even amongst this group since a large number of the members of these churches come from those people employed in "white collar" jobs which do not demand formal qualifications obtained through studies and apprenticeships. They suggest that this group feels more fearful of social changes in South Africa since their jobs would be more easily threatened by changes which open the jobs up to all sectors of the population (:65). In order to explain the growth of these churches, sects and New Religious Movements amongst more affluent people, the concept of deprivation has been widened beyond the economic to include "social", "ethical", "organismic" and "psychic" deprivation:

> Social deprivation consists of lack of power, prestige, status and opportunities for social participation afforded the high status members of society. Organismic deprivation is created by physical or mental deformities. Ethical deprivation is created by intense value conflicts where an individual has a firm commitment to a set of values but is unable to live according to these in his particular society (alienation). Psychic deprivation occurs where people are without a meaningful system of values by which to interpret and organise their lives (anomie). [Morran & Schlemmer 1984:25]

Morran and Schlemmer suggest that all of these with the exception of ethical deprivation, are playing a role in the success of the Neopentecostal ("new") churches in South Africa. They identify a "sense of powerlessness" as being the most important factor motivating people to join these churches in the Durban area. The world is seen as being "run by the few people in power and there is not much that the ordinary person can do about it" (:68).

Bradfield (1979) in a study carried out in the United States, suggests that ethical and psychic deprivation are playing a role in the growth of "neo-Pentecostalism" amongst middle class Americans.[1] For Bradfield "neo-Pentecostalism" refers partly to the incorporation of Pentecostal practices and experiences with mainline churches, principally through the Charismatic renewal. Experiences of baptism in the Holy Spirit and healing provide a new sense of purpose and meaning to life and the church provides the hope that society can be reformed through God's action. Morran and Schlemmer (1984:27) discount the role of ethical deprivation suggesting that the "value systems of members of the new churches prior to their conversion are not likely to have been dramatically at variance with the dominant values in white South African society." To some extent this latter statement may be true, but it is precisely the change in the values of society to which they react. This is occurring on two levels: White South African society is becoming more secular and Western and more importantly, the values of the "new South Africa" now emerging, but visible since the events of 1976, are clearly vastly different to those of people joining the "new churches". We suggest that ethical deprivation is indeed playing a larger role in the movement to these churches amongst Whites than Morran and Schlemmer suggest. Within the paradigm of sickness as social deprivation, the

Coping-healing phenomenon can be understood as a response to the deprivation through the reception of some compensating element which, in one way or another, restores the humanity denied by the deprivation.

5.3.2 Social Disorganisation Theories

Social disorganisation theories indicate that the more "economic and social unrest" there is in a society, the more certain kinds of religious groups increase membership. Morran and Schlemmer (1984:23) suggest that such theories "explain the growth of the new churches quite successfully" since Whites are experiencing the passing of the "old norms and values" of the old South Africa and the privileged position of Whites within it. Their research amongst "new church" members and members of mainline churches shows that the vast majority of all respondents saw the world as unstable and moving towards conflict and upheaval. However, the "new church" people felt that whilst most people should indeed "fear the future in this country" (:64), it was not necessary for them personally to be afraid. "The reason for their lack of fear is because of their membership in the new churches" (:64). Thus the churches were succeeding in removing a fear together with its concomitant stress factor.

Mary De Haas (1986:38) in a most perceptive article, brings together "two prevalent movements of an ideological nature which do indeed make very strange bedfellows: the 'Reborn Christian' movement and Marxism". She suggests that these provide two expressions within which people live out the same experience: "The ultimate truth behind outward appearances, a truth which guarantees their future redemption, an ultimate state 'where difficulties are overcome, happiness achieved' (Talmon 1965:526)" (De Haas 1986:43). Such truth and such need for redemption have become necessary, according to De Haas, as a result of the "situation of potential rapid social change, in which the very quality of their lives may be at stake" (:43). In the "Reborn" Christian movements, the importance of healing, a central theme, as well as the emphasis on the "Prosperity Gospel", emerge because these provide lived, "this world" experiences of the veracity of their choice: signs of the future redemption here and now.

Turning now to African Indigenous churches, Sundkler (1948:255) was well aware of the role of socio-economic changes and upheaval in the genesis of these churches. The resulting insecurity and uncertainty is interpreted as an increase in "threatening dangers from ill-omens to death". In the second edition of his work (1961:302) he suggests that these churches have become "adaptive structures" helping people to make the transition to a different way of life. J.C.Rounds (1982:85) researching the factors affecting religious choice amongst Zulus draws the same conclusion: "the Pentecostal sect, on the one hand offers solutions to the problems which arise in the lives of folk of rural background who have decided to move to the city and are trying to adapt to this new way of living".

5.4 Coping-Healing as a Sociological Phenomenon

5.4.1 Coping-Healing as Adapting to New Circumstances

The question of healing is central to the process of adaptation discussed above. Jules-Rosette (1981:127) points out that "coping with the urban environment and the adjustments that it necessitates, especially amongst new migrants, involves the individual's most basic perceptions of health and illness." This is so since health and illness theories are intimately tied up with the person and the network of relationships within which he or she lives (:127; cf. Bate 1991:59). Jules-Rosette (1981:146) concludes that people in urban areas experiment with different forms of folk healing, including religious faith healing, in an attempt to find ways to cope with rapidly changing social conditions. This attempt is made in order "to redefine a changing social world in terms of familiar avenues of recourse and associative networks." The familiar avenues are the methods used by the Zionists, as well as other traditional healers to whom they have recourse. Rounds' (1982) study also produces evidence to support the contention that healing is a means of finding ways of adapting to, and coping with, social change.

The experience of "baptism" as healing from socio-economic and political tension is emphasised by Oosthuizen (1989b). It is the "symbol which gives orientation and meaning; it changes chaos to cosmos" (:140). The chaos is described by him as ". . . their environment, work situation, living conditions and the foreignness of a secularised impersonal world . . ." (:140). This experience of social disorganisation is brought to the waterside and transformed through the ritual: ". . . an act through which balance is established; [having] not only great psychiatric value but also great physical value because of the influence of the psyche on the body" (:140). Clearly there are strong links between the Coping-healing ministry of the churches we have studied and the situation of social change. Healing here, is the providing of ways to cope with this change and remove the stress it generates.

5.4.2 Coping-Healing as Social and Personal Re-Creation

Comaroff (1985:229) suggests that "baptism is the act that initiates members into a cult of perpetual healing and reintegration." She affirms that both ritual and healing provide two responses to the society within which people live: an experience of resistance to the society on the one hand and an experience, on the other hand, of reconstruction of the human person (:228, 231). This reconstruction, both of dignity and of humanness occurs in the counter society, the church, within which such human dignity is both affirmed and enhanced.

These two responses can be seen as poles which outline a process of deconstruction and reconstruction which goes on in the healing. The reality which is deconstructed is the daily experience of the person in the alienating threatening society in which he or she lives and works. The reconstruction is of a new society in which the person is empowered to become filled with life within a community which affirms humanity. "In Zion, healing was the crucial act of innovative reconstruction; as a leader of the Z.C.C. put it, 'all we *do* is heal'" (Comaroff 1985:219). Comaroff (:197) suggests that "the Zionists construct rituals so as to reform the world in the image they have created, to establish a dynamic correspondence between the self and the structures that contain it " (:197). It is the reconstruction of humanity which provides a means for a person to emerge ready to survive within an alien environment without being totally destroyed by it. The origin myth of the church is "the exile from urban bondage to the site of liminal reconstruction" (Comaroff 1985:231) and the rites, dress and songs facilitate the move from *chronos* to *kairos* so that the metamorphosis may occur, transference may be enhanced and the personal and social fragmentation which is daily life may be subsumed and reworked through a process which transcends it.

> This unification, soon to be completed by the infusion of spirit, dramatically reverses the state of physical and social disarticulation that the testimonies expressed; it cuts across the fragmentation of person and community which pervades the experience of black South Africans under apartheid. [Comaroff 1985:233]

On a more general level Jones (1985:77) affirms that periods of rapid social change evoke the need to "turn inwards" in order to discover "a sphere of 'inner' integrity". Such a sphere is experienced in terms of prevailing cultural norms. In Western culture the emphasis is on the individual: "Jesus as personal saviour" and the importance of "personal healing". In African culture the emphasis is on the communal, the creation of an inner community of integrity, the Zionist band, as a source of life, strength and health. The role of the creation of a community within which healing occurs is also mentioned by Becken (1989:238) who considers the social aspect to have a healing quality in itself. Dube (1989:129-130) also emphasises the effectiveness of these methods in communities which find themselves socially disadvantaged.

The question of status and respect denied by the society and affirmed within the AIC communities is also highlighted by many authors. Williams (1982:40) considers this to be an important dimension of the healing process. He sees subordination as the "central principle in ordering social relationship in Zulu society" (:40) and that this is reflected in the structuring of Zionist ritual expression.

> When one first associates with a Zionist church, the newcomer is told to wear a specifically colored robe (the color of which has been prophesied) and to follow a certain treatment plan that is intended to bring not only relief but also to symbolize a process of becoming purified which entitles the patient to occupy a new status within the church. [Williams 1982:40]

The therapeutic process revolves around the growth in human dignity through a carefully graded series of steps symbolised by the acquisition of various statuses in the group. The need for such a structure in the healing process obviously bears on the question of fission in these churches since more status is obviously available to more people when more churches exist.

5.4.3 Coping-Healing as Power

The experience of joining the Neopentecostal churches is often expressed in terms of power returning to people's lives. The fear of the future which they formerly had is replaced by a sense of trust in God (Morran & Schlemmer 1984:64). They have experienced God most often in their own personal healing reported as miraculous by 47% of the "new church" members (:127). Many also reported how they too had personally healed someone else, thus affirming the experience of power operating in their own lives (:127). The "power variable" also plays an important role in African Indigenous churches. Martin West (1975:121-123) suggests that people are attracted to the prophet-healer because of "the ultimate power claimed by the prophet" (:121). This power is the power of God. Whilst the methods he uses may be similar to those of other traditional healers it is this recourse to God's power which sets him apart from them. West (:191) accepts the view which sees religion as "the systematic ordering of different kinds of power". He suggests that: "the work of the prophet . . . is perhaps the best example of this integration of power" (:193).

Comaroff (1985:260-263) suggests, in her study, that Zionism provides a framework within which the dynamics of resistance can be expressed. She argues that interpretations which dismiss these churches and the healing they provide as an escape from social responsibility: "merely finely wrought self-delusions, so entrapped within the structures of domination that they unwittingly put their imaginative power at the disposal of the regime they protest" (:261), do not take sufficient cognisance of the role they play in consciousness formation as well as the fact that they provide opportunities "to address and redress experiential conflict" within the "pitifully restrained circumstances" open to them. The Zionist movements have appeared within the context of the wider social community of which the Zionist members were also a part. That this social community was constantly a culture of resistance to colonialism, racism and exploitation is merely to state the obvious. Zionism should be seen within this context. The comments of Ngada (1985), himself a Bishop in one of these churches, are also significant in this regard.

> Our communities are sometimes accused of being too inward looking and people ask us what we think about *politics*. It is difficult for us to know how to answer this question. The members of our churches are the poorest of the poor, the people with the lowest jobs or with no jobs at all . . . Our people, therefore know what it means to be oppressed, exploited and crushed . . . But we also know that God does not approve of this evil and that racial discrimination and oppression is rejected by the Bible.
>
> And so what do our people do about it? They join political organisations or trade unions and take part in the struggle for our liberation. But it is a matter of individual choice. Members of the same Church will join different political organisations or trade unions and some will choose not to join anything. Politics is not a Church mat-

> ter. People meet together in our Churches to pray and to worship and to experience the healing of the Spirit. They go to political organisations in order to take action against the government ... The 'Churches of the People' and political organisations or trade unions of the people have different roles to play. It is often the same people who belong to both. [Ngada 1985:30-31]

For Comaroff (1985:261-263) Zionism is a "Body of Power": a system of implicit resistance to prevailing socio-economic and political conditions (1985:261). It is counter cultural in its nature (:194) and "its modes of practice . . . signify resistance to the institutions and categories of the dominant culture" (:255; cf. also Kiernan 1974). It is an attempt to regain control of life amongst a people whose daily experience confirms the opposite. This control, necessary for survival, employs the means and ways available to the people at a particular time (:262).

5.4.4 Coping-Healing as Social and Political Involvement

Gerrit Huizer (1987:89) notes that at the "Harare IAMS Workshop on the 'Church as a Healing Community' it was discussed that healing the effects of disruption and affliction at the individual or community level cannot be separated from healing the brokenness of societies as a whole." The notion of socio-economic and political involvement of the Church as part of its healing role is one which is currently gaining ground (WCC 1986; Diakonia 1991; Bosch 1988). When the society is perceived as dehumanising, this can also be interpreted as sickness and the remedial response to it on the social level, through political, social and economic involvement, can be interpreted as healing. Such a perspective raises the point whether the Coping-healing churches involve themselves in this type of healing.

A major question posed by Hollenweger (1972:465-472) in his comprehensive study is whether Pentecostalism leads to social involvement or social withdrawal. He affirms that in "certain societies the Pentecostal movement is a necessary island of humanity" (:467). When a society is dehumanising then the experience of having one's humanity affirmed is clearly necessary merely for survival and this is the point of Comaroff discussed in the previous section. However the question is whether the so healed are prepared to go into the world in order to heal what is broken within it. For Hollenweger, this question remains unanswered, for whilst he is able to find examples of this in some Latin American and European countries he suggests that the danger of Pentecostalism is the temptation of its members to close themselves off from the outside world (:467). Pentecostals experience the world as hostile (:484) and consequently they develop a response to it which mirrors their experience. As a result, the structures of the world are generally mistrusted and dismissed as evil and a pessimistic view of the present emerges. The focus is shifted to the *eschaton*, expected soon, in which everything will be transformed for the good. Clearly such a view of life mitigates against social involvement.

The situation of socio-economic and political deprivation can give rise to two responses both of which are found within Pentecostal and Neopentecostal churches. Either the things of this world are seen as of little value or as evil, or a system is developed which enables a person to get them. The former is evident in the rigorist ethic of some Coping-healing churches which ban smoking, drinking, cinema, cosmetics, fashion and the like whilst the latter is evident in teachings such as that of the "prosperity gospel" (cf. Hollenweger 1972:484). Several authors affirm that these churches promote political acquiescence in their members by "immunising" them to involvement by the substitution of coping mechanisms. Paul Gifford (1988) in a valuable, though rather one sided, etic analysis of the predominantly White Coping-healing churches suggests that the danger of these churches is that they inure people to mistrust an involvement in social struggle and reform and as a result "this Christianity can be used by those with interests to protect" (:109). These churches have been in the very thick of support for the "Pretoria regime of P.W.Botha" (:36-37) and are firmly anti-ANC, which was branded as part of the communist onslaught on the country and its people (:34-36). By learning to cope with the tensions of society such people are open to accept and affirm the status quo.[2]

Coming to the African Independent churches we have studied, we note, once more, the comments of Zulu (1986:152) who suggests that the "separatist churches" provide a place of retreat for Africans faced with the situation of socio-economic and political oppression. In this he follows many of the early Black consciousness writers (cf. Ndebele 1972, as quoted by Sundkler 1976:319). Matthew Schoffeleers (1991) in an important article, recently published, is also of the opinion that ritual healing churches give rise to political acquiescence. In his study he bases his thesis on the "general conclusion" of Max Gluckman (1965:216-67) that "healing practices not only restore order on a personal level but also maintain order on the societal level" (in Schoffeleers 1991:16). Gluckman's conclusion is based on studies of traditional healers and in his article Schoffeleers (:18) attempts to see if its conclusions are valid for Zionist churches. He concludes that this is indeed so. He identifies the healing ministry of these churches as "the root cause of their quietistic character" (:18), concluding from the research of Kiernan and West that Zionist healing "exhibits significant parallels with modern medicine. In both cases illness tends to be viewed in terms of deviancy . . . [and] healing involves a process of resocialisation in one form or another" (:16).

Schoffeleers (1991:15) suggests that Zionist healing sets up structures of social control and maintenance of the *status quo* within its subculture by prescribing the sick role as a form of social deviancy from its norms: ". . . among Zionists, social deviance is automatically defined as illness". Thus Schoffeleers maintains that healing in general and Zionist healing in particular is by nature destined for conservatism (:18). We have seen how social conflict can give rise to illness. Schoffeleers contends that healing depoliticises the conflict by individualising the problem as personal illness which is then controlled by the established healing structures of which Coping-healing churches are one example. The problem is not dealt with on the socio-political level of protest and thus this dimension is subdued by the presence of such healing structures (:18-19). On a more positive note he recognises that in the reconstruction of a "post - apartheid South Africa" the role of healing in social reconstruction becomes central and the social role of these churches may be essential as "stabilising agencies" (:19).

Other authors do not recognise the dichotomy between Coping-healing churches and social responsibility as being as clear cut as this. Already in the second edition of his book, Sundkler (1961:307) notes the protest character of these churches from 1913 to 1945 regarding the Land Act, White culture and the approach of the Mission churches. Itumeleng Mosala (1985:109) suggests that many Western approaches to African Independent churches lack an adequate social and cultural analysis of the issue. Such an analysis must be able to abstract the notion of working class and of Blackness as the keys to begin the investigation into African Independent churches and their practices (:109-110). The identification of the working class and its culture leads to the conclusion that the "African Independent churches and especially the Zionist churches are, in fact, in contradiction to all 'mainline churches', strictly speaking black working-class churches" (:110). As a result they are engaged in the historical struggle of the black working class for liberation since "culture is an arena of social struggle" (:111).

> [T]he new society into which they were integrated related to them as exploitable commodities, understood as labour power. In these circumstances the only available means of self-defence is cultural-ideological. Belief in God or gods becomes not a choice, it is a necessity. [Mosala 1985:110-111]

Mosala's invective is weighed against a "liberal" approach which tends to analyze through division into parts emphasising the role of the parts without recognising their interconnectedness. Jean Comaroff also argues against this approach. The Zionists she has studied find themselves in a historical process of "proletarianisation" to which they have to respond. The "Mission churches" as a result of their White leadership and imported practices were less able to do this but the Independent churches grew up within the proletarianisation experience since all its leaders and members were part of it.

> And, while the rise of the Independent churches might not have signaled the development of a "working-class consciousness," it objectified a cultural scheme that was to give more explicit voice to the conflicts inherent in the shared experience of wage labor. As Marks (n.d.:21) put it, this scheme "gave strategies for surviving in a new and harsh world, if not yet for transforming it." [Comaroff 1985:175]

The issue here revolves around the nature of protest and of struggle and the value given to its various expressions. Religious, cultural and ideological forms of struggle and protest may often be dismissed by those seeking more active political and social revolutionary approaches but the fact of the matter is that each has its own role to play within the totality. The question is very often one of timing: the *kairos*.

Healing is an important requirement in society and whilst it is true that medical systems, like those of the Coping-healing churches, are systems of social conservatism and may hinder necessary social reform, such a unilinear approach which sees only this negative dimension will not suffice. Social and political participation involves the commitment to, and establishment of, a society which promotes the common good and well being of all its members. Healing is not to be dismissed because of some links to political acquiescence. Clearly the cultural differences between Neopentecostalism and the AIC's are also playing an important role here. Neopentecostals tend to operate within the context of Western culture which is analytic and tends to situate religion in an "other worldly" reality. The AIC's, on the other hand, tend to operate within the more holistic African cultural framework where religion is perceived as part of life and is "this worldly". Nevertheless, this socio-economic mediation teaches us that society needs to be human and perhaps it is in this way, the restoration of humanity to society, that the Coping-healing ministry faces its greatest challenge, its clearest social role.

5.5 The Social Role of Coping-Healing Churches

The Coping-healing churches and the Coping-healing ministry do not only respond to the prevailing socio-economic and political context but they also contribute to that context. These churches have a social role which helps mould the society in which they exist. In a general comment on Pentecostal religion, Hollenweger (1972:460) suggests that "although in various countries it takes on a specific national colouring, its function of overcoming personal and social disadvantages by a religious experience is exercised amongst all nations." Hollenweger (1972:164) adopts Schlosser's (1967) analysis of Zionists in suggesting that Zionists have taken over social functions "which used to be that of the tribes" (:164). Martin West (1975:198-199) suggests that the African Independent churches fulfil several social roles in helping people to adjust to the urban environment they find themselves living in. One of their roles is to help in facilitating "interethnic contact" (:198) since he sees that the churches in Soweto draw members from all "tribal" groups. In this way he sees them aiding individuals in adjusting to the new multicultural and multi-traditional environment of the urban township (:198). The members of these churches also help one another in more practical ways such as with "employment opportunities", "getting information about the city and its ways" and through mutual financial help in times of crisis, illness, bereavement and other difficulty (:198-199). Finally, by offering opportunities for leadership they mitigate against a society in which so few such opportunities are available to Blacks (:199). Motala (1989:203) indicates four ways in which members of the Zionist Christian Church, studied by her, "take social responsibility for one another's needs".

> Firstly, the Zionist congregation is encouraged to act as a family, and to support and sympathize with fellow members. Secondly ZCC group members are encouraged to make friends within their church. In a small group, members are able to feel at home. The group is able to give both moral and material assistance in times of need, and assists individuals in their adjustment to city life. Thirdly, Little (1965) pointed out that the Zionist church offers supernatural protection to members through church membership and attendance at services. Lastly, the ZCC congregation also assists members in practical ways to deal with the urban situation. For example, members may be assisted by getting information about the urban situation.
>
> These factors indicate that membership in the ZCC and participation in the services help individuals who are placed in the urban situation to adjust and not allow external circumstances to influence their emotions to too great an extent.
>
> [Motala 1989:203]

Morran and Schlemmer (1984:100) contend that the ability of the churches they studied to provide clear answers, in simple contemporary language, to the complexity of life in today's South Africa, is one of their main appeals. They note that of all churches, "the new church charismatic group was the only group which had an absolute explanation for suffering" (:104). This explanation, imputing responsibility entirely to the devil, clearly assuages any guilt feelings Whites or other relatively rich people may have. Similarly, the emphasis on the "prosperity gospel" is an affirmation of the preoccupation with money or how to get it - a hallmark of Western culture (cf.: 104-109). Clearly these factors are performing the role of bolstering the political, social and economic values of the people joining them; values which are being threatened by prevailing social conditions.

The churches also provide a subculture in which persons can live their whole life without being involved in the world outside other than at work (Morran & Schlemmer 1984:134). This new subculture, within which they move, is described in terms of fellowship and love: "there is beautiful friendship there" (:151) and is considered a unique feature of the "new churches". In their conclusion, Morran and Schlemmer (:169ff) suggest that the "new churches" are performing the following social functions:

1) remedying the powerlessness felt by their members in the changing South African society (:170)
2) influencing their political attitudes in two ways : "by encouraging a very dismissive attitude to political issues" (:171) and by developing a "false sense of optimism and complacency regarding the future of this country" (:171-172).
3) influencing attitudes towards suffering, prosperity and poverty which takes them out of the sphere of human responsibility and into the supernatural (:172)

4) providing a sense of well-being, happiness and security in a fearful world (:174-175)

Clearly much of the above is expressed and experienced within the category of healing and this is why healing is such a central dimension of all these churches.

Feierman (1985), in his excellent article, is at pains to point out how healing and healers have always been caught up within a *complexus* of economic, political and social factors and that to isolate the healing phenomenon from these and consider only the question of whether the person is healed or not is to severely misunderstand it (:105-110):

> Both popular medicine and biomedicine are forms of ethnomedicine: they are embedded within a system of social relations, and give concrete form to assumptions about reality drawn from the wider culture which in turn influences the wider culture. [Feierman 1985:110]

He suggests that both are "traditional" in that they are "products of history" and make assumptions about the nature of the person, sickness and healing which are part of the history of the culture and society from which they have emerged (Feierman 1985:110). He contests that an analysis of the distribution and control of power and knowledge within a society provide an important understanding of the role of healing in society (:112-4). In traditional African Society, he indicates studies which show that health was "originally bound up with basic political and economic processes" (:116) and that "some categories of popular healers played a basic role in organizing production in the precolonial period" (:116). The important questions for Feierman are:

> Do healers find their interests linked tightly to those of ruling political elites or dominant classes? To what extent does healing serve the interests of privileged sub-groups within society? How does the place of healers influence the definition of public issues affecting health and illness? Can healers use their authority to help the oppressed win control over their own health? [Feierman 1985:114]

In answering these questions he affirms that the aim of healers is to achieve "cultural authority" which means that within the culture they are operating in, they are recognised as the "professionals". Such a culture or society will then assign control to this group: control over the allocation of resources, education in the area and so forth. It is interesting to note that the healers we have studied in the Christian Coping-healing phenomenon tend to do this by establishing a subculture: the Zionist band, the "born again" Christian community or the prayer group within which they are able to exercise hegemony. A further important question posed by Feierman revolves around the question of a conflict between the interests of healers and the interests of the sick. For example, he questions the "healing" achieved by a South African doctor who was able to find an organic cure for heart disease amongst workers in a Tongaat sugar mill who "live in compounds . . . rise at 4.30 in the morning . . . and work in the sun until late afternoon with only sour, watery maize porridge to eat until the evening meal" (1985:115). The doctor, whose interests coincide with those of the plantation bosses, may have solved the bosses' problem of too many people getting sick at work and thus being unable to produce effectively. However, Feierman suggests that an improvement in working condition may have more effectively led to the healing of workers.

The concern of some mainline church clergy regarding the damage done by Coping-healing churches, especially to individuals who are not healed or whose healing is temporary, also falls into this category of Feierman's analysis. It is in the interest of the pastor who wishes to build a strong church, that there be healings and miracles so that people may come. Most are not willing to listen to or acknowledge the failures. Feierman (1985:75) shows that the control of healing implies a concomitant rise in the power of effective healers to have control over other aspects of people's lives:

1) power over practical matters to decide when people can or cannot meet their social obligations
2) power over ideology: through their ability to explain illness in terms of a world view and morality, healers can actually change belief systems and value systems.
3) power over the psyche: through the therapeutic relationship the healer has power over people's self understanding and an ability to manipulate them.

Healers, when accepted by the culture as "the experts", become the health professionals (cf. Kleinman 1980) and when this occurs they exercise a power in society regarding the control of resources for well-being: a vital social role. These resources include the development of society's health infrastructure as well as decisions regarding the nature of illness and health in society. Clearly the healing role has powerful social consequences and religious healers are making a large impact on the moulding of the "New South African" society. They have a particular vision of how that new world should be and through their effective healing processes they are able to win people to their vision. Their vision is based on their world-view, their understanding of how the world operates and what underlies its meaning. This gives rise to philosophical considerations and it is to these that we now turn.

Chapter 6

The Philosophical Mediation of the Coping-Healing Phenomenon

6.1 Introduction

The importance of understanding and the role of shared world-view in the Coping-healing process has already been seen in chapter four. Nevertheless, categories such as "understanding" and "world-view" also raise philosophical questions of an epistemological and metaphysical nature. These questions revolve around the significance of a plurality of world-views and the epistemological keys that ground them, as well as the attempts to construct a metaphysics which can accommodate such a plural vision. These are issues which are becoming central in the theological and missiological debate today and are concerned with what has been called the "Paradigm Shift (Change)" in theology (Küng & Tracy 1989; Mouton, Van Aarde & Vorster 1988; Bosch 1991).

It is this author's contention that missiology, with its emphasis on the boundary between Church and "World" as well as its interdisciplinary nature (cf. Luzbetak 1988:12-15) is the field which can contribute most fruitfully to this debate. It does this precisely because it begins with an examination of a phenomenon at this boundary and then applies its method to understanding and grounding the phenomenon within the self-understanding of the community of faith moved by the presence of the Spirit. An adequate philosophical mediation, then, is a necessary part of any missiological investigation. In this chapter, however, we wish to consider the ramifications of world-view on the Coping-healing phenomenon and the consequences of this in identifying an epistemology that can meet the variety of world-views which ground the Coping-healing practices. We also show the importance of an epistemological grounding of the various methods and systems which are used to describe, interpret and explain the Coping-healing phenomenon. Several approaches have been used in this section: psycho-medical approaches such as the biomedical and systems approach; the psychological systems of Jung, Freud, behaviourists and existentialists; anthropological approaches such as structuralism, functionalism, semiotic symbolism; and, finally, sociological approaches such as neo-Marxism, Weberism, Gramscian hegemony theories and so on. It is important to acknowledge the fact of different approaches and their epistemological and metaphysical bases. In this chapter, we begin by indicating the role of world-view in both illness and disease and then go on to an epistemological consideration of world-view and its link with some of the methods used in our analysis so far. Finally we indicate the importance of searching for a metaphysics which could serve to ground the plurality which is emerging and address the issue of unity.

6.2 World-View and its Importance

The philosopher Dilthey, emphasised the tendency of humankind to "achieve a comprehensive interpretation, a *Weltanschauung*, or philosophy, in which a picture of reality is combined with a sense of its meaning and value and with principles of action" (in Edwards 1967:404). Geertz (1973:126) separates this totality into a number of dimensions suggesting that "recent anthropological discussions" refer to the moral and evaluative aspects of a culture as the "ethos" and the cognitive, existential aspects as the "world-view". "Their world-view is their picture of the way things in sheer actuality are, their concept of nature, of self, of society" (:127).

This "world-view" is made up of a number of perspectives "in terms of which men construe the world" (Geertz 1973:111). These are particular ways of looking at life and Geertz presents four major ones: the commonsensical, the scientific, the aesthetic and the religious. He suggests that each of these operates at different times under different conditions in order to respond to different preoccupations and goals. Thus the commonsensical affirms the "simple acceptance of the world, its objects and its processes as being just what they seem to be" (:111). The scientific perspective doubts this givenness and attempts to understand the world in terms of verified formal concepts which enable control and exploitation of it. The aesthetic perspective involves the "suspension of both naive realism and practical interest . . . in favor of an eager dwelling upon appearances" (:111). The "religious perspective" attempts to go beyond what is given in order to determine the "really real" which lies behind it and which gives fundamental meaning to the whole (:112).

Chidester (1989:16) suggests that the term "world-view" be broadened ("-unpacked") beyond its normal meaning of a way of seeing or thinking to include "a multidimensional network of strategies for negotiating person and place in a world of discourse, practice and associations". He then goes on to apply this semantically poetic construct in order to understand African Indigenous churches. In an article which makes up in erudition what it lacks in clarity, he proposes "Human", "Superhuman" and "Subhuman" as the terms which "are the three basic categories of classification in world-views" (:17). He suggests that African Indigenous churches are concerned with the process of re-establishing human identity for people whose daily experience is one of dehumanisation. This process occurs through contact with superhuman powers (:20). Clearly this is their healing function. He categorises the world-view of African Independent churches as a "religious world-view" and suggests that the essence of such world-views is that they are "complex strategic negotiations in which symbolic forms are formulated, appropriated, manipulated and mobilized to carve out a human identity and a place for that human to stand and act as a human being" (:21). The centre of Chidester's concept of world-view is the human person *qua* his or her humanity and world-view, for him, is about the establishment of humanity within the cosmos. In another exotic use of language, he refers to the way that the humanisation occurs as being through a "cultural process of stealing back and forth sacred symbols" (:22). This is because the process of appropriation of these symbols enhances the process of "becoming human" which is what the AIC group is concerned with. This could clearly be applied to the healing of people within those groups: the symbols appropriated are manifestations of power needed by the sick person for health.

Coming to a more prosaic level we suggest that some simpler comments with regard to world-view need to be presented at this time. Firstly, Hammond-Tooke (1989:45) affirms that "one of the most important functions of any religious system is to provide meaning to the world and to life." This is a cognitive function and an essential dimension of the religious. Both Oosthuizen (1989a:77) and Horton (1971:96) suggest that the African Independent churches have grown partly because they are prepared to take African cosmology and world-view seriously. Indeed, more correctly, we might say that they succeed because they work *through* this religious world-view. Lest we might be misunderstood on this point, it is also important to note that they do not merely take over a static African world-view and work within it to effect healing. As Sundkler (1961:260-264) points out, the religious world-view that Zionism employs manifests both similarities and changes to the traditional African world-view, which is obviously to be expected if, as Chidester (1989:20) says, world-view is "a process, not a thing: an activity, not an object". This process, of which healing is part, revolves around the "dynamic, complex and ambiguous . . . process of the emergence and appropriation of symbols . . ." (:24).

Horton (1971:96) indicates that the change in world-view of "main stream Euro-American Protestant Christianity" in the nineteenth century saw it "drop all pretence of providing a theory of how the world really worked, or a recipe for controlling the course of its affairs." This state of affairs, brought about by the scientific revolution in the West, severely hampered the appeal of the Church for Africans whose religious world-view included an "explanation - prediction - control" dimension (:96). He suggests that it is this lack which was remedied by the emergence of African Independent churches and which contributed to their growth; growth which resulted from them providing "this-worldly" experiences of God's power of which healing is the most important manifestation. Though Horton does not specifically mention it, one could easily interpret the emergence of Pentecostalism, with its stress on just these factors, at approximately the same time, in the same way.

6.2.1 World-View and Illness

Wellin (1977:50) indicates the role of world-view understandings of disease causation. He presents Rivers' conceptual model which points to three different world-view types: the magical, the religious and the naturalistic, and their role in indicating theories of illness and disease causation. The "magical" world-view leads to a theory of disease as caused by a human manipulation of magical forces as in sorcery and witchcraft. The Zulu understanding of *ubuthakathi* clearly has some links with this category. The "religious" world-view leads to a theory which sees disease resulting from supernatural forces whereas the "naturalistic" world-view indicates natural process as being disease causative. Clearly most cultures reflect an amalgam of these three models.

Cheetham and Rzadkowlski (1980:321-324) contrast Western concepts of mental health and ill-health with those in (what they call) the "preliterate society". The Western concept ranges between a biological model and a psycho-dynamic model. The biological model follows the mechanistic model of the disease entity, which is seen as having an independent existence (one "gets it" or "has it") (:322). The psycho-dynamic approach sees illness as a deviation from an ideal balance of normal mental functioning, caused by psycho-social factors. The authors suggest an approach which takes both of these into account proposing a "general systems theory" in which

> the human organism is viewed as composed of a number of hierarchically organised subsystems (particles, molecules, cells, organs) and itself belonging to larger systems (family, group, organisation society, nation, ecological environment) with each system relating reciprocally to the others. Health will be understood as a dynamic balance of the systems and illness as disequilibrium.
>
> [Cheetham & Rzadkowolski 1980:322]

In "preliterate society", they suggest, following the authors of the time, "mental illness is viewed in light of a threat to social order rather than as a cognitive malfunction *per se* " (:323). They conclude that such an understanding can be incorporated within the "general systems" model which they propose as a basis for cross cultural work in mental therapy.

African Traditional World-Views and Illness

In his early work, Oosthuizen (1968:136) emphasised the controlling role of the spiritual in the African world-view. Quoting Baëta (1955:139) he affirms that "In the traditional African world everything is controlled by the spiritual world 'which determines and awards weal or woe, abundance or work, illness or health, continuing life or death'". Sundkler (1961:225) says that the Zulu world-view incorporates a natural causation theory of disease (*umkhuhlane* -

nje) as well as a category of more serious illness, *ukufa kwabantu*, which is caused by some form of *ubuthakathi*. However *ubuthakathi* is divided into two types. The one is concerned with the natural realm in the manipulation of poisonous medicines (*imithi*) and is sorcery. The second, not mentioned by Sundkler, but referred to by Berglund (1976:267) is "witchcraft [which] assumes a supernatural and mystical character of the power and the witch." From this we can see that Rivers' three categories are present in the Zulu world-view. Janzen (1989) attempts to harmonise sub-Saharan "Bantu" understandings of sickness from an analysis of language. He suggests that the stem "thak" of *ubuthakathi* is found throughout this language group and refers to the malicious or destructive use of power, especially the misuse of powerful words in the sense of a "curse, spell or oath" (:233). Indeed, Janzen (:232) contests that "In Bantu - African thinking the interconnected fates of healthiness and of affliction or misfortune are traced to a central source of power (or life) in God and nature" (:232). Sickness is considered as part of evil or misfortune and whilst some of this may be considered as part of the natural order, "[m]uch of it, however is attributed to the evil and chaos in human nature and society rather than to an anti-God or devil" (:232). Sundkler, however, points out that Zionists have modified some aspects of this world-view especially regarding the issue of possession by ancestor spirits which is often considered as part of the therapeutic process in the traditional model. This is understood as demon possession in the Zionist world-view. The issue of demons does not normally occur in the African world-view and has been included in Zionism through the influence of Pentecostalism (cf. Sundkler 1961:226).

Pentecostal World-Views of Illness

Hollenweger (1972:377) says that the role of demons is central in the Pentecostal world-view: "That our battle is not against 'flesh and blood' but against 'principalities and powers', Pentecostals can testify from their own experience . . . There are demons of sickness, of lies, of fornication, Hitler demons and divorce demons." He then goes on to illustrate how sickness and suffering is fundamentally tied up with their activity in the life of people. At the same time, he points out that Pentecostals are not so much called to believe in demons but rather in the power to overcome them (:379). Demons, he suggests, are a way of explaining our inadequate understanding of reality (:381). He contests that whilst modern psychiatry can offer an alternative explanatory model, there still remains an "inexplicable remnant" which defies our current rational explanatory models. Hollenweger falls between two stools here and his attempt to justify the role of demons in Pentecostal theology without accepting their existence marks him firmly in the camp of second generation Pentecostals. For this group there is a change in world-view away from the more radical demon based model of reality which operates amongst original converts towards a more rational view amongst those who grow up in a more settled Pentecostal "denomination" (cf.:466).

Clark (1984) attempts to apply the personality theory of Rychlak (1973) to the writings of Neopentecostal faith teachers who have influenced churches like the "new churches" studied in the Durban area. Regarding their theory of illness, Clark (:282) suggests that faith healers such as Kenneth Hagin, E.W. Kenyon and Kenneth Copeland teach that "all sickness comes from 'the curse of the law' the effects of which are outlined in Deuteronomy 28." The curse is ineffective as long as people believe in God. "Satan, however, does everything he can to undermine the faith of the Christian and thus make the Christian subject to the curse" (:282). Now the sign of people's faith in God is determined "by what they audibly say about their situation . . . what a person says is what a person gets . . . and this appears to be the keystone of their system" (:282). So by accepting one's sickness one remains sick and by refusing it one is healed.

	Group A	Group B	Group C
a. Traditional African supernatural theories (ukufa kwabantu)	8 (22%)	21 (48%)	44 (62%)
b. Bio-psycho-socio-cultural psychiatric theories	12 (33%)	15 (34%)	15 (21%)
c. Combinations of (a) and (b) above	16 (44%)	8 (18%)	12 (17%)

Group A. Non-psychology students at the University (Psychology students were excluded as they might furnish biased answers on account of their knowledge of psychology) (N=42).

Group B. Urban residents of Esikhaweni township, some 5 km from the University (N=55).

Group C. Rural residents in the KwaDlangezwa and Ngoya areas adjacent to the University (N=86)

Fig. 6.1 Conceptions of Mental Illness - Beliefs concerning the etiology of madness (uhlanya). (Source Edwards 1985:10 & 7)

The question of the change in conception of sickness as a result of external factors such as history, progress in human knowledge and other acculturative effects is well known. S.D. Edwards (1985) examines this effect amongst Zulu speakers from three different backgrounds: university students (who have clearly been socialised into some Western value systems), urban township residents and rural residents. His results regarding the conception of mental illness are significant and are reproduced in fig. 6.1. The effect of Western influence is highest amongst the university students who accept the traditional explanation the least and go for a more holistic concept accepting both together. The less acculturated township dwellers find themselves in a dichotomy stage (thesis and antithesis) whereas the rural dwellers continue to accept the traditional explanatory model.

In presenting different world-views regarding illness, we have tried to show how world-views attempt to develop an explanatory theory for disease and healing. Horton (1967:53-54) shows how in both African Traditional thought and Western science, explanatory theories are developed in order to go beyond the limited understanding of reality offered by common sense. Such theories may be based on differing fundamental bases such as the personal and spiritual in African world-views and the material and natural in Western science, nevertheless both systems develop explanatory theories which can be effective in predicting and controlling the phenomena they are concerned with.

> I want to point out that it is not only where scientific method is in use that we find theories which both aim at grasping causal connexions and to some extent succeed in this aim . . . It is because traditional African religious beliefs demonstrate the truth of this that it seems apt to extend to them the label empirical. [Horton 1967:58]

We now go on to consider how these world-views explain and control healing.

6.2.2 World-View and Healing

In his powerful work, Edgar Jackson (1981:50-66) concludes that much of what is disease and illness is sourced in the experiences of anxiety, worry and guilt that afflict many people (1981:50-66). He suggests that many of these experiences are rooted in a sense of meaninglessness in life (:144). The realisation of a sense of purpose and meaning in life provides the catalyst for the release of healing power and consequently the healing of the person. Healing is a "release from meaninglessness" (:144). The issue of meaning in life is clearly tied up with the acceptance of a world-view which can provide such meaning. Once the sickness is understood in terms of such a world-view, the means for coping with it and thus of healing are assured. Both Sundkler (1961:232) and West (1975:122) attest to the necessity of understanding in healing. Sundkler points out that the move to the cities introduced uncertainties and perplexities into people's understanding of the world. The healing message presented by the Zionist churches "soon developed divining methods ('prophecy') which appealed to his inherent eagerness not simply to accept illness as such but to 'understand' and interpret its causation" (1961:236). West (1975:122) emphasises the role of the healer as a "reintegrative function":

> Through the diagnosis the unknown becomes known and fear is often replaced by understanding. Thus satisfaction may be given even if a complete cure is not achieved and this satisfaction can only come about if the diagnosis is meaningful to the patient - this is if the world-views of healer and patient in some measure coincide.
> [West 1975:122]

Jules-Rosette (1981:146) makes the same point, indicating that healing methods both of African Indigenous churches and other indigenous healing systems are part of a search to interpret changing conditions in terms of a familiar or meaningful world-view. Mkhwanazi (1989:265-266;271) points out that all forms of therapy involve a common sharing of world-view between the therapist and the client and that the therapist is able to name the disease within this world-view so that the person may understand his or her problem and begin to cope with it. Du Toit (1980:34) suggests that it is in providing a coping mechanism that world-view plays a role in the healing process. A disease that is unknown is itself a source of anxiety and the explanatory theory offered together with the means provided by the theory to deal with the disease, provide relief from this anxiety and synergistically from other anxieties and fears disturbing the person. A world-view helps a person to be situated within a whole: to find an acceptable place within the totality. The healer helps the lost person to understand where this place is and how to get there. Du Toit (1980:35) says that that process is expressed in two steps: "curing the ailment and restoring the balance of patient to ecology".

Janzen's (1989:232) analysis of health in "Bantu" languages concludes that health is described in terms of well-being "traced to a central source of power (or life) in God and nature. This source of life is modified by middle-range spirits, ancestors and consecrated priests who maintain contact with or receive inspiration from that source". He suggests that Bantu languages have two sets of terms for health, the first relates to a more narrow understanding ("*mavimpi*" in kikongo) whereas the second is concerned with a state of ritual "purity", "balance" or "coolness" which is a much wider term (:233).

Bührmann (1989:29) points out the importance of relationship in health within an African world-view. The necessity of maintaining good relationships with people living bodily in the world around and the ancestors, people living spiritually in the world, is essential to good health. "Any illness is therefore ascribed to a disturbance of the balance between man and spiritual or mystical forces and the aim of health seeking is to restore the equilibrium" (:30).

One of the apparent effects of acculturation in Africa has been the emergence of a therapeutic openness with people consulting a range of healers until a cure is found. Dorothy Farrand (1986:100) has studied this issue and concludes that the infiltration of Western attitudes and thought patterns has led to the emergence of a two stage process "in which the sick person first goes to a Western doctor to get the illness cured and then goes to an indigenous healer to determine and alleviate the cause of the illness". Her study also showed a move towards faith healers (*abaprofethi*) and away from traditional healers (*izangoma*). One reason given for this was that the former were considered more "oriented to an industrial and urban environment" (:101). Consequently they are seen to have more effectively amalgamated "the traditional black world-view and belief system with a western religious approach" (:102).

Janzen (1989:229-232) attempts to identify concepts of, and common approaches to, health in the Western and African world-views. He suggests six understandings of health which are found in both systems (:229-231):

1) Health is what healers do.
2) Health is the absence of disease.

3) Health is functional normality.
4) Health is adaptation to the environment.
5) Health is social reproduction.
   - as social well being and social continuity.
   - as the reproduction of labour.
   - as increasing fertility.
6) Health is well-being of body, mind and society.

Rappaport and Rappaport (1981) also concern themselves with the possibility of integrating Western and traditional understandings of healing. They suggest that previous models which understood traditional and Western healing systems as deriving from mutually exclusive world-views is unhelpful and that it is possible to develop a conceptual foundation which will incorporate the two and allow traditional healing to be integrated within the Western system. They note that the world-view and "entire sociocultural context" (:779) is essential to the healer, whether traditional or Western psychotherapeutic, and that therapy will be ineffective when the healer does not share the world-view of the sick person. This is the reason for the lack of success of Western psychotherapy in an African context (cf. Horton 1967:56). Consequently a model needs to be developed in which both world-views can function autonomously. Rappaport & Rappaport (1981:780) suggest that the incorporation of methods of dealing with psychosomatic illness into the Western model could be the starting point in the development of such a model.

The resemblance between African healing and Western psychiatry is noted by Horton (1967:57). He suggests that apart from the names given, the two operate out of closely parallel world-views:

> There are several points at which Western psycho-analytic theory, with its apparatus of personalized mental entities, resembles traditional West African religious theory. More specifically, as I have suggested elsewhere, there are striking resemblances between psycho-analytic ideas about the individual mind as a congeries of warring entities, and West African ideas about the body as a meeting place of multiple souls. In both systems of belief, one personal entity is identified with the stream of consciousness, whilst the others operate as an 'unconscious', sometimes co-operating with consciousness and sometimes at war with it. [Horton 1967:57]

Feierman (1979:277) has also highlighted the emergence of "a broad therapeutic pluralism in both the explanations of misfortune and the treatment of illness." However, he contests the attempt to identify explanatory models operating within various cultures and societies. For him, the explanation of healing and people's therapeutic choice in terms of such models leads to confusion rather than clarity. In particular, he criticises Horton's juxtaposition of Western scientific method and African world-view as comparable explanatory theories. He suggests that an explanation of the disease and its cause is not always necessary or central for the patient and cites the work of Lewis (1975) in which in "57% of the sickness cases he studied, the sufferers and their kinsmen were uninterested in the ultimate cause" (Feierman 1979:278). Feierman suggests that a better approach to understanding culture change and therapeutic preferences is obtained when the illness is defined independently of the society's own definition so that different cultural interpretations can be compared. Further he suggests, following a neo-Marxist approach, that the explanatory systems should be examined "in the context of social action" since socio-economic changes affect people's choice of therapy and the explanations for sickness and health.

> Contemporary African therapy must thus be understood within the context of capitalist relations of production, which have decreased the extent to which caregivers can influence the daily working lives or intimate living condition of the sick.
>
> [Feierman 1979:284]

One can be forgiven for imagining what Horton's response might be, given the fact of the Marxist explanatory model and world-view used by Feierman to organise his material!

Coming now to the specific manifestation of the role of world-view in the Coping-healing churches we have presented, we note that Dube (1989:119) points out that "the Zionist healer can be understood in terms of African religious consciousness. His healing power is not isolated from his understanding of his universe." He goes on to show that the power operated by the healer is of supernatural origin and linked to the notion of *umoya* (spirit). Now the understandings of *umoya* (spirit) and of Jesus as Messiah represent the specific difference in comparing the world-view of the Zionist with that of the traditional healer. The Zionist healer is ***called*** by *umoya* which is characterised as a whole array of mystical powers which effect the work of Zion (Dube 1989:120). *Umoya* is expressed in the Zionist healer through the channel of the healer's personal messenger (*isithunywa*) which "provides an avenue through which supernatural communication takes place" (:120). Now all of this means that most Zionists vehemently reject any kind of healing or medicine which invokes other spirits. This is "spirit possession" and demonic for them (Williams 1982:161; Du Toit 1980:42). Consequently Zionists are constrained by their beliefs to seek healing only from Zionist faith healers and not from traditional healers.

With regard to the Neopentecostal or "new churches", Clark (1984:282) indicates that the "faith teachers" he has studied (particularly Hagin and Kenyon) suggest that healing occurs when there is "hegemony of the spirit over the soul and body." When this occurs, cure of personality dysfunction is achieved. These authors stand as the main theoretical sources for the Neopentecostal churches we have studied (cf. McCauley 1985, 1989; Seago n.d.; Macdonald 1981). Hegemony of the spirit is achieved through a renewal of the mind by the Word of God: "just as sense knowledge is developed by reading sense knowledge literature, so the spirit grows by reading and meditating in the Revelation that was designed to be its food" (Kenyon 1966:16, in Clark 1984:283). Kenyon goes on to explain that the word effects the change by being spoken: "If Jesus were here,

He would say, 'Son, You are healed.' You say 'Son, by His stripes you are healed.' You are using his Word" (Kenyon 1970:106, in Clark 1984:283). The Neopentecostal healers posit a three-fold division of the human being: spirit, soul and body. The soul refers to the amalgam of mind, will and emotions in the person, and the body is the senses. The notion of spirit is the determinant one. God, angels, demons and humans are spirits. "Being a born-again spirit returns the personality to God's class of being, making possible communication between God and the believer" (Clark 1984:280). The cure is effected by the words spoken since this is what determines the orientation and growth of the spirit: "The spirit grows what it hears spoken; if words of fear, then fear grows; if words of faith, faith grows. You reap what you sow with your mouth." (:283). The techniques of healing revolve around a positive, persistent, affirmation of a clear goal: the healing, even before it is manifest. If such a goal is in line with the promises of Scripture, it will be manifest. The aim of the process is understood as to "build the Word of God firmly into the believer's consciousness" (:284) leading to a growth of the spirit in accordance with the word which then effects the cure since "God honors his Word spoken in faith from the spirit" (:284).

This attempt to indicate the various world-views operating in the Coping-healing churches we have presented, as well as our affirmation of the centrality of world-view regarding theories of illness and healing, together raise epistemological considerations on the nature and value of world-views themselves. It also poses the question whether there are certain epistemological keys which ground the various world-views. A short examination of these issues is the subject of our next section.

6.3 Epistemological Considerations

Chidester (1989:15) re-presents Ninian Smart's proposition that the study of religion is in fact "a discipline of world-view analysis". He suggests that the epistemological key to the understanding of world-view is the question of "human identity" and the "negotiation" of the make up of this term. The affirmation of human identity implies two necessary processes: Firstly, the determination (classification) of who is a person and what are the classes of person integrated by the world-view and, secondly, the question of orientation in time and space which creates the cosmos within which the person experiences self affirmation and self understanding as "person" within the chaos of the totality. In his analysis, Chidester (:20) suggests that African Indigenous churches are clearly involved in the process of negotiating "a human identity through contact with superhuman powers in a dehumanizing environment." Such a statement could also be applied to all the Coping-healing churches we have studied and to the Coping-healing ministry itself (cf. Comaroff 1985:219). For Chidester, the process of negotiating or affirming human identity occurs through the manipulation of symbols. The ownership of sacred symbols or their acquisition is an expression of power especially understood as the power which affirms humanity.

The understanding of life as a major epistemological key in healing and its acquisition through Zionist healing rituals (Dube 1989:135) would seem to be a clear affirmation of Chidester's analysis. He understands the manipulation of symbols as a struggle for the ownership of the symbols of humanity within the cosmos and differing world-views are in constant competition with one another in this struggle. Thus AIC's compete with the traditional African world-view, which it sometimes considers demonic, as well as with Western urbanised society which is polluting. Similarly, as Hollenweger (1972:414) points out, Pentecostalism is a reaction to the world-view of science and reason. Further, he suggests that African Independent churches represent a return to a non-literary form of Christianity in reaction to the literary form of the mainline traditional churches (:170).

A similar comment could be made regarding the Neopentecostal churches and their emphasis on the audio-visual expression of religion in the "post-modern" audio-visual emerging culture. These churches consider themselves to be responding to the dehumanizing effects of rationalism (Hollenweger 1972:218) and the scientific revolution (:293-5) which has removed God and his power from the natural arena. This fact is also responsible for the growth of African Independent churches which affirm supernatural power manifest in the natural world and which present a world-view which accommodates this fact as against the "main stream of Euro-American Protestant Christianity" (Horton 1967:96) which has lost this belief. Similarly, Oosthuizen (1975:176,331) indicates that one of the roles of Pentecostalism amongst Indians in the Durban area is to provide a world-view which enables the reappropriation of humanity in a way that traditional Hinduism is unable to achieve within the new, Western, urban reality people are living in.

Horton, however, contests that the symbolic model (used by Chidester) is weak in dealing with the reality of things as they are and in particular with the question of why a spiritual realm should be posited in the first place: "why should men have felt constrained to invent symbols with such very odd attributes as those of unobservability and omnipresence?" (1971:93). The question posed is in fact a metaphysical one although Horton's solution to it is an epistemological one and his own cultural limitations in this respect have been criticised (Morley 1978:12-13). Nevertheless, Horton (1971:94) suggests that an "intellectualist approach" is the only one which "takes systems of traditional religious belief at their face value - i.e. as theoretical systems intended for the explanation, prediction and control of space - time events." Horton's (1967:52) solution is that such an explanatory model renders the world intelligible in terms of a few basic, not directly observable, yet omnipresent elements called spirits in much the same way that atomic theory, wave theory and germ theory renders the Westerner's world intelligible in terms of a few basic, not directly observable, yet omnipresent elements called particles and vibrations.

In all the mediations we have studied in part II, we can detect underlying world-views to the understandings proposed. We have met explanatory systems such as the germ theory of disease, the biomedical theory of disease and, Freudian and Jungian psychiatric systems in our psycho-medical mediation. In our anthropological and socio-economic mediations as well, we have considered functionalist, symbolic semiotic, structuralist, Marxist and Weberian systems as well as various combinations of these grounding the discussion and conclusions of many of the authors we have cited. Clearly it is important to note the various epistemological systems supporting these discussions and the comments of Horton regarding explanatory models and systems are obviously important here. Just by way of example, we re-note the opinion of Feierman that the analysis of therapy is only effective if it is linked to an analysis of society's productive base. We also note the comment of Holdstock (1979:121) who summarises Illich's (1977) contention that the "mechanistic philosophy underlying health care" has led to the state of affairs where the Western medical establishment "has become a major threat to health". This results from the limitations of such a world-view in coping with psychosomatic and socially rooted illness and disease. Kleinman and Sung also note that with regard to healing:

> It only makes sense to talk of healing from the perspective of certain explanatory models . . . healing is not so much a result of the healer's efforts as a condition of experiencing illness and care within the cultural context of the health care system. The health care system provides psychosocial and cultural treatment for the illness *by naming and ordering the experience of illness, providing meaning for that experience* and treating the personal, family and social problems which comprise the illness. *Thus it heals even if it is unable to effectively treat the disease*. (My emphasis)
>
> [Kleinman & Sung 1979:23]

Armed with such an understanding of healing which is clearly applicable to the Coping-healing phenomenon we have studied, Kleinman and Sung (1979:24) conclude that indigenous healers ***must*** heal to the extent that they provide a culturally legitimate treatment of illness. Once the world-view is accepted and its procedures are followed so that the healing follows in terms of the world-view, then the person must be healed. Clark (1984) has pointed out how this process occurs within the churches he has studied. The work of the healer revolves around getting the sick person to accept the world-view of the church he represents. Faith, the Word of God, the Holy Spirit and so on are some of the symbols operating within the world-view. The healing occurs in terms of this world-view ("theory of personality, illness and cure" in his text) as it is accepted by the sick person.

The purpose of theory and explanatory models, according to Horton (1967:51) is to enable "the elaboration of a scheme of entities or forces operating 'behind' or 'within' the world of common sense observations" (1967:51). It attempts to place reality in a "causal context wider than that provided by common sense" (:53) so that reality may be rendered more fully intelligible and thus controlled more easily. The way that theory does this is by "break[ing] up the unitary objects of common sense into aspects [and] then plac[ing] the resulting elements in a wider causal context. That is, it first abstracts and analyses, then re-integrates" (:64). The usual way in which the analysis operates is through analogy with already understood phenomena. In contrasting Western and African culture, Horton attempts to show how such use of analogy may lead to different approaches. In traditional African culture, he posits, the world of the inanimate is considered quite unpredictable and mysterious, whereas the human network of relationships and community is seen in terms of order and balance. In scientific Western culture, the reverse is the case since scientific research has revealed the order and balance in inanimate things whereas people's human and social experience is one of disorder. Consequently it seems reasonable to expect, and it turns out to be the case, that African explanatory models of the cosmos are presented in a personal idiom whereas Western one's are presented in an impersonal one. Once this is seen, Western and African explanatory models are much more similar than a first sight would reveal. He shows parallels between African "religious" notions and Western sociological abstractions (:63) and it is easy to recall the work of Bührmann (1986a) in which she draws parallels between Xhosa traditional healing systems and Jungian psychology as well as between the two explanatory models supporting these therapies.

Horton (1967:169-172) is not so blinded by the similarities he sees within explanatory models from differing cultural backgrounds as to ignore obvious differences. He points to a particularly useful epistemological key which underlies processes of identification of sickness: processes usually referred to as diagnosis in Western models and divination in traditional African ones. He suggests that divination works within a framework of converging multiple causation in which one of a number of factors may cause the illness and the diviner's task is to discover which one this is. The multiplicity and complexity of causal factors allows for an "aura of fallibility" which makes it possible to "explain everything away" when the remedy is ineffective (:171). Diagnosis, however, works within a much stricter causal theory in which single causes are postulated for each illness condition. Thus the system does not allow for fallibility and the diagnostician merely has to elaborate the causal connection. Neo-pentecostal healing also seems to operate with the more diffuse multiple causation factors, including spirits, demons, sin and faith, in its system. Welbourn(1987:353-368) suggests that Western and African theories of illness can be incorporated within a single model where a graph with two axes is set up in which the X-axis represents disease and the Y-axis the involvement of mystical factors in illness and health (fig. 6.2).

Scientific approaches have normally only considered the X-axis whilst much of the religious healing we have considered is only concerned with the Y-axis. Wellbourne suggest that African approaches consider both dimensions and affirms that the "X-Y continuum illustrates most clearly the complementary factors in a process of healing" (Welbourn 1989:367).

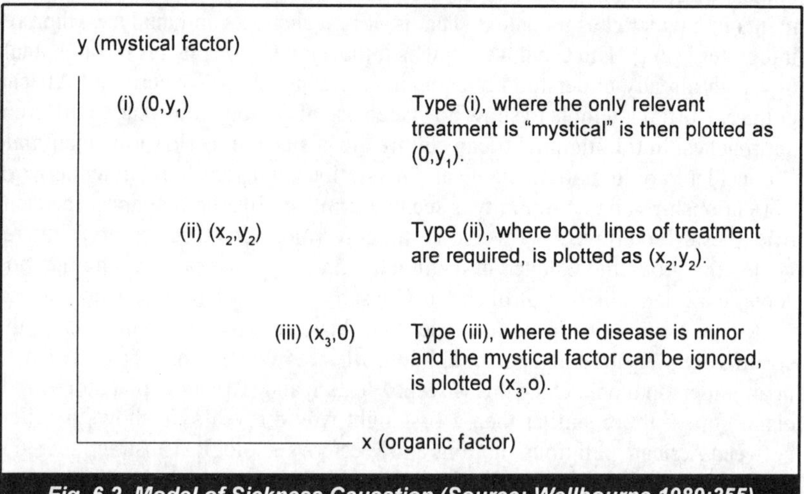

Fig. 6.2 Model of Sickness Causation (Source: Wellbourne 1989:355)

Clearly one could go on looking for fundamental epistemological keys which found or ground the explanatory models used to describe and explain healing in the world. The approaches of Douglas (1970b), Foucault (1970) and Berger (1966) spring readily to mind in this regard. However we wish to move from epistemological considerations to consider its own grounding in an adequate metaphysics. The metaphysical question is probably the most important one in the "post-modern" society which is emerging today. We have already noted how the Coping-healing phenomenon is one of the signs of that emergence and hence our interest to, at least, allude to the metaphysical dimension. There are, so far, no proposed solutions to this important philosophical question - indeed many would say that the metaphysical is merely an obfuscation. We, however, consider it important enough to present in our final section on the philosophical mediation of the Coping-healing phenomenon.

6.4 Metaphysical Allusions

In following the work of Lonergan (1971) in our methodology, we affirm the possibility of being able to move from the intelligible level to the level of judgement and reason and thus on to the level of responsibility. This process, we affirm with Lonergan, implies a metaphysics of allowal which grounds the whole process. Such a metaphysics affirms the human ability to transcend the phenomenal to arrive at the reasonable and thence the moral. That such a process is natural on the epistemological level has already been affirmed by the authors above. The metaphysical question revolves around the affirmation of this fact on the moral, practical (in the Kantian sense) or human level. Without the possibility of such a metaphysics, we contend that the plurality of experiences and practices which are manifest in the post-modern culture in general and in our studied manifestation of it, the Coping-healing phenomenon, in particular, can remain only that: plural. Relativism and freedom as licence become our only choice: whatever is meaningful (the epistemological) is permissible since the epistemological level is its own foundation.

Geertz (1973:101) sums this up as a "rush of metaphysical anxiety" which occurs when the explanatory apparatus which one is used to, fails. The resulting chaos coming from a failure of interpretability of the events which assail the human condition demands a new search for an adequate grounding of the rational, reasonable and ethical (:100). He suggests that the search for the metaphysical is the essence of religious action and the symbolic framework of ritual and practices is an attempt to formulate this.

> It is this sense of the "really real" upon which the religious perspective rests and which the symbolic activities of religion as a cultural system are devoted to producing, intensifying, and, so far as possible, rendering inviolable by the discordant revelations of secular experience. It is, again, the imbuing of a certain specific complex of symbols - of the metaphysic they formulate and the style of life they recommend - with a persuasive authority which, from an analytic point of view, is the essence of religious action. [Geertz 1973:112]

Clearly then, any work which is concerned with a powerful religious phenomenon such as healing needs to consider the metaphysical grounding of such a ministry. Matthew Lamb (1989:87-89) has shown how the scientific age (the modern age) resulted in two religious responses: a conservative one looking to the past and attempting to incorporate the new age into its existing framework, and a liberal one which embraced the new scientific paradigm and used it in an attempt to make Christianity relevant and meaningful to the new scientific world. As the ideological and non-objective basis of science itself has been called into question in the post-modern paradigm[1], a search has been made to ground Christian theology within a different framework to that of the reaction of the scientific age (or modernism). Lamb (:91-95) suggests that approaches such as those of Barth, Bultmann, Rahner, De Chardin, Pannenberg, Schillebeeckx and Küng have reflected this process.

> The very important differences and conflicts of interpretation among these and other theologians engaged in hermeneutical mediations of faith and contemporary human experience *cannot* be adequately situated within the framework of modern dichotomies between conservative or liberal orientations. The hermeneutical turn in the post-empiricist philosophies of science indicated how the ongoing projects of science imply a dialectics of questions and answers in which the heuristics of research programmes encourages pluralism without falling into the epistemological anarchism claimed by Feyerabend. [Lamb 1989:95]

He suggests that political and liberation theologies[2] are attempting to address these issues since they attempt to come to grips with the world and articulate its ideological distinction but at the same time do not lapse into a subjective pluralism as a result of affirmation of the truth and value of the gospels and of faith. They affirm a double dialectic reading through both the world and the Christian faith which refuses to accept either at its face value nor as base to the other.

> Academically, the many efforts to overcome the subject-object dichotomies which have artificially severed tradition and innovation, science and morality, theory and narrative, order and autonomy, technology and art, industry and environment, economic accumulation and social distribution, systems and life-worlds - all these efforts at truly post-modern intellectual transformations have to be encouraged. For only in such processes of intellectual transformation, conversion, or 'gestalt-switch' can these dichotomies be overcome to reveal their dynamic differentiated interactions which are the foundations of intersubjective creativity in communal quests for truth and freedom. In this context of differentiation and interaction the post-empiricist shifts toward praxis and dialectics are very important for complementary shifts in theology, and *vice versa*. Paradigm analysis in metascience and in theology exposes the illusions of monistic metatheoretical absolutism and dichotomous multitheoretical anarchism. Intellectual and religious praxis transcends those illusory alternatives towards the many forms of collaborative hermeneutics and dialectics. [Lamb 1989:102]

The whole of the methodology of this work is an inadequate attempt to recognise this fact (*supra* 1.5 - 1.8). We suggest that the phenomenological approach combined with the theological method of Lonergan provide a way forward in addressing the metaphysical problem. This is our methodology of contextual theology. The theological judgements made in chapters ten and eleven are an attempt to develop an approach to mission grounded in a metaphysics of responsibility which accepts the reality of the world, its phenomena and its methods of mediating, understanding and judging them.

Our *cursus* into metaphysics has led us inevitably to the question of God and religion and to issues of theology. It is now time, finally, to enter into this most difficult area. The theological understandings of the Church's healing ministry are as wide as the divisions outlined by Lamb. It is to a presentation and analysis of these understandings that we now turn in our final mediation of the Coping-healing phenomenon: the theological.

Chapter 7

The Theological Mediation of the Coping-Healing Phenomenon

7.1 Introduction

In this last chapter of part II we intend to present a brief analysis of some theological studies of the Coping-healing phenomenon, in order to develop theological understandings of what is occurring and eventually to pass some theological judgements upon it. We begin by considering some theological appraisals of the Southern African Coping-healing practices we have presented and then go on to a more general evaluation. In this chapter we are still concerned with mediating the Coping-healing phenomenon as in chapters 3-6. Here, we consider how theology and theologians understand the Coping-healing phenomenon and how they have attempted to build a theology of healing which understands and informs it. Our own theological reflection and judgement follows in part III.

7.2 Theological Comments on Southern African Coping-Healing Churches

The types of Coping-healing churches we have presented can be broken down into two: the African Independent churches and the Neopentecostal churches. We have consistently tried to treat them together because we believe that they are manifestations of an underlying common process. However, they have often had to be treated separately in our various mediations because most authors consider only the one or the other and from widely varying points of view. This is also the case when we look at how theologians deal with this phenomenon.

7.2.1 *African Independent Churches*

In general, the theological reflections and appraisals on the African Independent churches have revolved around the question of the adaptation of Christianity to Africa, and indigenisation.[1] Issues of syncretism have been brought in and healing has been linked to the perseverance of African cultural shamanistic practices within a Christian framework. In this regard, we note Sundkler's (1948:55) early comment that "[t]heologically the Zionists are now a syncretistic Bantu movement with healing, speaking with tongues, purification rites, and taboos as the main expressions of their faith." The Zionist church is identified with its healing. It is an "Institute of Healing . . . 'This is not a church, it is a hospital'" (:220). It has blended into a unique system: "two converging lines - traditional Zulu ideas of illness and healing, and the faith healing message of various radical American sects...the result is . . . a unique system in its own right . . ." (:221).

In the second edition of his book, Sundkler was to modify his views regarding the syncretistic nature of these churches, saying that his previous judgement was "too foreign, too Western perhaps" (1961:302). He suggests that the churches appear as "definitely Christian organisations, adapted to their own real needs, as bridges to a new and richer experience of life" (:302). He also makes the point that the healing activities of the church are not an end in themselves but a means to evangelisation. Many converts are made, both as result of people's personal experience of healing, and as a result of their testimony: a witness of their healing to others (Sundkler 1961:233). The testimony of healing is often linked to a testimony of liberation from sin (:235). Finally, Sundkler indicates a commonality between the Zionist and biblical interpretation of healing that is often missing in mainline churches and yet, as we shall see, turns up in the other Coping-healing churches:

> The Zionist way of healing also points to a common factor shared by traditional Zulu views on illness and healing and the Biblical interpretation. Through divining and prayer they procure the religious sanctions without which a Zulu does not really believe that healing can be secured. In European medical treatment the wholeness of man is seldom recognized. The appeal from the Zionist message undoubtedly comes from their insistence that both the practice of medicine and religious experience spring from a common root. A mission doctor who used to call nurses, patient and relatives together for prayer before performing an operation was often referred to by Zionists as a real Christian in whom they had confidence. [Sundkler 1961:237]

Oosthuizen has made a somewhat similar theological journey to Sundkler in his appraisal of these churches. In an earlier work he writes that they are

> theologically a new syncretistic African movement, concentrating on divine healing, triune immersion, purification rites, ritual prohibition, speaking with tongues, and witch-finding, and its indigenous approach to religious activities gives the right emotional atmosphere, e.g. in hymns and rhythmic movements. [Oosthuizen 1968:35]

He suggests that with regard to their Christology, the messianic type churches such as those of Shembe and Kimbangu tend to Nestorianism and Antinomianism whereas the more evangelical enthusiastic types such as Bhengu's church lead to legalism in morality (Oosthuizen 1968:189). Concerning the third person of the Trinity, he says that, together with many Pentecostal churches, they misunderstand the person and work of the Holy Spirit.

> In these movements the Holy Spirit receives the same uncertain position as is the case with their Christology and with the deity in general, although the uncertainty with regard to the Holy Spirit is more acute . . . The Spirits [sic] activity is not related to moral guidance but rather to vital force. The Spirit can be obtained before baptism while one is still a non-Christian, and a man may leave a wife of whom he is tired for another, younger one on the injunction of the Spirit. [Oosthuizen 1968:122]

> The Spirit is the channel through which ancestral ideas enter Christian concepts, with the result that something different is produced. [Oosthuizen 1968:123]

> The functions of the ancestor spirits have been transferred to the Holy Spirit, or simply 'the Spirit', so that in the independent post-Christian movements their 'holy spirit' is no longer the Holy Spirit of whom we learn in Scripture. [Oosthuizen 1968:129]

> A distinction is made between God and the Holy Spirit in the sense that they are not co-equal and co-eternal, as confessed in the Athanasian Creed.[Oosthuizen 1968:125]

In later works, Oosthuizen modifies his views and accepts African Independent churches as "indigenous churches" which "enhance the process of modernization . . . in changing attitudes advantageous to progress" (Oosthuizen 1986:238). His change of standpoint seems to manifest a growing openness to recognise that all churches express the Christian faith in ways that are historically and culturally conditioned. As an example he considers the case of baptism by comparing modern Zionist baptism and purification processes with those throughout Church history (Oosthuizen 1989b:137-188). He concludes from this comparison that AIC theology and practice seems to be closer to the "gnostics and scholastics who interpreted the act of baptism as freeing a person from guilt and punishment . . . They will agree with Thomas Aquinas that God is the Principal Cause and the baptismal water the instrumental cause of the spiritual work of grace" (:162). This he opposes to the Augustinian and subsequent Reformed theology that "the sacraments are the visible word. The sign (water) and the word (the baptismal formula) form an undivided unity" (:162).

Hollenweger (1972:161-171) presents a valuable survey of theological opinion available to him at the time. This indicates that whilst it is easy to apply Augustinian categories and refer to Ethiopian type churches as schismatic, having "cut the bond of love" and Zionist types as heretical, having "cut the bond of faith", doing so is not helpful. Theological knowledge is always fragmentary and it is usually unhelpful to condemn one theological interpretation from the standpoint of another. He affirms the necessity of critically assimilating African tradition into theology. But he also insists on a readiness to recognise the need to transform such tradition by the truth of the Christian faith. Two issues are highlighted: the importance of an eschatology which transforms a cyclical understanding of history and the importance of the *theologia crucis*. The former has been largely achieved whilst the latter remains "a stumbling block for the African, as for the European" (:163).

The AIC Theology of Sickness and Healing

In his early work, Oosthuizen (1968:88-89) says that healing and well-being are linked together with prosperity and having a good life, here-and-now, on earth. Salvation means the this-world realisation of strength and power in this-worldly benefits. He suggests that this is linked with the African cultural notion of "vital force". Prosperity is a sign of the presence of this vital force which Africans have recognised in the material benefits of Western culture and then attributed to Western gods and its religion: Christianity (:87-89). Consequently, for Oosthuizen, these movements have no place for the *theologia crucis*, for suffering nor even for the notion of a supernatural which is not here-and-now (:89). Oosthuizen maintains that this has led to a misunderstanding of the missionary message and the rise of the Zionist Churches.

> Putting away witch-craft means the end of the Old [sic]; the end of sickness and death, and freedom from total destruction. The missionaries are expected in their preaching to counteract it, but when they fail the prophets take their place and their eschatological promises are more effective than the ways of orthodoxy.
> [Oosthuizen 1968:98]

Oosthuizen (1968:191) notes that healing is often linked to a prerequisite confession of sin since "sickness is associated in the African mind with sin". The healing occurs through the spirit who possesses the sick person and who drives out any demons which may be present (:130-132). The adversarial forces confronted by the Zionist healer "are experienced so strongly that Bible study and prayer are considered to be inadequate . . . Rituals have to be performed . . . [which] have a miraculous effect when correctly utilised" (Oosthuizen 1989a:82). However, he maintains that the healing power is not recognised as being from Jesus but rather from the spirit, "which could either be the Holy Spirit or the ancestors" (:83). In these later works, however, Oosthuizen is much more circumspect in drawing theological inferences and conclusions from the phenomena he examines.

> The prophets/prayer healers take the world in which their people live seriously. The emphasis is never on "a pie in the sky when you die" but rather on the here and now. Theologically, certain issues may merit close scrutiny but, from a socio-psychological point of view, the prophet's position is firmly established in many indigenous churches.
> [Oosthuizen 1989a:89-90]

Msomi (1967:74) suggests that whilst the concern for the sick of these churches is laudable and love is manifest in them, "Healing has become an end in itself" and people are "taken into the church without any form of instruction. In fact some without any conversion." Their belief and faith is in fact syncretistic (:75).

H.J.Becken (1975:237), reflecting on the theological consequences of his observations at an AIC healing service, suggests that Western missionaries have often misunderstood the holistic concept operating in African Christian healing because of their own cultural experience of the division of functions between the medical and religious. His observations lead him to the conclusion that "in this AIC service we understand that God's Salvation in Jesus Christ is mediated to heal the whole person" (:237). This holistic approach to healing "is much closer to the Bible than our sophisticated Western ideas and concepts shaping our faith and life" (:239). He notes that "the literal translation of the term used by the AIC for healing is 'to be saved' (in the passive mood). The diseased person cannot save himself he can only be saved by God who is the center and giver of all life power"(:242). He also emphasises the important communitarian dimension of the healing process: the healing spirit is given to the community even when exercised by individuals: "'No healing without the congregation' is a well established principle in the AIC." (:240). Becken's theological appraisal of healing in these churches recognises it as a fulfilment of pastoral care of those who are sick. Such pastoral care occurs through and with the community of faith who mediate God's healing power to the sick who come.

M.L. Daneel also affirms the theological value of the healing ministry of the African Independent churches he has studied in Zimbabwe (1971, 1974, 1983a, 1983b). The starting point of his reflection is that "most of what we observe today in the independent churches concerns a genuinely contextualised and originally African response to the Gospel, irrespective of and unfettered by Mission church influence" (Daneel 1983a:58). He says that their emphasis on preserving life and well-being, of which the healing ministry is the major manifestation, can be interpreted as a living out of the liberating message of the gospel. In "Rhodesia/Zimbabwe" this liberation praxis has been carried out on the political, socio-economic and religious level as "the translation of the message of liberation in the concrete visible and physical activities of people in those fields of human experience that really matter" (:59). He draws the following conclusions from people's experiences of healing in AIC's (Daneel 1983b:29-30):

1) Western medicine has failed to effect a cure.
2) A strong sense of belonging and security is experienced in the AIC healing process.
3) Prayer plays a central role in the healing process.
4) "Coercion" to be part of the church, so that healing may be more effective, seems to play a role.
5) Healers are held in awe and respect.

In his evaluation of the phenomenon he concludes that:

> the overall impression which prophetic faith-healing makes on a person is one of a remarkable confluence of old and new, of traditional divination and a confirmation of God's Lordship over evil powers, in a typically African way. This is especially evident in the prophet's diagnosis and therapy. [Daneel 1983b:39]

He affirms that salvation is interpreted in the here and now: a "realised eschatology" (Daneel 1983b:40) but does not agree that this denies the reality of a future eschaton and the Christian understanding of the supernatural (:40). Daneel's theological conclusion is extremely positive:

> In conclusion, it should be emphasized that prophetic faith-healing practices provide African theologians with a vast field of interaction, dialogue and confrontation between the Christian message and traditional religion, between Christ and the ancestors - a field well worth serious consideration. For although the independents are not generally engaged in reflective theology, their intuitive enactment of theology at the grass-root level of their own world-view and philosophy, constitutes an enriching and original contribution towards a developing *theologia africana*, which should not be overlooked under any circumstances. [Daneel 1983b:43]

7.2.2 The Theology of Healing in Neopentecostal Churches

Much of what has been said above could also be applied to the Coping-healing ministry of the Neopentecostal churches we have studied. It is interesting that in the South African context this has not been the case. The emphasis of theologians who have studied these churches has been to reflect on their teaching and its orthodoxy. Theological reflections concerning the Neopentecostal type churches in South Africa have centred around an examination of their doctrines and their right wing ideological stance. The central reality of their Coping-healing ministry has been almost totally ignored. In an examination of "Why Some Catholics Join Evangelical Pentecostal Churches (SACBC n.d.) Verryn's study of the prosperity cult is scathing in its criticism, comparing the promises of health and wealth made by people such as Kenneth Hagin of Rhema church, and his followers, like Ray McCauley, to the devil's temptation of Jesus in Luke 4,9-12.

> If Satan had put his tempting word to Jesus in typically Rhema jargon, he would have said something like this:
>
> > 'Psalm 91 verses 11 and 12 state quite clearly that he will give his angels charge over you and they will bear you in their hands lest you dash your foot against a stone. You are entitled to this privilege as a child of God. Go on, confess your faith that this is so - then jump! Don't listen to failure-minded people who don't expect God's power to work for them!' [SACBC n.d.:27]

For Verryn, these churches operate out of a mistaken notion of faith which is based on miraculous powers. He assembles a number of texts which indicate Jesus' negative attitude to people who want miracles and signs indicating that

> Jesus saw that authentic faith in God involved a loving trust, not in marvellous powers but in a Person who would lead him to the rock of agony in a dark garden of Gethsemane, and thence to Pilate's court, to flogging, and to the Hill of the Skull. Faith walks that route in humble, unquestioning obedience. [SACBC n.d.:27]

In a more detailed study, Verryn (n.d.:1) opines that "Hagin's entire religion is built on his own interpretation of three verses in one chapter of St.Paul's letter to the Galatians". His central message "is that Christianity brings health, wealth and everlasting life." Verryn believes that this interpretation is based on two misunderstandings: Hagin's understanding of faith, and his interpretation of

Galatians 3,13. Rhema's understanding of faith is based on a faith in the miracle itself and works in the same way as the placebo effect in medicine. This is "faith in faith" rather than faith in God (:8-9). Faith as self-abandonment to God is what Paul is speaking about in Galatians. Now Hagin's understanding of sin is that it is a curse which makes us sick (:5). By using Galatians 3,13 he points out that this curse is now put onto Jesus which allows us to claim our health. Verryn presents a short study of Galatians showing how such an interpretation is incorrect (:6) and how consequently "Hagin's entire theological structure collapses" (:11).

Dan McConnell (1990) has made an in depth study of the "faith movement" as expressed by the churches dependent on the teachings of Kenneth Hagin and E.W. Kenyon. He is as scathing as Verryn in his criticism but his is a criticism from within since McConnell describes himself as "a confirmed, unapologetic advocate of and participant in the charismatic renewal" (:xx). His basic conclusion is that teachings of the "faith movement" are rooted in the 19th century metaphysical cult movements which gave rise to Theosophy, Jehovah's Witnesses and Christian Science and which are now animating much of the so-called "New Age" movement (:xix). In his analysis of the "doctrine of healing", McConnell brings out the important distinction between "Revelation knowledge" and "Sense Knowledge" as propagated by the faith movement. Revelation knowledge refers to the "claiming" of one's healing by faith even before it is manifest "in fact", which is Sense Knowledge. "The point is that those claiming these healings believe that they have been healed, and nothing, not even pain and continued symptoms of illness, will convince them otherwise" (:148).

Through an analysis of the writings of Kenyon and Hagin, McConnell points out that their faith doctrine of healing is based on a dualism which attributes all sickness to spiritual causes and God's method of healing to the purely spiritual. Since the possibility of healing is rooted in the atonement, "the Faith teachers conclude that the atonement had to be a spiritual act and not physical" (McConnell 1990:150). They believe "that diseases are healed by Christ's *spiritual* atonement in hell, not his physical death on the cross" (:150). He shows how such a world-view is actually rooted in the teachings of Quimby and Trine, major voices in the "metaphysical New Thought" movement of the 19th century. He goes on to parallel the teachings of the metaphysical cult movements and the faith teachers, Kenyon and Hagin, showing their correspondence in a number of areas (:149-158):

- disease is spiritual not physical
- negative confession produces disease
- believers should deny symptoms
- believers should endure pain
- medicine has no curative value for disease is spiritual not physical
- believers should never die of disease
- believers should never die before seventy years of age

He concludes that these parallels have distorted and deformed the churches' healing ministry.

> Because of its metaphysical background, the Faith theology has transformed healing, a biblical practice of long standing in the church, into a cultic obsession. Healing is, indeed, a gift of the Holy Spirit (1 Cor. 14:9). The church has been commissioned to pray for the sick (Jas. 5:14,15). Signs, healings and exorcisms do often follow those who preach the gospel (Mk 16:15-20). These supernatural experiences and ministries are the heritage of the people of God. This heritage is not, however, the gospel itself. Christianity is not a healing cult and the gospel is not a metaphysical formula for divine health and wealth. The Faith theology's inordinate emphasis on healing is a gross exaggeration of the biblical doctrine and distorts the centrality of Christ and the gospel. [McConnell 1990:158]

McConnell goes on to show how this teaching contradicts the Bible at a number of points citing texts to justify his position. He shows that to suggest that healing is a "cause-effect" formula which must always work for a believing Christian is to actually deny the lordship of Christ to whose will we must abandon ourselves. "Any doctrine of healing that teaches, as does the faith theology, that 'we don't have to wait until the Spirit wills' is not true faith" (McConnell 1990:159). Suffering of the body in this world is part of Pauline teaching on bodily redemption (Rm 8; 2 Cor 5; 1 Cor 15). Paul himself experienced illness and suffering (Gl 4; 2 Cor 12). Neither is there any place in the teaching of these healers for the book of Job and its message. "The faith teachers have committed the error of Elipaz, Bildad, Zaphar and Elihu." (:164). Finally, McConnell (:165-166) concludes that the healing doctrine of the faith teachers leads to serious pastoral care problems since the sick are blamed for their sickness: "they do not have enough faith" and they are often discouraged, until it is too late, from seeking the kind of medical care which might help them. The terminally ill have no place in such a movement and receive no experience of cure and concern from it.

7.2.3 Similarities in Coping-Healing in AIC's and Neopentecostal Churches

The difference in emphasis on the theological comments on the Coping-healing ministry in the AIC's and that in the Neopentecostal churches masks a number of striking similarities between them. Many of the comments of McConnell regarding the centrality of healing could be applied to the AIC's. A similar emphasis on the spiritual source of sickness and its spiritual cure can also be found in both types of churches. It is less easy to attribute the doctrine of "faith in faith" to the AIC's. Nevertheless, one can also detect an implicit notion of causality based on the methods they use which seems to be quite far from those of Jesus.

In the same way many of the positive comments of Daneel and Becken on the AIC's could be applied to the Neopentecostal churches. They do seem to be building up healing communities of care and concern within their churches.

There is an adaptation and assimilation of the emerging post-modern cultural system to the Church in these churches as other authors have noted (cf. Morran & Schlemmer 1984; Easthope 1986). They are concerned with the day to day issues of the well-being of people as are the AIC's (Daneel 1983a). We indicate these similarities, not in an attempt to falsely harmonise what is happening in the various churches, but rather in order to eliminate the impression of an exclusively positive theological evaluation of the AIC combined with an exclusively negative one of the Neopentecostal churches which in our opinion does not reflect the true situation.

Before leaving this section we wish to note the plethora of books and reflections emerging out of the mainline church traditions of late. The concurrence of ministers and theologians in these works is that there is a tremendous upsurge in the Coping-healing ministry right throughout God's church at present. Authors such as Hollenweger (1972) and Dale (1989) (both of the Reformed church), MacNutt (1974) and Häring (1984) (both Roman Catholics), Kelsey (1973), Parsons (1986) and Maddocks (1981,1990) (all Anglican), Booth (1987) (Methodist) and many others affirm the reality of this ministry, its efficacy and power as well as the need for the Church to incorporate it more into the day-to-day pastoral involvement of its ministers. Interesting in this regard, is the way in which the ministry is being incorporated efficaciously into the existing traditions of these communities of faith and indeed how it is also a means of bringing together Christians of different traditional backgrounds for a perceived greater good. These two dimensions: charismatic (in the traditional sense of the word) and ecumenical are surely signs of the presence of the Spirit.

7.3 Developing a Theology of Healing

Faced with the upsurge of healing churches theologians have been attempting to come to grips with the whole gamut of experience, controversy and concern which has arisen around the Coping-healing phenomenon of late. It is an incipient attempt to develop a theology which responds to the *sensus fidelium* which much of what we have been presenting seems to represent. The major issues with which this theology seems to be grappling are the following:

- Developing an adequate biblical foundation for the ministry.
- Examining the historical development of the ministry in the Church and the theological responses to it throughout history.
- Attempting to develop a contextual understanding of the ministry as it is emerging today. Especially important here is the notion of *kairos*: the Spirit operating in a time; as well as the attempt to grasp what exactly is meant by the notion of healing itself.
- Concern regarding practical and pastoral consequences of the ministry: how it should be effected, by whom and through what means.

Probably the classic work in this field is that of Morton T Kelsey (1973) who set about the task to "provide a theological foundation, based on historical and scientific understanding, for a serious ministry of healing today" (:viii). Although neither "a paragon of physical health, nor . . . unusually gifted as a healer" (:viii), his own experiences of this ministry as well as his observation that "modern theology on the whole has avoided the subject" (:viii) led him to at least attempt to set about the task. Kelsey is an Episcopalian (Anglican) minister and his theology reflects the historical emphasis of the Anglican and Catholic theological tradition especially in the body of his work. In building up his theology of healing he uses the following framework.

1) The healing Ministry in the O.T. and Ancient world (ch.3).
2) The healing Ministry of Jesus (chs.4&5).
3) Healing at the time of the Apostles (ch.6)
4) Healing in the History of the Church (chs. 7&8).
5) The Modern Problematic (chs. 9-13)

The whole is prefaced by an examination of the situation today and especially of conflicting attitudes to the healing ministry in the modern Church (his starting point: ch.1) and the antithetical "case against healing" in the Church tradition (ch. 2). Since many other authors have subsequently followed a similar kind of theological framework, we will take Kelsey as the basis of this section. In the following section we will present some of the main contributions of other authors.[2]

7.3.1 Healing in the Old Testament

All authors concur that the healing ministry of the Church is rooted in that of Jesus and the particularly new understanding he gave to healing. Nevertheless, Kelsey (1973:33-45) points out that two distinct theological perspectives on healing can be apprehended from the Old Testament. The first and more fundamental perspective indicates that the omnipotent Yahweh is the author of both life and death, sickness and health. His purpose in sending sickness is to chastise his people in order that they remain true to him and united as a people. The stress is on the group and the disciplining nature of sickness:

> Deuteronomy 32:39 pretty well summarizes the basic attitude of most of the Old Testament: "It is I who deal death and life; when I have struck it is I who heal (and none can deliver from my hand)." This was essentially the same thing Yahweh had affirmed to Moses earlier, when he asked, "Who makes him dumb or deaf, gives him sight or leaves him blind? Is it not I, Yahweh?" (Exod. 4:11). This understanding of good and evil was practically the theme of the prophets. "Does misfortune come to a city if Yahweh has not sent it?" Amos demanded (3:6), while in Isaiah 45:7 it was Yahweh who declared: "I make good fortune and create calamity, it is I, Yahweh, who do all this." God, the giver of all good things, was seen equally as the dispenser of misfortune and pain, including sickness of all kinds. [Kelsey 1973:34]

Kelsey also detects the existence of a second, different perspective which challenges the more widespread orthodox position as exemplified by the Deuteronomic redactor. Here the whole question of evil and sickness as basically good and acceptable, because it comes from God, is challenged. Clearly the book of Job is the most obvious manifestation of this perspective. But Kelsey shows that throughout the Old Testament, a strand can be detected which indicates that healing is God's will for people whereas sickness is against his will. The many healing stories[3], some of the Psalms[4] as well as some of the writings of the prophets[5] indicate the perseverance of this strand of thought throughout the Old Testament. It is this strand that Jesus takes up in his preaching and ministry.

7.3.2 The Healing Ministry of Jesus

No-one denies that at least the early part of Jesus' ministry emphasised two realities: the preaching of the Kingdom of God and its manifestation in signs, principally healings. Kelsey (1973:55-57) adapts Dearmer's (1909:137) listing of 41 healing works carried out by Jesus as attested by the evangelists. In answer to the questions what, how and why did Jesus heal, Kelsey (1973:69-103) concludes as follows:

> If we accept the stories at all, we must conclude that Jesus healed all kinds of disease and that we do not know how he did it, for we are still not able to follow in his steps. Most attempts to rationalize these miracles do not make sense for they are based more upon wishful thinking (in a negative sort of way) than on the facts as stated in the stories themselves. While there may be uncertainty in certain instances, the plain sense of the Gospels is that Jesus healed all kinds of ailments, and that what he did had the effect of true healing, not just of alleviating symptoms. [Kelsey 1973:78]

Attempts to demythologise these stories reflect a theological position which is "entirely theoretical" denying experiences which do not fit in with "what seems impossible to us" (Kelsey 1973:79). Jesus' method of healing was quite varied: he called upon the faith of the sick person, he spoke words and touched people with his hand (the most common method) and he used physical media such as saliva, mud and possibly oil (:79-80).

> Instead, the methods Jesus used with such effect upon the sick were actions which appear to have done two things. They awakened the spirit that lay deep within these people, waiting to be touched. And at the same time his actions, words, and attitudes brought contact with the Spirit of God, the creative force of reality, which sets men's minds and bodies aright and recreates them. Deep spoke to deep, through sacramental action. The nature of his healing, its essential method, was sacramental, religious. Through him the power of God broke through into the lives of men, and they were made whole. There is little more that one can say. [Kelsey 1973:86-87]

In response to the question why Jesus healed, Kelsey (1973:88-89) gives three answers. Jesus healed because he cared for people, because he was hostile to what made them sick and because he wished to bring them to repentance for their sins and conversion to the Kingdom. Jesus' caring is a manifestation of his compassion: the experience of suffering with those who suffer which is a direct consequence of the Incarnation and which attitude is brought to fullness on the cross.

Jesus' hostility to the source of sickness points to his understanding of a demonic role in sickness and the link between sickness and evil. This evil source, expressed as "demons" and "Satan" in the New Testament was seen as the antithesis of the Spirit of God and part of Jesus' mission was to do battle with these forces and ultimately conquer them. Healing those possessed by such demons was thus part of his mission (Kelsey 1973:89-90).

However, Jesus also saw that human beings were not passive vessels in the battle between good and evil and that much suffering was sourced in the active turning towards evil through sinful acts and attitudes. Sin and sickness are expressly related by Jesus although not in the way that sin is the sole cause of sickness. Jesus did not follow the absolute Deuteronomic position that all sickness was the result of sin. In Luke 13,2-5 he repudiates this position and in John 9,3 he offers another reason for blindness. Kelsey suggests that Jesus' position was that sickness basically resulted from a "force of evil loose in the world which was hostile to God and his way" (Kelsey 1973:95). This evil could cause sickness directly and also could tempt people to orientate themselves towards it resulting in sinful attitudes. Such sin could also open a person to sickness. Jesus' attitude was one of compassion to sin and sickness: to heal both and then call for conversion to the Kingdom.

7.3.3 Healing in the Church

Kelsey (1973:123) shows that healing was an essential part of the Church's teaching and ministry from the beginning. The Acts of the Apostles continues the story of these healings: "In a simple, almost offhand way it affirms that the ministry carried on by Jesus was continued among his followers. They did not go out of their way to make a point of the matter. It just *was*."

The writings of Paul, especially the early ones, also testify to the continuation of the ministry and identity as power (*dunamis*), sign (*semeion*) and marvel (*teras*). Paul refers to the ministry of healing as a gift (charism) of the Holy Spirit (1 Cor 12). The classic healing text is the prescription of James 5,14-16 which indicates a procedure, clearly part of the early Church tradition, to be followed in praying for healing. Kelsey notes the unfortunate rendering of the Greek (*sosei*) which means to save, to cure and to heal by the Latin (*salvare*) which means only to save (Kelsey 1973:115). The more holistic Greek understanding is today being recovered.

Drawing on the work of Frost (1940), Kelsey also presents evidence to show how the practice of healing continued uninterrupted between 100-250 AD. Then, after the Edict of Milan in 313, he notes that despite a diminishing of enthusiasm with the large number of nominal Christians entering the new religion of the Empire, the ministry continued and some Church Fathers, particularly in the East, developed a theology of healing.

Amongst the earlier Church Fathers, Irenaeus stands out in his description and affirmation of a healing ministry in which "all kinds of bodily infirmity as well as many different diseases had been cured."[6] The whole attitude voiced by Irenaeus was that healing is a natural activity of Christians as they express the creative power of God, given to them as members of Christ (Kelsey 1973:150). Origen, Cyprian, Clement of Alexandria and Lactantius are some of the other Ante-Nicene theologians who affirm the healing ministry as an essential aspect of the Church. Chrysostom, Basil, and Gregory of Nyssa continued to affirm the same in their own time. Gregory of Nyssa dealt with the issue of healing in developing his theological synthesis (:174). He says that healing is a manifestation of "the way Deity is mingled with humanity" and an affirmation of the Incarnation. Healing as a gift of divine life to the natural becomes "the main door through which a knowledge of God reaches men" (:174). In the Scriptures, the healing miracles are central to people's faith and open their eyes "to knowledge that the resurrection was a possibility."[7] Chrysostom also emphasises that healing comes only through God's power. He affirms the value of prayer for healing.

In the West, Augustine's change of mind regarding healing is particularly significant. In his early writings he is quite clear that "Christians are not to look for continuance of the healing gift" (Kelsey 1973:184). However, an ongoing experience of many healings in his own diocese of Hippo, sometimes before his own eyes, caused him to change his mind and affirm that miracles were still taking place in his time in the name of Christ (Retractationum I.13.7: PL32 c604f). Despite this, Kelsey detects a "drift of reasoning" within the Church which whilst continuing to acknowledge the existence of divine healings and even recounting them, interprets the gift as of little importance or necessity since what is important is not the healing of the body but the saving of the soul (Kelsey 1973:191-194). Healing is seen by authors such as Jerome and Ambrose in this light.[8] The bodily healing is merely a symbol of this greater reality and not necessary to be sought. John Cassian was the major exponent of this neo-Platonic theological viewpoint. Kelsey quotes his comments on the gifts of healing possessed by some of the desert monks and goes on to show how Cassian's position leads to a negative view of healing gifts:

> . . . when they did possess them by the grace of the Holy Spirit they would never use them, unless perhaps extreme and unavoidable necessity drove them to do so". These miracles, as Cassian saw it, were performed to demonstrate the power of the Lord to heretics or scoffers, or because a monk was "pestered" for healing. He thus expressed the most correct theology - the works were accomplished by the compassion of the Lord and not the merit of monks - but he himself seemed to have learned little about compassion. From this point on, the purpose of his discussion is clear. It was necessary to warn the church about the dangers of using the gift of healing. If one were not fully aware of them, he might lose not only his humility but his inward purity and perfect chastity. Indeed, the implication was that one could lose his very soul by too much attention to healing men's bodies. [Kelsey 1973:195]

This theological position was enshrined by Gregory the Great in his "Book of Pastoral Rule". The influence of this book during the time of the Church's missionary endeavour in northern Europe at this time can scarcely be overestimated. For Gregory, illness was a sign of God's chastisement for sin in an attempt to discipline and reform sinners.

> The sick are to be admonished that they feel themselves to be sons of God in that the scourge of discipline chastises them." He understood illness as one more blow of the hammer in shaping the stones of humanity be placed in the heavenly wall on the other side [sic]. Sickness brings a man to himself so that he can ponder his sins and repent.[10]
> [Kelsey 1973:196-197]

With the re-adoption of the Deuteronomic position by Gregory, the stage was set for the demise of the healing ministry in the official Church although it was to re-emerge from time to time in the more charismatic fringe groups and movements. Within the official Church, the sacrament of anointing became a preparation for death in "Extreme Unction" and the emphasis was placed on the forgiveness of sins in the sacrament of Penance.

The reformers, too, were extremely circumspect on the role of healing in the church. Luther dismissed miracles in his own time believing that "the great miracles like healing were given in the beginning so that church people could later do 'greater works than these' by teaching, converting and saving men spiritually" (Kelsey 1973:221). Calvin was similarly unenthusiastic about healing gifts. Luther, however, was to mellow his position and even wrote an instruction of how to pray for the sick based on the letter of James. His change of viewpoint, like Augustine's, was based on a personal experience of healing (:233).

It is only in the 20th century that the healing ministry begins to re-emerge as a powerful force in the Church. The beginnings can be traced to the emergence of the "Healing sects" and the Pentecostal movement at the beginning of the century. It has continued through the Neopentecostal eruption since the 1960's which has seen the movement of the ministry into the mainline churches as well as the emergence of another wave of "new churches".

7.3.4 Kelsey's Implicit Theology of Healing

Kelsey does not provide a developed theological understanding of the healing ministry in his book but from his excellent historical survey we are able to abstract some elements of what such a theology would comprise. It seems that two theological bases or emphases persevere from the Old Testament through to the present day and these influence the understanding of the healing ministry. They can be outlined as follows.

1) Both good and evil (health and sickness) come from God and sickness is seen as the punishment/chastisement for sin.
2) Sickness is rooted in an evil which is against God's will and God actively fights against it.

Healing was central to the ministry of Jesus and also to the commissioning of his disciples who were told to proclaim Good News and to heal the sick. The Apostles and the early church naturally continued this ministry. Theological interpretations were influenced both by prevailing philosophical systems as well as by social circumstances. Here we note the role of especially Platonic and Aristotelian systems in the interpretation of the healing ministry. The former by Gregory of Nyssa and the early Fathers, the latter by the later medieval Doctors especially Thomas Aquinas. Regarding social conditions, we note the changes brought about when Christianity became the official religion of the empire in 321 AD, the disruption brought about in the time of Augustine and Gregory as a result of the break up of the empire, and the Islamic onslaught. These events can also be correlated with changes in theological interpretations. Healings and other miracles are accepted by all the theologians presented by Kelsey as a manifestation of God's *power* operating in the world. Interpretations of its meaning and the reason for it seem to change from age to age as do opinions regarding its necessity. We are now in a period in which the ministry is viewed more positively.

7.4 Contemporary Contributions to a Theology of Healing

We continue to build on the framework abstracted from the work of Kelsey by adding the contributions other theologians have made to a contemporary theology of healing. Four major authors, coming from different traditions, are presented here as a representative sample of current theological reflection. In addition, we note some contributions from Africa as well as some reflections on the social implications of healing amongst liberation theologians.

7.4.1 The Contribution of Morris Maddocks

Morris Maddocks (1981,1990), an Anglican Bishop, has made a major contribution to the theology of healing. Following much of the historical perspective of Kelsey, he makes some important additions. Chief amongst these are: the perspective of the Kingdom of God, the role of Calvary, the healing dimension of the sacraments and, finally, the image of the Transfiguration as the symbol of the healing ministry.

Maddocks (1990:3-93) situates his discourse within the context of the Kingdom of God. Jesus came both to preach the Kingdom of God by word and to make it manifest through signs, of which the healings were a major manifestation particularly in his early ministry. Further to this, Maddocks suggests that healing is linked to creation since the power used is the creative power of God (:9-10). Healing is a particular manifestation of the restoration of all in Christ so that everything is good as it was in the beginning (cf. Gn 1,13). The concept of wholeness is derived from this as a wholeness which is achieved only in the Kingdom. Wholeness is Holiness and is the goal for which Jesus came. Healing is a manifestation of this wholeness in the life of a person (:13-18).

The passion and death of Jesus is a sign pointing to the fulfilment of the Kingdom of God and implies the unleashing of God's power through weakness. This is a power that heals (Maddocks 1990:66). Following O'Collins (1977:76) he notes that "the uncrucified is unhealed" and this tells us something both about the reality of the mission of Jesus and the commission to his Church.

> 1. Before Jesus could cause our healing, he had to be crucified. His execution prompted the healing. In that sense, if uncrucified he would not have been our healer. Being made perfect 'through what he suffered', he could become 'the source of eternal salvation to all who obey him' (Heb. 5.8f). 2. It was the whole Jesus who was crucified, not - so to speak - just some part of him. Crucifixion destroyed his entire human existence. What remained uncrucified in him would be unhealed in us.
>
> [O' Collins in Maddocks 1991:67]

In his teachings Jesus exalts the weak and poor and the same vision is evident in his works. The signs, of which healing is one of the main, are addressed to those who find themselves in weakness of body, mind or soul, or to those who are oppressed whether by the powerful or the demons. It is this state which is transformed by the paschal mystery. The healing signs are precisely signs of this truth.

Maddocks indicates seven forms of healing in the Church's healing ministry which he refers to as teaching signs. The first three are the sacraments: Eucharist, Anointing of the Sick, and Penance. These are recognised as special means of God's healing grace responding to different forms of illness.

> The Eucharist is *the* healing sacrament for it is a making present of Christ and his Grace . . . [it] proclaims the present reality of the beginnings of the Kingdom . . . [and] is a participation in the words and works of Jesus, until his coming again . . . [it] must again become the anticipatory celebration of a healed creation . . .
>
> [Maddocks 1991:113-116]

The Sacrament of "Anointing of the Sick" is described as "a healing explosion" (Maddocks 1991:121) which has healed many people, physically, emotionally and spiritually, from their illnesses. The "Sacrament of Penance" with its emphasis on the confession and forgiveness of sins is also seen as a privileged means of healing for those who are burdened by a life of sin. The priest's role of healer and counsellor is manifest in the irruption of God's power to forgive those under sin and to remove that sin so that they might begin again as renewed people.

Besides the three sacraments, Maddocks (1990:122) indicates "laying of hands accompanied by the prayer of the Church" as a theologically justified method of healing, as well as "exorcism" (:127) for the possessed. The latter is a ministry which should be exercised with care: "It is essential that this ministry should be firmly under the discipline of the church" (:129). Finally he affirms two ministries of pastoral care as part of the healing ministry: post-healing aftercare, and helping people to prepare for death (:130-135). These, he notes, are both specialised ministries which require training and preparation.

Maddocks (1990:192) suggests that the transfiguration is "a helpful model for healing." The transfiguration unveils a vision of the Kingdom to the disciples as they prepare for the journey to suffering and death which Jesus has revealed. It provides a sign of what lies beyond that suffering and death, a manifestation of God's Reign not yet fully realised. He argues that this is a valuable model for the healing ministry whose goal is similarly to manifest a vision of the Kingdom in the lives of people who find themselves caught up in the suffering of sickness.

> The transfiguration event underlines the necessity of Jesus being in the midst. It also clearly demonstrates that not only weak human beings can be sharers in the glory and healing of the cosmic Christ. He is able to use any channel for his power and that healing and transfiguring power can also shine through a distorted universe, through a world in conflict, and still reveal the glory of God. [Maddocks 1991:198]

The transfiguration points to the kind of fullness, wholeness and health we are called to in the Kingdom. But more than that, it provides a source of renewal and enthusiasm which, as it motivated the disciples to persevere on the journey with Jesus, motivates today's minister "to spend one's life in the service and healing of others, suffering gladly if need be in union with the 'exodus' sufferings of the Master, whose power and glory would always be at hand" (Maddocks 1991:205). This, too, is transfiguration for Maddocks. The healing which is required is an affirmation of a new humanity restored in Christ. Such a new humanity manifests itself on the individual, interpersonal and social levels with the transfiguration as model for all of them.

7.4.2 *Healing as God's Freedom in Creation: Walter Hollenweger*

Walter J Hollenweger (1972) comes out of the Pentecostal tradition and his work is a definitive text on the Pentecostal movement. In his theological assessment of the healing ministry he is remarkably low key, recognising a reversal in traditional Pentecostal teaching regarding the use of medicine and the acceptance of divine healing "without making it a doctrinal principle" (:359). "Purely as a phenomenon, healing through prayer can be seen to be an effective form of support, and in some cases a substitute, for medical healing" (:359).

In a later work Hollenweger (1989:166,168) affirms that theology must take account of healing. However he cautions against the use of ontological categories in developing a theology of healing especially when it comes to the category "super-natural": "thoroughly unhelpful . . . a construct of a specific European scholastic approach which has now been superseded" (:167). He suggests that a functional approach is more useful as well as being more biblical. As a basis for his theology, he recognises that all healing comes from God even though the means He uses are various and yet of equal merit "whether someone is healed by an operation, by a reasonable diet, by prayer or by a combination of these different therapies" (:168).

In developing his theology of healing, Hollenweger (1989:172-173) stresses the following:

1) "A Christian theology of healing must start with creation . . . we live because God has breathed his spirit into us. If he takes his spirit away we die" (:172).
2) "The Spirit of God liberates forces of healing in Christian and non Christian alike" (:172).
3) "Christian healing is rooted in the belief in God's freedom and sovereignty" (:173).

From these three basic parameters Hollenweger (1989:173) draws three major conclusions relating to sin and sickness; faith and healing; and the role of the worshipping community in healing:

1) Whilst there is a connection between sin and sickness it is not a direct causality. "[I]t is not those who 'sin' that necessarily become sick. It is often the innocent who are affected."
2) Similarly, whilst faith and health are also linked this connection is also not direct causation. "Faith does not automatically lead to health, nor is unbelief automatically the cause of illness . . . There are many healing stories in the New Testament where faith plays no role."
3) The worshipping community is the place where healing "can and should be expected . . . not in a *virtuoso* healer."

7.4.3 The Contribution of Bernard Häring

Häring (1984) in his little book, makes two important contributions to the theological debate: the understanding of Christ the Healer deriving from the paradigm of the Good Shepherd and the notion of the wounded healer in a wounded society deriving from the image of the suffering servant of Isaiah.

Christ is the Good Shepherd who takes care of his flock (Häring 1984:10-25). This is the major theological key which Häring uses to interpret Jesus' healing ministry and Christ's ministry through his body, the Church. Starting from the image as presented by the prophet Ezekiel (Ezk 34,11-16) he goes on to show that it is this fundamental attitude of caring for his people which roots the healing ministry, in all its various forms, in God himself (:11-17). Jesus is Good Shepherd because he is the incarnation of this attitude of God here on earth. He is redeemer for the same reason. He redeems creation by healing it (:17-18). He restores broken relationship as Christ the reconciler. In his presentation, Häring adopts a wide notion of healing, incorporating the personal, interpersonal and social dimensions of humankind.

Häring's (1984:72-97) second insight is the notion of Christ as "wounded healer". This is an essential aspect of the healing ministry and is present in all ministers who participate in it.

> The Saviour of mankind is himself the archetype of the "wounded healer". In Christ we see the fulfilment of what Second Isaiah foretold about the Servant of God: "A man of sorrows and familiar with suffering, a man to make people screen their faces

> . . . And yet ours were the sufferings he bore, our sorrows he carried . . . through his wounds we are healed" (Is 53:3-5). Jesus, the divine and human Physician, is more deeply wounded than any other human being and all his wounds and sufferings are intimately linked with his mission as saviour and healer. The mystery of this utter solidarity between the healer and those to be healed should be seen as the key to authentic healing in a perspective of salvation. [Häring 1984:72]

Häring goes on to indicate the ways in which this woundedness is manifest in many healing ministries. Amongst these are the experience of depression and suffering common amongst men and women of the helping and healing professions. Another occurs in organisations such as Alcoholics Anonymous where the sick are helped by those who have the same sickness. There is much here which relates with Daneel's comments regarding an African Christology based on Christ the healer as "*nganga*". Most African healers have to be called by the ancestors and this call is manifest by a sickness which is healed through the "*thwasa*" experience of being apprenticed to another healer and gradually becoming a healer oneself. The point is that, in some sense, one cannot be a healer without having been through the sickness experience and having been healed of it.

7.4.4 Developing a Method: The Contribution of MacNutt

Francis MacNutt (1974) in his classic work deals with several of the issues we have presented above and in many ways was the first to attempt to bring the various strands of the healing ministry into some kind of coherent methodological whole. MacNutt is clear that

> although I am aware that some prayer can have a psychological effect through the power of suggestion, I am convinced through my own experience that prayer for healing brings into play forces far beyond what our own unaided humanity contributes. The results of prayer have been extraordinary - so much so that what once would have astonished our retreat team we now take almost for granted. The extraordinary has become ordinary. And that's the way I think the healing ministry should be: an ordinary, normal part of the life of every Christian community.
> [MacNutt 1974:14-15]

He describes four basic types of sickness (:162):

- sickness of spirit caused by personal sin.
- emotional sickness caused by emotional hurts of our past.
- physical sickness caused by disease or accidents.
- demonic oppression which can cause any of the above.

These lead to four types of prayer for healing (:163):

- prayer for repentance: (for personal sin).
- prayer for inner healing (healing of memories) (for emotional problems).
- prayer for physical healing.
- prayer for deliverance (exorcism).

SICKNESS	CAUSE	PRAYER REMEDY	APPROPRIATE SACRAMENT OR SACRAMENTAL	ORDINARY HUMAN REMEDY
1...of the *spirit* -often contributing to emotional sickness -sometimes contributing to bodily sickness	*Personal sin*	*Repentance*	*Penance*	
2...of the *emotions* -often contributing to *spiritual* sickness -often contributing to *bodily* sickness	*Original sin* (i.e., the person has been hurt by the sins of *others*)	Prayer for *Inner Healing*	*Penance*	Counseling (psychiatric & spiritual)
3...of the body -often contributing to *emotional* sickness -sometimes contributing to *spiritual* sickness	Disease, acccidents, psychological stress	*Prayer of Faith* for physical healing	*Anointing of the sick*	Medical care
4...any, or all of the above can, upon occasion be	*Demonic* in its cause	Prayer of *Deliverance* (Exorcism)	*Exorcism*	

Fig. 7.1 Ministerial Response to Sickness (Source Macnutt 1974:166)

These are linked to sacramental healing practices as well as to human healing methods as indicated in fig. 7.1. MacNutt's other major contribution revolves around the issue of faith as it links to healing. We have already seeni some of the difficulties regarding the role of faith in healing. MacNutt (1974:115) also recognises such difficulties and as a response in order to "avoid some of the oversimplification that has ended in harming people's faith instead of helping it" he describes four possible faith attitudes towards healing (:115-118):

1) Healing is simply man's responsibility
2) Healing by faith is possible but extraordinary
3) Healing by faith is ordinary and normative but does not always take place
4) Healing always takes place if there is faith.

MacNutt (1974:120) situates himself in the third of these attitudes. He suggests that the fourth limits God's freedom and leads to faith in faith and not faith in God. We have to "leave the results up to God". He makes an interesting distinction between the "gift of faith" and the "virtue of faith" (:125-126). The latter refers to the normal faith given to every Christian whereas the "gift of faith" as listed in 1 Cor 12,9 is only given to some Christians: "a ministry gift which God imparts to help us pray with confidence and 'no hesitation in our hearts' for a given intention" (:126). He makes a similar distinction between the prayer of petition by which an ordinary Christian asks God for a healing and the prayer of command prayed by the minister who has the "gift of healing". The latter ministers in the name of the Godhead through His power: "in the name of Jesus" or "by the power of the Holy Spirit". These two models are each perfectly valid for MacNutt although "one is deeper and better than the other; yet it cannot be forced, for it is a gift" (:128).

A further important issue raised by MacNutt is the question of those who are not healed. This has been the subject of much debate and hurt amongst many people who have considered themselves duped and exploited by some of the more extreme practitioners of faith healing. Both Carmen Benson (1975) and Robert Wise (1977) have written sensitive and insightful books on this issue. In order to respond to this debate, MacNutt (1974:248-261) proposes eleven reasons, from his own experience in his own ministry, why people are not healed:

- a lack of faith
- the redemptive value of suffering
- a false value attached to suffering
- sin
- not praying specifically
- faulty diagnosis (e.g. praying for physical healing when inner healing is required)
- refusal to recognise medicine as a way God heals
- not using the natural means of preserving health
- now is not the time
- a different person is to be the instrument of healing
- the social environment prevents the healing from taking place

The fact that people are sometimes not healed indicates the "sense of mystery" which should surround the healing ministry. We are called to ask God to meet our needs with confidence but not to "expand any one method or experience into a universal method" (MacNutt 1974:137). Indeed he questions any tendency of universalising and absolutising anything linked with this ministry since to do so is to limit God's freedom.

7.4.5 African Contributions

Perhaps the main African voice in this field is that of M.L. Daneel and we quote him at some length. Regarding healing, he suggests that the appropriation of the role of traditional healer by the prophet healer in AIC's indicates the emergence of a Christology, based on Christ the healer, which may be a major contribution of African theology to the Church as a whole (Daneel 1983a:86). He points out how the affirmation of the power of the Christian God through Christ the healer presents an effective means of conquering the spirits which trouble people (:87). This role was traditionally that of the healer (Shona, Kikongo: *nganga*) in African society. Drawing from the work of the African theologian Buana Kibongi, Daneel indicates the theological framework around which the theological notion of Christ the healer may be developed:

> Buana Kibongi shows that the Congolese *nganga* was never a mediator between *Muntu* (man) and *Nzambi* (God) but only between man and the departed spirits. The *nganga*'s activities drew out the concepts of liberation and redemption. "*Nganga* is certainly the saviour or the liberator of *Muntu*", says Kibongi [1969:54]. Thus the *nganga* is the predecessor of the minister and priest. It was after all the *nganga* who established the "theological" framework on which the missionaries could build. Even more important, the *nganga* is the predecessor of Christ in Africa: He, as the new *nganga*, is the fulfilment of the past traditions. "*Nganga* willed to save man, but did not succeed in doing so; Christ did so fully once for all. Christ has therefore accomplished the work of *Nganga*" [Kibongi 1969:55]. The prophetic Independent Churches, which can also be described as "healing institutions", have placed the paradigm of Christ as the "healing *nganga*" in sharper relief than any other church in Africa.
>
> [Daneel 1983a:86-87]

In a somewhat cautious though very balanced reflection, Mbonyinkebe Sebahire (1987) also indicates the emerging theological emphasis of Jesus as healer and doctor in the African context. However, he is also careful to note that this emergence mirrors a resurgence worldwide of the ministry of healing and its theological consequences. Besides the christological dimension, he also recognises the importance of the pneumatological and ecclesiological dimensions of this ministry, emphasising that healing involves the whole community:

> Indeed, it is the support of the believing community which makes health and salvation available. The faith which founds and which structures the new community is the very source of healing. [Sebahire 1987:14]

He concludes that healing is part of the ongoing process of total liberation and salvation to which the Church should be committed. He sees certain "excesses" in this ministry, in particular an over-emphasis on spiritual powers and especially demons and in this respect he is critical of Archbishop Milingo's healing practices. He sees the emerging Independent healing churches as a challenge to the Roman Catholic Church to increase its involvement in the therapeutic faith healing ministry (Sebahire 1987:25).

The 1985 International Conference on Mission Studies in Harare focused on the issue of the Church's healing ministry. The following comments emerged:

> We understand the term Faith Healing as using the dynamics of prayer and community support to directly calling [sic] upon the power of Christ as an agent of healing. Faith healing is to be considered as an important aspect in the concept of Christian healing and is applicable in every kind of brokenness. Some important aspects of Faith Healing are:
>
> - it acknowledges the supernatural factor in healing,
> - it ought not to be performed by amateurs, and
> - it also has political implications for the medicine of poverty.
>
> Faith healing is understood as supportive to the healing process but not an absolute substitute for medicine. [in Becken 1989:236-237]

Author's such as Ngada (1985) and Makhubu (1988) provide a more practical rather than reflective theology of healing. For Ngada (1985:27), the centre of the healing ministry is the Spirit: "It is the Spirit who heals us when we are ill." Illness comes from evil spirits or demons who "can take possession of a person and . . . can cause illnesses." People are healed when the demons are cast out "in exactly the same way as we read about in the gospels" (:28). He describes the different rites of the AIC's as "healing, exorcism, *isiwasho* (purification), baptism . . . but there is only one Spirit who does all these things. In a way all these things are healing or salvation." Makhubu (1988:77) also emphasises the importance of visible signs in the healing ministry: "elements used symbolically unite the sick person to God." He goes on to outline the role and significance of 10 of these elements. Makhubu suggests that the AIC's emphasise the essential role of healing which speaks to African life and culture and suggests that these churches had to emerge because in mainline churches the healing ministry is "practised at a very low key" (:77). Given the widespread nature of the Coping-healing phenomenon among Christian groups and movements in Africa, the development of a coherent and widely disseminated theology of healing by African theologians is clearly of paramount importance.

7.4.6 Healing in a Social Perspective

All the authors we have considered above allude to the social dimension of the healing ministry. Gerrit Huizer (1987:75) makes this the centre of his healing paradigm. He says that the Church is called to be a healing community "preserving or bringing wholeness to the disharmonious community as well as to the sick individual. Over the last centuries this function has been lost to a large extent." He argues for the Church to become a healing agent in a broken Western society since this sick society extends its influence into every other society on earth (:89). Such a healing ministry needs to be concerned with the modes of production in society and their effects on the well-being of people. Health is intimately linked to the socio-political reality of people's lives and any authentic healing ministry needs to recognise this social dimension (:92). Consequently, any kind of emphasis on personal healing mitigating against an involvement in society must be questioned (:94).[11]

Huizer's comments echo the earlier analysis of Hollenweger who, coming out of the Pentecostal tradition himself, confesses its weakness in this regard.

> We must look beyond the gifts of the Spirit which are manifested in the Pentecostal movement to find modern gifts of the Spirit: the gifts of service to society and science. That is, we need gifts that will help us to understand better our sick world of politics, economics and science and to contribute to the task of healing it.
> [Hollenweger 1972:373]

Clearly this much more complex healing ministry of the Church is one which has hardly begun. Nevertheless it is interesting to note that the Durban Christian social agency, Diakonia, an ecumenical organisation primarily involved in the Church's role in society, chose as its theme in 1991: "Heal, Build, Reconcile" with precisely this social emphasis (Diakonia 1991).

This attempt to reflect the process of developing a theology of healing has clearly only touched the surface of the many issues involved. Nevertheless it has helped to illustrate that theologians are already attempting to come to grips with the fact of this ministry and its consequences for the mission of the Church. The theology which evolves must concern itself with the reincorporation of the missionary mandate of healing, as articulated in Luke (9,1-6) Matthew (10,6-7) and Mark (16,17-18), into the more currently accepted and practised missionary mandates of preaching, teaching and baptizing of Matthew (28,19-20) and Mark (16,16) (cf. Häring 1984:viii citing McGilvray 1981:1).

Conclusion to Part II

This long section has clearly revealed to us the complex nature of the phenomenon we are investigating. If nothing else we have discovered that simplistic solutions and explanations of the Coping-healing phenomenon are of little help. Nevertheless the complexity which our analysis has revealed is not a sign of despair. The comments and reflections presented in our various mediations can help us draw clear conclusions from the breadth of investigation we have presented here. In this way we are now in a position to describe the phenomenon with some confidence. This phenomenological description of the Coping-healing practices of the churches we have investigated will be the subject of our next chapter. Our description will serve to inform our own theological judgement regarding the Church's healing ministry and the position of the Coping-healing phenomenon within it. The construction of this theological judgement is the aim of Part III.

PART III

TOWARDS A THEOLOGICAL JUDGEMENT

Introduction: Theologising on Mediated Phenomena

The phenomenological movement considers phenomenological description to be "primarily . . . based on a classification of the phenomena . . . presuppos[ing] a framework of class names" (Spiegelberg 1982:693). Description can also be by negation to show the unique dimension of a phenomenon as well as, more guardedly, "by metaphor and analysis" (:694). Clearly the chapters of part II constitute a beginning of this process especially as regards description by classification. What we wish to do now is to bring together the major elements of this initial classification in an attempt to look for commonalities, relationships, complements and even contradictions in order to synthesize these elements into a single description. Our understanding of phenomenological description goes beyond that of Spiegelberg (1982:696-708) and includes, to some extent, steps two to five of his method: investigating general essences; apprehending essential relationships; watching modes of appearing (our mediations) and exploring the constitution of the phenomenon in consciousness. Regarding the "Phenomenological Reduction" (:708) we contend that *epoché* has been applied at each step in the process from chapter two to chapter seven as we move from one mediation to another attempting to view the phenomenon in different ways. Against Spiegelberg and following Husserl we maintain that the operation of *epoché* comes earlier in the phenomenological process and occurs throughout the process, a procedure we have attempted to follow in our long journey to the description.

In this third part we aim to describe the Coping-healing phenomenon from our own standpoint. We begin this process by bringing together the various elements of the mediated phenomenon as perceived so far. Chapters two to seven have provided us with these elements. In chapter eight we attempt to see how these factors come together in relationship to one another.

The results of chapter eight will provide the matter upon which we can begin our theological reflection. Our theological judgement is clearly part of the description of the phenomenon since we are ultimately speaking from the standpoint of faith. Developing our theological judgement will be the aim of chapters ten and eleven where we will be attempting to do Boff's (1987:78-84: cf. xxvi-xxvii) "second theology", based on the fruits of the description obtained in chapter eight. Since this description will be in terms of the inculturation model, the thesis of this work, it will be necessary to ground it on an adequate understanding of 'culture' within the South African context. We hope to develop this understanding in chapter nine.

In this way, chapters eight to eleven form an ensemble leading up to a presentation of the phenomenological description in a theological key: our theological judgement. The judgement takes the form of a theological model which we develop in chapters ten and eleven and which, we believe, will allow us to indicate the criteria by which we can indicate to what extent the Coping-healing phenomenon we have studied, forms part of the Church's healing mission and ministry. This judgement clearly extends the scope of theology into the other disciplines considered. We see this process to be at the very heart of missiology, the theological discipline which finds itself on the boundary between "Church" and "World". Any true missiology must be multidisciplinary if it is to respect the world it meets and the world's understanding of itself which is, at least on one level, expressed through the ways it categorises its thought in academic disciplines. We close this part and the study in chapter twelve by drawing some conclusions which have emerged.

Chapter 8

What is the Coping-Healing Phenomenon?

8.1 Essential Elements of Coping-Healing and their Relatedness

Our aim in this chapter is to summarise the major conclusions of part II by identifying the main factors or essential elements of the Coping-healing phenomenon as revealed by the five mediating perspectives. We have attempted to organise these in terms of three main areas: the epistemological paradigms operating in the mediation, the factors involved in illness causation and the factors involved in the healing process. Besides indicating these elements we also consider some of the important relationships between them and some of the main conclusions which emerge from this relatedness. In this way we attempt to describe something of the content and the structure of the phenomenon. We also enhance our description by indicating some important predications which have emerged.

8.2 Essential Dimensions Revealed by the Psycho-Medical Mediation

The psycho-medical mediation showed a number of factors operating within the Coping-healing phenomenon. These factors impinge upon the mechanism, the patient, the healer and the context within which the healing occurs. It also revealed several intellectual paradigms within which psychology and medicine organise their thought. An awareness of these paradigms helps to explain some apparent anomalies and contradictions in the opinions expressed by the researchers.

8.2.1 Intellectual Paradigms Operating in the Psycho-Medical Mediation

These paradigms are important to identify at the outset since they form the epistemological lens through which the phenomenon is mediated. We identify three in our psycho-medical mediation.

The Medical Model

Following Boucher (n.d.) we recognise a "Medical Paradigm" which understands disease as a physico-chemical process and curing as physico-chemical intervention. Knowledge is obtained through experimentation: the scientific method. In this model, psychology and medicine attempt to search for "objectivity", "repeatability" and "verifiability" within a modern scientific world-view. The apparent subjectivity and varied nature of both the illness and treatments in the Coping-healing phenomenon render "objective" judgements very difficult. It is for this reason that authors such as Stumpf, Levin and Rose are unable to substantiate any miracle cures.

The Psychological Model

There is a growing recognition, within the medical and psychological professions, of the limitations of the defined boundaries of their own disciplines. These are no longer seen to coincide totally with the fields of illness and healing. Frank (1961), Kiev (1964) and others have affirmed the therapeutic value of healing paradigms operating outside those recognised by Western medicine and the scientific method. In this way, a "Psychological Paradigm" or "Psychological Model" has emerged in which the mutual influence of psyche and soma is recognised. The notion of healing is widened to include the psychosomatic in a recognition of the power of the mind to control the body.

Clearly categories such as psychosomatic disorder, psychogenic disease, stress and intropsychic balance are difficult to deal with using the scientific method. The psychological model has a greater openness to less easily verifiable categories and attempts to incorporate them within its understanding. The psychological model is stretched further to incorporate the more mystical categories of Jungian psychologists such as Bührmann. Here, the model is extended to include the religious and cultural. Bührmann recognises the importance of religious healing methods in allowing the emergence of forces operating within the unconscious to come through the ego defences and thus effect healing. The religious is specifically incorporated into this system "as a psychic instinct" (1989:34) and religious healing "as a psychological healing process within a particular cultural framework."

The "Holistic" or "Systems" Model

Several of the authors presented in chapter 3 have indicated the need to move beyond normal medical, scientific and even psychological models in order to understand the phenomena they study. Cheetham and Rzadkowolski "opt for an eclectic Holistic approach and in particular a general systems theory". Here, systems of elements are themselves elements of larger systems with reciprocal relationship between the systems right through from atoms to cells to organs to individuals to families to groups to society and, finally, to the ecosphere. Such a holistic approach is also affirmed by Holdstock (1979:120).

Bührmann refers to Jung's conception of the "transcendent function as the major unifying determinant in the life of a person". This provides a cue for the emergence of models which include a "spiritual" dimension. The "spiritual" is not just incorporated into the psychological, but becomes a separate category. In this regard, a series of witnesses from the medical and psychological fraternity testify to the efficacy of a spiritual dimension of healing where the agent is referred to as "prayer" or "God". Other authors prefer to speak of "unknown natural forces which are at work".

8.2.2 Factors in Illness Causation

Besides organic factors, the following psycho-medical factors have been identified as operating in illness causation: psychogenic factors, stress, psychosomatic factors and cultural factors. Psychogenic factors link illness directly to a person's psychological make-up. These are factors such as personal psychological history, arrested psychological development and other psychological problems. Factors such as these can lead to illness or illness susceptibility which may manifest itself in organic symptoms. It is often possible to "cure" the organic symptoms without dealing with the underlying cause and real sickness. Stress is the name given to those factors: personal, historical, interpersonal and social, which give rise to a disturbance in the intropsychic balance of a person. Such a disturbance may lead to the manifestation of organic symptoms through psychosomatic mechanisms. Much of religious healing is helping people to develop mechanisms for coping with stress. The relationship between psychological and physiological mechanisms in the human person has been increasingly studied in recent years. The division of the person into psyche and soma is today seen as an artificial one imposed by the particular way that scientism looks at the human person. The mind can and does affect the body and emotions and feelings can also operate on this level. The way in which psychosomatic factors work is not yet clear although theories of chemical transfer in the hypothalamus have been propounded (Moerman 1979:61-2). Cultural factors can influence the way physical symptoms emerge. Research has shown that the physiological symptoms emerge in the way that the culture expects stress based, psychological sickness to be manifest in the person's life. So *amafufunyane* is a Zulu disease whereas "Depression" and *Anorexia Nervosa* are Western ones. The etiologies of both types could be strikingly similar whilst the symptoms are very different and culturally conditioned.

8.2.3 Factors in the Healing Process

The psycho-medical mediation has revealed many different factors operating in the healing process. All of these would seem to apply to the Coping-healing phenomenon we are studying. They can be sorted into four main categories: contextual factors which describe the environment in which the healing occurs; factors which affect the healer in the process; factors which impinge upon the patient or sick person and, finally, factors which affect and describe the mechanism by which the healings occur.

Sharing the Same Cultural Framework

The importance of a shared cultural framework between healer and patient has been stressed throughout. The cultural system provides the understandings which help to alleviate fears by making the illness intelligible. It also provides accepted symbols which the healer uses to manipulate the emotions and psyche of the patient. The cultural framework provides the medium through which the suggestions are received and the catharsis can be experienced. Whilst the Zionist *umprofethi* and Neopentecostal healer are often bringing people through the same healing process, they are clearly working in widely different cultural contexts and would find it difficult to heal one another's patients.

Holistic Healing

The type of healing that is occurring is seen as holistic healing. It is an attempt to deal with the whole person within a personal and social environment. The psycho-medical mediation recognises the challenge that this kind of healing poses to traditional Western healing techniques.

Availability of Services

This simple practical issue is nevertheless important. It seems that people use the services provided by the Coping-healing phenomenon on an ad-hoc basis. Sometimes, there is no healing. But when there is, there is often a resulting commitment, on the part of the healed person, to the person, church or ministry of the healer. Such a commitment enhances the reputation of the healer or church. One could say that what we have here is a market providing services on a supply and demand basis with product loyalty forces also operating.

The Status of the Healer

Researchers have indicated repeatedly that the prestige and competence of the healer as well as the ability to maintain a powerful persona in the presence of those seeking healing, is an essential component of the Coping-healing phenomenon. The role of the healer is to inspire trust and confidence so that the method used will be viewed as a powerful intervention into the life and sickness of the patient. Competence is measured by the healer's effectiveness in being able to enter into the world of the sick person providing, firstly, understanding of the illness and then the way to conquer it.

There is a large amount of agreement amongst the researchers that the healers they have studied are operating on a psychotherapeutic level. They often seem to be more effective, in less serious cases, than their Western trained counterparts.

The Therapeutic Relationship

The healer has to build this relationship in order to be effective. It is described as a relationship in which confidence, trust and expectancy are enhanced thus providing the conditions where healing can occur. It is within such a relationship that the process of psychological transference can occur. The therapeutic relationship also has a communal dimension which creates a therapeutic atmosphere which enhances the healing process. This is clearly the case with "healing services". The group, be it the Zionist band or the Neopentecostal prayer group, allows the person to be healed within an atmosphere of support and care. The effective healer is at pains to provide such an environment in which to work.

The Personality Type of the Patient

It has been suggested that certain personality types are more open to faith healing methods and this type is variously described as "one oriented about external factors"; "the simple, extroverted, neurotic, guilt ridden person"; "the traditionally religious person with a capacity for faith, a mood of expectancy and hope and an ability to relate one's self to others". Hollenweger (1972:491) comments on the preponderance of this type of person in Pentecostal churches compared with traditional churches.

The Attitude of the Patient

Botha (1986:182-83) summarises the importance of patient attitudes in healing: "all healing, including medical or surgical, is facilitated by attitudes of compliance, motivation and faith and retarded by anxiety and guilt feelings." Faith in this sense indicates an attitude of expectancy on the part of the patient that the cure will be effected. Such an attitude of mind is in itself a powerful healer working synergistically with trust in the healer to effect the healing.

Naming the Illness

The first step in the healing process is to name the illness and thus bring it from the realm of the anxiety laden and fearful unknown into the realm of the known where it can be dealt with. Psychological mechanisms of displacement and projection often operate here. The cause of the illness is shifted onto some element like a spirit, a demon, or another person or agency. This element, once named, is then dealt with by the healer in terms of the framework of his speciality: in our case, religious healing.

Suggestion and Psychosomatic Mechanisms

All the authors point to the importance of using the mind to control the body in the operation of healing mechanisms. The ability of the healer or the healing service to induce suggestions and positive feelings into the mind of the patient will be directly proportional to the effectiveness of the healing.

Expression of Emotions

Part of the healing process has been identified as the ability to help the patient express emotions which may be at the root of physiological symptoms. Bührmann emphasises the importance of catharsis and confession in this process and the therapeutic effect of emotional expression in Pentecostal churches has been mentioned by Hollenweger (1972:372). Frank points to the importance of emotional manipulation to achieve status feelings as central to the healing process.

Provision of Success Experiences

The healing process needs to provide success experiences for the patient. Success experiences can be such things as positive emotions, feelings of esteem, growth in status and remission of symptoms both psychological and physiological. Such experiences are signposts to the effectiveness of the healing process.

The Role of Consciousness

Several authors refer to the way consciousness operates in the healing process. Consciousness is used in helping the patient to re-experience those memories and events which have affected the sickness. This re-experiencing leads to emotion transfer which can effect the healing. The power of suggestion and positive thinking also operate on the consciousness (at least at one level). Here the aim is to achieve a change in consciousness in order to acquire new attitudes and behaviours in accordance with the new, healthy, (saved) lifestyle which the healing has effected. Consciousness is also involved at a level where ego defenses and identities which make up the old sick persona have to be broken down in order to begin the re-creation of the new person. Ritual, dance and music are used in the Coping-healing phenomenon to enhance this process. Holdstock speaks of moving from left hemisphere to right hemisphere domination whilst Karagulla (in Jackson 1981:88) speaks of the superconscious state. Boucher and Easthope indicate that "Altered States of Consciousness" provide the condition where identity change in consciousness can occur .

Physico-Chemical Factors

It has been pointed out that psychological, emotional and spiritual processes often correlate with physical and chemical ones which are not well understood. It is the inter-relatedness of these processes which makes authors like Cheetham and Rzadkowolski (1980) opt for a systems approach which acknowledges, without specifying, these relationships.

Unknown Factors

Several authors conclude to the operation of "unknown", "not yet discovered" or "transcendent" factors in the healing process. This factor is experienced as a healing power, as heat or as an energy. It seems to be manipulated by certain gifted individuals. It is also noted that this power is not specifically confined to religious healing or an acknowledgment of God.

Finally we note the caveat of some authors that apparent cures of physiological symptoms do not always mean a healing of the person either on a physical, emotional, psychological or spiritual level. The manipulation of emotions may cure physical symptoms by making the person feel spiritually blessed. However, these feelings may also feed an inherent egoism which is actually a manifestation of deeper psychological or spiritual sickness. The danger that religious healing can attract and worsen hysterics, neurotics and psychotics of all kinds needs to be clearly stated and recognised.

8.3 Essential Dimensions Revealed by the Anthropological Mediation

8.3.1 Introduction: Religious Healing is Cultural Healing

Anthropology views the Coping-healing phenomenon as a cultural phenomenon. It shows us how illness itself is a cultural construct, how the criteria used in choosing health care are culturally determined and how the healing process is made up of culturally determined mechanisms.

8.3.2 Paradigms Operating in the Anthropological Mediation

Our mediation identifies three anthropological schools: the functionalist, semiotic and structuralist. The functionalist paradigm is frequently employed by the South African authors probably reflecting the British orientation to their training. Authors such as Kiernan, West, Oosthuizen and Dube are usually concerned with the purpose and functions of the behaviour they observe. They identify the needs of people and the processes which respond to these needs. The value of this paradigm is that it remains close to the ground in its method and interpretation and sometimes provides a useful control on the more esoteric flights of fancy of the other two paradigms. Its weakness is that it is sometimes unimaginative and has been accused of being ethnocentric in the ascribing of functions to non-Western cultures.

American authors like, Moerman (1979), Landy (1977) and Dow (1986) use an Intellectualist-Semiotic approach. Here culture is fundamentally communication and the symbols of illness and healing both describe and actualise the process of becoming ill and becoming well. Horton's (1967; 1971) intellectualist approach, whilst more dated, relies on concepts rather than symbols. Whilst it is perhaps less comprehensive it is sometimes helpful in clarifying (whilst clearly simplifying and reducing) this complex process. The work of Williams (1982) in this section is useful since it combines the approach of someone trained in the semiotic school operating in an area where the functionalist school seems to predominate. His perceptive work provides a useful synthesis of these two approaches.

The structuralist approach used by medical anthropologists such as Kleinman (1980) and Dow (1986) attempt to go beyond cultural trappings in order to identify the common human process which is going on in the illness/health paradigm. Such attempts have been criticised as the search for the centre of an onion. Nevertheless, they provide important insights regarding the psycho-medical process which are going on and which are expressed in cultural categories. The section on the structure of symbolic healing is particularly helpful in this regard. The structuralist approach seems weak in recognising the human person as community as well as individual. The indication of communal human structures which impinge upon the healing process seems to be lacking in structuralist approaches which become largely psychological.

8.3.3 Anthropological Factors Operating in the Coping-Healing Phenomenon

Illness is usually defined as the perception of and response to disease. When illness is understood as the process of becoming aware, making intelligible, and determining a behavioural response to disease, stress or other debilitating factors, then illness is always a cultural construct. Disease too, may have a cultural component. The culture bound syndromes we have discussed indicate behavioural, physiological and social responses to cultural factors. Culture influences disease in two major ways. Firstly, sickness and health are identified, understood and dealt with in a culturally conditioned manner. Secondly, cultural factors can themselves be pathogenic through the operation of the psychosomatic mechanisms seen in the psycho-medical mediation.

The role of a common world-view between healer and healed has emerged throughout as an important cultural factor influencing the experience, interpretation and diagnosis of illness. The explanatory models which are developed within the common world-view give sense to the worrying symptoms and provide a means of inserting them within a coping structure (the explanatory model) which gives hope of successful resolution. The explanatory model is composed of a series of symbols and healing metaphors accepted by both sick person and healer. This acceptance provides the healer with a path through which he can heal by means of the manipulation of these symbols. Conversion in religious healing is seen as the acceptance by the sick person of the healers world-view and symbol domain in order to open this path.

The semiotic school understands symbols in a very wide sense as "articulated carriers of meaning" and thus words, actions, objects and intellectual constructs may all be symbols. Through processes like prayer, laying on of hands, stepping into a healing circle, confessing sins and so on, a series of illness and healing symbols are articulated. This creates the framework through which healer-patient communication occurs. This process occurs in steps, each of which is expressed symbolically. Examples include the diagnosis of illness in terms of the explanatory model, the changing of clothes in purification rites, the use of prayers and dance, the altar call and so on. These symbols are utilised and manipulated by the healer as the patient is moved through the process. From the standpoint of the patient there is a gradual construction of healing symbols and it is this construction process which is the healing. This manipulation and construction process has consequences on the emotional, psychic and physiological make-up of the patient. These are weii known to the healer but usually a revelation to the sick person as health returns.

The Coping-healing phenomenon has some important functions in society. This ministry is meeting the needs of people on a very basic and accessible level. People experience the healing of their illnesses through the interventions of the Coping-healing churches even though the healings achieved are often disputed by other healing groups (notably the medical profession). Particularly in African Independent churches but also in the Neopentecostal groupings, healing has an important role in the restoration of disturbed relationships. The illness of an individual has consequences on a whole group: family, friends, other church members and so on. The healing process is a healing for the whole group. In this way, the Zionist band or the Neopentecostal church becomes the community of the "saved", the "healed" or the "pure" and is reconstituted as such in each healing ritual.

The Coping-healing churches are also seen as adaptive structures which provide a "coping" social environment that operates within an easily understandable, simplistic cultural framework. This provides a refuge for those unable or unwilling to cope with the complexity of modern life. These churches are thus identified as subcultures within the prevailing culture providing an acceptable social environment for their members to live in. The time spent within the subculture is a time of reconstitution of humanity: healing in order to be able to go back into the chaos of the world, sufficiently purified and protected to withstand its polluting, sickening, demon ridden, assault.

Anthropologists see the following mechanisms operating in the healing process. Firstly, it provides culturally determined explanatory models of illness and health which determine the framework within which healing can occur. These models operate both on the epistemological level of helping people to understand what is happening to them as well as on the behavioural level indicating the process to follow in becoming healed. The second mechanism is that of symbol construction and manipulation in the healing process. Healing is the construction of these symbols for the sick person and the manipulation of them by the healer. Thirdly, healers are seen as mediators of culture. They are able to indicate, articulate and manipulate the symbols of healing. Through this process they are said to enact cultural physiology. Finally we note the important social role of healing indicated by the anthropological mediation. The healing process helps the group or community to: "expel evil", "feel good about itself", "restore harmony", "reconstitute itself", and "re-incorporate the healed person within itself". Terms such as these are used to express how this social dimension of healing occurs.

Some anthropologists look for the common human processes and mechanisms, expressed in the various cultural keys they have studied. On the level of the individual they isolate the importance of identity change as central to the healing process. The process of the movement of consciousness from being-as-sick person to being-as-well person is a culturally mediated common human process in healing. Dow outlines the steps in this process as follows:

1) Construction of the cultural myth of health with its healing symbols.
2) Persuasion of the sick person that the sickness can be explained and cured by the myth.

3) Attaching the emotions of the sick person to particular symbols within the myth.

4) Manipulation of the symbols to effect the healing.

Clearly this model can be applied to the Coping-healing phenomenon we have studied as can Kleinman's model of the five core functions of all cultural healing systems.

Structural interpretations on the social level are much less evident and apart from Douglas's comments on the importance of taking this dimension into account, very little is mentioned. It is clear that common transcultural structural processes are operating on the social level in the healing process and it would be valuable to identify something of their nature.

8.4 Essential Dimensions Revealed by the Sociological Mediation

8.4.1 Introduction

Chapter five limited the notion of sociology to socio-economic and political considerations. As Feierman points out the issue of healers and healing has always involved economic, political and social factors and to ignore these is to misunderstand the phenomenon in its totality.

The focus of this mediation tends to be a study of churches rather than ministry. The Coping-healing phenomenon is seen as what these churches do since they are referred to as healing churches. They are seen as communities, subcultures or societies within society as a whole. This mediation identifies two ways of seeing "healing". Firstly it is seen as what the Coping-healing churches do. Here, the focus is on why society needs this type of healing today. Questions regarding its purpose, role and efficacy are asked. On a second, more general level, the focus is the role of illness and healing in society. Here the emphasis is on whose interests are being served by the political decisions made regarding health care.

8.4.2 Epistemological Paradigms

We identify the operation of three major epistemological paradigms. Whilst a distinct bias towards one or other of these is noticeable in the various authors, very few of them operate entirely within only one of them.

The liberal-empirical paradigm approaches society by analysing it into constituent manageable parts. It then attempts to use the modern scientific method usually through surveys, questionnaires and the like to determine objective conclusions about the area it is examining. The works of Morran and Schlemmer, Seedat and Meer, Rounds, and Sales tend to follow this approach. The value of this model is that of all research which uses the scientific method. It is the search for verifiable repeatable conclusions. Its weakness, as emphasised by Mosala, is the lack of recognition of the influence of the various parts of a phenomenon on one another. This leads to unilinear analyses and reductionist conclusions.

Mosala and Comaroff use a cultural-epistemological approach to social analysis which brings their work close to that of our anthropological mediation. However we include it here because they deal with many of the same issues raised by the sociologists. The cultural-epistemological approach stresses the importance of consciousness, values and culture as they determine people's social behaviour. It serves as a form of Weberian critique to the liberal-empirical paradigm.

The third paradigm comprises the neo-Marxist models operated by authors such as Feierman and Leger and used to a lesser extent by authors such as Gifford and Schoffeleers. The focus of these researchers is the analysis of power and its movement in society. They are concerned with identifying the groups and individuals whose interests are served by the decisions made and behaviours encouraged in society.

8.4.3 Sociological Factors Operating in the Coping-Healing Phenomenon

This mediation sees sickness and health as sociological phenomena. Health is seen as normal human participation in the life of society whereas sickness is seen as a form of deviance leading to withdrawal or antagonism towards normal social roles. Consequently it is society which proscribes "the sick role". The reasons how and why sick roles are socially determined rest on cultural, economic, political and physical criteria. Cultural factors comprise beliefs and values regarding traditionally right and wrong behaviour. Economic and political criteria are tied up with preserving the economic and political interests of the controlling group and persons with society. Physical criteria include the effects of disease on other members of society, through contagion and contamination as well as environmental factors such as access to infrastructure, pollution, climate and other geographical factors.

The sociological mediation recognises the source of illness to be bound up with social deviance. Besides its normal meaning of a person not conforming to society's norms, "social deviance" can also be understood as "social deprivation" where the "deviance" refers to the person's situation as one who does not receive the normal benefits of society. It can also be understood as "social disorganisation" where the society as a whole "deviates" from what a normal society is and finds itself in crisis. Social deprivation can operate at many levels. Environmental and demographic deprivation, resulting from overcrowding, poor land use, pollution and so forth, are directly pathogenic. Economic and political deprivation also results in the emergence of all types of illness. Social deprivation and alienation, which occurs as people feel powerless and alienated from the societies they belong to and the values they profess, may also give rise to illnesses of various types.

In order to heal people it is important to respond to the deviance. With regard to social deprivation, the Coping-healing church directly fulfils these needs by being a supportive, caring, giving group. However, indirect means are also used. These usually revolve around sublimating the need by responding to it on another level. Thus hierarchy, status and dress within African Independent churches provides the esteem which blacks do not find in South African society whereas the prosperity cult assuages the guilt experienced by rich people in some Coping-healing churches by providing legitimating justifications for wealth.

The research in this mediation indicates that the social instability experienced by people in the prevailing South African situation generates a search for social and personal stability amongst those most affected by it. Social disorganisation impinges upon people in different ways. There is the disorganisation experienced by traditional rural blacks who move to urban areas and who experience cultural, economic, political, and environmental changes. There is the disorganisation brought about by the context of growing violence within the society and there is the disorganisation experienced by Whites as control of society moves from their hands.

Finding stability within all of this is experienced as healing within the Coping-healing churches and the Coping-healing phenomenon is seen to be providing this sought for stability. The stability is expressed as balance, orientation, meaning, coping, healing, power, adaptation and the removal of fear. Healing is in fact the prevailing metaphor for this experience and the reason why healing has become so important in these churches.

Some authors, particularly Comaroff, Jones, Becken, Dube and Williams, recognise that the healing process is a humanisation process in which both the person and the society are involved. On the negative level it is a form of resistance to the evil, chaotic, threatening reality of society as experienced by those who come for healing. This reality is not accepted and is challenged by the Coping-healing church and the forms of its ministry. On a more positive level the Coping-healing ministry is an attempt to reconstruct the humanity of the sick person according to the values the healer and church espouse. The aim is to heal the person rather than to cure the disease. The healing is done through various processes: helping a person acquire dignity and self respect, a sense of power and well-being and through the status acquired in the group. On a third level, the healing process is seen as the reconstruction of society. This is done in a metaphorical and exemplary way through the creation of an ideal community within the subculture of the church or Zionist band.

On a further level, authors such as Easthope (1986) argue that the healing process is concerned not only with healing the person but actually healing the society itself through the "re-integration of a society disrupted by the illness of one of its members". This social function of the Coping-healing phenomenon is articulated in how African Independent churches have taken over many of the social functions of the tribal system. The Neopentecostal churches also substitute their own system of social functions for the rejected ones of the perceived chaotic society they wish to counter. In this way they help people re-adjust to the new threatening social reality and to find ways of coping with it.

If the members of the Coping-healing church are the community of the healed, then the question is posed whether they move beyond the confines of their group in order to have a healing impact in the greater society to which they belong. No, say authors like Zulu and Schoffeleers, suggesting that movement into these churches is a quietistic withdrawal option to the prevailing socio-political tensions in society. It is an escape from political and social responsibility into conservatism: a way of living with the present reality and thus, ultimately, of accepting it. Authors such as Comaroff, Daneel and Mosala disagree with this analysis. They see the African Independent churches as participants in the struggle for liberation operating on the level of consciousness and culture as sites of resistance. Furthermore, they show that the members of these churches are often the same people of the oppressed class who find themselves involved in overt political and social roles in other contexts. Involvement in the cultural struggle and resistance creates a consciousness which strengthens people to engage in more overt forms of social transformation as the occasion arises.

On a broader political level we note the role that "interests" play in the setting up and maintenance of society's health roles. Decisions made in this regard are political ones which serve interests. The interests of healers are not always the same as those of the healed. The search for legitimacy, power and wealth on the part of healers can also obscure and deform the healing process as such. The mediation informs an important caveat here on the aim, purpose and value of the Coping-healing phenomenon we are studying.

8.5 Essential Dimensions Revealed by the Philosophical Mediation

8.5.1 Philosophical Factors Grounding the Coping-Healing Phenomenon

World-view

Dilthey's original conception is at the basis of three approaches to sickness and health. The first is in the use of explanatory models which situate sickness and health within a cosmology of understanding. In this regard the failure of the Western scientific model to assign a religious role to these realities and the success of both African Spiritual cosmologies and Pentecostal cosmologies to fill this lacuna, has helped to legitimise and render this phenomenon effective amongst those accepting the grounding world-view.

The second usage is the attempt, as elaborated by Chidester, to mediate the conception of world-view in order to abstract the idea of human identity and humanisation as its fundamental epistemological key. Healing in this model becomes humanisation which is achieved by incorporating the superhuman into what has been rendered subhuman through contacts with the world. This incorporation process is achieved through symbol manipulation in ritual, prayer and religious experience. Healing is then humanisation through those symbol manipulations which reinforce the humanity of the sick person.

The third approach to sickness and health based on world-view is apparent in the emergence of holistic type system theories. Several types of systems are proposed. The multi-layered system of Cheetham and Rzadkowolski allows illness in any part of the system but recognises that all the parts are interconnected. The tripartite system of Wellin sees illness as magical, natural, religious or some combination of these. The eclectic borrowing system of Edwards allows mixing and matching of illness from traditional and Western sources depending on people's experiences and needs. The holistic system theories attempt to respond to the reality of eclecticism and consumerism within the Coping-healing phenomenon in which people go for what seems to work for them.

Janzen uses Linguistic Analysis to get to understandings of healing. He analyses the use of common stems and roots in various African languages and through comparison with other words using the same stems and roots he attempts to bring important nuances to the meaning of sickness and health.

The various Marxist philosophical approaches indicate the importance of concrete material bases when seeking to understand this phenomenon. Factors such as economic possibilities and the lack of time available to the working class in a capitalist society can explain the emergence of much of the AIC's Coping-healing ministries. The role of Neopentecostal churches in legitimising privilege also explains much of their popularity. The analysis of socio-economic interests being served by this ministry also goes some way to explaining its growth and efficacy.

Metaphysical Factors

The metaphysical questions attempt to address the issue of eclecticism in the Coping-healing phenomenon by indicating that the criteria for judging sickness and health are more complex than epistemological considerations may indicate. Eclecticism and a plethora of epistemological models aimed at understanding sickness and healing inevitably run the risk of lapsing into cultural relativism. Unfortunately, this fails to deal adequately with the fact that most in the Coping-healing phenomenon are claiming both power and results in terms of the Absolute: the one true God. They refuse relativism being largely dismissive of groups other than their own. Clearly the metaphysical ramifications of this need addressing. Some of the studies in "paradigm shift" in theology seem to be an attempt to address these issues.

8.5.2 Philosophical Factors in Healing Mechanisms

The epistemological keys which underlie notions of divination in traditional African culture and diagnosis in Western culture have repercussions in the determination of the cause of sickness and its nature in all the churches we have studied. Central to the healing process is the ability of the world-view to incorporate the sickness and its healing so that as the sickness is known it enters into the realm of "that which can be coped with". The understanding either effects or empowers the healing. Healing is achieved in this way when a person accepts the world-view of the healer which gives a "sense of meaning and purpose" to the sick person's life. It is having "meaning and purpose" in one's life that effects or empowers the healing. Linked with this is the important corollary that, in a sense, shared world-view is the necessary condition for healing since it forms the common ground or framework within which the healing can occur. The importance of the acculturated world-view in AIC healing is a valuable testimony to this truth.

Health is seen as "power" in all the Coping-healing churches we have studied. This power is linked to "God" as well as to the notion of "*uMoya*" and to the "Word". In all these cases it is this power which effects the healing. The word has important connotations in African traditional culture as well as in Pentecostal theology. Similarly the key of "life" which is linked to human identity in "Bantu" languages and to new life in the Johannine vocabulary is also ascribed to the healing process. Health is life and this is being fully human.

8.6 Essential Dimensions Revealed by the Theological Mediation

8.6.1 Introduction

Theologians agree that there has been a tremendous upsurge in the healing ministry throughout the Church. The ecumenical and charismatic dimensions of this growth are seen as indicators of the presence of the Holy Spirit. The ecumenical sign gives the phenomenon theological breadth whereas the charismatic sign points to a particular manifestation of the Spirit: a gift offered in response to our times. They also note a link between healing and life, a correlation which appears closer to the biblical concept than some of the modern western theological understandings.Through this correlation healing is linked to creation. Finally, there is also consensus that healing has a supernatural dimension linked to God's will although some authors point out that whilst God's will is always for healing there are cases where people are called to sickness for other higher purposes.

8.6.2 Paradigms Operating Within This Mediation

Theological language is notoriously difficult to deal with on the level of mediation since it demands a leap of faith and so always transcends the level of the *intellectus*. It is by its nature open to misunderstanding and is often dismissed as mere opinion. Much of theological language and judgement ***is*** opinion and is often influenced by personal, cultural and ecclesial factors without these being acknowledged.

We note a major difference in the approach of the authors to this ministry. On the one hand, many of them operate from a predominantly etic standpoint at varying distances from the phenomenon they are observing. There is also, however, a group of authors who theologise from an emic standpoint: within the phenomenon. They attempt to explicate their experience and theologise about it.

Predominantly Etic Theological Reflections

a) The Modern Theological Paradigm (the Search for Objectivity)

Several theological methods operate from this most distant standpoint. The historical-critical method with its roots in Gadamer and Ricoeur amongst others, is used by authors such as Kelsey, Hollenweger and to a lesser extent McConnell. The search here is for understanding of what is happening and for reasons which make it happen. The reasons are linked to historical, sociological and philosophical forces which shape the phenomenon and which root it in a tradition.

Authors such as Häring, O'Collins and Huizer also operate within this paradigm but their concern is the development of over-arching intellectual theological concepts which can explain and theologically root the phenomenon. It is an intellectualist framework (in the Lonerganarian sense).

b) Ethno-Centric and Ecclesio-Centric Models (The Clash of Subjectivities)

Some authors tend to make judgments on the phenomenon based on their own subjective (which they may perceive as objective) criteria. These criteria may be personal, as a result of their own training and upbringing, cultural or ecclesial. The early works of Sundkler and Oosthuizen fall into the ecclesio-centric category as does that of Msomi and to a more nuanced extent Sebahire. Ethnocentricism appears when theological judgements are based on the particular cultural upbringing, education and theological training of the authors. These are usually ethnocentric from a Western, White centre.

c) Participant-Observer Phenomenological Type (The Recognition of Subjectivities)

Authors such as Daneel, Becken, the later Sundkler and the later Oosthuizen attempt to incorporate the theological self-understanding of the phenomenon within their own theological reflection. The fact that they refer to those with the phenomenon as "they" renders this still an etic theological approach. It is, nevertheless, the closest of the etic approaches to the phenomenon itself.

Predominantly Emic Theological Reflections

Authors such as MacNutt, Maddocks, Makhubu and Ngada are clearly doing a different type of theology from those above. They are attempting theology from the standpoint of belief in the healing ministry in which they are personally involved. As those who have received this "gift of the Spirit" (as they believe) they are the only ones who can speak with authority about it. They do theology within the *fides quaerens intellectum* paradigm where the *fides* is their own belief in the gift God has given to them. It is an articulation of the communal experience of faith within the healing group or church they belong to.

8.6.3 Theological Factors Affecting the Coping-Healing Phenomenon

It is very difficult to identify the theological mechanisms operating in the Coping-healing phenomenon because of the transcendental nature of the theological factors which affect this phenomenon. In general, we can say that the theologians see that healing occurs through God: Father, Son and Spirit, operating in people's lives, through faith, explicitated by prayer, and other signs like sacraments, within the community of faith: the church, in order to realise the Kingdom of God in society. This is healing. Clearly, each of these theological terms requires its own analysis. We also note that they are sometimes used by our authors in differing senses.

Theologians recognise physical, emotional and psychological etiologies of illness whose treatment may benefit from physical, emotional and psychological remedies. However they are unanimous in also attributing theological categories to illness etiologies. In line with tradition, the major theological causes of sickness are expressed as sin and evil. Evil is often expressed as demons, evil spirits or Satan.

Sin and sickness are linked but not just in a simple causal way. Sin may cause sickness in the sinner and often does, but it also has consequences throughout the community and sometimes it is the innocent who are affected. Most of the authors, including all of those in the emic paradigm attribute some sickness to the action of evil, Satan or demons within the person affected. However, most point out that these possession type illnesses are relatively rare. Finally, some authors note that sickness may also be God's will for a person. This may result from higher purposes such as the person's vocation and mission or simply for the lordship of God.

God's will may be both for sickness or for health and Kelsey indicates the two strands in the Old Testament which explicate these two experiences. Healing is seen as a manifestation of God's power. Concomitant with the expression of this power is, however, a recognition of the operation of God's freedom in giving his gifts for his own sometimes mysterious purposes. Jesus' option for healing in his ministry and his delegation of this ministry to his apostles is a fundamental New Testament teaching. Jesus healed because he cared for people. He was the Good Shepherd. The healings he performed were a manifestation of the Kingdom of God in the world. Christians today are encouraged to call upon the name of Jesus when praying for healing. This power is seen to be rooted in the passion and death of Christ on the cross and one author expresses this as "the uncrucified is the unhealed". Another author sees the Transfiguration as the model of healing but clearly the Transfiguration also points to the Calvary experience. Häring's category of the wounded healer also resounds with that of the cross. This finds an echo in the role of Jesus as "*nganga*" (healer) that the African theologians are attempting to develop. An important link is the sickness and suffering process that the traditional healer goes through before becoming a "*nganga*". Finally, we affirm that Oosthuizen's caveat regarding the problem of the *theologia crucis* applies not only to those churches he was studying but probably to all of the Coping-healing churches.

The gifts used for healing are seen as gifts of the Holy Spirit and some of the churches we have studied refer to themselves as "Spirit Churches". There seems to be some confusion between Spirit as Holy Spirit and spirit as healing spirit especially where the term *uMoya* is used. This word seems to have a wider meaning than the English word "spirit". Nevertheless there appears to be consensus that it is the Holy Spirit who is working to effect the healings manifest in these churches.

The healing ministry is recognised as an essential part of the Church's ministry. This ministry was clearly visible during the first four centuries of the Church and then somewhat overshadowed for many years. It is re-emerging more strongly in recent times. The ministry offers signs of the Kingdom of God here and now: a form of realised eschatology, without denying a future eschaton. The community dimension of this ministry is an essential part of it. It demands a worshipping community and the healing is achieved with reference to the Church and its faith. The Church is in fact called to be a healing community, involved in the healing of all levels: personal, interpersonal and societal. Such healing is seen as a means to evangelisation. It is necessary to reappropriate the missionary mandate to heal given in Matthew chapter ten to add it to the more familiar one of preaching and making disciples.

Most authors also note the effect of cultural factors in the Coping-healing phenomenon. In some of the earlier authors these factors operate in judgments regarding the syncretistic nature of these churches. More recently, cultural factors have led to a more positive evaluation since there is a recognition of the cultural conditionedness of all ecclesial expression. The holistic healing models operating within this ministry are usually seen to be closer to the biblical cultural framework than the Western scientific model. The signs through which the Coping-healing ministry operates are varied but include prayer, the laying on of hands, as well as sacramental means.

Clearly the role of faith is central to the Coping-healing process and this is acknowledged by all the authors. Attempts are made with varying degrees of success to explicate this role. It is noted that faith and healing are linked but not in the direct causal relationship that some of the more extreme faith healers would espouse. This latter attitude is summed up as "faith in faith" rather than "faith in God" and is criticised by almost all the authors presented. It is attributed to influences of dualism and the metaphysical healing movements of the late nineteenth century as well as to an over-emphasis or obsession with healing in some churches. In its worst form, it can result in the sick being blamed for their illness since they are considered to be weak in faith.

MacNutt distinguishes between the virtue of faith, as the faith experience of all Christians, and the gift of faith, as a gift given for ministry. It is this gift which operates in the Coping-healing ministry. He suggests that the correct faith attitude is one which accepts that healing is ordinary and in fact the norm in the Church's ministry but that this does not imply that it will always occur.

8.7 Describing the Coping-Healing Phenomenon

This survey of the essential factors in the Coping-healing phenomenon has revealed a plethora of elements within it. We now bring these elements together in a description. In particular, we hope to highlight other dimensions of their relatedness which transcend the mediations we have used so far. We will also indicate some basic predicates and metaphors which we are now in a position to assert.

8.7.1 The Complexity of the Phenomenon

Our mediated manifestation of the phenomenon which is the Coping-healing ministry of the Church has revealed a large number of elements and factors operating within it and impinging upon it. Indeed the whole of our study so far has been an attempt to allow these elements to appear. Whilst we do not make any claim to comprehensiveness in the task undertaken in these eight chapters, we are nevertheless in the position to state with some confidence that the Coping-Healing phenomenon in the churches we have studied is an exceedingly complex reality. This is nevertheless an important inference since it is often claimed within the churches that the phenomenon is actually very simple: being a direct intervention of God, usually as Holy Spirit but also as the risen Christ, who suspends natural law with a supernatural, often miraculous, intervention. Clearly we have shown that such an interpretation is at best simplistic and at worst, as Verryn would have it, downright malign.

Our analysis has shown that a large number of psycho-medical, anthropological and socio-economic mechanisms are operating within this ministry. The study of these mechanisms is relatively new in all of these human sciences and the conclusions reached are often only tentative. Nevertheless we believe that the insights from these disciplines illuminate our phenomenon giving some reason and clarity to, as yet, poorly understood issues.

8.7.2 The Non-Specificity of the Phenomenon

It seems fair to draw a second conclusion regarding the non-specificity of the Coping-healing phenomenon in the churches. The study in our mediations has shown that the kind of healing that goes on in the Coping-healing churches is not particularly specific to them. The authors have shown that there is considerable overlap between the kind of healing that goes on in the African Independent churches and the Neopentecostal churches with that which occurs in other kinds of folk healing, shamanistic healing, spiritualist healing, psychosomatic positive thinking healing, as well as other health and healing practices. This is true both with regard to the type of illness healed as well as the mechanisms operating in the healing process.

Clearly any claim that this ministry is a specific one linked to particular confessions of faith and specific worshipping communities could not be accepted. It is more reasonable to suggest that this ministry is rather a tapping into the methods of psycho-somatic, cultural and folk healing within particular theological interpretative keys.

8.7.3 The Role of the Theological Key

It seems that the most evident factor which renders the Coping-healing phenomenon specific, is the use of a particular theological key or framework to experience, understand and interpret it. The ministry occurs within an experience of a confession of faith which re-orientates and redefines what is happening. It is this factor which introduces an element of specificity. For Christians, the whole of life is called to be lived within this re-interpretation and in this way, the ministry is a legitimate living out of the gospel and the Church's missionary mandate. Within this understanding, God's intervention in human life is a natural event. The Holy Spirit dwells amongst Christians and within the Church, having a marked effect on life. The Coping-healing ministry can thus be understood as a manifestation of the attempt to extend that mandate into a new or forgotten dimension of Christian healing. Such a dimension can be seen as a complement to the more current expressions of healing in the Church's medical mission seen in hospitals and clinics. Also important here is the fact that the cultural trapping for this ministry seems not to be in "modern" Western culture (where the hospital model would find its roots) but rather in the contemporary eclectic "post-modern" emerging culture where a re-appropriation or integration of other historical (Western) and geographical (non-Western) cultural expressions is occurring. We will say more of this in our chapter on inculturation and healing.

8.7.4 An Unexplained Remnant

We acknowledge the existence of the mysterious within this phenomenon. Many authors have pointed to verified, unexplained forces and unusual manifestations of healings and healing powers. Two approaches are offered by the authors presented in dealing with this fact. The first is to consider the powers and forces as natural but part of the natural world which we have not yet understood. The second approach is to consider them as spiritual in nature, either linked to God or to other spiritual forces. Here is the closest we come to direct spiritual intervention in a way which does not appear to be normal. This is a question which our work has not answered and it is necessary to indicate this as a recognised, albeit rather rare, element of the Coping-healing phenomenon.

8.7.5 Factors and Elements in the Coping-Healing Phenomenon

In chapters two to seven we indicate the elements which make up the Coping-healing phenomenon and the factors which operate within it. Clearly this process was already the beginnings of a description and as the elements or fac-

	Psycho-Medical Mediation	Anthropological Mediation	Sociological Mediation	Philosophical Mediation	Theological Mediation
Organic Factors	-biological dysfunction -infection	-specific culture organic disease	-socio-specific organic disease		
Cultural Factors	-role of culture in disease and illness	-illness as cultural construct -culture bound syndromes		-role of world-view in illness determination -role of lang-uage in illness determination	
Emotional Factors	-stress and psychosomatic illness	-symbols of illness -culturally caused psycho-somatic illness			
Identity Factors	-psychogenic illness		-illness as social deviance		-sin as illness causative
Contextual Factors			-illness as social deprivation -illness as social dis-organisation		-Evil, Satan and demons as illness causative

Fig. 8.1 Factors Operating in Illness Causation

tors emerged through the various mediations so another part of the description was achieved. In this chapter we have tried to distil out the essential parts of this description. At the risk of reductionism, we think that it is useful to attempt to tabulate some of these factors. In fig. 8.1 we have attempted to indicate the major factors operating in illness causation as revealed by our five mediations. In fig. 8.2 we show the major factors operating in the healing process.

The tables are meant to be read in reference to the headings of the various sections within this chapter where we have attempted to abstract the major conclusions of chapters three to seven. In fig. 8.1 we indicate that the theological mediation is generally open to accept scientific factors without concerning itself with them since they are usually considered to fall outside its competence. We have also attempted to box together factors having some commonality across the different mediations. These figures then provide us with a useful, though perhaps simplistic, indication of the make-up of the Coping-healing phenomenon we have been describing. The mediations (columns) indicate something of the internal structure of the phenomenon as does the attempt to box together some common factors across the mediations (the rows).

8.7.6 Other Relationships Between Elements of the Healing Process

Figs. 8.1 and 8.2 help us to explore in a tentative way, other possible relationships between essences which may not have appeared before: part of the phenomenological method. This is the purpose of our attempts to box together similar factors across the mediations. Thus cultural factors operating in both illness causation and healing are indicated in all the mediations. The role of emotions in the healing process has psycho-medical and anthropological dimensions to it. Persuasion factors in the healing process appear to have psycho-medical, anthropological and theological dimensions to them.

The importance of identity reconstruction in the healing process both on a personal and social level has psycho-medical, anthropological and sociological dimensions to it. The importance of success factors in healing are dealt with in both the psycho-medical and anthropological mediations whereas the importance of healing as meeting people's needs especially in times of crisis appear in the anthropological and socio-economic mediations. Clearly some factors are specific to the particular mediation concerned and these have been indicated where necessary.

The appearance of factors across the mediations clearly lends weight to their importance and so it is perhaps useful to list these factors which are operating broadly enough within the phenomenon to manifest themselves through more than one epistemological lens. We can say that these factors play a large role in the Coping-healing phenomenon in the churches.

- Cultural Factors (5 mediations)
- Identity Factors (4 mediations)
- Success Factors (3 mediations)
- Persuasion Factors (3 mediations)
- Emotional Factors (2 mediations)
- Adaptation and Needs Factors (2 mediations)

8.7.7 The Cultural Factor

One important fact which has emerged from our study is the predominance of the cultural factor in the healing process. Its role has emerged in differing forms within each of the five mediations. It is clearly a major factor in the Coping-healing phenomenon. In our own theological reflection and judgement on this phenomenon we intend to pursue this cultural factor in some depth. As we already indicated in the first chapter it is our view that "the healing ministry in

	Psycho-Medical Mediation	Anthropological Mediation
Cultural Factors	-Role of Culture -sharing of culture -naming of the illness -quality of the therapeutic relationship	-shared world-view and explanatory model -positive explanatory model of health
Emotional Factors	-expression of emotions and catharsis	-attaching emotions to symbols -symbol manipulation as emotion manipulation -role of symbols in healing: construction of cultural healing myth
Persuasion Factors	-suggestion and psychosomatic mechanisms	-role of persuading the sick person to believe in the cultural myth and the health symbol
Identity Factors	-status of the healer -consciousness, re-experiencing & identity change	-identity change in accepting cultural myth and new healthy (saved) lifestyle
Success Factors	-provision of success experiences -attitude of patient	-meet affirmation and other cultural needs
Contextual Factors	-availability of services	-restoring disturbed relationships -move to interiority in times of crisis -healing churches as adaptive structures which help people cope
Other Factors	-personality type of sick person -physico-chemical processes -unknown factors	

Fig. 8.2 Factors Operating in the Healing Process

Sociological Mediation	**Philosophical Mediation**	**Theological Mediation**
-Healing as fulfilling cultural and social deprivation and deviance	-shared world-view as essential in healing -healing as coming to understand the illness -healing as release from meaninglessness	-healing and the Church: role of cultural factors
		-Healing and faith: faith in faith or faith in God?
		-Healing as good news.
-healing as personal and social reconstruction		-healing and conversion -healing and faith
-help group feel good and pure in an impure society -healing as search for stability in instability		-prosperity gospel -healing as blessing
-healing as responding to deprivation and fulfilling deprivation needs -social role of healing churches: do they heal society		
	-epistemology of divining and diagnosis -linguistic understandings of "power" and "life" in healing	-Healing and the Father: -His power -His freedom -Healing and Jesus: -power of the cross -wounded healer -good shepherd -Healing and the Holy Spirit: -Spirit heals today -*uMoya* and the Holy Spirit -Healing and the Church -part of the Church's mission -importance of community dimension -Healing and faith

the church . . . can be best understood by means of a cultural analysis of the South African context." Our subsequent analysis has indeed borne out the necessity of a cultural approach. As we intimated above, we believe that the cultural paradigm within which the Coping-healing ministry is emerging is the post-modern cultural paradigm as opposed to the modern paradigm which gave rise to the Church's medical ministry as its healing ministry.

The theological key we choose is that of inculturation as indicated in chapter one and it is to this task that we now turn. Inculturation implies a theological approach starting from culture. This has been an abused and neglected area in South African theology. Abused in its appropriation by apartheid theological ideologues and neglected by others precisely because of an antipathy to the caricatured understandings of culture which emerged. Nevertheless the role of culture is becoming more and more important in theology today amongst both Protestants and Catholics (Ch 1 nn. 4,6) as a growing explicitation of what was often implicit takes place. Our first task then is to re-appropriate the understanding of culture in a way which will help our theological discourse and which will be true to current anthropology. This, then, is the task in our next chapter.

Chapter 9

Towards an Understanding of Culture which can Inform a Theology of Inculturation

9.1 Introduction

The theological model which will encapsulate our theological judgement on the Coping-healing ministry finds its interface with the mediated phenomenon in the notion of culture. The mediations in part II have indicated the commonality of the cultural dimension throughout and it is this dimension which provides the largest door through to our judgement. However if culture is our door, it may also be a trapdoor leading into a hall of mirrors which need to be negotiated carefully if we are to arrive on the other side. The purpose of this chapter is to negotiate the pathway that is culture, noting the abberations, illusions, confusion and obfuscations which abound around the term. We aim to provide a simple map of culture as it is discoursed in the South African context in order to arrive at an understanding which will validly inform the theology of inculturation which is to be the framework of our theological judgement on the Coping-healing phenomenon.

There are four steps in our mapping process. Firstly we will indicate some of the popular uses of the term culture in South Africa today. After a shaky past, the term is becoming more fashionable although it is used in many diverse senses. These will be indicated to avoid subsequent confusion. Our second step will be to provide a brief overview of some of the current (and varied) academic understandings abstracted from recent South African literature in the various fields and disciplines which operate the term. The aim of the first two steps is to provide the context within which an adequate understanding of culture informing theological anthropology may emerge. It is an attempt to indicate, if you will, the South African culture of "culture". From here we move to our third step, which is to indicate some of the important understandings of culture which are emerging in theological anthropology. Finally we hope to synthesise the elements of our own understanding of culture: adopted to inform the model of inculturation which will be developed in the next chapter.

9.2 Popular Usage of "Culture" in South Africa Today

9.2.1 Culture as "The Arts"

Reference to any South African newspaper will illustrate this usage of the term. Culture here is seen to refer to "song, dance and painting, that sort of thing" (New Nation 1992a:13). Within this general understanding, Tomaselli (1992:61) sees two approaches. On the one hand culture is seen as " 'improving the mind' during leisure time, that is paradoxically, mainly the privilege of the ruling classes". Culture is what the ruling classes do in their free time and its pursuit is considered the finer aspect of the "civilisation" that they represent. Culture columns of the English press aimed at Whites would pursue this understanding of culture in their reviews of theatre, ballet, opera, literature, Fine Art and so on, comparing the situation here to the standard at the metropole (New York, London or Paris).

Events in the latter part of the internal liberation struggle in South Africa have shown how theatre, dance, music, literature and other forms of the arts have participated in forming the consciousness and solidarity of the oppressed. This emergence of culture yardsticked to the process of socio-political change and struggle from below as well as to local forms and criteria in performance has clearly given culture-as-the-arts a new meaning. "Culture in this paradigm, then, has to do with making and contesting meanings, making sense of material conditions and offering ways of coping with and overcoming oppression" (Tomaselli 1992:61). Culture, then, is seen as an expression of the hopes, aspirations and struggle of a people engaged in a process of socio-political change. It is an articulation of the conscious and unconscious elements of a community's self understanding and it succeeds when it mirrors that reality. Culture is understood in this way in newspapers like New Nation and in the ANC's Department of Arts and Culture (ANC 1990:43).

9.2.2 Culture as The People

The many years of apartheid socialisation as well as the effects of anthropological notions of culture as *ethnos*[1] has taken its toll in the popular South African usage of the term culture. South Africa is popularly seen as made up of a number of "cultural groups" which more or less coincide with the ethnic groups of apartheid ideology. The official year book of the Republic of South Africa explains as follows:

> Cultural diversity is an everyday reality within the South African context. This can be attributed to the complexity of the country's population, since many cultural groups have immigrated to South Africa over the years, introducing their traditions in the process. These cultural heritages are mutually respected and there is extensive communication and cultural interchange, although each cultural group is still clearly distinguishable. [Kayter 1992: 27]

This leads to a common popular usage (across the socio-political spectrum) of terms such as Zulu culture, Xhosa culture, Indian culture, Afrikaner culture, and so on. South Africa is seen as being made up of many cultures or as a "multicultural" reality. "Coloureds", however, in popular language, are not considered to have a culture - a source of much distress to many of them.

Within this context the whole question of "intercultural" communication and relationships becomes important. As well as this, however, an important question is currently being raised regarding the issue of a common South African culture. Positions on this question vary enormously. The official 1991 government line suggests that:

> Owing to the disparate cultural backgrounds of the various peoples of South Africa, there is no uniform, distinctive South African culture as such, but rather a rich conglomeration of cultures reflecting the diversity of the population.
>
> [S.A.C.S. 1991:n.p]

On the other hand, organisations such as Azapo call for "the building of a National culture" (Streek 1990:2). Indeed liberation is seen to be "about the creation of one culture and one history by one people in one country under the same set of material conditions" (:23). Between these two extremes, we note the attempt to look for signs of commonality emerging as a result of the process of socio-political change currently underway. It is suggested that one can detect the emergence of a set of common values which could form the basis of a future South African culture.

> The task of upholding the peace cannot be approached without examining the underlying questions of the individual's relationship with the state and this, in turn, has compelled a commitment to a set of core values. From all quarters of the political compass, South Africans are converging on the belief that in so deeply divided a society only the tolerance of diversity, underpinned by the protection of the individual, can offer a shield against the centrifugal forces of communal violence.
>
> [Sunday Times 18 Aug. 1991:20]

The article uses the National Peace Accord[2] as a practical expression of these values. The Centre for Contextual Hermeneutics at Stellenbosch University attempts to indicate a set of social values around which a future non-racial South Africa could emerge. They suggest that both Black and White people in South Africa are already articulating aspirations which "arise from values which do not differ significantly from so-called 'common Western values'" (Lategan et al 1990:ii).

The commonality observed by the Sunday Times and the Stellenbosch project seem to revolve around traditional, liberal, Western values based on individual human rights. The Sunday Times lauds this apparent convergence as "a matter of rare satisfaction to South Africa's tiny, oft defeated, usually self deprecatory, liberal community" (Sunday Times 1991:20). Not everyone would see the commonality in liberalism

9.2.3 Culture as Attitude Formation Describer

The discourse on values within culture leads us onto another popular understanding of the term which is becoming ever more prevalent in the media. This is the use of the phrase "culture of . . ." when attempting to describe a process of attitude formation which is going on in society. Examples of this neologism are boundless as any perusal of the local press will show. We are encouraged to move towards a "culture of democracy"[3], a "culture of tolerance", a "culture of justice"[4], a "peace culture" or "culture of peace"[5], a "culture of learning"[6] and an "entrepreneurial culture"[7] in South Africa. Many other examples could be quoted.

These expressions refer to a process of internalisation of values aspired to within the emerging new cultural framework. The term is also used to refer to negative attitudes or "disvalues", as I will call them, which have emerged in the present society. On the question, for example, of the restructuring of education in a New South Africa, some in the ANC point to the danger of following the example of the United States "where (black) inner city schools foster a culture of deprivation while the rich (white) suburbs provide the tax basis for decent education" (ANC 1990:22). Similarly, terms such as "culture of recklessness and resistance"[8], a "culture of exile"[9], and "culture of violence"[10] are used to refer to unacceptable emerging attitudes within society. Manganyi (1981:67) refers to the "culture of the gun and prayer" as the prevailing mindset of the early White settlers in South Africa. And Challenge magazine, in an article on wife beating, exhorts women to speak out and stand up for their rights since "The culture of silence must be broken" (Dangor 1992:4).

The neologism "culture of . . ." seems to wish to express two basic realities: an attitude (mind-set) as an expression of a value or "disvalue" on the one hand, and a historical process of transformation on the other as society moves towards the attitude referred to. It is a recognition of the historical groundedness of attitudes in tradition, history and experience. It also expresses a *telos* or goal for the historical process in terms of the value to aim for or the disvalue to move away from.

9.3 Academic Understandings of Culture in South Africa

The surge of academic interest in culture and the cultural is a major feature of recent South African studies in many fields. There seem to be two major reasons for this. The first relates to a general upsurge of interest in cultural studies internationally especially in the growth of semiotics within cultural anthropology, media, and cultural and literacy studies. The second relates to the role of the cultural as expressed in dance, drama, music and art in the liberation struggle. The effectiveness of this role in South Africa is of particular interest to academics who had severely discounted this dimension in early social analyses of the South African Context (Clingman 1991; Tomaselli 1987).

This increased interest has led to an examination of the notion of "culture" in general and a recognition of the multifacetedness of its nature. Characteristically, this has led to the emergence of conflict amongst academics regarding the nature, meaning and dynamic of culture so that "what we are witnessing is a conflict over the very *definition* of culture and of what it can be" (Clingman 1991:Introduction n.p.).[11] In order to inform our own notion of culture we need to unravel some of the strands which are pulling on the knot of culture to identify some of the underlying forces which are pulling them taut.

9.3.1 Culture as Volkekunde

The apparent villain of the piece is the understanding of culture linked with *ethnos* and nation as developed by Afrikaner Nationalist ideologues Eiselen, Coertze, Diedericks and Cronje as based on the ideas of Kuyper, Fichte and Shirokogoroff (Sharp 1981). In this understanding, culture is linked with clearly identifiable bounded groups. Culture is somehow seen as a measure of the distinctiveness of human groupings.

> Ethnos theory starts with the proposition that mankind is divided into *volke* (nations, peoples) and that each *volk* has its own particular culture, which may change but always remains authentic to the group in question. The entity comprising a group and its culture is an ethnos, which, viewed over time and in relation to its physical and social environment, forms a life-process within which individuals exist. An individual is born into a particular *volk*; its members are socialized into its attendant culture; therefore they acquire a *volkspersoonlikheid* (a volk-personality). It follows that the most important influence on an individual's behaviour in any social context is his ethnos membership. [Sharp 1981:19]

A country like South Africa is seen as being composed of a number of these ethnic groups: a number of cultures. A major question then clearly revolves around the relationship between these groups living together in one country. Here the concept of "acculturation", understood in a particular way, is employed and a number of factors are indicated which influence these relationships (Sharp 1981:24).[12] In its earlier form, *Volkekunde* argued for a genetic dimension to culture expressed in physical and mental characteristics and the "level of civilisation which the ethnos has attained" (Sharp 1981:25). However this element seems to be discarded by later authors in the discipline.

The influence of the *Volkekunde* understanding has been immense in South African society. It informs the vocabulary and behaviour of many who would consider themselves fundamentally opposed to Afrikaner Nationalist ideology and forms part of the under the surface rhetoric of many South Africans of all walks of life. Groupness and discreteness is part of South African self-understanding today however much lip service may be paid to visions of non-racialism and common nationhood. Apartheid has socialised all the peoples to greater and lesser degrees into this mindset and behaviour.

9.3.2 Culture and Groups (Continued)

The identification of culture and group which gives rise to the model of South Africa as an agglomeration of different cultural groupings is not limited to academics of the *Volkekunde* persuasion. It also crops up in the writings of

South African academics of widely differing backgrounds and persuasions. Thus we might perhaps expect that the "standard" South African definition of culture as provided by the UNISA[13] study guide in socio-cultural anthropology in 1988 suggests that "culture . . . includes all the standardized mental and material products of a *particular group* of people" (Jonas and De Beer 1988:7) (my emphasis). However similar understandings emerge in traditionally more "liberal" forums. In a University of Cape Town summer school focusing on "Group identity and National interests",[14] Prof. Johannes Degenaar of Stellenbosch quotes Harvard scholar Nathan Glazer as follows:

> Nathan Glazer's thinking is representative of the new awareness of the role of ethnicity in politics. The term 'ethnic' refers to "a social group which consciously shares some aspects of a *common culture* and is defined primarily by descent" (Glazer, 1975:8) (My Emphasis). [Degenaar 1980:33]

Writing from a South African liberal perspective, we note that Van Zyl Slabbert and Welsh (1979) in their analysis of possible power sharing options in a future South Africa begin with the following social analysis:

> For purposes of this analysis we define an ethnic group in the broadest of terms as group that is bounded off from other comparable groups or population categories in the society by a sense of its difference, which may consist in some combination of a real or mythical ancestry and a common culture and experience.
> [Van Zyl Slabbert & Welsh 1979:10]

More radical South African authors have also operated this understanding of culture. Rick Turner's seminal work on participatory democracy (1972, 1980) deals with the question of culture and conflict. However the notion of culture he adopts is also tied to that of group so that the conflict is between the cultures, races or groups and is explained within the Marxist key of economic and power interests.

> Cultural, racial, or religious differences, per se, are not a cause for conflict. They only become significant when these differences overlap with other significant differences of interest . . . Nor do I mean to deny that the co-existence of different language, cultural, and religious groups can pose certain political problems . . . But these kinds of conflicts are of a very secondary nature as compared to the major black-white confrontation over wealth. [Turner 1980:32]

Finally we note that some Black theologians also operate a notion of culture as group in their analyses. Thus Dwane (1988:19) in an article on the relationship of the gospel to culture, informs us that "culture is the expression of group loyalty, a common identity, and shared memories and ideals." Tlhagale in an article on Transracial Communication suggests that:

> The preservation of group identity is closely related to the issue of culture in South Africa where each group has its own traditions, language, customs, socio-political institutions and a collective historical experience. In order to survive, each group should preserve its own culture. [Tlhagale 1983:113]

Clearly the above rapid survey indicates that the correlation of culture and group is widespread in the South African academe indicating the perseverance of an important South African understanding of this term throughout the society.

9.3.3 Culture in South African Social Anthropology

In his inaugural lecture as Professor of social anthropology at the University of Cape Town, Martin West (1979:3) observed that "Social anthropologists see culture as a means to ends." It sees the cultural as the framework within which human behaviour as social relationships and social institutions can be explained. Since human behaviour changes over time, culture is seen to have a fluid dimension. West contrasts social anthropology in South Africa with what he calls "Cultural Anthropology" in South Africa. For him this latter is anthropology based on *Volkekunde* to which he reacts very negatively. He is also quite negative about notions of culture which are linked to an "interest in language and to structuralism of the Levi-Straussian type". He suggests that this is an unfruitful area for South African anthropology being at best an "arcane pursuit of little relevance to the modern world with its rapid changes" a prophecy which was to prove alarmingly off the mark.

Mary De Haas[15] stresses that culture is "only a theoretical construct, a tool used by anthropologists to describe and analyze what is taking place in society" (De Haas 1989:2). She notes that so-called cultural groups like the Zulu, Xhosa, Sotho, Tswana and so on, are merely constructs placed on the people by nineteenth century anthropologists which were then subsequently used by politicians in a kind of divide and rule policy. These groups, divided on a linguistic basis, have much cultural uniformity between them and also many cultural differences within them. Culture tends to be situational in nature "that is people everywhere operate their lives through drawing on different sets of norms and values which are appropriate to specific situations, to different spheres of their lives" (:7). These sets of norms and values operate as structural sets within which people live.

9.3.4 Culture as Structure

The structuralist position on culture is reflected in the work of Levi-Strauss. Its influence on cultural studies in South Africa has been minimal. Muller and Tomaselli (1989) suggest that it was imported into South Africa as a form of pessimistic Althusserianism used by "historians and historical sociologists who sought explanation for the quiescence in popular resistance of the 1960's" (Muller & Tomaselli 1989:311). "Structuralism holds that individuals can only live and experience conditions in and through categories, classifications and frameworks of culture" (Tomaselli 1987:2). Its value is that it provides an analytic tool for understanding human behaviour in a particular context and for comparing peoples in differing contexts. Its weakness is that it offers a static view of society - a weakness which was startlingly evident in the South African context which saw Althusser's views propagated in the academe whilst society was involved in a process of massive change in which the cultural played a major role.

9.3.5 *Culture as Praxis*

A large number of South African authors point to the dynamic nature of culture in the process of social transformation. They adopt a "culturalist" position indicating that culture has a dynamic component of process and transformation to it. Here culture, largely perceived as the arts, is seen as a means of consciousness raising: "for us culture must be a weapon that we use effectively to raise the awareness of people about their sufferings" (Muller and Tomaselli 1989:315).[16]

Steadman (1988) has analyzed this mobilisation of the arts and suggests that it is rooted in both aesthetic and social factors which lead to the emergence of a "popular culture" which is an expression of resistance to and rejection of the perceived dominant culture. The socio-political *status quo* forms both the framework and the content of the new resisting culture so that "what defines popular culture is its relation to a dominant culture . . . Popular culture feeds off the dominant culture [and] . . . is therefore defined in a continual dialectical relationship with the cultural forms of the dominant group" (Steadman 1988:114). This is expressed in the aesthetic root as a "rejection of the hegemony of Anglo-American artistic norms and values" (:114). Thus popular dance, theatre, music and art deal with the same situations and socio-political issues but from the experience and world-view, and within the artistic forms, of the people they represent: "the people".

Clingman suggests that the relationship between culture and politics expressed through praxis as transformation may be applied to understandings of culture which transcend "the arts". In a diverse collection of historical, cultural and political studies edited by him he notes that:

> the essays show the centrality of cultural politics and political culture both within academic study and in South African existence and struggle today. Furthermore, they show part of the legacy which has *led* to that struggle and to its very *forms* of current enaction. The paradox is this: that scholarly studies as diverse and (perhaps) apparently arcane as this are connected at deeper levels not only with one another but with the prevailing forms of cultural and political activity in South Africa at large.
>
> [Clingman 1991:n.p.] (16)

Clingman uses the notion of "repertoire", borrowed from the arts, as a guiding concept which can inform the behaviour of people in situations as diverse as gang subcultures, student forms of protest, music groups and traditional dress. The repertoire forms a kind of historically developed cultural matrix which informs social behaviour patterns. Groups of people develop structured ways of responding to particular situations which are triggered by the repetition of the situation or ones analogous to it. These patterned responses are often symbolic of deeper and more traumatic situations which are less easily dealt with. Thus the patterned response of food riots in boarding schools as researched by Hyslop (1991) is also a protest against the society and oppression within it as a whole.

Other Black authors have referred to this culture from the underside. Manganyi (1981:68) refers to this "protest culture" as "in important respects a survival kit". Mosala (1989:2) suggests that "one of the critical tasks of black theology would be to work toward the cultural autonomy of black people . . . creating autonomous weapons of social and cultural struggle." The dynamic category of struggle (in the Marxian sense) is seen, by him, as the major hermeneutic key for culture (:9). Similarly Goba (1988:13) suggests that theology can only respond to the "socio-cultural revolution going on in Africa" when it becomes "cultural revolutionary praxis".

> The point which needs to be emphasized is that our cultural experience has not been static or for that matter disappeared into oblivion. Rather there has been an emergence of dynamic cultural experience grounded in the immediate past and grappling with the present contemporary situation. Our culture, in other words, provides an orbit of meaning, one which synthesizes our past and present. It is a kind of a dialectical process which affirms and negates certain crucial and unimportant aspects of our cultural experience. [Goba 1988:13-14]

It is interesting to note how a similar type of culturalism has also informed the emergence of Afrikaner hegemony through organisations like the Broederbond, FAK, SABRA, AHI [17] and so forth (cf. Muller & Tomaselli 1989:306, 315).

9.3.6 Culture and Semiotics in South Africa

Tomaselli (1986:3) and others [18] in his Contemporary Cultural Studies Unit at Natal University cite "Richard Johnson's landmark statement 'Neither structuralism nor culturalism will do'" as they present their own theory of culture which rests largely on the semiotic model of the American anthropologist Charles Pierce. Pierce's semiotic model is preferred to those of the Europeans, De Saussure and Barthes since, besides the subject/object dimensions of sign as signifier and signified, it also includes a historical dimension to it understood as habits (Tomaselli and Shepperson 1991:4-8). Such an approach provides a way of analysing meaning in terms of processes of signification which describe and predict the "social responses of particular groups to specific historical conditions in all their meaningful particularity" (Tomaselli 1988:38). These processes can be analyzed into a network of historically generated signs accepted by a group of people (the signifiers) as referring to specific realities (the signified). Tomaselli defines culture as:

> the ensemble of meaningful practices and 'uniformities of behaviour' through which self-defined groups within or across social classes express themselves in a unique way or locate themselves within an identifiable 'field of significations'. It is the process which informs the way meanings and definitions are socially constructed and historically transformed by social actors themselves. Cultures are distinguished in terms of differing responses to the same social, material and environmental conditions. Culture is not a static or even a necessarily completely coherent phenomenon: it is subject to change, fragmentation, reformulation. It is both adaptive, offering ways of coping and making sense, and strategic, capable of being mobilised for political, economic and social ends. Culture may also be limiting, reducing awareness of potential options. [Tomaselli 1988:39]

This cumbersome definition attempts to root culture in social practice and expression in an attempt to incorporate an ontological dimension to the epistemological one emphasised by semioticians such as Geertz who restrict culture to patterns of meaning which inform communication, knowledge and attitudes.[19] Tomaselli's definition allows him to adopt a "historical realist" approach to people and their condition.

> We want to be able to make sense out of the stories told by the women, the children, the aged, and those disabled by war, famine or poverty, who might want to motivate a different order in the world. More, we in the privileged reaches of higher education must learn a whole new language if we are to be able to negotiate relevant new ways of living with and for these people. They and we have to talk about *real* action in real situations so that some kind of future is possible which will be a result of something done by themselves within their own contexts.
>
> [Tomaselli and Shepperson 1991:10]

Tomaselli's project is to centre culture as a site of struggle through which a process of transformation to a better world may occur. Within his Marxian framework he chooses the underclass of society as the agent of this transformation and cultural studies examine the significations of the processes in this struggle.

9.3.7 The Common Culture Discourse

Some academics are also exploring the emergence of a common culture within the "New" South African societal paradigm. The Centre of Contextual Hermeneutics at Stellenbosch aims is "to contribute to the development of a common loyalty in South Africa based on commonly accepted social values." (CCH n.d:1). This somewhat artificial task is seen in terms of a subscription "to the ideal of a democratic culture in which race is not a determining factor and in which universally accepted human rights are upheld" (:1).

The values examined and accepted by the centre seem to revolve around those of the liberal humanism of Europe and the United States and one is reminded of Manganyi's comment in this regard.

> The white geo-political identity and its exclusive cultural idiom is successful in so far as it can assert itself in terms of its military power, the potential vitality of its economic and technological advances, the visibility of its secular shrines and the diminishing power of its psycho-social dominance of the blacks. What we blacks absorb from this culture are not white South African cultural specifics but universals from such imperialistic cultures as that of the United States. What remains of the local variation of Western culture is soured for us by its intransigent preoccupation with exclusion and self-preservation. [Manganyi 1981:68]

De Haas (1989:8) attempts to indicate elements of such a common culture from a descriptive rather than a prescriptive perspective. She suggests that "there are *far more* commonalities, based on common interests, common belief systems (e.g. Christianity), common value systems (political, educational, consumerist) than there are differences, between whites and blacks." Participation in the economic sector through work and consumerism and access to the mass media also enhance the emergence of common lifestyles and value systems.

The South African (predominantly White) predilection for emphasising differences has tended to mask the commonalities which already exist. These commonalities form the basis for the emergence of a South African culture. De Haas also notes that culture has a strong situational dimension to it and that people operate out of differing cultural frameworks depending on the situation in which they find themselves.

In a series of twelve theses which express "value-terms required to measure any path to the creation of genuine nationhood in an embattled and deeply divided South Africa", Cochrane (1991) attempts to indicate the parameters of "national culture" necessary for the reconstruction of national life: "the regeneration of a meaningful common life for all" (:21). Elements of such a national construction process would include, the following:

- freedom for all persons and life worlds as constitutive.
- allowal of the suppressed voices of the past to emerge as constitutive of public discourse.
- respect for the individual within the plurality of world-views.
- acceptance of the plurality of life-world in society and the development of mechanisms for sustaining a unity within the plurality.
- an inclusivist rather than exclusivist ethic.
- accountability within power structures.

The attempt by academics to both describe and prescribe commonalities within South African society indicate the importance of the discourse on a common culture. Clearly such a discourse is only beginning but as it starts, it describes the pathways which map out the journey that the nation is being ever more urgently called to make.

Unfortunately, however, many of the commonalities which exist amongst South Africans are not so positive and reflect a socialisation into "disvalues" rather than values. We have already noted the terms "culture of deprivation", "culture of recklessness", "culture of exile", and "culture of violence" in this regard. Many other commonalities reflecting this negative side could be found. They reflect the history of a dehumanising social context, a context which has seen the emergence of some of the world's highest rates of such social ills as murder, suicide, violence, divorce and even road accidents. This reflects something of the dark side of the emerging South African culture, a culture which is in need of healing and saving.

9.4 Culture in Theological Anthropology

The contributions of Cochrane (1991) and the Centre for Cultural Hermeneutics (CCH) presented in the last section are written within a theological framework. The role and understanding of culture within theological anthropology impinges directly upon our own aim of developing an understanding of culture which will inform our own theological judgement on the Coping-healing phenomenon. The task of this section will be to present some of the more important contributions to this discourse in recent times. Clearly we do not aim to do justice to this vast field here. Rather, we hope to indicate some of the major contemporary contributions to the cultural discourse in theological anthropology. Specifically, we examine seven sources which provide an overview of different approaches to this issue from different traditional, and contextual standpoints.

9.4.1 The Contribution of Richard Niebuhr

In Niebuhr's (1951) classic work, an early attempt is made to explore the relationship between Christ and culture. Niebuhr understands culture as an "environment" for humankind, superimposed on the natural world. "Culture is the 'artificial, secondary environment' which man superimposes on the natural" (:32). It is through this "environment" that humankind knows nature for "we do not know a nature apart from culture" (:39). Rather than present a formal definition, he draws on the work of Malinowski and Ruth Benedict to describes five characteristics of this human environment which is culture:

- Culture is social and relates to the organisation of people into groups. It is transmitted and received social heritage (:32-33).
- "Culture is human achievement" (:33).
- "Culture is a world of values" (:34).
- "Culture . . . is concerned with the temporal and material realization of values" (:36).
- Culture is pluralistic (:38).

In going on to develop a theological anthropology, he presents the two realities, Christ and culture, and examines their relationship in various theological approaches running from the extremes of Christ and culture being opposed, where culture is identified as the evil of the Johannine "World", to Christ and culture being synonymous where Jesus is seen as the fulfilment of humanity and the summit of culture. He opts for a position between these two seeing Christ as both above culture but operating through it to transform it.

9.4.2 Kraft's Extension of Niebuhr

Charles Kraft (1979:104-115) builds upon Niebuhr's bipolar model finally accepting a synthetic model for theological anthropology as a "God-above-but-through-culture position" (:113). "This model assumes that, though God exists totally outside of culture while humans exist totally within culture, God chooses the cultural milieu in which humans are immersed as the arena of his interaction with people" (:114). In Kraft's model, God is transcendent and absolute. Culture is the

> vehicle or milieu, neutral in essence, though warped by the pervasive influence of human sinfulness . . . in which all encounters with or between human beings take place and in terms of which all human understanding and maturation occur. The human psyche is structured by culture as is every expression of groupness including family, community and church. [Kraft 1979:113]

Consequently the relationship between God and humankind is always a cultural one from the human point of view. Kraft follows the work of Kroeber and Kluckhohn (1952:35) in which culture is understood as patterns of ideas and their attached values which are historically and symbolically derived and transmitted and which determine behaviour. The centre of culture is the world-view understood as "the central systemization of conceptions of reality" (:53). Its role is to explain and evaluate behaviour.

Kraft's analysis provides him with some very useful tools for understanding culture. He distinguishes four component entities of culture. These are "cultural forms", "cultural functions", "cultural meanings" and "cultural uses". "Cultural forms" are the observable parts which make up a culture: the implements, customs, works, and other symbolic forms. Each form serves a particular "cultural function" some of which are universal to all cultures such as the need for food, clothing, shelter and so on whereas others are particular to a society or group such as symbols of identity. One of the important functions of cultural forms is to convey "cultural meaning" since "In many ways 'culture is communication'" (:65).[20] The meaning is attributed to the form by the group through a historical process of comming to understanding. Clearly forms also change through time. "Cultural use" makes the actual involvement of humans in culture more explicit. The cultural forms are used by people and the styles of usage are part of the process of cultural learning. This culturally patterned usage may also have individual variants. Cultural patterning provides a series of boundaries within which forms may be used and comprehended.

Kraft does not adopt a static understanding of culture since he accepts that culture may change and suggests various reference points for such change (Kraft 1979:72-77). He also points to the existence of a human commonality underlying cultural diversity and suggests that this commonality can give some clues regarding the nature of humanity (:84-86). In his view, such commonality can operate on the biological, psychological, spiritual and socio-cultural levels. He posits four categories of common universal human needs which are linked to a set of universal cultural functions. These are biological needs, psychological needs, socio-cultural needs and spiritual needs. These needs are expressed and articulated within the patterning of cultural forms and are thus dependent on the world-view and traditions for their articulation.

9.4.3 Luzbetak's Approach

Luzbetak (1988) has a somewhat a similar approach to Kraft and is included here for the sake of completeness. His analysis is slightly different in that he sees three levels to culture. The first level is that of the culture forms, and provides only an etic superficial understanding of culture as what is observed. The second level is the level of meanings expressed and carried by the forms as determined by the functions of the cultural forms. On a third level Luzbetak moves to the "basic psychology" which manifests the underlying why's of society, the mentality of a people, their world-view, mythology and religion (Luzbetak 1988:223).

Luzbetak (1988:223) sees culture as essentially a system. This system is "strictly speaking . . . restricted to social groups speaking the same language and having more or less similar economic, social and ideological systems". But he also admits of an extended analogical sense to culture where a number of similar cultural systems are related. Western culture, Oriental Culture, and African culture would be examples of the analogical use of the term. In developing a perspective of culture which will inform missiology, he suggests that culture is essentially a "design for living" (:139). This design comprises a plan or blueprint for life consisting of "norms, standards, notions, and beliefs for coping with life" (:156). The design is shared by a group of people and learned by the individual from the society. Thus culture is a societal possession (:172) made up of patterns which guide behaviour and which are transmitted in tradition which is open and adaptive (:172).

9.4.4 The Riano Consultation of WCC

The strength of the approaches of Kraft and Luzbetak is the analysis and understanding of culture which is imported from cultural anthropology and applied to theological anthropology. The weakness, in our opinion, is that they remain within a bipolar paradigm of God and humanity, Christ and culture. The World Council of Churches consultation at Riano in 1984 indicated the weakness of such approaches in its appraisal of the Vancouver 1983 definition of culture.[21] Without themselves giving a definition they concluded as follows: "We agreed on the urgent need to redefine culture and the relation between gospel and culture in a new theological approach . . . [which] has to focus on creation and on the incarnate, suffering and risen Christ" (WCC 1985:264). At the consultation, the Orthodox writers Meyendorff (1985) and Yannoulatos (1985) stress the essential unity of culture with humankind's creation in the image and likeness of God.

> Culture, as an act and attainment of humankind created in the likeness of God, is not outside the rays of the divine energies; it is not unrelated to the breathing of the Spirit who controls all things, "the visible and the invisible." The creative work of people upon nature is a gift, a commandment and a possibility given to the first created couple, a consequence of being "in the likeness of God" (Gen. 5:1). The Orthodox tradition holds that this "likeness" was not lost, nor made useless following the Fall. Thus, humankind remains the recipient of the messages of God's will and of the energies of his Spirit. In the roots of culture there is a gift and a command of God: he gives human beings the right and the possibility to reign over creation (Gen. 1:28-30).
> [Yannoulatos 1985:187]

Meyendorff extends this to the incarnation and the union this creates between the human and the divine.

> If the divine Logos becomes flesh, there is no more and can never be an incompatibility between divinity and humanity. They cease to be mutually exclusive. For us Christians God is not only in heaven, *he is in the flesh*: He is with us first because he is the Logos and model of creation, and second because he became man. In Christ, we see God as the perfect man. Our God is not "somewhere" - in heaven. People have seen him, we see him - in Jesus of Nazareth. [Meyendorff 1985:254]

9.4.5 The Contribution from Roest Crollius

Descriptive understandings of culture, whilst necessary and helpful, are never sufficient for an understanding of culture which will serve theological anthropology. With this observation in mind, Roest Crollius (1980) presents an understanding of culture linked to a theology of the human person. Using the Thomistic anthropology of Rahner (1968) he suggest that "The self-realisation of man in his world will be understood here as culture" (Roest Crollius 1980:259). Self realisation is understood as the actualization of human identity and can be analyzed in three perspectives: The human person as a) Being-in-the-world (:259); as b) Being-with-others-in-the-world. (:260) and as c) transcending the world through his spiritual nature (:261). This three-fold delimitation expresses the fields within which human culture manifests itself. The self-realisation of the human person within and through the world implies a concomitant humanisation of the world expressed in the symbols and forms people create: as work, as community and society, as technology and as "the arts". These symbols and forms are interlinked in an "inherited system of meanings - which are expressions of its finality - embodied in symbols" (:266).

9.4.6 Culture in Local Theology: Robert Schreiter

Schreiter (1985) suggests that certain criteria are necessary for an understanding of culture which will serve the creation of local theology. Since this will be our purpose in chapter eleven when we attempt to articulate the Coping-healing phenomenon within the theological key of inculturation, his comments are most pertinent. Schreiter's theological approach to the study of culture emphasises listening for Christ who is ***already*** present in a culture. This implies a particular focus on "those cultural realities that cluster around the theological concepts of creation, redemption and community" (:40). At the same time such a focus should not be exclusive since in cultural analysis one wishes to avoid a reductionist approach which "concentrate[s] solely on one part of a culture and exclude[s] other parts from consideration [or]. . . see[s] one part of the culture as nothing but another manifestation of some more important part of the culture" (:43). The exclusion of popular piety as a means of dealing with oppression within some forms of liberation theology is given as an example of this, a point which clearly responds to the debate between Schoffeleers and Comaroff noted in chapter eight.

Besides a holistic approach to culture, Schreiter (1985:43) recognises that an adequate cultural approach should also focus on the questions of "the forces that shape identity in a culture" and "the problem of social change". This is because two of the major purposes of local theology are to confirm and describe the identity of the local Church community in terms of group boundary and world-view as well as to render intelligible the dynamics of social change which constantly challenge the same local community. According to Schreiter, a model of culture which can inform local theology needs to include the following parameters:

-listening for Christ already present

-local understandings of creation

-local understandings of community

-A holistic approach to culture

-Indicating identity factors
  - group boundary formation
  - world-view

-Understandings of social change

Schreiter indicates the value of functionalist, ecological, materialist and structuralist approaches to the study of culture but adopts a semiotic approach giving three reasons for its suitability to the construction of local theology.

> First, its interdisciplinary approach and its concern for all dimensions of culture, both verbal and nonverbal, both empirical and non-empirical, represent the kind of holism that is important when it comes to listening to a culture. It allows study of the so-called high cultural elements (art, poetry, music, religious belief) and the so-called popular elements (customs, superstitions), and other elements of the cultural systems (social organization, economic and political organization) in a way that allows them to be seen as interlocking and interdependent. In so doing, it lessens the risk of reductionism and determinism.
>
> Second, its concern for observation of the various sign systems in a culture, and their configuration, allows for a closer look at how the identity of the culture and the identity of members of the culture are constituted. By studying not only the sign systems (which functionalism also does in one kind of way), but the relations among the signs given in the syntactic, semantic, and pragmatic rules, the culture is allowed to emerge in its own configuration, and still be reasonably comprehensive to the outsider. While there has been some argument that semiotics still represents a Western mode of explanation, it is fair to say that the risk of Western ethnocentrism is significantly reduced below the level of other competing explanatory and descriptive possibilities. For this reason, using methods of cultural semiotics seems to provide a better possibility for local communities to describe their own cultural uniqueness, and at the same time to put it into a form that may have a better chance of being intelligible to others.
>
> Third, the concern for patterns of change is very strong in semiotics. Trying to define trajectories of change, the limits of such trajectories in relation to the problems of identity, and the mechanisms whereby cultures cope with chaos and change are all of

> central importance in the investigation. In view of the importance of these areas for local theology, an investigative method which sees change as more than deviance from identity is of importance. [Schreiter 1985:52]

The semiotic approach to culture attempts to create a "semiotic description" of the culture. It does this by identifying "culture texts which is the basic unit of analysis" (Schreiter 1985:61). A culture text is made up of "a series of interlocking signs held together by a set of codes or a common message" (:61) Gestures in ritual are an obvious example of such a text. It then looks at how these texts reinforce group identity, indicate group boundaries or respond to social change.

An analysis of the culture text reveals the signs which make it up and the codes which determine the way the signs are put together. Signs are the bearers of meaning. The codes can be understood as "answering the questions: How are things done?" (Schreiter 1985:67). Codes and signs transmit messages which reveal meaning within the culture. Thus semiotic analysis is concerned with the identification of codes, signs and messages within the culture text. Central to the semiotic approach is the concept of metaphor. Metaphors help to relate signs which would not normally be seen together and so help to weave the fabric of the culture linking it together as a whole. Schreiter gives the examples of Jesus as Son of God or bread becoming the Body of Christ as examples of such metaphorical union (:69). Metaphors operate within "semiotic domains whic Schreiter defines as

> an assemblage of culture texts relating to one set of activities in culture (economic, political, familiar), which are organized together by a single set of messages and metaphoric signs. Often the semiotic domain is governed by what Turner has called a root metaphor, which gives direction to the signs to be included and the codes to be developed. For example, a root metaphor for the economic domain in capitalist societies is the marketplace. [Schreiter 1985:69]

A culture is then understood as "a series of linking (sometimes hierarchically organized) semiotic domains: religious, economic, political, social, sexual, and so on" (Schreiter 1985:69).

Social change is seen as the transformation of sign systems and can occur both through the transformation of the relationship between the sign to the message as well as the transformation of the code which governs the interaction of the signs. This process can occur in two ways, either through the incorporation of new sign codes within existing systems or through a process of conflict where one set of signs is replaced by another. Chidester's (1989) analysis of the world-view of African Indigenous churches in terms of the appropriation of sacred symbols is an attempt to analyze such a process of social change and its effect on world-view. Schreiter outlines four basic rules of transformation which govern semiotic change:

> 1. Change is initiated when a boundary is transgressed. The transgression of a boundary calls for a reorganization of the semiotic domain.

> 2. Because of the binary nature of many signs, depending upon contrastive elements, it is not unusual for a sign to reverse itself in a situation of change. What was good becomes bad, what was dominant becomes recessive.
>
> 3. Structuralism has taught us that two irreconcilable signs can be mediated by a third sign that somehow incorporates the first two. This has also been a common principle in dialectics.
>
> 4. Change can be expressed in the semiotic system by changing either the spatial metaphors or the temporal metaphors. [Schreiter 1985:73]

The understandings of semiotic domain and culture text provide us with a methodology for analysis of the Coping-healing phenomenon where Coping-healing practices can be seen as culture texts operating within various semiotic domains of healing. The link to local theology in Schreiter's work also provides a nexus into the study of inculturation and healing.

9.5 Our Approach to Culture

The purpose of the foregoing complex overview of ways of understanding culture was to show how they can be classified into three main types. The first type comprises those which impinge upon the context within which the Coping-healing phenomenon we have studied has emerged: South African society in general. The second type comprises those understandings of culture which are emerging from the context of the Church in general within ecclesial cultural studies. Our final group comprises those understandings of culture which inform current studies in theological anthropology. They are presented because these are understandings which, in one way or another, interact with or overlap the site of our own study. They are thus important for our study. In indicating an understanding of culture which will inform the rest of this work, we need to take into account the insights of the understandings presented above as well as to highlight the more important contributions which will play a major role in our own understanding of culture. In this way we will take a position within the complex discourse on culture in the South African ecclesial context. Our position identifies the following parameters as central:

1) Culture on the epistemological level is fundamentally communication.
2) Culture on the ontological level is the humanisation of the world.
3) Culture requires a metaphysical dimension which grounds it and which is interpreted as the sanctification of the world.

In choosing these three levels or dimensions we return to the thought of Bernard Lonergan already presented as providing part of the framework within which we are working. In what follows we will try to flesh out these parameters indicating their importance and the way in which the preceding analysis can be incorporated within them.

9.5.1 Culture as Communication

Together with Tomaselli, Kraft, Luzbetak, Schreiter and those who follow a semiotic approach, we affirm that culture is fundamentally communication. Within the South African context we suggest that this approach is, at this time, more important than particularist approaches to culture which search for identity, groups and *ethne*. The réason for this is two-fold. Firstly, it counters the overemphasis which has been give to these particularist approaches and secondly, the current emphasis on social change and crisis within the society is rendering such group understandings of culture relatively ineffective in responding to the current context. This is especially the case when we study phenomena such as the Coping-healing practices which appear to be directly related to such social change, and which are occurring within different groups with apparently different "cultures".

We affirm, then, an understanding of culture as communication and say that people share a culture to the extent that they communicate or understand one another and that they do not share a culture to the extent that they misunderstand and fail to communicate with one another. Such a misunderstanding/understanding paradigm is essential to effectively deal with many of the dynamics which are going on in South Africa today: negotiations, political realignments, economic changes, peace accords, women's issues and so on are all an expression of culture as communication. An analysis of signs, codes, symbol, meaning, culture texts, semiotic domain and the like can indicate the lines and contours of communication and misunderstanding going on. Together with Schreiter we affirm the efficacy of the semiotic model in dealing with the process of social change currently underway in South Africa and of which the Coping-healing phenomenon is one such sign. Within such a framework, what is happening within the Neopentecostal churches, the mainline churches and the AIC's can be linked within a single semiotic domain or better, using the mathematical terminology of Venn diagrams, within a set of overlapping semiotic domains. The signs and symbols which operate within these domains serve to enable the communication of the meaning of life and death, sickness and health, good and evil, truth and lies within a context where communication of these realities has broken down in the lives of the people concerned. This in a very real sense is the role of the Coping-healing practices in this context.

The value of the "culture as communication" model on the epistemological level is that it is able to incorporate the reality that the same sign may signify different realities to different people in different contexts. Even words may be misunderstood and people who think they are sharing a common symbol system such as a language, religion, or behaviour may often misinterpret and misunderstand one another. This apparently obvious statement is very often ignored in basic human relationships leading to much conflict.

9.5.2 Culture as the Humanisation of the World

Together with Roest Crollius, we affirm that descriptive understandings of culture do not suffice. Our understanding of culture should reflect an ontological dimension which tells us something of the human person. Even on the intellectual level, Geertz (1973:76) points out that "the human brain is thoroughly dependent upon cultural resources for its very operation." Roest Crollius (1980:259) describes the ontological dimension of culture as a "single historical process, which is at the same time the self-realisation of man by means of the world and the humanisation of the world through the self realisation of man." Thus we affirm that culture is praxis, both as consciousness raising and as an "arena of social struggle" (Mosala 1985:111). "Culture is not only the outcome of a people's history. It is a determinant of that history . . . Commitment to a people's liberation is reflected by commitment to their culture" (Mosala 1986:98).[22]

We have already noted how popular theatre and other cultural repertoires have played a vital role in consciousness raising and values transformation within the current South African context. The ontological dimension of culture as humanisation indicates and articulates the human values by which such a process is guided. This is the significance of the phrase "culture of . . ." which describes those attitudes (representing values and what we have called "disvalues") which inform the process of human existence within society. It is important to note that the so-called "disvalues" described in terms like "culture of violence, culture of deprivation, culture of exile" express a life style which whilst judged negatively by the commentator is not necessarily seen as such by the perpetrator. One person's disvalue may be someone else's value. The search for common values within a common culture impinges upon this discourse.

It is also on the ontological level that the affirmation of human identity occurs. The need for a group to belong to, and be part of, forms part of what it means to be human. However we also note that the expression and understanding of this reality occurs on the epistemological level. *Volkekunde*, ethnic groups, church denominations and the varying groupings within which identity is expressed are profitably categorised as the symbolic, epistemological expression and understanding of an ontological reality which is human identity. It is the reification of these realities which has obfuscated attempts to understand humanity in the South African context. We note however, with Lonergan, the mutual penetration of the metaphysical, ontological and epistemological dimensions and affirm that the categorisation we adopt is a tool for understanding reality rather than a description of it. The ontological dimension also endorses the value of structural approaches to culture in which the search for common human expression and behaviour is affirmed within cultural plurality. The approach of medical anthropologists (cf. Kleinman 1980; Dow 1986) has indicated the importance of this dimension in any understanding of culture.

In summary then we see that culture on the ontological level affirms the human and ecological process which is the mutual dialectal relationship between humanity and the *oikos* understood as both ecosphere and ecosystem. Within this we may note that culture is intimately human identity and human process; human structure and human expression; human attitude and human attitude judgement; human repertoire and human transformation. Clearly the way such realities are expressed and understood forms the epistemological dimension of this ontological reality.

9.5.3 Culture as Sanctification: the Metaphysical Dimension

Finally we affirm the transcendental dimension of culture as revealed by theological anthropology. We have noted that the metaphysical dimension grounds the ontological and epistemological. It provides the condition for the possibility of the affirmations we make on the ontological and epistemological levels.[23] The metaphysical dimension indicates what is central, what is important and what is basic. It provides the ground upon which the humanisation which is culture occurs and the root metaphors, root values and root meanings from which common understandings can emerge. The process of secularisation and modernity have tended to discount the metaphysical confusing it with the loss of meaning which previous "spiritual" realities have undergone in the modern period. However in a very real sense the modern age has continued to operate out of its own metaphysics: a metaphysics of the physical in which the material has been sacralised whether in Marxist Dialectical and Historical Materialist philosophy or in the sacralising of money, profits and the banks in the West. In both cases science and technology were raised up as the new absolutes, the new panaceas to the human condition and the new solutions to the human problem, a sacralisation out of which they are only haltingly emerging. The sacral as the organiser of being and meaning did not disappear in the modern age but rather changed its guise. Any analysis of culture which discounts it will eventually end up in mere relativism and opinion.

Culture in theological anthropology cannot be seen outside the relationship between God and humankind. This relationship has three essential dimensions: Creation, Redemption and Community. Thus together with Yannoulatos we affirm the "essential unity of culture with humankind's creation in the image and likeness of God." And together with Riano we note that the definition of culture has to "focus on creation and the incarnate, suffering and risen Christ" (WCC 1985:264). This soteriological dimension of culture indicates both the value of suffering and struggle in the redemptive work of Jesus on the Cross and the Father's work of transformation in the Resurrection. The old Pentecostal adage "No Cross, No Crown" expresses a reality of human existence which only the life, death and Resurrection of Jesus can inform sufficiently.

This is so since this reality is lived once again in the human community which is the Body of Christ, the Church. This Body of Christ is called to the same journey as Jesus made; to Good News, crowds following; Journey to Jerusalem, crowds deserting; suffering, death and then Resurrection through the

Father's transforming power. This imitation of Christ is an event in community, for that is where he is found: "when two or three are gathered". Clearly culture is a communal reality as well since there is no individual with a private culture. It is here where culture and Church meet in the following of Christ as his body and it is here in the relationship between Body of Christ: the Church, and culture, that we find a valuable theological key, inculturation, which can help us understand, rationalise and render reasonable, the Coping-healing phenomenon we have studied.

9.5.4 An Emerging South African Culture

Within the understanding of culture presented above we are now in a position to affirm the emergence of a "South African" culture. The tremendous social upheaval that the country is going through in the 1990's is accompanied by changes in modes of relating and communicating as well as in the understanding which is given to the humanisation and sanctification process. Common values and processes are emerging as we have seen above. But the process is also accompanied by the emergence of common understandings and behaviour based upon what we have called "disvalues" or on dehumanisation processes. This could be described as an "anticulture" rather than a culture or a culture in need of redemption. It is a culture in need of healing, a culture in need of transformation. The role that the Church plays in the transformation of culture has been described in terms of the inculturation model. It is also the model we adopt to make our theological judgement on the Coping-healing phenomenon since we wish to ask if the Coping-healing phenomenon is an adequate response to this need for healing. We turn now to an examination of the inculturation model.

Chapter 10

Inculturation as Key to the Theological Judgement

10.1 Introduction

The discourse on culture presented in the last chapter has enabled us to infer three dimensions of an adequate understanding of culture. In indicating the metaphysical dimension as describing or realising the organising, centralising and rooting dimension of culture, we give weight to the transcendental dimension of the human condition. It is clearly here that the discourse on faith finds its own centre especially when expressed as the conversion moment where, in the process of becoming Christian, a person or more importantly a group of people, re-orientates itself, re-grounds itself and, to a certain extent, re-founds itself. Nevertheless we affirm, once more, the mutual interpenetratedeness of the three dimensions which make up our model of culture. Consequently the discourse on faith finds a home within each of the dimensions of communication, humanisation and sanctification since faith penetrates the whole of human life. Indeed the historical journey of a people, which includes such a conversion moment, is a single process which can be described as having two parts. The first part comprises all that is involved in the coming to awareness of the presence of God in Christ as he has been revealed. The second part involves the expression of the effects of this coming to awareness in the life of a community as the consequences of faith affect the behaviour of the community.

The first part is more rightly evangelisation expressed as *Ad Gentes* whereas the second is the concrete expression of faith in community: the emergence of a community of faith, the Church, in a place and time. What we are describing here is the process of the emergence of this local community of faith amongst a people: a people, on a journey. It is a journey in communication and understanding, and in striving to become more fully human. It is a sanctifying journey, in which the sanctification is experienced both as goal and as holy presence. In other words, the journey is a cultural journey. The procession of this journey which leads to the emergence of a local community of faith: a local Church, is what we wish to call "inculturation".

10.2 The Term "Inculturation" in the Literature

The term inculturation is very new in missiology. Its appearance can initially be linked to the attempt to find a model whereby "the Church becomes part of the culture of a people" (Roest Crollius 1978:725). An analogy is made with the process of "enculturation" apparently coined by Herskovits (1952:39) to describe "the aspects of the learning experience which mark off man from other creatures, and by means of which, initially, and in later life, he achieves competence in his culture."[1] The term emerged during the period 1974-1981 when it was the subject of some theological enquiry particularly amongst Jesuits as a result of discussions on the role of culture in the Church in the 32nd General Congregation of the Society of Jesus (Roest Crollius 1978:722).[2] This enquiry culminated in an interdisciplinary seminar on inculturation in Jerusalem in 1981 and the emergence of the series of "Working Papers" on inculturation.[3]

Since then, the theme has been taken up particularly by Catholic missiologists, throughout the world. It has, however, also entered into Protestant missionary discourse so that by 1991, Bosch (1991:447) could say that inculturation "is today one of the most widely used concepts in missiological circles." The rapidity of its dissemination has, however, meant that the term has become multivocal and it will be necessary to indicate something of the multivocality before proceeding to our own understanding.

10.2.1 Bipolarity in the Inculturation Model

Definitions and understandings of inculturation revolve around the dynamic relationship or interpenetration of two elements: a religious one and a worldly one. The latter is normally expressed as "culture" or "cultures" although some authors (cf. Waliggo 1986:13) prefer the term "people". The other pole of the relationship is more problematic being expressed diversely as: the faith (George 1990:124; Shorter 1988:11; Bosch 1991:453 Lineamenta 1990:52)[4]; the Christian message or gospel (Shorter 1988:11, 60; Azevedo 1982:7; Arbuckle 1990:7; CT 53); Jesus Christ (Shorter 1988:61; Okure 1990:59) and the Church (Roest Crollius 1978:725; Mutiso-Mbinda 1986:81; Onwubiko 1992:166; RM 52). Most of these authors nuance the religious pole of the relationship by including more than one of these terms within it and so it is important not to read the understandings expressed above as exclusive. Nevertheless, the choice of theological category to describe the inculturation relationship does involve a theological judgement and leads to theological conclusions in the understanding of the term.

10.2.2 The Subject of the Inculturation Process

Inculturation is always seen as a process and we have commented elsewhere on the importance of the diachronic dimension of the inculturation model against the usually more static approach of most forms of contextualisation (Bate

1991:98-99). However, as with the bipolar model, there is divergence as to the subject of this process. Variously it is seen as the gospel, Christ, Faith, People and the Church. We intend to briefly examine these divergent, though in some ways complementary, approaches.

The Gospel as Subject of the Inculturation Process

Approaches which consider the relationship of the gospel to culture are similar to those which speak of "contextualisation of the gospel" (cf. Bate 1991:88-97). The image here is that of the Incarnation and in this model inculturation becomes evangelisation (De Napoli 1987). This model informed much of the earlier understanding of inculturation before the distinction between inculturation and "evangelisation of cultures" had been clarified. Thus in *Cathechesi Tradendae* (CT 53) Pope John Paul II refers to inculturation as a "neologism . . . [which] expresses very well one factor of the great mystery of the incarnation." He goes on to point to the role of catechesis as evangelisation in bringing "the power of the Gospel into the very heart of culture and cultures" (CT 53.) The relationship with *Evangelii Nuntiandi* on the evangelisation of cultures (EN 20) is clear. The incarnational model appears regularly in papal documents[5] and forms part of John Paul II's understanding of the term "inculturation" which he defines as "the incarnation of the Gospel in native cultures" (SA 21).

In Africa, Theresa Okure leans strongly on this model. Following Sarpong (1988) and the teachings of John Paul II and Paul VI she affirms that "our understanding of the mystery of the Incarnation should serve as the solid foundation for understanding inculturation" (Okure 1990:57). As the Good News of Jesus Christ meets the African reality of peoples of different cultures there is a mutual enrichment which occurs. This meeting and enriching process is what is meant by inculturation. However at the centre of this process is not only the Good News, but Jesus himself.

Jesus Christ as Subject of the Inculturation Process

Okure's incarnational model of inculturation goes beyond the Evangelisation of culture's discourse to posit Jesus Christ as the real subject of inculturation.

> Inculturation functions as the process by which Christ becomes "native to or incarnated in" particular African cultures. Without it Christ remains an outsider or a foreigner to a culture, he does not become a citizen; and then the culture itself cannot be redeemed by him. [Okure 1990:59]

The approach which considers Christ as the subject of the inculturation process is also supported by Shorter (1988:61). Nyamiti's work (1991) focuses on the developments within African Christology in providing understandings of Jesus which relate to African cultural categories. He points out that "christology is the subject which has been most developed in today's African theology" (:3).

This model of inculturation sets itself two tasks. Firstly it attempts to discover the Jesus who is already present in the culture and to allow him to come into view. This is the attempt to allow the risen Christ, who has already redeemed Africa to be manifest from within the traditions, history and culture of the people. The works of Pénoukou (1991), Sanon (1991) and Bujo (1992) would be examples of such an approach. The second task of this model revolves around the attempt to transform the Christ who has been preached within a Western cultural matrix into an African. This is not so much an attempt to express Christ and Christianity within African cultural forms but rather the attempt to ask:

> whether or not any of us wants Christ to assume his or her culture, so as to become substantially part of it, to enrich it and be enriched by it, and transform it from within, so that it can become the Yoruba, the Kikuyu, the Zulu or any other Christianised culture. [Okure 1990:59]

The incarnational and redemptive dimensions of the Christian message both play an essential role in the process of inculturation which has Jesus Christ as its subject. The incarnational dimension expresses the truth of the manifestation of the Fatherhood of God and the brotherhood of Jesus for all peoples and cultures and the kenotic effort required to enable this manifestation. This implies much deconstruction, purifying, clearing away and cleaning up of the structures, vessels and containers which were the vehicles in which the missionaries brought Jesus. These were forms of the missionaries' own experience and articulation of Jesus and were themselves cultural artifacts. This deconstruction process is only a first step in allowing Christ for Africa to emerge. It is also easier said than done and a highly emotive issue, since the missionaries did also bring Jesus and their own faith experience of him. This faith experience has transformed, and continues to transform, the lives of many people. Often the conversion in Africa has meant a rejection of the past and attempts to recover a perceived "pagan" past seem strange to many who have associated Christianity with progress, prosperity and freedom from the curse of magic and spirits.

The redemptive dimension of the Christian message and its role in inculturation implies all that the transformation of the cross means. Incarnation always points to the Cross and the Resurrection. Redemption is won through the power of the Father raising up Jesus on the third day. This central Christological dimension is essential to the understanding of inculturation as the transformation of a people and its culture (Shorter 1988:83). The people and their culture is called to die and rise with Christ in order to become a Christian people: a Christian culture.

The Faith as Subject of Inculturation

Writers with a more Western background tend to this model of inculturation (Shorter 1988:59; George 1990:31;4; Bosch 1991:452). Faith in this sense is described by Shorter (1988:59) as "a religious tradition or affiliation . . . a broad and undefined concept". Traditionally the term has two senses: in its objective sense it refers to the body of truths, practices and traditions as expressed in the Scripture and tradition of the Church's teaching: Scripture, Creeds, Council definitions, Magisterial teaching and so forth. It is a *complexus* of doctrine to which one is called to assent to when making a profession of faith (cf. Livingstone 1977:188). In its second, more subjective sense, it refers to the personal act of assenting to God's presence in one's life. Such an act of faith is the result of grace and is itself a gift of God. It occurs both on the personal and communal level.

Now "faith" in both these senses is seen, in this model, to be in dialogue with the culture of a people. But faith, particularly in the second sense, is also understood as the coming together of the divine and the human in the human response of faith to the divine, of faith which is also itself, in some sense, a divine gift. So it is "the faith" itself, understood in the complexity of both senses, which is called to become a culture. George (1990:40) asserts that "the faith needs to be part of a cultural synthesis" and quotes Pope John Paul II in this regard: "a faith which does not become a culture is a faith not fully received" (:44)[6]. He goes on to define inculturation as "the process by which the faith becomes culture, thereby synthesizing man's entire existence around Christ the wisdom of God" (:44).

The People as Subject of the Inculturation Process

Although it does not appear much in the literature, a model of inculturation which sees "the people" as a theological category as subject of the inculturation process would seem to be useful. This is perhaps more true in South Africa where "the people" as a category already exists both within the religious and non-religious discourse about the human person.

Gaybba (1990) and Nolan (1988) use the concept in the sense of the poor and oppressed: "any exploited group " (Gaybba 1990:68). One may argue that such an exclusive understanding could not inform a theology of inculturation, but a moment's reflection on the meaning of the Incarnation and the Kenosis as well as the declared mission of Jesus (cf Lk 4, Mt 5) indicates the importance of this understanding for any person or group or culture which wishes to be Christian. In a specific reference to inculturation, Waliggo (1986:13) asserts that "Inculturation, therefore, is that movement which aims at making christianity permanent in Africa by making it a people's religion and a way of life which no enemy or hostility can ever succeed in supplanting or weakening." He goes on to affirm that "it is the inculturated christianity that can attempt to give an answer of hope to the anxieties and anguishes of the people of Africa" (:24).

The discourse on "the people" also raises the vexed question of "the people and the peoples" (*ochlos* against *ethne*). Moltmann (1978:100) raises this crucial issue indicating the importance of the emergence of "the people, that collective identity made up of the various nations languages and races . . ." in the Christian discourse. He concludes that "There is hope only in a new collective identity of the people which takes up into itself also the ethnic and religious identities" (:101). It is from such a people that the Church emerges. Indeed it is a Church ***of*** these people rather than one ***for*** them which identifies the true nature of the Church: "The true Church is where Christ is . . . His community is . . . the brotherhood of the believers and the poor, the lovers and the imprisoned, the hopers and the sick . . . The least of these are already subjects before the missionaries and helpers come" (:105).

The Church as the Subject of the Inculturation Process

The discourse which sees "the people" as the subject of the process of inculturation is clearly related to the vision of the people of God on their journey to the Kingdom: the promised land. This is an image which comes from the book of Exodus and which also reflects Paul's teachings (Rm 9-11). It was one of the major understandings of the Church to emerge from Vatican II (LG 9-17). In itself the term reflects the two poles of the inculturation dialectic: "The people" on the one hand and "God" on the other. The step to a model which recognises the Church as the subject of the inculturation process is then a relatively short one.

Nonetheless, Shorter (1988:60) rejects this model: "we do not usually speak about the Church being inculturated." This is surprising since he both indicates and seems to affirm the other models which we have presented thus far. On the other hand, Mutiso-Mbinda (1986:81) suggests that "[i]nculturation must lead to a truly authentic African Church" and Onwubiko (1992:166) points out that "[i]nculturation is concerned then, not with the individual as such but with the community in which he lives his faith . . . [it] demands the correct understanding of the Church, Religion and Culture and how they are related."

The value of the inculturation model which sees the people or the Church as the subject of the inculturation process is that it is the same community of people who both live within the Church and live within the culture: "the community links the Church and culture firmly" (Onwubiko 1992:171). This apparently simple and obvious statement is nevertheless very important. People are already living and expressing inculturated faith to the extent that there is a coherence or integrity within their personal and community life. Whilst dichotomies and compartmentalisations do exist and need to be dealt with in the inculturation process, much of lived Christianity, albeit often in a simple, unreflective and localised way, already manifests inculturation. The recognition of the life and practice of the community of faith and the affirmation of this as Christian life and practice is essential to the process of inculturation understood in this way.

Roest Crollius' (1978:728-729) original understanding of inculturation fits within this model: "the term 'inculturation' refers primarily to the dynamic relationship between the local Church and 'its own culture', i.e. the culture of its own people" (:728-729). He understands the process to be analogous to the process of enculturation whereby a person grows up and becomes inserted into the culture of the people. By analogy "we can speak of the Church becoming inserted into a given culture" (:726).

In Roest Crollius' work the concept of the local Church emerges as the central theological category:

> One of the characteristics of the local Church, in a developed status, is precisely that it is "already rooted in social life and considerably adapted to the local culture" (AG 19). This note was also stressed by the Bishops of Asia at their meeting in Taipei in 1974: "The local Church is a church incarnate in a people, a church indigenous and inculturated. And this means concretely a church in continuous, humble and loving

> dialogue with the living traditions, the cultures, the religions - in brief, with all the life-realities of the people in whose midst it has sunk its roots deeply and whose history and life it gladly makes its own". The present day discussion on inculturation, therefore, has to be seen in the context of the new awareness of the reality and the mission of the local Church. [Roest Crollius 1978:727-728]

The concept of local Church at the centre of the inculturation process is also seen in the work of Onwubiko (1992:111): "the inculturation of Christianity . . . leads to the Incarnation of the universal Church in a local culture to give birth to a local Church into which individuals old and new are enculturated." We consider the concept of local Church to be essentially correlated to that of inculturation. The local Church is seen as the manifestation of the universal Church in a place (cf AG 20; LG 26). The Church is deemed to be fully present when the local Church exists in a place. This process involves the:

> Church's insertion into peoples' cultures . . . [which] means the intimate transformation of authentic cultural values through their integration in Christianity and the insertion of Christianity in the various human cultures . . . Through inculturation the Church, for her part, becomes a more intelligible sign of what she is, and a more effective instrument of mission. [RM 52]

We contend that the historical process which is the emergence of a local Church in a place is the best model to describe inculturation. The Church model is the best model to work with because it roots the process in the same common denominator: human beings. It is human beings as community who make up the Church and it is human beings as community who live within a cultural matrix. The community based model avoids analogical jumps and provides a common ground where the discourse of the human sciences can meet the discourse of theology: "In the venture of inculturation, the central point is neither Evangelisation nor Context but the human person . . . The human person is the way of the Church" (Roest Crollius in Bate 1991:VII).

Nevertheless, the category "the people" is not enough to capture the symbol "Church". Nolan (1988:166) uses "the people" in the sense of the poor of Yahweh, those somehow favoured by him and even equates "the power of the people that is manifest in the struggle" with "the power of God". Gaybba (1990:71) cautions against an over-identification of these since it "comes perilously close to placing 'the people' as a concrete entity beyond all possible criticism." Gaybba's comment is perhaps a little unfair since all theological appropriations run the risk of exaggeration and absolutisation. Nolan clearly feels that the theological category "the people" is one whose time has arrived in South Africa. But he does not equate the concept to the Church since he devotes a full chapter of his book to the "role of the Church" which he defines not in terms of the people but through its specific difference, the gospel. "The Church is defined and constituted by the gospel" (Nolan 1988:210). The ability of the category "Church" to encompass and transcend the various symbols of a people communicated to, humanised and sanctified; communicating, humanising and sanctifying, makes it the best model to adopt for our understanding of inculturation.

A decision to adopt the model of Church does not in anyway negate the other models which have been presented and which illuminate the inculturation process from different perspectives.[7] However in choosing the Church based model we take a clear standpoint within the discussion. We say that inculturation is a word which describes a process. This process is the emergence of the local Church in a place. Clearly such an affirmation requires a clear statement of what we mean by the term local Church and we hope to provide this in the next section. We also affirm that our choice is particularly important within the South African context. This is because of the large gap between the disunity manifest in a context which comprises some five thousand separated ecclesial traditions and the growing unity of purpose and action thrust upon this tattered fabric by the situation it finds itself confronting as a result of the *kairos* it finds itself living within. The development of an ecclesiology which can speak to the South African context is both urgent and difficult: a challenge whose time has come.

10.3 Inculturation as the Emergence of the Local Church

10.3.1 A Notion of the Church

The discourse on inculturation as the emergence of the local Church demands an adequate ecclesiology and clearly it is impossible to develop such here. Nevertheless we need to at least indicate some parameters. Firstly, we affirm a notion of the Church as "the community of faith" (De Gruchy 1986:27, 35-38); "the community of faith, hope and charity . . . one, holy, catholic and apostolic" (LG 8). Such a statement is already a challenge to the fragmentation we see in South Africa. We also affirm the notion of the Church as the People of God on the journey to the promised land: a people somehow searching to express the unity of the common journey led by one Spirit and motivated by the incarnation, life, death and resurrection of the one Lord Jesus Christ (cf. UR 3). At the same time we affirm the diversity expressed by contextual, historical, traditional and cultural factors. The model is then one of Unity in Diversity, of a community of communities, of a family of families, which is called to manifest and express the Unity and Trinity which is itself part of the Mystery of God, a mystery also reflected in God's image: the human family.[8]

Fig. 10.1 attempts to express the essentials of the Church's praxis in the world. The diagram is a modification of Alberich's (1987) model of Ecclesial Practice. The figure indicates three levels of ecclesial praxis. The first level shows that the Church does not exist for itself but is at the service of God's divine plan of salvation which is expressed as his Kingdom. This is the Kingdom which Jesus preached and which was actualised through his life, death and Resurrection and which is now manifest through the Holy Spirit in the world. It is the Church which is called to be the medium of the manifestation of the Kingdom in the world (cf. also Verkuyl 1973:197-204). The second level articulates, on the existential mediated level, how the Kingdom is manifest through the gospel values of *martyria* - witness; *koinonia* - relatedness; *diakonia* - service; *kerygma* - message and *leitourgia* - worship or sacrifice. The diagram also indicates some of the ways in which these gospel values are articulated in the Church's praxis. The third level points to the fact that there is a diversity of groups, agents, institutions and communities called to the various dimensions of praxis. Each group or community may emphasise one or other aspect according to its charisms and its context. The articulation will always be culture-conditioned. These groups are called to praxis within a totality: a unity. This unity expresses the relatedness both of the one Holy Spirit which animates the Church as well as the recognition of the participation in such unity by all the groups and agents.

LEVEL 1 Fundamental commitment and Final Objective	AT THE SERVICE OF THE KINGDOM OF GOD				
	THE KINGDOM OF GOD IS MANIFEST IN THE CHURCH				
	it is witnessed in	it is lived in	it is realised through	it is proclaimed by	it is celebrated through
LEVEL 2 Dimensions and means of Church Mission	MARTYRIA	KOINONIA	DIAKONIA	KERYGMA	LEITOURGIA
	Giving ones life for the Lord. Faith	Community Fraternity Unity Related-ness Communi-cation Communion	Service Charity Liberation Justice Develop-ment	Word Prophecy Doctrine Preaching Cate-chesis Evangel-isation	Eucharist Sacraments Feasts Celebra-tion Prayer Spiritua-lity Piety
LEVEL 3 People Groups	PEOPLE, GROUPS, ORGANISATIONS MOVEMENTS, PARISHES, STRUCTURES				

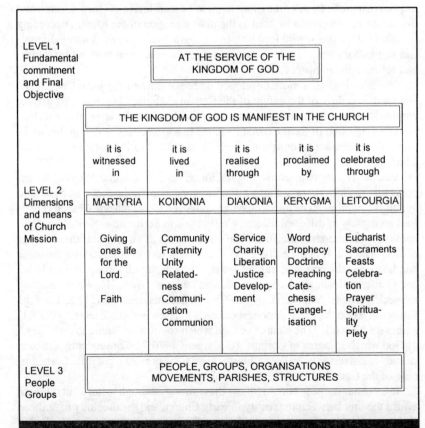

Fig. 10.1 THE CHURCH IN THE WORLD TODAY
(Source Alberich 1987:19 with modifications)

10.3.2 The Local Church

Coming to the question of the local Church, we wish to emphasise the understanding of this concept which sees it as the fullness of the Church in a place rather than a piece or section of the Church covering a certain area. Kalu's (1978:164) comments are enlightening in this regard. Speaking from an apparently Protestant perspective, he bemoans the division and factionalism brought by the importation of "the implacable war in Europe among these confessional groups". However he points out that unity does not mean a mere merger of denominations but is "a process of establishing a community in order that a humane future may be developed . . . Christ prescribed one-ness as the *esse* of His Church, the people who know and celebrate His task of reconciling the world to His Father" (:174). Clearly such a demand for unity as communion implies that the fullness of the Church has to be manifest in the local Church and that inculturation cannot be seen as the diversification of the Church according to culture since this would lead us into a geographico-culturo-denominationalism somewhat parallel to the historical fragmentation brought about by schism and reformation in history.

Since Vatican II, a more developed understanding of the local Church has emerged. Because of the nature of the Roman Catholic Church and its greater emphasis on preserving and safeguarding visible unity, the attempts to accommodate the notion of local Church have led to a greater focus within this tradition on the question of unity and diversity as related to the nature of the local Church.

Vatican II uses two terms: "local Church" and "particular Church" to express this reality. There are also a few references to "indigenous", "new" and "young" Churches.[9] The meaning being conveyed is that the one Church is realised concretely in different places. We find this in Scripture as well. Thus Paul speaks of "the church of the Thessalonians" (1 Th 1,1, 2 Th 1,1) and "the churches of God" (2 Th 2,4) in the earliest New Testament references. Acts, on the other hand, stresses the one-ness of the Church: "So the church throughout all Judea and Galilee and Samaria had peace and was built up" (Ac 9,31). When referring to specific places, Acts refers to "The Church in Jerusalem" (8,1; 11,22) and the Church at Antioch (13,1). Amongst the early Church Fathers, Clement (PG 1,1) addresses his work "The Church of God which sojourns in Rome to the Church of God which sojourns in Corinth" (cf. Jurgens 1970:7). Consequently the twin strands of universality and particularity seem to be present right from the beginning of the Church.

It is not our purpose here to follow these strands through history but rather to affirm the link between the reality in early Church and the theology of Vatican II. *Lumen Gentium* suggests that "This multiplicity of local Churches, unified in a common effort, shows all the more resplendently the catholicity of the undivided Church" (LG 23). This reference to local Churches - the only specific one in *Lumen Gentium* - refers principally to the emergence of different rites, traditions and Patriarchal Churches throughout history. This document refers more often to "particular Churches" and here, as well as in other documents (CD, AG. Code of Canon Law), the reference is mainly to a diocese: "A diocese is a section of the People of God entrusted to a bishop . . . formed by him into one community in the Holy Spirit through the Gospel and the Eucharist, it constitutes one particular church in which the one holy, catholic and apostolic Church of Christ is truly present and active" (CD 11, cf. LG 25, AG 19; CCL 368-374). *Evangelii Nuntiandi* (EN 62) says that "this universal Church is in practice incarnate in the particular Churches made up of such and such an actual part of mankind, speaking such and such a language, heirs of a cultural patrimony, a vision of the world, of an historical past, of a particular human substratum." At the same time the letter points out that the universal Church is not a federation or a sum of particular Churches but remains One, present in a particularist reality. This reality is socio-cultural, theologico-christological and juridico-geographical (cf. Wolanin 1987:99-112).

Ad Gentes (AG 19) refers to "a definite point" which the "assembly of the faithful" reaches in a historical process which begins when a community of the faithful is raised up in a place through the work of missionaries sent there. This "definite point" can be said to be linked to the emergence of a "young Church", a "particular Church" or a "local Church".[9] The text goes on to indicate ten characteristics or criteria which can be said to describe this "definite point" as follows (cf. AG 19):

The assembly of the faithful

- -is rooted in the social life of the people
- -is to some extent conformed to its culture
- -enjoys a certain stability
- -enjoys a certain permanence
- -has its own priests (although insufficient)
- -has its own religious and laity
- -has its own ministries and institutions
  - -to lead the people of God
  - -to spread the faith
- -is under the leadership of its own, autochthonous bishop
- -is involved in civil and apostolic action in the state
- -has fostered its own theological, psychological and human studies which allow elements of the "tradition to be grafted onto their own culture".

Redemptoris Missio (RM48) also refers to this point as a "precise stage" which "is hard to identify" in the "great and lengthy process" of the formation of a local Church. Further to the above criteria, this document points to the "evangelising activity of the Christian community, first in its own locality, and then elsewhere as part of the Church's universal mission . . . [as] the clearest sign of a mature faith" (RM49). The Church is missionary by its very nature and the manifestation of a missionary dimension beyond itself is a further necessary sign that the "definite point" has been reached.

The notion of local Church is clearly extended beyond that of a particular Church in the work of George (1990:233-250) who bases himself on the teaching of John Paul II. In a review of this Pope's teaching on the "local Church as inculturated Church" he concludes that "cultural unity is . . . a legitimate basis for describing a group of culturally similar dioceses as a 'local Church'" (1990:247). George makes this statement in the context of his affirmation that "attention to culture entails rethinking theologically the relationship between the universal and particular in all areas of human experience" (:233). Such an enquiry impinges on the impact of the cultural upon the very nature of humankind. This issue was dealt with in our previous chapter where we concluded that the cultural dimension is indeed part of what it actually means to ***be*** human. Only a small reflection leads us to see that this conclusion is already a theological judgement and is the reason why we included a theological-anthropological analysis in our analysis of culture. George points out, however, that the same debate also impacts upon the question of unity and plurality in "the faith" and in "the Church". This occurs firstly in the local component of both the understanding and expression of the "universals" or "sources of our faith unity" (:234) which emerge in the local context. It also appears in the manifestation of the one Church as expressed in the local Churches linked together in an essential communion but where each reflects the presence of the risen Lord within a locally constituted community of faith. Each particular community of faith is a community of people whose particularity is manifest most fundamentally through their culture.

George (1990:240ff.) indicates the theological weight of culture as it relates to the translation of the message of the gospel and the tradition (cf. also Sanneh 1989:1-8; 200-209). But he also points to the contribution of different cultural expressions both in the formulation as well as the illumination of the one faith as expressed in, for example, the creeds. In this way he shows how culture has already contributed to the Church's understanding of revelation:

> A new expression of the faith in a new inculturation may, in fact, be more adequate to the objective content of the faith than an older expression. The Church's understanding of revelation can never be complete, although it is always accurate. [George 1990:235]

People who have heard the Good News, accepted it, and been born again into the community of the faithful, actually find, when the local Church emerges in the sense we have indicated, that it is their culture which "becomes, analogically a kind of theological *locus*, a place to look for a deeper understanding of what God has revealed" (George 1990:242). It is in this sense that Roest Crollius (1978:728-729) explains inculturation as the "dynamic relationship between the local Church and 'its own culture' i.e. the culture of its own people." Culture thus becomes a theological category, playing a part, although not an exclusive one, in indicating the nature and praxis of a local Church.

It is probably an affirmation of the historical and contextual conditionedness of much of the fragmentation that has occurred in the Christian Church that the teaching of the "Faith and Order Commission of the World Council of Churches" (WCC 1991) reflects an almost identical understanding to that which has been presented above from a Roman Catholic perspective. The Church is seen as "the community of those who are in communion with Christ and, through him, with one another . . . This community finds its full manifestation wherever people are gathered together by word and sacrament in obedience to the apostolic faith - i.e. in a local Church" (:84).

Hoedemaker (1991:626) points out that the World Council of Churches has focused on the local Church as "the basic unit of unity". The 1975 assembly at Nairobi understood the One Church as "a conciliar fellowship of local churches which are themselves truly united" emphasising that "each local church possesses, in communion with the others, the fullness of catholicity" (:626). Hoedemaker points out that as a result of historical ecclesial developments the notion of local Church has come to be multivocal referring to "dioceses, archdioceses, parishes, national churches and other territorial-ecclesial units" (:627). Whilst indicating the revival of the understanding of the Eucharist as a core determinant of unity (cf. also LG 23, CD 11; Lima:E19 in WCC 1982:14) he suggests that other factors are also emerging pointing to: "a new emphasis on the missionary quality of church structures . . . and to a proliferation of small groups intent upon a creative interaction between church and context" (:627).

Clearly these two large ecclesial bodies are moving towards one another. The Roman Catholic Church is moving towards a more pluriform understanding of its visible unity and the World Council of Churches towards a more united vision of its own pluriformity. The pluriformity is being seen as a response to context and mission within the WCC milieu and towards culture in the Roman Catholic milieu.[10]

The terms context or culture would seem to represent different expressions of the same wish that a local Church should be responding to the world where it finds itself: being in but not of the world. Schreiter (1985:1;5-6;12-16;21), amongst others,[11] suggests that the two realities, context and culture, are fundamentally the same but opts, as we do, for the notion of culture as being "the concrete context" in which the Church, the gospel and theology happen. Culture represents "a way of life for a given time and place, replete with values, symbols and meanings, reaching out with hopes and dreams, often struggling for a better world" (:21). Culture represents the human locus of a people's context. It is the site of the humanisation of the *oikos* and thus the site where the meeting occurs between the Church as the human community of faith and the world as the human community in life. This being so, we see that, in fact, to some extent, every local Church is inculturated, whether acknowledged or not, since culture is part of the human condition, whether acknowledged or not. Yet it is the dialogue of Church and culture as the explication of this otherwise hidden or implicit relationship which is what marks the inculturation process. It is in the coming to consciousness of identity as a people through the affirmation of humanity and the local expression of values, attitudes and behaviour, redeemed through conversion and commitment to the risen Lord, manifest as a willingness to do his will, which marks the inculturated Church.

This coming to consciousness of a community's own humanity is at the same time an affirmation of the humanity of other peoples. The tragedy of apartheid was that rather than being built on this principle, the identity of a people and its church was instead built upon fear and group interests to the detriment of others. This has often been the case in denominationalism and the rivalry between church groups. Within denominations in South Africa, this demon has also been active in church structures such as parishes which have emphasised division by class and race by conforming to the geographical entities set up by the state (cf. De Gruchy 1986:37). Such facts within our own history should warn us to the dangers of the inculturation process and in particular they illustrate the necessity that such a process must always affirm and manifest the essential unity both of the human community and of the Church. Any inculturation process which leads people and churches to deny this unity needs to be questioned regarding its premises. The affirmation of our own humanity and goodness as image of God is surely the pathway to the recognition of the same humanity and goodness expressed in different ways in others and is a challenge to communication, to community and to unity as a human family: the one people of God, the one Body of Christ.

10.3.3 Inculturation and the Emergence of the Local Church

We have tried to show how culture provides a valid key for understanding diversity in the manifestation of the One Church from one site to another. Since culture is part of what it means to be human, so culture is called to die and rise with Christ to new life and become a new creation. This is the meaning and purpose of the evangelisation of cultures. We re-affirm an unwillingness to reify the concept of culture by indicating that such a process occurs in the human person or rather in the community of human persons. So inculturation is the dialogue between the community of the saints[12]: the Church within a context, and others of the same culture. In this way inculturation is mission. This mission is carried out by bringing good news to the culture and in this sense, inculturation is evangelisation: the evangelisation of culture. This evangelisation leads to conversion and the acceptance of the new faith both within the cultural categories in which it has been preached but also beyond these to a recognition of the universality of salvation and communion beyond one's own culture within the fellowship of the sons and daughters of God.

Further to this, inculturation also has a mission *ad intra*, to affirm the values, attitudes and culture of those people who already belong to the Church. It is an affirmation of all that is good as well as a challenge to reject what is evil and redeem what has been distorted by sin. This is an ecclesial process since the local Church needs to dialogue with its own culture in order to make these theological judgements under the guidance of the Spirit it has been given and in the presence of the risen Christ now revealed. Such theological judgements inform a local, contextual theology. So inculturation implies the construction of local theology. It is a theology which reveals the presence of the risen Christ already in the culture before the missionaries came, as well as articulating his incarnate presence in the now present community of faith.

Local theology is not only christology but also pneumatology and ecclesiology. This latter has important practical consequences since inculturation as a process guides the praxis of the Church as it sets up the structures and institutions which allow it to be the Church in the world responding to the "joy and hope, grief and anguish of the men of our time, especially those who are poor and afflicted in any way" (GS 1). This transformational role which is the Church's praxis is also part of the process of inculturation. The Church's praxis is bound up with its ministry and the ministries which articulate it. As a consequence any process of inculturation will clearly impinge upon ministry and the ministries of the local Church both in regard to their nature as well as their form and style.

In this way, then, we come to our own theme. We have seen how the various Coping-healing ministries are apparently attempting to respond to the needs of people within the South African context. We now have to ask the question to what extent is this is an inculturated ecclesial ministry, a manifestation of the emergence of the local Church? Obviously such a theological judgement does not depend upon a simple yes or no answer.

Our work so far has indicated both the complexity of the Coping-healing phenomenon as such as well as the multiplicity of elements which impinge upon the inculturation process understood as the emergence of the local Church. Nevertheless, we have been able to indicate a number of factors which determine the inculturation process thus enhancing our understanding of it. Before moving on to the encounter of inculturation and healing in the next chapter, it is necessary to draw up a model of inculturation which will facilitate our understanding of the factors, both causative and consequential, which affect this encounter. This is a model of inculturation which will inform ministry.

10.4 A Model of Inculturation to Inform Ministry

The process of the emergence of a local Church can be described in terms of a series of significant historical events which have an effect on the relationship between a local Church and the culture of the people in which it is emerging. In fig. 10.2 we describe this relationship in terms of four major elements: the identity and function of the missionary, the identity and role of the local people, the praxis of the local Church and the understanding of the local culture by the local Church.

The process is described in terms of seven moments or events which are experienced in different ways from the perspective of different agents or elements of the process. The diagram provides a simple schematic map of the inculturation process. The model is an expansion of Roest Crollius' (1978:733) model of inculturation which comprises three moments. In the *translation* moment the evangelisation and Church implantation occur in the categories of the sending Church. In a second, *assimilation* moment the Church is assimilated into the local culture and ethos. In the third, *transformation*, moment the local Church in dialogue with its own culture seeks to transform that culture into a genuine Christian culture. Clearly the moments are not discrete in actuality and occur at differing rates in different contexts of the culture. In our own model (fig.10.2) steps 1-4 would roughly correspond to the *translation* moment, steps 3-6 to the *assimilation* moment and steps 4-7 to the *translation* moment. Clearly, the discrete steps of our analysis shown in the model, would be more holistically related in reality.

In looking at the relationship between ministry and inculturation it is the third element, the identity and praxis of the new Church, which is of particular interest. We note that with step 4, a set of indigenous Christian practices and ministries begin, which find their source in the group which is reacting to the missionaries. Since the missionaries lead the emerging Church whose identity is that of a translated Church (translated from the sending Church), these practices occur either on the fringes of or outside the emerging local Church. This is clearly the case with much of the Coping-healing phenomenon we have been investigating amongst both Blacks and Whites. It is experienced as a reaction and a resistance to the "official" way of being Church amongst a group of people who have nevertheless discovered Christ and received faith in some way. The medium through which ministry is expressed in these reacting groups is primarily the local cultures involved, together with some acculturated elements of the new transformed culture and the emerging local Church.

In the assimilation moment (steps 3-6), the grip of the sending Church is loosened as the new Church becomes predominantly of the people of the area and leadership moves into local hands. At this point, as a result both of osmosis and of the reflection of Christian communities on their experience of God, there is a greater openness to, and acceptance of, the local culture. Those ministries which respond to the real needs of people persevere and some of these are the indigenous Christian practices and ministries of step 4. These are reflected on and theologised about, to the extent that they have affected the life of the Christian community. This reflection process, carried out in the light of faith, is a process which takes the ministry through steps 5 and 6 so that the ministry may become part of the praxis of the emerged local Church in step 7.

Event or step	Identity & Role of Missionary	Identity & role of local people	Identity & Praxis of new Church	Role of local culture
1. Sending church called to mission	Christians of the sending church	Not Christian	None	Seen as pagan
2. Sending church sends missionaries	Christians of sending church and explorers	Not Christian	None	Seen as pagan
3. Missionaries arrive and evangelise using mode (culture/vision) of the sending church	Evangelisers: witnesses of faith as expressed in the sending church	Followers of missionaries or not Christian	Follows that of the sending church	Seen as pagan - all practices to be dropped on conversion
4. Church implantation; acculturation process occurs	Leaders of emerging local church	Followers of missionaries and reacting group (against missionary style approach)	Follows that of the sending church; some specific local practices begin causing tensions with the official local church	Officially pagan but many cultural religious practices continued; some cultural values and some of cultural world-view enters into the practice and self-understanding of the local church
5. Transition moment. Change in church leadership	Some leaders Differing vision and praxis	Some leaders	Follows that of the sending Church with emerging local structures & ministries	Greater openness to and participation of the local culture & world-view in the local church
6. Inculturation process is more explicit and urgent local church emerges	Some local people become missionaries. They open up the inculturation process	Leaders	local identity emerges with a growing awareness of requirement to respond to local needs	More values of the local community accepted into Church praxis. New ministries are approved but some tensions remain in the relationship with universal Church.
7. Local church	Local people sent as missionaries	Leaders	Local identity affirmed; unity with Universal Church affirmed; missionary ideal emerges	Acceptance of local culture; transformation of it through Christian witness within; emergence of new Christian culture; Affirmation of difference and reaffirmation of unity. Sending of missionaries.

Fig. 10.2 The Process of the Emergence of the Local Church

This reflection process is the process of pastoral praxis as outlined by Vela (1984). The reflection on pastoral praxis starts from an analysis of pastoral practices using the human sciences, where necessary, and then moving on to a theological reflection on each particular practice and the context within which it occurs. This meeting of practice with faith leads to new praxis.[13] Theological reflection on the institutions, ministries and practices of the local Church forms part of pastoral planning and is an essential part of step 5 if a truly local Church is to emerge. It needs to take into account a large number of factors and at the risk of appearing to make the matter extremely complicated we wish to illustrate these through a series of models.

The process of the birth of a local Church has both diachronic and synchronic dimensions to it. Our first diagram (fig. 10.2) indicates some of the diachronic elements. In figs. 10.3-10.5, we attempt a synchronic presentation of the process from step 4 to step 6 of fig. 10.2: i.e. during the assimilation moment where the importance of the translation moment is receding and that of the transformation moment is increasing. Here we show in more detail some of the factors which influence this process as well as the relationships between them.

Fig. 10.3 describes something of the human condition in a particular area. We identify three major parameters in this diagram. The context refers to the events, situations and forces in the life of the people of the particular area.[14] Such a context has physical, geographical, socio-economic, political, cultural, religious and philosophical dimensions to it. It forms an *oikos*. Some events in

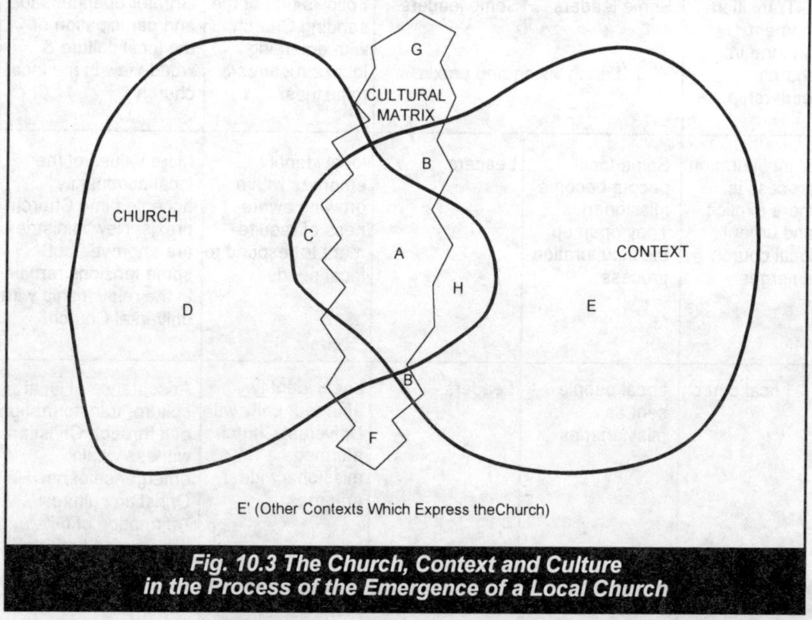

Fig. 10.3 The Church, Context and Culture in the Process of the Emergence of a Local Church

the *oikos* are relatively transient. Others are more permanent and become situations which can affect the cultural matrix.[15] The cultural dimension provides the epistemological lens through which the context and the Church are both accepted and understood. It also informs the behaviour of the people through the value and attitude system it affirms. Context and culture work upon one another as indicated by regions A and B in a kind of dialectic. Crises and short term events in the context will affect the culture to the extent of their intensity whereas longer term events and situations even though less intense can have an equal or even greater force through the effects of inertia.

The Church gradually inserts itself into the context-culture matrix as people are evangelised and join it. As the insertion increases so the intensity of its own dialectical relationship with both the context and the culture increases. The reaction to context tends to be swifter and clearer as needs are quickly perceived and responded to. Intensity tends to be the yardstick here. So floods, drought, famine, a new group of evangelised people, violence, detentions and so on elicit an immediate response. These tend to occur in regions C and H of our diagram. More long-lasting situations within the context lead to the establishing of min-

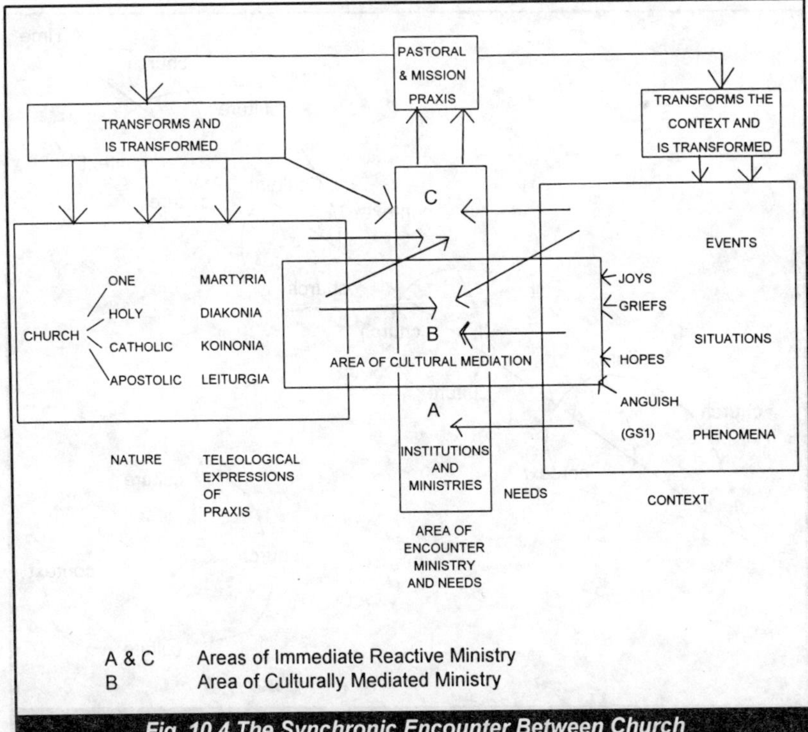

Fig. 10.4 The Synchronic Encounter Between Church and Context as Mediated by Culture

istries and institutions to deal with them and it is this level that we are most concerned with. The more long-lasting situations also affect the culture in a deeper way since they eventually generate the required inertia to be able to dialogue with it. These ministries and institutions enter into region A where context, culture and Church meet. The region is one of mutual interpenetration or dialogue, not one of identity. The Coping-healing ministry we have been discussing is one such ministry.

Fig. 10.4 is a schematic expansion of fig. 10.3 attempting to explicate some of the important dimensions of culture, context and Church which are dialogueing in this process. Again we emphasise that the model is reflecting life and that any separation and categorisation is clearly both artificial and reductionist. A model is not reality but attempts to deal with some aspect of it. Its purpose is merely to indicate elements and the differences between them as well as to illustrate relationships. We note in fig. 10.4 that the context generates a set of events, phenomena and situations expressed in *Gaudium et Spes* (GS1) as joys, griefs, hopes and anguishes. These are variously mediated and immediate. The immediate ones present areas of need which are often responded to in a direct

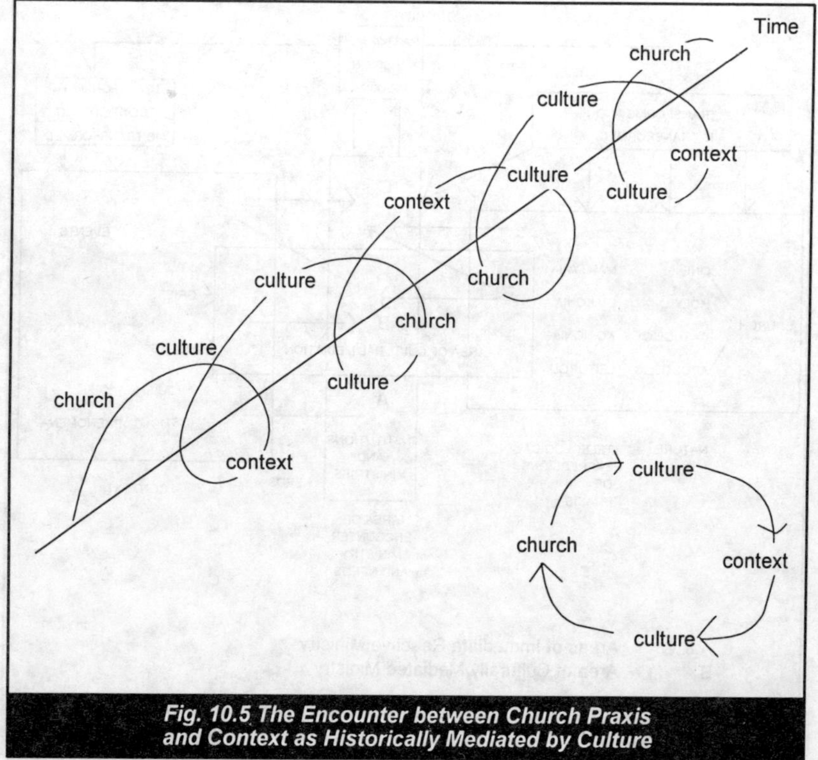

Fig. 10.5 The Encounter between Church Praxis and Context as Historically Mediated by Culture

1. CHURCH.

Nature:	One Holy Catholic Apostolic	act as a litmus test for praxis
Telos of Praxis:	Martyria Diakonia Koinonia Leitourgia Kerygma	Express goals of all ministries and institutions

2. CONTEXT.

Events, Situations, Phenomena
Experienced as Joys, Griefs, hopes, anguish
Expressed as needs.
Needs are of different kinds:
- Short term, urgent
- medium/long term, urgent
- medium/long term, less urgent
- chronic, of varying intensity

3. CULTURE.

Culture mediates longer term needs, ministries and institutions more powerfully since they contain the inertia required to affect the culture in its historical dimensions i.e. they can affect tradition.
Culture is communication, humanisation, sanctification

Fig. 10.6 The Role of Church, Context and Culture in Determining Criteria for Mission

way as "reactive ministry". The mediated ones are of more interest to us here. The mediation occurs in various ways and we have discussed this with regard to the Coping-healing phenomenon in chapters two to seven. Of particular importance for the Church is the cultural mediation for reasons already discussed. We emphasise once more the heterogeneous nature of culture and that the cultural mediation aims to facilitate the process of communication, humanisation and sanctification.

The mediated needs encounter the Church on the level of its praxis. This praxis has the categories we have described: *martyria, diakonia, koinonia, leitourgia*, and *kerygma*. The response occurs on this level. However in its reflection on its ministries, the Church is always thrown back onto its nature to be one, holy, catholic and apostolic. The ministries are themselves a challenge to the Church's self understanding as one, holy, catholic and apostolic and the Church's nature is a challenge to the form nature and style of its ministerial praxis. It is the dialogue of this mutual challenge which informs the inculturation process. The encounter of needs with praxis gives rise to new forms of praxis which then occur and live. In this way they become part of the context of the people and move through the model once more influencing the needs and mediated response to these in terms of ministry. The model in fig. 10.4 is synchronic. However inculturation is quintessentially diachronic: historical. The inculturation process occurs through the ongoing cultural mediation of needs and ministries. As time goes on the cultural dimension of the need and its expression, as well as the ministry and its expression, become clearer. This is the time at which the assimilation phase occurs (cf. fig. 10.2). From there we move on to the transformation phase and it is this historical process which gives rise to inculturation in ministry. This process is schematised in fig. 10.5.

Our model, then, comprises the following elements: Church, context and culture as explicitated in fig. 10.6. The encounter of Church, expressed as ministries and institutions, and context, expressed as needs occurring within a cultural medium, allows the emergence of an inculturated ministry which, as praxis, returns both to the context, to become a new event or phenomenon within the context, as well as to the Church where it challenges the nature and praxis of the Church (cf. fig. 10.4). In this way ministry is transforming both of the context and of the Church whilst it is itself once more transformed by these encounters. It is this process which gives rise to inculturated ministry.

It is on the level of mediated needs, responded to as pastoral practice, and thus emerging as a phenomenon within the context, that we encounter our own phenomenon: the Coping-healing ministries as we have met them. These ministries occur within area B of fig. 10.4 since they are culturally mediated. And it is on the level of a taking cognisance of the elements presented in our model that we will be able to perform our theological judgement on them. This judgement is concerned with deciding to what extent the Coping-healing phenomenon is a genuinely inculturated manifestation of the Church's mission to heal the sick. Such a theological judgement is itself part of the inculturation process, part of the construction of local theology, and is our own contribution to this inculturation process. It will help to inform the praxis of the Church leading to practices which reflect the steps taken so far in the emergence of the local Church. This, then, is the task of our next chapter.

Chapter 11

Inculturation and the Healing Ministry

11.1 Introduction

In this penultimate chapter we wish to bring together the conclusions of section III in order to form our theological judgement on the Coping-healing phenomenon as we have presented it in sections I and II. In coming to our theological judgement we have been concerned about developing a phenomenological description. This description has been performed from two perspectives: that of the phenomenon itself within its context and then from the perspective of the Church since it refers to itself as a ministry of the Church.[1]

In chapter eight we presented the essential elements of the phenomenon as gleaned from the mediations of section II together with something of the relationship between these elements. This relationship also allowed us to describe something of the structure of our phenomenon. In order to illuminate the structure further and to situate the phenomenon in its dynamic relationship with its context, we have attempted to indicate something of the context both of the society, which we have called culture (ch. 9) and of the Church of which the phenomenon is a ministry, which we have called inculturation as the emergence of the local Church (ch. 10). The dynamic relationship between the phenomenon and its context clearly affects, and even, to some extent, determines something of the elements and structure of the phenomenon itself. Thus the investigation of the dynamic relationship between these three descriptors is essential. These three descriptors, presented in chapters eight, nine and ten, are tied together in the model (fig. 10.4) which then forms the basis of our descriptive model of this phenomenon.

Our purpose in this chapter is, then, to perform a theological judgement on the phenomenon we have described in order to say how and to what extent this phenomenon is a ministry of the Church and a challenge to its mission. We are aware that the movement into judgement is fraught with difficulties not least of which is the conditionedness of all theological judgement. Accepting this fact, we do feel that the approach adopted has led to the emergence of many factors within the Coping-healing phenomenon which allow for a kind of comparative judgement by predication. These can be said to be logically drawn conclusions which, we believe, can effectively inform our own judgement.

Our first task is to situate the Coping-healing phenomenon in terms of both the conclusions of chapter eight and the model in fig. 10.4 referred to above. We hope to indicate the culturally mediated needs that this ministry is responding to as well as the culturally mediated forms that it takes. We then hope to be able to make some tentative judgement regarding its effectiveness in responding to these needs. From there we will indicate the challenges that this ministry is making to the whole Church in terms of fulfilling the Church's mission.

After this first situating of the phenomenon we will move on to a judgement of the ministry by predicating it against some of the criteria indicated in chapter ten. We will consider the phenomenon within the model of inculturation as the emergence of the local Church in a place. Here we will examine the phenomenon in terms of the five goals of the Church's ministries and institutions as presented in chapter ten: *martyria, diakonia, koinonia, leitourgia and kerygma.* We will also consider how these ministries inform the inculturation model of translation, assimilation and transformation and what this says to the local Church in South Africa.

Finally we will attempt to consider what consequences these ministries have on the level of the universal Church. Here we will predicate the Coping-healing phenomenon in terms of the four marks or notes of the Church as enumerated in the Nicene creed: One, Holy, Catholic and Apostolic, in order to see to what extent our ministries reflect the Church whose nature is so bound up with her mission. From this we hope to draw some challenges that the Coping-healing phenomenon poses, as a ministry, to the whole Church.

11.2 Situating the Phenomenon of the Coping-Healing Ministry

11.2.1 Introduction

We said in the conclusion to chapter ten that the Coping-healing practices we have studied are a response to culturally mediated needs emerging from the current South African context. Such needs, which we identified in our various mediations of the phenomenon find their commonality in the fact that they are all culturally mediated in terms of the understanding of culture that we developed in chapter nine. The various Coping-healing practices that we have described are similarly culturally mediated pastoral responses to these needs. This shows the centrality of the concept of culture in our discourse and of inculturation as the major theological key we have adopted to describe the Coping-healing phenomenon as a theological reality. Having demonstrated the importance of culture in this phenomenon we now need to situate it as Christian praxis since those whose ministry we have examined claim to be exercising Christian ministry and thus fulfilling the mission which Christ has given to the Church.

The model, presented in the last chapter, of the process of the emergence of the local Church (fig. 10.2) predicts that in step four within the new Church praxis "some specific local practices begin causing tension with the official local Church". Step four refers to the acculturation process which occurs during Church implantation. Similarly in the succeeding step, the transition moment, "local structures and ministries" begin to emerge. As a starting point for our discussion we shall situate our Coping-healing phenomenon within the practices and ministries of step four and step five. Consequently, we say that the Coping-healing phenomenon we have studied fits into the steps of the inculturation process as a combination of practices and ministries, within the local Church praxis. Some of these result from the acculturation phase and are not fully accepted by the new Church, whereas others are more accepted practices and ministries forming part of the emerging structures and ministries of the local Church. To the extent that our phenomenon is placed in the latter category it is accepted as part of the Church's mission and to the extent that it is placed in the former category it is still in tension with the emerging local Church and its role within it is not yet clarified nor even, in some cases, accepted.

Within the three steps of the inculturation process: translation, assimilation and transformation, we can situate our phenomenon largely within the assimilation phase. Here the translated, implanted Church begins to assimilate elements of the local culture.[2] Whilst this point may be relatively easy to see for the AIC healing ministries it is also true for the Neopentecostal churches since they are successful precisely because they reflect elements of late 20th century Western culture more easily than do the traditional churches.[3]

The fact that we can situate our phenomenon within a reasonable model of the Church's emergence in a place, lends considerable weight and legitimacy to our phenomenon as an ecclesial phenomenon and as part of the process of Christian praxis. Indeed, our model predicts that such phenomena should occur: they should be expected within the inculturation process. However, our model also predicts that these phenomena will give rise to tensions with the "official" new Church (fig. 10.2), and this turns out to be the case. It is to an analysis of these tensions that we must now turn. Before doing so we should note that as the inculturation process moves through the assimilation moment, when the transition step (step 5 of our model) is reached, acceptable local structures and ministries are predicted to emerge with the emergence of the local Church. At this point, the tension moves to one *ad intra* between the local Church and the universal Church. In this way it becomes an ecumenical issue.

11.2.2 The Coping-Healing Ministry as Ecclesial Praxis

The analysis of the Coping-healing phenomenon made through the various mediations has helped us identify the elements and factors which make it up (part II). We now need to ask the question whether or not those elements and factors could be considered to be part of ecclesial praxis and indeed ministries of the Church.

At the outset we recall our affirmation that the Coping-healing phenomenon is ***not*** normally a "direct intervention of God, usually as Holy Spirit but also as the risen Christ, who suspends natural law with a supernatural, often miraculous, intervention" (*supra* 8.7.1). Since this is often the claim, we can clearly make the judgement, based on our own research, that except in a small number of cases (what we have called an "unexplained remnant")[4] such claims would be untrue and thus would offend against the kerygmatic dimensions of the Church's mission (cf. fig. 10.1). Another factor which impinges upon the nature of this phenomenon as an ecclesial practice is our conclusion that

> the kind of healing that goes on in the Coping-healing churches is not particularly specific to them . . . there is considerable overlap between the kind of healing which goes on in the African Independent churches and the Neopentecostal churches with that which occurs in other kinds of folk healing, shamanistic healing, spiritualist healing, psycho-somatic positive thinking healing as well as other health and healing practices. [*supra* 8.7.2]

This conclusion allows us to make the judgement that claims to the Christian specificity of this ministry are at best dubious. The best Christian interpretation which could be put upon the results of our analysis is that to the extent that these phenomena are indeed true healing (something which we must still examine and thus do not yet concede) they can be said to be manifestations of the power of the risen Lord and his Kingdom. In this case, the Christian ministry of healing makes explicit a truth which remains implicit in the other healing methods and styles. If this is indeed the case with the Coping-Healing practices we have studied, then we can say that they are true ecclesial ministries since they reveal the presence of the risen Christ in the world. However any claim to exclusivity and any condemnation of other healing forms would clearly go against the facts which have emerged in our study and would be unacceptable. Indeed we have suggested that a further interpretation would be that this ministry is rather a tapping into the methods of psycho-somatic, cultural and folk healing within particular theological interpretative keys. This is tantamount to the process which gives a theological interpretation to the medical curing of disease within a Christian context: for example, a Christian mission hospital using Christian mission doctors. Clearly this is a legitimate exercise within the Church's mission since mission is concerned with the aim and purpose of such work rather than the means. Much of the Church's missionary endeavours in schools, hospitals and other institutions have operated on this principle.[5]

The fourth and final affirmation we wish to make regarding the Coping-healing phenomenon as ecclesial praxis is the clear centrality of the concept of culture, and thus the ecclesial model of inculturation, in understanding this ministry. Our study has shown that healing is always a cultural construct and that the healing process always involves culturally determined mechanisms. Consequently only an ecclesial model of ministry which takes the cultural factors into account will be able adequately to interpret, found and direct this ministry. This model is, we contend, the inculturation model we have presented. With this in mind we can affirm that to the extent that such cultural healing is Christian healing then the Coping-healing practices are an ecclesial ministry. Here we are saying that it all depends what one means by healing. Authors such as Kleinman and Sung have shown that cultural healers are always successful in terms of the understanding of healing operating within the cultural framework. However such an understanding of healing may not necessarily be a Christian understanding of healing.

Here we are concenrned with the transforming role to which Christianity and the local Church is called in its dialogue with the local culture. Clearly during the assimilation phase, it is possible that cultural practices, values and modes of healing may be incorporated into the emerging ecclesial practice and that some of these may still need to be contested, adapted, transformed rejected or purified as the ministry of the local Church emerges. This step is a necessary part of the inculturation process without which the local Church cannot emerge and the new Church just becomes identified with the local culture and a sect or a separate fragment results. This has clearly been the case in the South African context precisely because an adequate model of inculturation was unavailable to affirm and incorporate the factors and forces which have been part of the emergence of Christianity in this part of the world.

In summary, then, we identify the various Coping-healing ministries which are emerging in terms of four foundational ecclesial parameters:

1) It is not normally a direct supernatural intervention.
2) It is not normally a practice which is specific to Christianity but an incorporation by the Church using a theological key, of folk healing practices in both African and Western cultures.
3) The Coping-healing ministry is making explicit what is implicit in other non-Christian healing forms: the presence of the risen Christ and the Kingdom of God in healing.
4) Culture is central in healing and the inculturation model is the best theological key for understanding it.

11.2.3 The Coping-Healing Ministry as a Culturally Mediated Pastoral Response to Culturally Mediated Needs

We suggested in the last chapter that the Coping-healing ministries we have been studying are found in area B of fig. 10.4. This means that we describe them as culturally mediated pastoral practices responding to culturally mediated needs emerging from the context. Now we shall examine this assertion to enable a fuller understanding of the ministry and an examination of the extent to which it can be inserted into a valid pastoral and mission praxis of the Church.

In a very real sense we can say that the model in fig. 10.4 summarises the work we have been trying to do in this thesis. After a presentation of the phenomenon in chapter two we have attempted, through the various mediations of part II, to describe both the needs and the pastoral response to them. Our description has attempted to explore, through the phenomenological method, the internal structure of both the needs and the ministries. From the description we have concluded to the centrality of culture as the kind of human medium through which both needs and response are somehow negotiated. This has led to the adoption of a theological model built on culture, inculturation, as our way of understanding, explaining, reflecting and coming to theological judgement on our phenomenon. We now wish to recapitulate, within this model, the culturally mediated needs to which the ministry is responding and then to identify some of the parameters of the cultural mediation of the various pastoral responses to these needs.

We have said that the process of being ill is concerned with the perception of a person as she comes to an awareness of not being well and she names herself as "ill". We have also said that this process is culturally determined since the perception of illness is one which has been learned through the socialisation or enculturation process. The way the illness is dealt with also follows culturally determined patterns within which the recourse to the Coping-healing ministry type may be a particular step in the process. Normally we have found that it is only certain types of illness which are brought to the Coping-healing ministry. One type comprises illnesses which have been unsuccessfully treated elsewhere through recourse to resources in the home, the hospital, medical doctor or clinic. The other type comprises illnesses which are seen as being specifically within the field of competency of the Coping-healing ministry, such as perceived possession, witchcraft, or other evil related or sin related illness. Thus people making use of the Coping-healing ministry are coming as a result of perceived needs which they feel this ministry can fulfil. In our mediations we identified these needs. It is important to note the extent of overlap and interrelatedness of all these needs which we categorise here to provide a model for understanding.

Psycho-Medical Needs

These can be expressed in terms of four interrelated and overlapping categories:

(i) The need for a "miracle" cure of incurable disease.

-the need to hope for the seemingly impossible.

(ii) Emotional needs:

-the need to satisfy unexpressed emotions which may result in illness through psychogenic, psychosomatic and stress mechanisms.

(iii)Identity and ego needs:

-the need for affirmation, dignity, self respect, a sense of personal well-being and strength.

-the need for success experiences.

(iv) The need for caring others:

-the use of those services which are available.

-the value of the therapeutic relationship.

-the importance of a caring group of like minded people.

Anthropological Needs

These can be expressed in terms of three interrelated, overlapping categories which are also related to the needs expressed in the other mediations.

(i) The need to articulate perceived unwell-being:

-the need to construct illness and healing symbols.

-culture-bound syndromes.

(ii) The need for understanding (To move from the threatening unknown to the known which can be dealt with):

-to find acceptable explanatory models.

-to find acceptable symbols to believe in.

(iii) Needs coming from culture change and acculturation:

-The need for new symbols to replace ineffective old ones.

-The need for identity/belonging in the new situation.

-The need to resist a threatening, alienating dominant culture:

-The need to create a resisting counter culture (subculture).

-The need to create a coherent acceptable life style in a threatening/dominant culture.

Socio-Economic Needs

These can be categorised in the two main socio-economic understandings of illness: social deprivation and social deviance:

(i) Deprivation needs emerging from socio-economic conditions:

-poverty, overcrowding, poor hygiene, lack of education, contagion etc.

-poor health-care infrastructure and poverty leading to the search for alternative, cheaper healing.

(ii) The need to move from perceived social deviance (ill) to social acceptance (well):

-The search for stability in social crisis.

-The need to move to interiority in social upheaval.

-The search for subcultures and groups where acceptance is given.

Philosophical Needs

These tend to be closely related to the anthropological ones since philosophy is largely a Western cultural approach to understanding and humanisation:

(i) The need to understand the illness and how to heal it:
-The need to move from the unknown to the known:
-naming the illness and describing its cure.
(ii) The need to be released from meaninglessness:
-anxiety and other psychological needs can be tied up with this.
(iii) The need for healing as humanisation.

Theological Needs

Theological needs tend to be tied with the struggle with sin and evil and the experience of God's transcendent power in one's life:

(i) The need of forgiveness from sin and guilt.

(ii) The need to fight and conquer demons and evil.

(iii)The need to experience God's power in one's life:
-the need to believe in the spiritual and have this belief confirmed.

In this way we see that the needs emerging from the context can be described in terms of fifteen types of needs which are interrelated amongst themselves and indeed which overlap. These fifteen needs emerge from the five epistemological mediations made in chapters three to seven on the Coping-healing phenomenon.

Once more we stress our contention that whilst the anthropological mediation remains one of the five, all of these needs are in fact culturally mediated when presented to the Coping-healing ministry. This is because illness is always a cultural construct and is confirmed by the appearance of cultural factors in all our mediations. Consequently we are predicting that the psycho-medical, anthropological, socio-economic, philosophical and theological needs we have presented will be perceived, experienced and identified in terms of the patterns of understandings expressed in symbols (cf. Geertz 1973:89) which are available to the person. This may be in terms of the cultural understanding of the person at the time but normally it is an extension of knowledge starting from the person's culture but somehow different to it, encompassing new elements which require "acceptance", "belief" or "conversion" by the sick person. It is this process of acceptance through the construction of new symbols in terms of acknowledged and understood old ones that effects the healing. For this reason the Coping-healing ministry is itself always culturally mediated. But it tends to incorporate, within its cultural horizon, some elements of the sick person's cultural horizon together with some new elements.

In a parallel fashion there seems to be some overlap and some diversity between the "culture" of the Church and that of the healers. This need for newness or diversity through which to express the mystery of the healing or in order to have "something" to "accept" or be "converted to", seems to be an essential part of the Coping-healing ministry and may go some way to explaining its fissile, sectarian nature. New, slightly differing groups seem to be always emerging and seem to need to be always emerging. Nevertheless, the healing is in this way also always a cultural construct and so the Coping-healing ministry is always a culturally mediated response to these culturally mediated needs. We now go on to examine the nature of the cultural mediation of the ministries.

The Culturally Mediated Pastoral Response

In our chapter on culture we indicated that a "group" understanding of culture is unhelpful in understanding the Coping-healing phenomenon and we opted for a semiotic understanding of culture on the epistemological level where we said that culture is basically communication and is oriented within an "understanding/misunderstanding" paradigm.To the extent that people understand one another or communicate, they share a culture and to the extent that they misunderstand or fail to communicate they do not share a culture. Thus culture can be described in terms of a field of continuous overlapping intersecting and interrelated semiotic domains within which people live. The nature of the field and the domains is their openness so that people may move in or out of them at will. For the purpose of analysis it is possible to construct models which categorise groups of people as sharing certain semiotic systems and in this way one identifies "cultural groupings". But one can only legitimately do this if one acknowledges the model as a "reduction" of reality and accepts the fundamental openness of the semiotic field: i.e. people can move in and out of it.

In this way, the Coping-healing ministry can be seen, on this epistemological level, to be operating within a semiotic domain which contains signs and symbols of sickness and healing. Through our own mediations we have attempted to identify and categorise these. Given this fact we now also need to indicate that within the totality of the semiotic domain of the Coping-healing phenomenon, there are sub-domains in which differing symbols and signs may represent the same processes. This is as a result of the heterogeneous nature of South African society. Thus whilst we can say that often, basically the same processes, the same kinds of needs and the same kinds of responses are occurring within the African Independent churches, the Neopentecostal churches and the other Coping-healing ministries we have investigated, we also have to say that some of the sign/symbol systems are shared, some are different and in some cases the same symbol/sign is carrying different meanings in different contexts.

For example, the symbol: "laying on of hands", is expressed and interpreted differently in different contexts. It is a simple action in the mainline church healing ceremony. It becomes a more dramatic pressing or pushing gesture in the "Miracle Tent Crusade" where people fall backwards and are caught by others standing behind them for this purpose. Finally, in the Zionist service, the action is expanded to include spinning the sick people and the "touching of the various parts of the body as well as slapping of the shoulders, back, arms and base of the head" and "hold[ing] the hands or forearms of a person, pull[ing] them in a kind of extending exercise". Clearly here we have a common biblical symbol which is being used in widely differing ways and which is communicating an understanding to the three groups which has some element of commonality (as a healing action) as well as a large measure of diversity. God's healing would probably not be communicated to the mainline church member in a Zionist Service and the converse would probably also be true.

The semiotic domain within which the African Independent churches operate is strongly influenced by what is normally referred to as the move from an African traditional culture to a Western culture and in particular an urban township cultural paradigm. That which still communicates from the cultural root is retained in the AIC practice whereas that which does not is discarded. Examples of the latter would be the expense of the traditional healer or the fact that since one is away from "home" and therefore one's ancestors, it is more difficult to communicate with them. The elements of Christianity which the AIC has adopted supply the new cultural elements or semiotic system which provide the requisite factor of newness which enables the construction of new symbols and in particular the necessary conversion process which we have identified as part of the Coping-healing phenomenon. We have also seen how the Coping-healing phenomenon constructs symbols of resistance to the perceived alienating dominant Western cultural paradigm within African Independent churches. It would seem safe to assert that similar symbols of resistance form part of the cultural parameters of the Neopentecostal churches and this would explain the emphasis on the anti-technological, anti-scientific standpoint of many of these organisations. Within these churches we also see a movement of culture change but in this case the move is from the dominant modern Western culture to the setting up of an

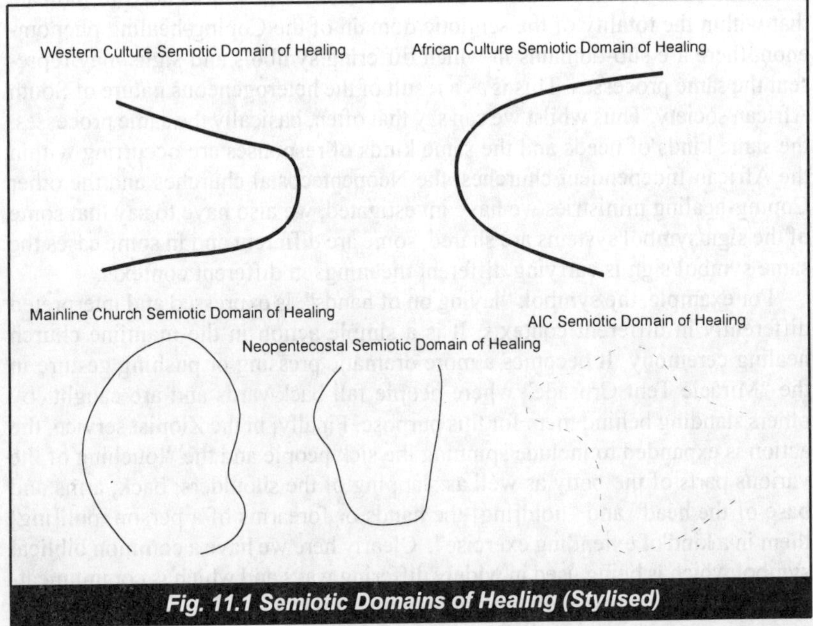

Fig. 11.1 Semiotic Domains of Healing (Stylised)

acculturated subculture stressing particular non-Western features and symbols. These include things like the direct manifestation of God's power in physical miracles, the theocratic nature of society, the attempt to demonise some Western values and forms such as computerisation, medicalisation, scientific method and conclusions, and the attempt to create an elite who are saved within the mass of society who are not.

The mainline churches on the other hand find themselves, largely, comfortably within the dominant Western cultural paradigm. Consequently if one were to draw a "culture map" of the various types of healing ministries we have considered it may look something like fig. 11.1. The diagrams are purely stylised representations, in the form of Venn diagrams, to indicate the differences between each domain. In fig. 11.2 we have combined the five domains into one map to indicate the overlapping of these domains as well as the areas of difference.

We note that the domain boundaries are open and not rigid for the reasons indicated above. We have illustrated five semiotic domains of healing: the Neopentecostal church, the African Independent church, the mainline church, African traditional cultural healing and Western healing. Clearly the three "categories" of church that we consider respond to the types of ministry we have investigated but are again only theoretical models for the purpose of analysis. Reality is naturally more complex. Given this caveat we note that each type of church is working within a particular semiotic domain of healing which informs its own ministerial approach. In this way the ministry itself is a culturally mediated response to the culturally mediated needs.

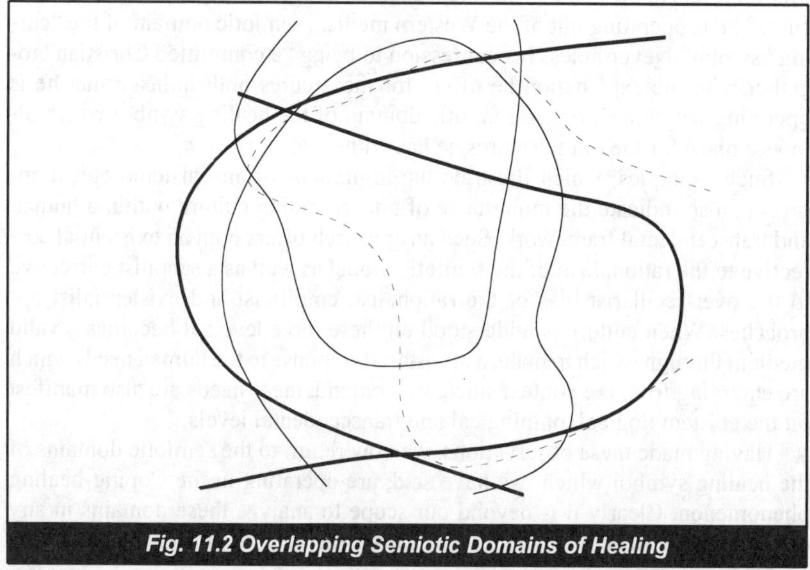

Fig. 11.2 Overlapping Semiotic Domains of Healing

It should be clear that the semiotic domain of healing out of which a member of a certain church who is looking for healing is operating need not necessarily be the same as the one out of which the church is itself working. But we can assume that the healing would not be effective if the minister/preacher cannot convince the sick person to accept the church's position and move within its semiotic domain of healing. This is usually the role of the conversion process and explains why a perceived experience of healing usually goes together with conversion and adherence to the church. By the same token, someone operating within a semiotic domain of healing which is very different to that accepted by the church would find it very difficult to be convinced by its arguments. This helps to explain the position of authors such as Stumpf, Levin and Rose. Normally one would assume that the presence of the ill person at the healing service presumes a certain openness to the process and a willingness to move within the horizon of the minister and his ministry, a willingness fuelled by the hope for healing. All of these factors work synergistically to catalyze the process of convincing.

Nevertheless, the evidence of Knight and Proctor is more difficult to fit into the analysis offered above and reminds us of the limitations of a semiotic analysis. These are important limitations which we need to take seriously. It is for this reason that we have referred to an "unexplained remnant" and "unknown factors" as operating within this ministry. Knight's experience of seeing the physical healing of a medical condition before his eyes on national television clearly violated his own understanding of healing and forced him to widen his own understanding apparently against any predisposition to do so. Similarly, when Proctor refers to the healings he has witnessed as "genuine inexplicable miracle cures" he is operating out of the Western medical semiotic domain of the "curing" symbol. Nevertheless his confession to being "a committed Christian" together with the explanation he offers for these cures both indicate that he is operating within a Christian semiotic domain of the healing symbol which allows a place for the miracle cures he has witnessed.

Such examples, which illustrate the limitations of an epistemological approach, also indicate the importance of understanding culture within a human and transcendental framework. Such an approach offers both an existential corrective to the rationalism of the semiotic model as well as a sacralist corrective to the over-secularist bias of the rationalist, empiricist and existentialist approaches. When culture is understood on these three levels it becomes a valid medium through which to make a ministerial response to the human needs which are emerging from the context since, we contend, these needs are also manifest on the epistemological, ontological and transcendental levels.

Having made these observations, we now return to the semiotic domains of the healing symbol which, we have said, are operating in the Coping-healing phenomenon. Clearly it is beyond our scope to analyze these domains in any detail but nevertheless we feel that it is necessary to at least indicate, in a very general way, some of the factors which play a role in an adequate understanding of the healing ministry. These factors make up the structure of the healing symbol within the domain. Clearly there will be a lot of overlap between the various domains, representing areas of commonality. These may be historically conditioned like the symbol of "demon" which is found in both AIC and Neopentecostal semiotic healing domains and to a much lesser extent the mainline churches. The symbol is both biblical and part of the Western culture of the middle ages. This latter has been diminished by the role of secularisation in modern Western culture but it has persevered through groups which have resisted secularisation. It is thus available to be transmitted to those who feel alienated by modern Western culture: a process which goes on in the Neopentecostal type churches. In the AIC's, the symbol is also related to traditional African cultural systems where it is tied into such factors as "witchcraft" and "sorcery" *(ubuthakathi)*, ancestors (but of another family or tribe - since a person's own ancestors could not be seen as evil spirits) and avenging spirits of one or other type. Usually spirits are identified with people who have passed away whereas in the Neopentecostal churches the demons are not given a human characteristic but are often identified with the sickness and evils which befall people.

Another symbol which is used differently within the three Coping-healing ministry domains is the Bible. Within the Neopentecostal church the Bible is seen as a direct immediate fixed communication of God's truth to be literally believed. Within the mainline churches the Bible has to be interpreted or mediated. So the truth of the Bible depends on the interpreters. Interpretation in mainline churches ranges from the informality of the ministers or congregations on the one hand to the dogma of the enshrined tradition as interpreted by the Magisterium on the other. In the African Independent churches, the Bible is largely a symbol of God's presence and power. It is an audio-visual symbol rather than a written one and the reader will often be quoting only learnt texts rather than reading from the book.

This discussion on the symbols of "demons" and "the Bible" serves to illustrate the way in which particular symbols which operate with the semiotic domains of healing are themselves symbolising both overlapping and intersecting human understandings. That is to say that together with some commonality one can also identify some diversity. The ministry which is informed by such a semiotic domain will also reflect these variations in its execution. We will now briefly indicate some of the important factors operating in the main semiotic domains of healing:

The AIC Semiotic Domain of Healing

The AIC understanding of the healing ministry includes the following factors, signs and symbols:

(i) From African Traditional Culture:

-Sickness which is cured by medicine *(umkhuhlane)*.
-Sickness which is personal and relational *(isifo sabantu)*.

-The role of ancestors, spirits, alien pollution from spirits/ people of other groups nations etc.
-Dreams.
-Community/group emphasis.
-Role of dance, music, touch in acting/living out the sickness and the healing.
-Power *(amandla* sourced in *USomandla).*

(ii) From Christianity:
-Healing by the Holy Spirit/Spirit of Jesus.
-Healing by God's power.
-The Bible.
-Rejection of "witchcraft", "sorcery" and any form of ancestor possession.
-Demons.
-Laying on of hands.
-Prayer.
-Sacramentals.
-holy water.
-ash.
-crucifixes, candles, rosaries.
-uniforms.

(iii) From Western Culture:
-Use of hospitals and medicines (not all AIC's accept this).
-Resistance symbols to the dominant culture
-night services.
-healing by closing out the alien outside.
-closing doors and curtains.
-removing shoes on entrance.
-symbolic changing of clothes in purification ceremonies.

The Neopentecostal Semiotic Domain of Healing.

The Neopentecostal understanding of the healing ministry includes the following factors, signs and symbols.

(i) From Western Culture:
-Acceptance of the Capitalist system.
-Use of music, decor, electronics to create atmosphere.
-Use of psychological methods like counselling, group therapy etc. under different names.
-Symbols of resistance to Western culture.
-world-view which is:
-anti-intellectual.
-anti-scientific.

-anti-secularist.

-Allowing and fostering emotional expression.

(ii) From the Church Tradition:

-Prayer.
-The Bible.
-Non-conformist/Protestant ethos.
-Laying on of hands.
-Hymn singing.
-Healing by God's power.
-Demons.

(iii) Particular to the Church:

-Theocratic world-view.
-Immediate rather than mediated relationship with God.
-"God said to me" sermons.
-Bible as literal word not to be interpreted.
-healing as God's direct intervention.
-Faith as "ask and you will receive"
-faith as power.
-Wealth as a sign of blessing.

Mainline Churches' Semiotic Domain of Healing.

The mainline churches' understanding of healing includes the following factors, signs and symbols.

(i) From Western Culture:

-Medical model of curing.
-Growing importance of psychology and counselling.
-Accept "reality" as it is.
-Miracles don't happen.
-Secularism.

(ii) From Church Tradition:

-Value of prayer/sacraments/sacramentals.
-The Bible (which must be interpreted).
-Accept God's will even when it is not your will.
-God can intervene in exceptional very rare cases.
-Importance of development, social upliftment and justice.

Our description of the factors making up these three semiotic domains, which are intended to be indicative rather than comprehensive, show how there is a measure of agreement and diversity within the three types of church. An analysis of different types of mainline church, or different types of African Independent church or different types of Neopentecostal church would also show areas of agreement and disagreement. Nevertheless the three groups do represent three major categories of pastoral approach. The ministries operating within these three semiotic domains of healing would then clearly determine their pastoral response using the symbols operating within the relevant semiotic domain. Finally we note that within the South African context these three ministries are influencing one another since they are operating within the same context and people are related to one another within this context in many ways such as family, work, social relationships and other types of contacts.

11.2.4 Other Factors Operating in the Coping-Healing Ministry

To conclude this section on situating the Coping-healing ministry we wish to mention briefly four other factors which need to be considered in making our theological judgement upon it. The first two of these concern the way in which we ascribe religious and theological categories to the ministry. The next factor concerns the essential role that success factors play in this ministry. Finally we consider the challenge that this ministry has on the whole Church.

"Religious" and "Secular" Characteristics of the Ministry

We have noted that amongst the Coping-healing ministers, the articulation of what happens in the ministry occurs within the particular religious and theological world-view that they subscribe to and we have analyzed how this type of healing works in terms of psychological factors, anthropological factors, sociological factors philosophical factors as well as theological factors. If factors from each of these epistemological domains can be found to be operating in this ministry, we should be cautioned about the immediate ascribing of transcendental and supernatural mechanisms to what can be understood through natural mechanisms. This is a simple application of the philosophical principle of "Ockham's Razor".[6] Clearly we subscribe to a theological position which sees the presence of God in the natural and the natural as reflecting God through his creation (cf. Ps 8; Ps 19). But to ascribe direct supernatural intervention resulting from faith to what are mechanisms which can be described by natural factors would seem to be unacceptable. What we are saying here is that much of what happens in the Coping-healing ministry can be explained by non-transcendental natural mechanisms and that there is a danger in ascribing religious categories involving God's direct intervention through faith, prayer and so on to what is actually a manipulation of natural forces.

Having said this, however, we wish to add that most Christian ministry operates through using natural forces. When we help people, serve them, love them; when we visit the sick and the prisoners and fulfil all the injunctions of the Lord's commands to love people we are able to use natural forces and indeed have to use them since ministry and mission is the Church in the world. Consequently ministry is always a marrying of the natural and the supernatural. This marriage occurs in two main ways. Firstly we ascribe religious significance to our actions through our faith. When a Christian loves, serves or helps as a Christian, this loving, and serving becomes ministry. Secondly, we accept the fact that God, through his Holy Spirit, continues to work in his ministers to build his

Kingdom and continue Christ's work. By attributing healing in this way to the power of God operating in the world, the Coping-healing ministers are correct and we need to hear their word.

We have emphasised two points here. Firstly we note the danger of ascribing supernatural categories to natural phenomena but on the other hand we stress the importance of seeing that ministry is always a mixture of the natural and supernatural. Although it may seem that we are condoning two contradictory positions, the contradiction only exists when one absolutises one or the other of the two particular world-views or semiotic domains out of which each of these points come.

The first point is a critique emerging from a Western scientific world-view whereas the second comes out of an attempt to construct a holistic religious world-view. We contend that it is the acceptance of differing "standpoints", "fields of semiotic domains" or "cultures" within a greater whole and yet recognising the value in itself of each perspective and the danger of absolutising each perspective which provides one of the keys to situating and understanding these ministries.

The Importance of Success Factors

The importance of success factors in this ministry is crucial. It is clear that not all who ask for healing receive it. It is also clear that in the churches we have examined, success is achieved when people receive what they want. The process of the cultural mediation of needs produces "wants". When people receive what they want then a "success" experience occurs. When success is achieved, energy is produced which helps bind the person to the organisation fulfilling the wants. This is the language of consumerism and we have deliberately employed it in describing this process to indicate its inherent ambiguity and the necessity of providing some criteria of judgement. What people want is not necessarily what they need and someone's "want" may deny another person some other necessity. The evils of apartheid, capitalism and communism have taught us this lesson. Some so-called healings inflict psychological damage on individuals. We have also seen the opinion of some authors that the Coping-healing phenomenon tends to produce "subcultures" of groups alienated from society whose withdrawal allows social evils to go unchallenged. Needs are hardly being fulfilled in such cases though "wants" may be. On the other hand, "wants" do often reflect needs and responding to them is the best way of building up the society or establishing God's reign. This relationship between "wants" and "needs" requires careful analysis when making theological judgements on ministry.

The Challenge to the Church

To the extent that the Coping-healing ministry is responding to real needs, it is offering a challenge to the whole Church and in particular to those sections of the Church which do not practice this ministry. The Scriptures clearly testify to the missionary mandate to heal and this ministry is an essential part of the Church's total ministry. It is perhaps the boundness of the mainline churches to modern Western culture and its scientific world-view which has reduced this ministry to the medical missions. The new Coping-healing churches have provided a challenge to once more examine the necessity of this ministry within the whole Church and the search for the varied cultural forms of its realisation from place to place would now seem to be essential. This is the task of a true inculturation of this ministry, a point we now go on to examine.

11.3 The Local Church as the Locus of the Healing Ministry: An Inculturated Ministry

11.3.1 A local Church Differentiated by Culture

We have already presented George's affirmation that "cultural unity is . . . a legitimate basis for describing a group of culturally similar dioceses as a 'local Church'" as well as our own affirmation that "culture thus becomes a theological category, playing a part, although not an exclusive one, in indicating the nature and praxis of a local Church". Within the South African context, one aspect of the particularity of our situation and indeed one aspect of the "South African culture" which is emerging is the reality of unity and plurality which permeates it. The structure of the plethora of linking semiotic domains which operate within this context can be referred to as the "South African culture". The Coping-healing phenomenon also needs to be seen within this unity in diversity paradigm. Indeed, one of the aims of our work has been to indicate the underlying unity, also emerging from the context, which surrounds the Coping-healing ministry as experienced in the different churches we have considered. In the past, as a result of more traditional, rather ethnic, cultural understandings, Coping-healing approaches in African Independent churches, Neopentecostal churches and mainline churches were treated as mutually exclusive things. It is the reappropriation of culture as communication, humanisation and sanctification which allows what were formerly seen as different to manifest their fundamental relatedness. It is culture understood in this way which can inform the nature of the local Church. Thus we are moving from an awareness and understanding of a plethora of "cultures" and indeed "churches" within the South African context to the search for an underlying unity which relates the particularities without denying them. It is in this way that we understand a local Church, differentiated by culture, emerging in the Southern African context.

Consequently, it is in this way that we see an inculturated Coping-healing ministry of this local Church. We suggest that the Coping-healing practices we have studied present some signs of the emergence of this inculturated ministry. The extent to which this ministry is truly the ministry of such a local Church may be judged by comparing the way in which this ministry manifests the Kingdom Of God in the world. In the previous chapter we indicated five ways in which this manifestation may be judged. We now wish to apply these criteria to the Coping-healing ministries we have considered so far.

11.3.2 Coping-Healing at the Service of God's Reign

In fig. 10.1 we indicated that the fundamental commitment and final objective of the Church was to be at the service of the Kingdom of God. The Kingdom of God, in fact, is manifest in the Church through five principal dimensions and means. In *martyria*, the Church witnesses its faith in the risen Lord and people give their lives to and for the Lord to allow his Kingdom to be manifest through them. In *koinonia* the People of God manifest the essential communal nature of God's Kingdom living the truth of being one body in one Lord. In *diakonia* the Kingdom is realised through the command to love and serve others and in particular the poor. In *kerygma* the Kingdom is proclaimed as Good News for the people of all places, times and contexts. In *leitourgia* the Kingdom is celebrated as the living presence of God amongst his people through worship and prayer[7].

All ministry seeks to realise God's Kingdom in one or other of these means and thus all ministry can in some way be measured to the extent that it actualises one or more of these five dimensions. It is thus our intention to compare the Coping-healing ministry to these criteria to see how and to what extent it manifests them.

The Coping-Healing Ministry as Martyria

Martyria refers to the witnessing of the Kingdom of God and the risen Christ in the lives of believers. It is rooted in a living faith. When the ministry of the Church is genuine it witnesses to Christ in his death and resurrection. This witness is the full offering of the ministers to be followers of Jesus as they themselves offer their lives to his service. This is what we refer to as *martyria*. The martyrs may be witnesses through the shedding of their blood for the Kingdom of God as Jesus did, but this dimension of the Church's praxis may also be fulfilled by those who offer their lives to Christ in the lifelong fulfilling of the Father's will. Indeed anyone who witnesses to Christ and the Father is living out this dimension of the Church's mission.

In the various practices of the Coping-healing ministry we have studied, we have seen that healing can be understood as a witness to the manifestation of the Kingdom of God in the life of a person or community. The ministry offers signs of the Kingdom of God here and now. We have noted that the healers heal in the name of Jesus Christ, and through the power of the Holy Spirit. We also recognise that healing "demands a worshipping community" and that the healing is achieved with reference to the Church and its faith. Indeed the role of faith is central and where the healings are achieved through faith in Jesus Christ then the ministry truly witnesses to the power of the Lord. Many who are healed give their lives to the Lord. They are converted and become Christians. In this way the ministry is a means to evangelisation as it was in the Acts of the Apostles. Moreover, we have seen that the healing achieved in the Coping-healing ministry often reflects a praxis which is closer to the biblical cultural framework than to the Western cultural framework. In this way such healing witnesses the need for Westerners both in and out of the Church to transcend their own limited horizons. Finally, the tremendous upsurge in this ministry is seen as an indicator of the presence of the Holy Spirit and the ministry thus witnesses to him.

On the other hand we have seen that many of the conversions are not permanent and that many become disillusioned and leave when so-called miracle cures are only temporary remissions. Others become disillusioned when they are told that their faith is not strong enough for healing. This false use of faith which runs the risk of becoming "faith in faith" rather than faith in God is a counter witness to the Kingdom. This can also be said of all ministers who raise false hopes of healing in people when such healing cannot be guaranteed. To be healed is not always a witness of following Jesus by accepting the Cross and God's will. In such cases there is a counter witness to the Kingdom. A false witness to the Kingdom of God seems also to be given when healing caused by other psychological and anthropological factors is attributed directly to God's power. In such cases one can speak of a counter witness to truth.

The Coping-Healing Ministry as Koinonia

We say that the Kingdom of God is manifest in the Church when the Church is a site of *koinonia*. By *koinonia* we understand all that impinges upon true community. Community implies relatedness, unity, sharing, concern for one another and openness to others. The Coping-healing ministry usually operates within the framework of a community of believers and usually attempts to situate the sick people within community so that they become part of it. In this way those who are ill have the opportunity of being part of a caring, affirming, loving group of people and this experience is itself therapeutic. Clearly this is an experience of *koinonia*.

We have also recognised that some of the healings achieved are related to the restoring of disturbed relationships between people as well as to the experience of personal and social reconstruction within a context of personal, interpersonal or social crisis and fragmentation. In this way, the ministry provides a site of resistance to the evils of society and a place of refuge amongst a group of caring others in which people may be renewed and refreshed in order to go out once more to confront the alienating, dehumanising world. In all of these ways then we can say that the Coping-healing phenomenon manifests the gospel value of *koinonia*.

However we have also noted areas within this phenomenon which seem to militate against this value and its full expression. Several authors have shown the danger of groups which close themselves off to the outside world in order to create artificial subcultures which then do not participate in the world and its transformation but become alienated from it. Clearly religious withdrawal from a society in which people still have to live is not a true manifestation of real adult communion but can rather be a regression into an acceptance of a simplistic subculture within a complex world. In this case one has to question whether true communion, which is an expression of human freedom and maturity, is not replaced by an adherence to a simplistic, immature lifestyle which destroys rather than transforms adult human freedom and which is therefore not true communion nor community. Such a conclusion is reinforced when communication is used for the manipulation of emotions and not for true human liberation . The danger of too much control by the leader within the group and the arbitrary use of psychological techniques of emotional manipulation without a true understanding of their mechanisms can lead to the formation of unhealthy rather than healthy groups of people. When this occurs the Coping-healing phenomenon is destructive of *koinonia* and is not ministry.

This point is related to the dissociative nature of these churches. Emerging new leaders tend to split off to found their own separate communities which become discrete independent bodies with little or no relationship to the whole. Some of these groups then become highly sectarian in nature, denying the legitimacy of other Christian groupings and setting themselves up as the sole possessors of truth. Clearly such attitudes are divisive of unity and in particular deny the fundamental fact that the Church of Christ is one. A country with over five thousand separate Christian churches could hardly be said to be living in *koinonia* on this greater level.

The Coping-Healing Ministry as Diakonia

Diakonia refers to the way in which the Church attempts through its praxis to make the Kingdom of God manifest in the world. It refers to all those attributes of care, concern and service which the community of faith is required to bring to its actions. *Diakonia* is manifest in service, charity, justice and peace and in all which promotes human liberation and development. The Coping-healing ministry clearly manifests *diakonia* when it helps in the personal and social reconstruction of people and in their humanisation. We have also seen how the ministry responds to people by responding to their need for esteem, belonging, hope, dignity and self-respect. It also provides a place of refuge for those who find themselves in times of crisis where the move to interiority and re-assessment is necessary. In this way it provides a means of coping with the complexity and anxiety of life and is valuable for the short term reassessment needed from time to time. In its fight against sin and evil it also promotes the realisation of God's Kingdom and manifests service. Some describe this process as realised eschatology. Clearly the ministry is fulfilling an important social role in "overcoming personal and social disadvantage by religious experience." Finally it has also fulfilled the role of helping people adjust to the new social environments they find themselves living in as a result of migration.

On the other hand, some authors have questioned some of the practices operating in the Coping-healing phenomenon indicating how people can also be rendered a disservice through them. It has been suggested that these churches and the so-called healing they give provides a means of helping people to cope with evil without confronting it and defeating it. These churches have been accused of supporting a form of political quiescence and of the fact that they mitigate against the necessity to heal society of its ills by encouraging social withdrawal. In this way the value of a temporary withdrawal in order to deal with personal and social crisis through personal and social re-assessment is transformed into a disvalue by making this withdrawal permanent. Coping-healing then becomes distorted into disability: a permanent refuge for those who cannot cope with reality and who are confirmed in their inability to find ways of coping with the complexity of life in the affirmation of the withdrawal from it.

We have also pointed out the dangers of a consumerist approach to religion in the Coping-healing phenomenon where people's "wants" are dealt with rather than their needs. Such an approach manifests itself in the justification of non-Christian attitudes such as those of the prosperity creeds. This too is clearly not serving people. Finally, we note the conflict of interests which may exist between healers and patients. When the healer uses his gifts to satisfy his own interests rather than those of the patient, then manipulation will occur rather than healing. Such a conflict may also hamper the Coping-healing ministry when the search for success in order to have bigger and better churches, a secure healing practice, a good reputation and financial stability may result in a lack of care for those who are not healed and even a rejection of them and their faith. When such things occur, the Coping-healing phenomenon does not demonstrate *diakonia* and is no longer ministry but something else.

The Coping-Healing Ministry as Kerygma.

The *kerygma* is the message which is to be preached. It is the good news in all its fullness that Christians believe in and are called communicate to all people to the end of time. This good news manifests itself as the "Word", the gospel, the Bible and all that teaches us about God's presence in our lives. The Coping-healing ministry proclaims the *kerygma* when people are truly healed through God's power, His message is communicated into the lives of people and they are evangelised. We have seen that Christ as healer is preached in this ministry and that the Church's missionary mandate to heal is fulfilled. Clearly the *kerygma* is being proclaimed when people are being brought to conversion and when the role of God and particularly the risen Lord is given the priority in the exercising of the ministry. The emphasis on faith in the Lord and his power to heal is also a practical manifestation of the acceptance of the message in the life of a person or community.

However, when faith in Jesus becomes faith in faith then a message other than the *kerygma* is being preached as several authors have pointed out. Here we are seeing the influence of persuasion, positive thinking and other metaphysical cult movements rather than the gospel. A similar judgement must be made when the sick are blamed for their illness for not having enough faith. Other authors have indicated the falseness of the prosperity gospel as not being of the *kerygma* and the lack of an adequate *theologia crucis* in the message proclaimed. Such a selective use of the Scriptures can lead to a deformation of the *kerygma* and the preaching of another message. Many authors have expressed concern in this area. It seems that here we can recognise the incorporation of cultural factors in the inculturation process. These cultural factors, however, have not yet been transformed by the inculturation process. Perhaps the concern of the authors already reflects a step in the transformation process. Finally we note the confusion which surrounds the issue of "spirit" in the African Independent churches and the tendency to over-emphasis of the spirit and under-emphasis of Jesus in its ministry. All of these factors need to be taken into account when making a judgement on the difficult issue of the extent to which the Coping-healing phenomenon proclaims the *kerygma*.

The Coping-Healing Ministry as Leitourgia

We use the term *leitourgia* to refer to all which has to do with the worship of God in prayer, ritual, praise, ceremony, spirituality and piety. The Christian community is called to be a prayerful, worshipping community and all Christians are called to a relationship with God expressed in prayer and worship. Since the Coping-healing phenomenon we have been studying is almost entirely expressed within the context of prayer and worship, it is useful for us to make a comparison of the ministry we have presented with how we would expect the church to celebrate the presence of God's reign through *leitourgia*.

All that we have presented leads to the conclusion that worship is truly happening within the Coping-healing ministry. The ministry "demands a worshipping community and healing is achieved with reference to the Church and its faith". The transcendence of God and God's power to intervene in power for the wellbeing of His people is both celebrated and often realised in the Coping-healing services. God's presence and power is acknowledged as operating through believing people to actualise the ministry. The means of healing are through prayer and ritualised action such as the laying on of hands, touch, blowing and so forth. Sacramentals such as holy water, ash and prayer chords are also used. We have also seen that the services and ceremonies used correspond to the culture of the people involved. There is a high degree of the use of cultural worship forms in the rituals of both the African Independent churches and the Neopentecostal churches. In the former this is seen in the use of dress, dance, music, the healing circle and so forth. In the latter we see the sophisticated use of electronics, music as community singing, music as concert, and the use of atmosphere-creating decor. Many of the cultural forms manifest here belong to show-business and drama forms which speak powerfully to Westerners of the 1990's (cf. n.2).

Such cultural forms are valuable and have their role. Drama, for example, will always be a part of *leitourgia* due to its ability to open us to the transcendent. Nevertheless, we also need to be aware of the inherent dangers. There is no doubt that part of the purpose of the Coping-healing services is the ability to move people out of the ordinary to a state of being able to experience "otherness". If the aim of this is to open people up to the transcendence of God, this may be a valuable exercise but when the focus changes and the aim becomes the pure manipulation of people's emotions to achieve particular psycho-emotive effects then the negative side of this process may emerge. Psychology teaches us of the processes and mechanisms which can cause people to emote and how emotions can be manipulated. When this is done by untrained, unaware people who ascribe all that happens to "the action of the Holy Spirit and God" we have moved away from *leitourgia* and into the dangerous field of amateur group dynamics.

Finally, it seems to us that in most of the Coping-healing churches there is a disproportionate emphasis on healing. Whilst this is clearly an important part of the Church's ministry one would question the fact that almost every service should always end up in healing. There is also the danger that the positive emphasis on claiming a healing which God always gives mitigates against a spirit of prayer and worship which is always focused on finding God's will for the worshipping community and then doing it. Prayer is always praise, thanksgiving and petition. And petition, the least important third dimension of prayer, is always a request in accordance with the will of the Father. We need vigilance to ensure that prayer remains true to its nature.

This reflection on the Coping-healing ministry in terms of the five means and dimensions of ecclesial praxis in manifesting God's Kingdom through the Church, has shown us that the Coping-healing ministry is indeed a true ministry of the Church implementing *martyria, koinonia, diakonia, kerygma*, and *leitourgia* where it is practised. At the same time we have also noted areas where it is also countering the implementation of these five dimensions. We believe that the reason for this is that the ministry is not yet fully inculturated within the South African local Church. In the inculturation model we have presented we would say that it is the manifestation of a ministry emerging within the assimilation phase of the inculturation process. We now briefly examine this statement.

11.3.3 Coping-Healing: A Partially Inculturated Ministry

In the diagram illustrating the process of the emergence of a local Church (fig. 10.2) we indicated that after Church implantation, an acculturation process occurs in which there is tension between the culture of the sending Church and the local culture. As a result of this, specific local practices emerge which are frowned upon by the "official" new Church. This is the process which has given rise to the growth of the independent churches of which the AICs and Neopentecostals are examples. The Coping-healing ministry presents the clearest manifestation of this process. By and large, the ministry has grown up within these churches. They have been successful precisely because they are responding to culturally mediated needs within the local context when the "official" Church does not.

As the inculturation process continues, however, it moves from a translation phase to an assimilation phase where the Church becomes more open to receiving from the local culture and where more dialogue between the local Church and its culture occurs. This is usually dependent on the presence of local people in the leadership of the Church. This phase is illustrated as step 5 in our diagram (fig. 10.2). Coming from the context and its culture, such people have themselves experienced the culturally mediated needs in question and will have had some experience of culturally mediated responses like those of the Coping-healing ministry. It is our contention that we find ourselves at this stage in the inculturation process with regard to the Coping-healing ministry in South Africa. Our analysis in the last section has shown that in many respects it conforms to the nature of a true ministry in the One, Holy, Catholic and Apostolic Church.[8] However we have also noted that it retains elements which still need to be transformed since they reflect impure and non-Christian values. Our model predicts that such a process only occurs in the transformation moment after assimilation and so the Church should not be closed to this ministry for those reasons. As the local Church emerges there is a "growing awareness of the requirement to respond to local needs" (step 6 fig. 10.2). This, we contend, is our present situation. We suggest that the Coping-healing ministry bears the signs of an inculturated ministry within the local Church and all attempts at its assimilation and transformation should be promoted.

This, we suggest, is particularly the case now within the South African context. The country finds itself within an assimilation and transformation phase as a New South Africa is being born. The events of the last few decades have impressed upon us how sick the country and its peoples really are as a result of the imposition of inhumane, devilish systems upon all people. Black and White, rich and poor, in their own different ways, have been infected with this sickness and the context as a whole cries out for healing. In fact we should be astonished if there were no healing ministry around with such sickness in the society. The need for healing is perhaps the greatest need for all our people at this time. If this is the case then we can say that inculturation today should be focused on healing.

The transformation which needs to go on within the people, can be described within a healing paradigm, as can the centrality of the Church's mission to its people at this time. Inculturation as healing and the emergence of the healing ministry in the South African local Church seems to be a sign of the Kingdom whose *kairos* has arrived.

11.4 Conclusion: Healing and the Universal Church

We have already stated that healing is an essential part of the Church's mission as it was of Jesus' own ministry. We have seen how the missionary mandate of Matthew's tenth chapter is often overshadowed by that of his twenty eighth chapter in the Church's understanding of mission. Consequently, we have affirmed that the mission to heal the sick and cast out demons forms an essential part of the missionary task. Such a task needs to be part of the nature of the One, Holy, Catholic and Apostolic Church since mission is part of the Church's nature (AG2; WCC 1990b:34; Lausanne 1974:n.6 in Scherer & Bevans 1992:256). At the moment, the mission to heal seems to be focused on the periphery of the Church in the multitude of separate churches whose very separateness provides a counter witness to the oneness of the Church. The ministry represents a challenge to this oneness through greater openness and dialogue and an acceptance of the sign which this ministry is making to the whole, One, Church of Christ.

A similar comment could be made with regard to the catholic nature of the Church. Catholic in its true meaning relates to the universality of the Church and is always a challenge to the community of faith which is continually called to respond to the prompting of the Holy Spirit who is never confined to the boundaries of the Church. In the Coping-healing ministry we suggest that we are seeing the working of the Holy Spirit challenging the Church to openness to His/Her presence and the presence of God's reign within this ministry. This is a call to greater catholicity in the Church's mission. It also reflects how the true process of inculturation occurs through the onward leading of the Spirit as the pillar of cloud led the people of Israel out of Egypt.

Similarly we need to see the exercising of the ministry as the manifestation of the Church's holy nature. By healing, the people are sanctified and the Church too is sanctified when it creates ways for God to heal people through its ministry. It is "realised eschatology" where God's sanctifying presence to people is effected. Finally we note how this ministry responds to the Apostolic Nature of the Church. The ministry is apostolic in that through it the Church does what the apostles did (cf. Lk 9-10; Acts) and it is apostolic in that it reaches out in service to others so that the power of God may reach them through the apostles of today.

The Coping-healing ministry we have studied forms, then, a part of the total healing ministry of the whole Church of God when it is understood in the way we have presented it. In fig. 11.3 we attempt to represent the totality of the healing ministry that the One, Holy, Catholic and Apostolic Church is called to. The diagram which is partly new is also partially indebted to MacNutt (1974:166) and to the class notes of a former professor at St Joseph's, Cedara: Fr. Theo Kneifel who himself was inspired by the need of people for healing in their life, who worked for their liberation and who was expelled from South Africa by the apartheid regime in 1986. In this diagram we situate the Coping-healing ministry within the totality of the Church's healing ministry in the hope that this work has helped to clarify something of the nature of this ministry, its importance at this time in our country, South Africa, and to indicate the areas of purification and transformation it still needs to undergo.

South Africa is a microcosm of the world context where the need for healing on a world-wide scale is being reflected in the growth of all kinds of healing movements and churches. Some of these are professedly Christian, others are not. In attempting to clarify the nature and necessity of the Coping-healing ministry within the South African context we hope that we have also contributed to an understanding of this ministry, its value and its limitations, within the greater global context. What is clear is that both nationally and internationally there is a growing awareness of the necessity to rekindle this essential dimension of the Church's mission to all to whom apostles are sent.

Sickness	Diagnosis	Human Therapy
Physical Sickness	Organic factors	Medical / Surgical Intervention (Western and African)
	Psychological factors • psychogenic • psychosomatic	Psychotherapy
	Social factors: (See Social Sickness)	
	Cultural factors	Cultural (Folk) Healing
	Spiritual factors: (See Spiritual Sickness)	
Emotional Sickness	Original Sin (Person hurt by the sin of others)	Psychotherapy Counselling
	Organic factors (see above) Psychological factors (See above) Cultural factors (See above) Social factors (See Social Sickness)	
Social Sickness	Original Sin (See also above) Sinful/Evil social structures: • economic • socio-political • interpersonal	Conscientisation Socio-political action for justice
Spiritual Sickness	Personal Sin	Confession and reparation
Demonic Sickness	Demonic • possession • obsession	

Fig. 11.3 Dimensions of The Healing Ministry

Prayer	**Sacraments and Sacramentals**	**Communal Service / Worship**
Prayer for physical healing by: • individual or • group	Anointing of sick Holy water, ash *iziwasho*	Healing Services
Prayer for inner healing Prayer for forgiveness	Penance, Anointing	Healing Services Penitential Services
Prayer using culturally significant healing symbols by culturally significant religious leader	Laying on of hands Penance, Anointing, Holy water, *iziwasho*, "casting out" and "binding sick-ness"	Healing Services Penance Services
Prayer for inner healing Healing of memories	Baptism Penance	Healing Services Penance Services
Prayer for inner freedom and integrity Prayer for social justice Prayer for prophetic discernment	Baptism Penance Prophetic signs	Services for: • social awareness • conscientisation • justice • reconciliation Social healing Penitential Services
Prayer of repentance Prayer of contrition Prayer of forgiveness	Penance Baptism Holy water, Ash Laying on of hands	Penitential Services
Prayer for deliverance	Exorcism, Holy water crucifix	Communal Prayer for deliverance from Possession/Obses-sion

Chapter 12

Inculturation and Healing: Conclusions

12.1 The Inculturation Model: A Powerful Missiological Tool

The inculturation model is particularly valuable in helping the Church identify the scope and nature of its mission: its praxis. We have seen how it does this by taking into account the context and cultural matrix within which a local Church finds itself together with the historical process which has brought it to a particular moment. Included in this historical dimension is the role of the Holy Spirit who continues to be with the Church enlightening, sanctifying, counselling and comforting the people of God as they journey onward. It is the Spirit which reveals the *kairos* in each historical period. By taking both synchronic and diachronic dimensions into account the inculturation model roots the *kairos* in praxis, and the praxis in *kairos*. It is the ability to analyze this dialectic which gives the inculturation model its value.

Our work has attempted to analyze this dialectic from the perspective of a South African context which has been sickened by the sin of apartheid and racism over many years. This sickness has exacerbated the social and personal sickness which exists here as it does elsewhere throughout the world as a result of the sin and selfishness of the modern era. Consequently the South African context has a universal component as well as a specific one. This context describes the natural dimension of the *kairos*. Within the context, Christian Coping-healing practices have become more and more prominent so that today the largest grouping of Christians in South Africa belong to Coping-healing churches and probably the majority of Christians in the country have experienced these practices in one form or another. The extent of the Coping-healing phenomenon, involving the majority of Christians in South Africa, is probably unique in the world.

The healing ministry represents, in all its varied forms, the praxis of the Church as it attempts to respond to the presence of the Holy Spirit in this situation of sickness. And discernment of the Holy Spirit within a context reflects the supernatural dimension of the *kairos*. However the question arises whether or not the plethora of Coping-healing practices which have emerged, appropriating to themselves the label Christian, are in fact manifesting the Church's healing praxis. This is the subject of our investigation.

12.2 Coping-Healing and The Healing Ministry

We have seen that South Africa is indeed a sick society currently undergoing transformation. Part of this transformation is seen in the efforts being made to heal the sickness brought about by the dehumanisation of all our people. The Church's role in this transformation process is clearly one of being a healing presence since only in that way can it respond to the manifest needs of this particular context. In this regard we have seen how wide the etiology of sickness can be. Our investigation has shown how physical, psychological and social sickness can be caused by physical, psychological, cultural, social, economic, political and theological factors. Consequently, we have determined that both sickness and health are holistic phenomena involving the whole of humanity, body soul, spirit, person, family, community and society. We have also noted the weakness and culture conditionedness of the Western model of sickness and health and the need to develop an adequate cultural response to sickness and healing.

Similarly, we have shown how the various Coping-healing practices of the various churches are themselves always mediated by culture. A large measure of their effectiveness is concerned with convincing the sick person to accept the world-view, symbol system and healing myth of the "healer" and his or her church. We have also seen how much of the Christian Coping-healing phenomenon can actually be subsumed under cultural healing practices of which it is a particular form employing Christian world-views and symbol systems.

This in itself does not denigrate the value of the Coping-healing phenomenon since we have seen that any local Church must operate within a local cultural matrix. However part of the process of inculturation is also the ability of the local Church to transform its culture in accordance with its faith and the gospel in order to create a Christian culture. This task still remains.

12.2.1 Some Difficulties with The Coping-Healing Phenomenon

Our investigation has pinpointed some areas where the Coping-healing phenomenon needs to be challenged. On the level of truth, some Coping-healing churches fail in that they do not accept the value of human efforts in wisdom and understanding which come from the sciences. They call people to an inhuman simplistic world-view which does not reflect the wealth and complexity of current human insertion into truth. We have also seen how some churches err with regard to the truth of the gospel in the propagation of prosperity gospels and in supporting the apartheid status quo. On the level of human freedom we would need to pose serious questions regarding the use of techniques of manipulation, emotional control and pseudo-psychological management in Coping-healing processes. In this regard, too, the whole question of a conflict of interests between the sick person and the "healer" can arise where the "healer" needs the sick person to fulfil financial, status and esteem needs. This situation can be exacerbated further when the "healer" has unhealthy psychological neuroses and psychoses which can be projected onto the sick person thereby worsening the sickness. There is much evidence to support the contention that the Coping-healing phenomenon can worsen hysterics and neurotics of all types.

On the social level, too, we have seen how the Coping-healing practices and its churches can provide a quietistic withdrawal from the reality of society preventing people from becoming involved in the ongoing struggle against evil, especially social and structural evil, in the real world. In this way Coping-healing can deepen the sickness on a social level by devising ways and means for people to cope with sin and evil instead of fighting to eradicate it.

12.2.2 The Value of the Coping-Healing Phenomenon

Despite the above difficulties our analysis has shown us that the Coping-healing phenomenon is a genuine attempt to respond to the needs of peoples and communities living within this context. Too many people have experienced healing in their lives on a personal and social level for us not to take the Coping-healing practices seriously. On the social level, many of the Coping-healing churches have provided sites of resistance where people's humanity has been reaffirmed in a context which continually denies it. The Coping-healing phenomenon is also important on the level of truth since it helps us to move beyond the narrow confines of modernism which have constricted the Church's openness to the sacral and the spiritual and often strongly influenced its ministry towards pastoral practices which are merely rational and secular. This greater openness to the sacred forms part of the manifestation of the post-modern era which has consequences for the universal Church. In this way the emergence of Coping-healing practices in the South African local Church has worldwide ramifications for the Church's self understanding in a post-modern era.

12.2.3 The Natural and The Supernatural

Our study has been an attempt, within this post-modern paradigm, to give appropriate weight to the "natural" and the "supernatural". We are aware of the limitation of this terminology but we adopt it *ad cautelam* for its simplicity.

One of the weaknesses of the Coping-healing churches is their tendency to ascribe all that occurs to the supernatural order. By contrast the weakness of modernist approaches (which infect most mainline churches) is the tendency to ascribe everything to the natural order. Clearly neither approach is sufficient. Our work has been an attempt to address this deficiency. On the natural level we have seen that the Coping-healing phenomenon can be understood and explained to a large (but not entire) degree through the operation of psycho-medical, cultural-anthropological, socio-economic and philosophical factors which affect the etiology of both sickness and healing. On the supernatural level we have seen that the Coping-healing ministry is responding to the missionary mandate of Jesus to manifest God's power in the world. Those Coping-healing practices based on faith in Jesus and openness to the Spirit have had an effect on people which is experienced as personal and social healing in terms of the irruption of the Spirit into their lives. Many people have been evangelised through this ministry and have become Christians and even healers themselves. We know that the experience of God's power working in the life of people is an essential dimension of evangelisation. Finally, even the investigation of the phenomenon using natural sciences has turned up an "unexplained remnant": something which goes beyond their grasp.

12.2.4 Final Conclusion

We conclude that the Coping-healing phenomenon reflects a partially inculturated ministry in which culturally mediated needs are being responded to by empirically based culturally mediated pastoral responses. As such, it needs to be accepted and incorporated into the Church's praxis. However, we have also found that the Coping-healing practices are themselves in need of evangelisation and purification particularly in the areas we have indicated above. As this is done we hope that the Coping-healing practices will become a true and genuine pastoral praxis releasing people from the sicknesses which bind them, limit their humanity and destroy their freedom. This is the task of the local Church as it emerges in our context. In our time, our place, and in our local Church, inculturation is healing.

> As you go, proclaim that the Kingdom of Heaven is close at hand. Heal the sick, raise the dead, cleanse the lepers, expel devils. You received freely, so give freely.
>
> [Mt 10:7-8]

Notes

Notes to Chapter 1

1. The data for this section is taken from the South African Christian Handbook edited by Marjorie Froise, 1992 Addendum 3 pp. 292 & 293.

2. The terms "contextualisation" and "contextual theology" seem to have entered into the missiological debate during the early 1970's in documents emanating from the World Council of Churches in Geneva (Roest Crollius 1978:723n.7). Shoki Coe (1976:20) explains how the term was used to replace the term "indigenization" in theological education. This latter term based on the metaphor of the soil was considered too static since it was interpreted as applying a static gospel to a static traditional culture and too regional since it was applied only to Africa and Asia. Contextualisation was considered a more dynamic concept since contexts change and exist everywhere. Whilst we concede the changing reality of contexts, we contend that it is text and not context which is the root metaphor of contextualisation. Otherwise contextual theology is really "situational theology". The text-context paradigm informs the "contextualisation" model especially as text relates to the Scriptures.

   In South Africa, the terms "contextualisation", "contextual theology" and "contextualisation of the gospel" are used to describe the process of relating the gospel (the text) to the response to it within varying contexts. Thus Boesak (1977:14) calls "Black theology" a contextual theology and Bosch (1976:83) sees contextualisation as "relating the gospel message to the entire existential content of a group". Most South African authors are Protestant and the priority of "*sola Scriptura*" is evident in their emphasis on the relationship between the Scriptures and their context in the life of people. However a different emphasis is given to contextual theology by those authors influenced by the liberation theology of Latin America. Here the starting point is the community of faith and its experience of faith. The gospel becomes the good news of the events taking part within that experience interpreted in the light of faith which the gospel illuminates (Nolan 1988:22). The "Institute of Contextual Theology" also understands contextual theology in this way. It is "essentially group theology, group reflection on the meaning and problems of our faith in a particular context" (ICT nd:1). In this second emphasis, the root metaphor is almost lost and the focus is, in fact, the community. Since culture is a better root metaphor when considering community of persons, we contend that the inculturation model can inform and expand this second emphasis. Hence our thesis. Within the parameters of the second understanding of contextual theology this work is an exercise in contextual theology (see 2.1.1).

3. It is necessary at this stage to indicate the somewhat complicated system employed when referring to the Church in this work. When referring to the One Church founded by Christ the term is capitalised and always singular: the Church. Similarly, capitalization is employed when referring to the fullness of the Church as present in a place in a local Church, particular Church or new Church. Here, capitalization is employed since these terms all refer to the One Church of Christ (see ch. 10). When referring to official names of churches, capitalization is also employed but for a different reason viz. that proper nouns are capitalised: thus the Methodist Church, Roman Catholic Church, Presbyterian Church, and so on. In all other cases the lower case, church, is employed. Thus lower case is employed in phrases such as "mainline churches", "Coping-healing churches" and "African Independent churches" as well as in sentences such as "The Roman Catholic Church is a church which stresses the role of sacraments". We have attempted to be consistent throughout in this usage. In quotations we have followed the usage of the authors where

there is little consistency a fact which is particularly visible in the English translation of the Vatican II documents (Flannery 1984). For example the term local church found in *Ad Gentes* and *Christus Dominus* is rendered local Church in *Lumen Gentium*.

4. Schillebeeckx (in Küng & Tracy 1989:312) points out that all revelation is necessarily mediated through cultural forms and that whilst God's revelation in Jesus Christ is, in a certain sense, "independent of men and women and their experiences and history", nevertheless, it is experienced and put into words in terms of the culture in which it is received. This is as true for the writers of the Scriptures as it is for the readers in each age. It is also the case within each denomination since each denomination carries with it a kind of particular "subculture" of historically transmitted patterns of understanding which sets it apart, or "denominates" it. Through a recognition of these subcultures as well as a need to move beyond them as history continues and new unities emerge as new communities are formed, we are able to transcend the past and move into the future. This is the meaning of the transformation moment in the inculturation process (see 10.3). In South Africa, De Gruchy (1986:35) has indicated that whilst the Catholic Church is moving towards a greater emphasis on the local community of faith - what he calls the "Congregationalist" element in Catholicism - the Congregationalists are moving towards a greater emphasis on the catholicity of the Church. It is clear that both movements represent the one process of the emergence of the importance of unity in plurality.

5. The term "horizon" is used in the sense understood by Lonergan (1971:235-236). Lonergan follows a basically Gadamerian understanding. For Gadamer (1975:269), the "horizon" is "the range of vision that includes everything that can be seen from a particular vantage point". This vision metaphor is transferred to the levels of knowledge and experience (Lonergan 1971:236; cf. Gadamer 1975:269,273).

6. Cf. Roest Crollius 1986b:3-7. Francis George (1990:233-240) indicates that importance of the role of culture in the dialectic of universality and particularity. Küng (in Küng & Tracy 1989:450) suggests that the new paradigm in theology requires a move from particularist to universal thinking whereas, at the same time, the "*Indian* (or Chinese or Japanese or African or Latin American) '*way of reading the Bible*' is not merely legitimate. It is necessary." At the same time he notes that: "a number of different theologies are possible within the one . . . model" (:451). The ecumenical Boston Theological Institute has also contributed to this debate with its work "One Faith Many Cultures" (Costa 1988).

7. An exposition and analysis of this model is the subject of chapter ten. Here we indicate that the process of inculturation is basically linked with the process of the emergence of the local Church in a place. Roest Crollius (1978:735-736) explains this process in terms of three moments: translation, assimilation and transformation . Such a description is particularly useful in Africa since the first two steps refer to realities already experienced when the Christian faith was brought by the 18th, 19th and 20th century European missionaries. African theologians such as Sanneh (1989), Ela (1986) and Eboussi Boulaga (1984) have addressed these realities. The transformation moment relates to what these same authors and many other African theologians are more and more concerned with today: the importance of praxis and change in a new reappropriation of culture in Africa (cf. Ela 1986:87,113,119; Eboussi Boulaga 1984:166,196-7; Nkéramihigo 1986:73).

8. Liberation theology has been weak in its consideration of the role of culture in the liberation process. This may often be laid down to an uncritical appropriation of Marxist philosophy into its method. Within the Marxist movement itself, the work of Gramsci has indicated the importance of cultural analysis. Amongst South African theologians the question of culture has tended to be discussed in terms of African traditional culture (cf. Setiloane 1978, Dwane 1988 Mofokeng 1983:22-23). However some Black theologians have begun to emphasise the importance of recognising the emergence of a new culture amongst blacks resulting from the acculturation process (Goba 1988, Mosala 1989). Tlhagale (1985) has attempted to indicate some of the values from traditional African culture which are persevering in the new Black culture. It is our contention that many of the debates regarding the priority of race and class in an analysis of the life of the oppressed reflect an inadequate appropriation of culture into contextual analysis (cf. Sebidi 1986:14-22; Goba 1986:66).

9. The term "community of faith" is useful since it has acquired an acceptance which transcends denominations. De Gruchy (1986:17,25,27,44,45 etc.) uses the terms "church" and "community of faith" interchangeably, indicating that this is his major metaphor. On the Catholic side, prescinding from the texts cited from the documents of the Second Vatican Council, African theologians such as Eboussi Boulaga (1984:167ff.) have emphasised this understanding of Church. George (1990:284) has pointed to the fact that "communion" has "only gradually . . . come to be generally recognised as the controlling notion of the Second Vatican Council's teaching on the Church." This issue is dealt with more comprehensively in chapter ten (cf. 10.3).

10. The methodology of Vela is gleaned both from the notes of a class of the professor followed by this author as well as from the article cited in the Bibliography. The following quotes summarise his methodology. Concerning the starting point of pastoral reflection he writes:

> El Pastoralista no es un "vulgarizidor" de los planteamientos hechos por el teólogo dogmático, sino un agente de reflexión teológica en relación con la práctica pastoral. Hace Teología a partir de una praxis "situada" en la realidad social. Sólo ésto salvará a la Teología de la ideologización. El Pastoralista no es sólo un "práctico", sino también un teólogo que reflexiona a partir de la práctica.
> [Vela 1984:141]

Concerning the intellectual (in the Lonergarian sense) mediation of pastoral praxis by the human sciences he writes:

> Ante la dificultad de una relación "ingenua" con la realidad, el Pastoralista busca establecer *un discurso "objetivo"* con la situación. Quiere delimitar científicamente el campo de su reflexión. Adopta la "epistemología" de las ciencias humanas y sociales, dando primacía a sus métodos, para garantizar el conocimiento objetivo de la realidad. En 2o. lugar, aplica los principios teológicos a esa realidad conocida "científicamente". [Vela 1984:144]

Concerning the method of the theological reflection leading to praxis he writes:

> De aquí surge una posible Práctica Teológica:
>
> 1) Se parte de la Acción Pastoral de la Comunidad cristiana, no de un conocimiento "científico" de la realidad social.
>
> 2) Se reflexiona sobre la doble implicación de las dos variables - cultural y social - sobre esa acción pastoral. Esas dos variables modifican nuestros planteamientos pastorales.
>
> [. . .]
>
> 4) Esta acción pastoral, así implicada en la realidad cultural y social, ayuda al pastoralista a encontrar datos importantes *para una exégesis bíblica que facilite una praxis pastoral de liberación.* Praxis que busque caminos de consonancia entre el proyecto social y el proyecto cristiano. [Vela 1984:146]

11. Phenomenologists are not in full agreement regarding the admitted steps and processes of the Phenomenological method. Spiegelberg (1982:682) has, however, attempted to synthesise the major elements of the method. Our own analysis attempts to broadly follow this sequence without pretending to be rigorous in its application. He describes the method as follows:

1. The Investigation of a Particular Phenomenon.
   a) Phenomenological Intuiting: opening the eyes, listening, reflecting, intuiting.
   b) Phenomenological Analysis: Tracing the elements and structure of the phenomenon.
   c) Phenomenological Description:
      -predication in terms of known classes
      -negative predication in terms of known classes
      -predication by metaphor and analogy.
2. Investigation of general essences (eidetic intuiting)

3. Apprehending essential relations amongst essences.

These steps correspond roughly to what will be the subject of chapters two to eight of this work.

12. This understanding corresponds to Boff's (1987:208) "minor key" of dialectic in which the process is an epistemological one from the unknown to the known.
13. The work of Küng & Tracy (1989) on paradigm shifts in theology relies heavily on the work of Thomas Kuhn (1970) who seems to have had a greater effect on theological reflection than within his own field. Küng's work on paradigm shifts in theology has found a ready echo in South Africa where change is so clearly part of the context and Bosch (1991) as well as other South African theologians have given much thought to it (cf. Mouton et al 1988).

Notes to Chapter 2

1. Many different terms have been used to describe these various churches. In this work we have tried to follow the following system of nomenclature which is largely based on the definitions of Morran and Schlemmer (1984:iii-iv):

Pentecostal churches:
The established distinct Pentecostal denominations coming out of the Pentecostal and Holiness movements of the late 19th and early 20th century. They hold to the classical two or three stage spiritual experience which includes the Baptism of the Holy Spirit (cf. Bond 1974:15).

Neopentecostal churches:
We use this term to refer to the "independent", "non-denominational", "new" churches which have emerged or grown as a result of the Pentecostal or Charismatic revival since the 1960's. The term "Neopentecostal" is used in different ways by different authors. More restrictedly, it refers to those groups who accept pentecostal experiences and practices but remain within mainline churches (cf. Barrett 1982:835). It is also used in a wider sense to refer to the whole revival of Pentecostal gifts experienced since the 1960's (cf. Müller 1974:41; Bond 1974: 16-17). This revival has led to the incorporation of Pentecostal practices within mainline churches as well as the emergence of new groups and churches. The term is used in this wider sense in our study. Thus the churches we call Neopentecostal churches are churches which are either growing or emerging as a result of the Neopentecostal revival (See also Lederle 1986:64-65 for a complementary use of this terminology).

New churches:
This term is used by some authors (e.g. Morran & Schlemmer 1984) to refer to the churches we call Neopentecostal. These churches are sometimes called non-denominational churches (cf. Lederle 1986: 64,67)

African Independent (Indigenous) churches:
These churches form the largest grouping of Christians in South Africa in some five thousand different churches. They have emerged in South Africa both as a result of dissatisfaction with mission church approaches and as a result of the stress on healing. They tend to be small groups although one or two large "denomination" types have emerged. There is confusion regarding nomenclature of these churches. Up until recently African Independent churches was the more frequent term. Some authors prefer the term African Indigenous churches to refer to them suggesting that the word Independent has a negative connotation since they are part of the Church. In this work these two terms are used interchangeably usually following the authors cited.

Zionist churches:
The large group within the African Independent churches which refer to themselves as such

and which to a greater or lesser extent can trace their roots back to John Dowie's Christian Catholic Apostolic Church in Zion. They have developed a synthesis between traditional African Values and Christianity. They stress the role of the Spirit and of healing.

Mainline churches:
This term is used to denote the mainstream traditional denominations of Christianity such as the Anglican, Presbyterian, Methodist and Roman Catholic Churches.

Coping-healing churches:
These churches stress healing as a major part of their ministry and offer regular "healing services" to people. They comprise both the AICs and Neopentecostal churches.

2. It is not our intention at this stage to comment on the effectiveness of these practices since the study of this ministry is the work of the whole thesis. Here we merely present the phenomena as they manifested themselves to us.

3. The quotes come from a pamphlet advertising the "Jesus Miracle Crusade" between 25 August - 1 September 1991 at the "circus site" Stanger Street, Durban.

4. The term "altar call" has come to mean the call for people to come to the front or stage area of the church, hall or tent where they then are called to "give their lives to Jesus" or where they receive prayer, usually for healing. There is normally no altar in churches of this kind as they deny the sacrificial dimension of worship in the form it takes in churches such as the Roman Catholic Church.

5. The service I participated in was held on Thursday August 29th. A video tape of the service was later available for purchase and this has assisted me in being able to quote from the minister's words. See MacDonald 1991 in Bibliography.

6. The notion of "cultural paradigm" will prove important in the later part of this work (see ch. 8). It will be explained then in more depth. At this stage we use it to refer to the cultural system of intelligibility within which people develop their understanding of the world and their dialogue with it. It is the ordering of symbols, understandings and experiences within a whole which enables a person to find meaning for him or herself and within the group that he or she has relatedness to. This is close to the meaning Clifford Geertz gives to culture (1973:89). We add the word paradigm here to emphasise the fact that different groups of people operate out of a different *complexus* of understandings within which there may be similar kinds of things such as "life" and "healing", for example which are understood, expressed and even patterned differently within different paradigms.

7. Daneel (1971, 1974, 1983a, 1983b) has also done extensive work on the Coping-healing ministry in Zimbabwe. His material is used extensively in our later reflection (see ch. 7).

8. The audio tape "Ministry in the Supernatural" distributed by Dove Ministries in Natal has helped in the presentation of this section. It is a recording of a talk given by De Gersigny in which he relates some of his beliefs, experiences and methods especially with regard to healing. For reasons of space I have paraphrased De Gersigny in this section since the rendering of the spoken word into print is often repetitive and long.

9. The method outlined here by De Gersigny and attributed to John Wimber is presented in depth in Wimber and Springer (1987:208-244).

10. Bonnke is referring here to Joash, king of Israel in the story of his meeting with Elisha in 2 Kings 13,14-17. This text, with the command of Elisha to Joash to "Open the window eastward" has fascinated Bonnke and he devotes a whole chapter of his book to his interpretation of it. His point is that we are called to open our minds to the Spirit and his power if we are to perform miracles. This is paralleled with the commands to "open the window eastward" (i.e. open our minds to the spirit) and "shoot our arrows" (i.e. perform the miracles) cf. Bonnke 1989:138-148.

11. The terms well-being (*inhlalakahle*) and life (*impilo*) have broader meanings in Zulu than they do in English. When a person is alive and well he is said to "have life" (*unempilo*). When he is sick he does not live well (*Akaphili kahle*). The notion of well-being is also tied up with this. So sickness is directly related to life or its lack. A person who has life is one

who is naturally in harmony with his world. This world includes himself and the network of relationships that a person has with those around him both living in this world and those who live beyond it, principally ancestors (cf. Setiloane 1975:29-38).

12. Harriet Ngubane (1977:22-24) explains sickness in Zulu culture in terms of the following categories:

    "*Isifo*" (English closest equivalent: sickness)
    This is a generic term which refers to all forms of sickness. It refers not only to illness but also to various forms of misfortune as well as the disposition of being vulnerable to misfortune and disease.

    "*Izifo*" (Plural of "*Isifo*"). These can be of two kinds:
    (a) "*Umkhuhlane*". This is a bodily sickness which is due to the ordinary breakdown of the body and is not attributable to external forces. It is cured by natural medicines (imithi) which are effective in themselves and whose use is not ritualized. Western medicines and procedures are accepted by Zulus and usually understood as fitting into this kind of healing process.

    (b) "*Izifo zabantu*" or "*Ukufa kwabantu*" lit. "sicknesses of the people" or "death of the people". This kind of sickness is much more tenuous for people of Western culture. It is tied up with the idea of not living well and not being in harmony with one's environment especially in relationship to others both the people around and the ancestors.

    It is important to note that what we have distinguished above is not normally distinguished within a traditional Zulu cultural paradigm and so both "sickness" and "healing" will not correspond with Western understandings.

13. The term "*inyanga*" refers to the traditional Zulu doctor who treats people with various herbs. "*umkhokheli*" was originally applied to the leaders of women's societies especially in the Methodist Church. It is now often applied in a generic sense to women having some kind of leadership role within many different churches.

14. The survey was distributed to ministers and priests in charge of congregations or parishes within the Roman Catholic, Anglican and Methodist Churches. 80 copies were distributed to Parish Priests of the Archdiocese of Durban of which 27 were completed and returned. 60 copies were distributed to ministers of the Natal Coastal District of the Methodist Church of which 23 were completed and returned. 44 copies were distributed to Priests in the Durban and Pietermaritzburg area of the Diocese of Natal of the Church of the Province of South Africa. 18 of these were returned. Thus 184 questionnaires were distributed and 68 were returned giving a total return of 37%. Of those returned, 28 were from predominantly Zulu speaking congregations and 40 from predominantly English speaking parishes. 36 returns were from mainly urban areas, 18 from semi-urban areas and 14 from rural areas. The Roman Catholic sample was over-represented amongst rural areas whereas the Anglican sample was very under-represented in both Zulu speaking congregations and rural congregations.

Notes to Chapter 3

1. Geertz is speaking about similarities between diverse phenomena whereas we are concerned with studying one phenomenon from different perspectives. The citation abstracted is prefaced as follows:

    > In short, we need to look for systematic relationships among diverse phenomena, not for substantive identities among similar ones. And to do that with any effectiveness . . . (our quote continues as in the text)

    It might be argued that we are taking Geertz out of context in order to apply his quote in support of our method. Our contention is that this same method needs to be applied when analysing similar phenomena as well as when looking for relationships between diverse phenomena. From a philosophical point of view, it can well be argued that as such relationships are identified, so the diverse phenomena are actually seen as part of a greater whole.

2. Boucher (n.d.:10) indicates the following studies which have "produced evidence of psychological elements in clinical entities". Duodenal ulcer, multiple sclerosis, asthma and heart disease: Paulley 1975; Witkower and Wormes 1977 (missing from her bibliography).

3. Jackson (1981:41-42,157) reports on the following studies which relate physical symptoms and psychological etiologies:

    diabetes: Johnson 1950

    ulcerative colitis: Lindeman (source not cited in bibliography)

    cancer: Le Shan 1977

    tobacco & alcohol addiction: Menninger (source not cited in bibliography)

    rheumatoid arthritis: Alexander 1950

    Heart disease: Dunbar 1954

    skin disease, congestion of the respiratory tract and spastic colon: Research of Mayo Clinic cited by Jackson 1981:157.

4. *Amafufunyane (amafufunyana)* (cf. *ufufunyane* in fig. 3.2) is diagnosed as "Brief Reactive Psychosis" or "Hysterical Psychosis" in Western psychology. Clearly the diseases understood within the Zulu world-view form part of the "*Izifo zabantu*" (people's sicknesses) (cf. ch.2 n.2). See also 3.5.1 for a discussion of Conversion Disorder.

5. The hysteria referred to by Weatherhead is meant in the technical psychological sense of the word rather than its more common usage which is often also applied to such gatherings. See section 3.5.1 for a discussion of this disorder.

6. These are discussed in more detail in our anthropological mediation (cf. 4.3.1).

7. By "religious healing" we limit ourselves in this context to the type of healing we have been studying as the "Coping-healing" phenomenon. We recognise that this is a narrow understanding and does not take into account all the various healing endeavours that religious institutes have been involved in. It specifically excludes the Church's medical ministry in hospitals, clinics and the like but does include all forms of healing through prayer and faith.

8. Healing without outside intervention has been reported by Botha (1986:184) in the following sicknesses:
    - primary shoulder dislocations.
    - ulcers.
    - bone fractures (hook of hamate)
    - Intracranial bleeding resulting from perforated aneurysms.
    - Bladder gangrene.
    - Gangrenous cystitis.
    - Tuberculous meningitis.
    - Bleeding of the spleen.

Notes to Chapter 4

1. The question of "culture" is central to this thesis and will be dealt with in chapter eight where a fuller analysis and description will be presented.

2. *ukuthwasa* refers to the process of becoming sick and responding to the sickness as the call from an ancestor to follow a particular lifestyle as a healer. The traditional healer who is possessed or under the influence of an ancestor spirit through whom he/she does the

healing is called an *isangoma* in Zulu and *igqira* by Bührmann in the Xhosa context she has worked in. In Xhosa the term *igqira* also has a wider meaning as a generic term for all types of healers.

3. DSM-III refers to a listing of mental disorders within the framework of Western psychiatry. The *Diagnostic and Statistical Manual of Mental Disorders* of the American Psychiatric Associations is the standard for the categorising of mental disorder within this discipline. "III" refers to the latest (III 1985) and "greatly revised editions, 'DSM-III', being the most comprehensive and conceptually innovative" (Simons & Hughes 1985:3).

4. Type A refers to the 'achiever' personality type which has tended to be idealised in Western culture. Single mindedness, aggression, hard-work, selfishness oriented towards success are descriptive of this personality type. Such types often fall foul of conditions such as "burn-out", heart attack, "mid-life crisis" and other illnesses which could probably also be characterised as Western culture bound syndromes.

Notes to Chapter 5

1. For Bradfield, Neo-Pentecostalism refers to the incorporation of Pentecostal practices and experiences with mainline churches principally through the Charismatic renewal. Note that we are using the term in a different sense. (See ch. 2 n. 1).

2. The political position represents conventional government ideology and White thinking during the early 1980's, the time of Gifford's study. Since then the political reality has changed with the unbanning of the liberation movements and the setting up of transitional structures towards a "New South Africa".

Notes to Chapter 6

1. Kuhn's work (1962, 1970) is concerned with showing the effect of world-view and standpoint on the nature and conclusions of scientific research. He shows how the logical empiricist and "objective" nature of science is often an illusion and that science is far more influenced by "subjective" cultural and non-rational factors than has been conventionally accepted.

2. In the South African situation, the favoured term is contextual theology. This is the term we have adopted in our work. The methodology referred to by Lamb would equally apply. See also our use of Boff (1.2.2).

Notes to Chapter 7

1. See chapter 1 note 1 for a discussion on indigenisation.

2. In this section we are not attempting to develop a full theology of healing but rather concerned with presenting in our mediation the contribution of several theologians working in the field.

3. Kelsey lists the following Old Testament healing stories. The healings of barren women are described in Gn 20,18; 30,2; 18,10-14; Jdg 13,55-24; 1 Sm 1,19-20; 2K 4,16-17. The healings of Elijah and Elisha are other examples found in 1 K 17,17-23; 2 K 4,188-37; 2 K 5,1-14; 2 K 13,21. Other healing stories cited by Kelsey include Nm 16,47-50; Nm 21,9; 1 Sm 6,4-5; 2Sm 24,10-25; 2 K 20,1-7; Is 38,1-6,21; and the book of Tobit.

4. Kelsey cites the following Psalms which refer to healing as God's will: Pss 103, 91, 41, 46, 62, 73, 74, 94, 116, 121 and 147.

5. Hs 6,1-11; 13, 12-15; Is 26,19; 29,18; 61,1-11; 35,5-6; Ezk 37.

6. Irenaeus, *Adv. Haer*. II.6.2; II.10.4; II.31.2; II.32.4; III.5.2.

7. Quotes from Gregory of Nyssa, *The Great Catechism* XI, XXXIV; *On The Making of Man* XXV,6ff. as cited by Kelsey 1973:174.

8. Jerome: *Letter* III.2; *Letter* CV III. Ambrose: *The Sacraments* I,5,13ff. as quoted in Kelsey 1973:192 nn.55 & 56, 194 n.58.

9. The quotation at the beginning of this citation comes from John Cassian, *The Conferences*, The Second Conference of Abbot Nesteros XV.2. as cited by Kelsey 1973:195.

10. The quotation at the beginning of this citation comes from Gregory the Great, *The Book of Pastoral Rule* II.13 as cited by Kelsey 1973:197. The sentence following the quotation does not read well and we suspect that it should read ". . . shaping the stones of humanity *which are to* be placed in the heavenly wall . . ."

11. cf. Also J.M. Ela 1983 who makes a similar point regarding the churches' social responsibility as part of the healing ministry (in Sebahire 1987:3).

Notes to Chapter 9

1. *Ethnos*, from the Greek term for nation, is used by some anthropologists to indicate a cultural approach which links culture with a nation: a defined group of people having similar notional, attitudinal religious and even physical characteristics. Sharp (1981) shows how this cultural approach is rooted in the German Romantic movement of the 19th century particularly as articulated in the writings of Fichte and Kuyper and as articulated in the work of the pre-World War II German anthropologists such as Muhlmann (cf. 9.3.1).

2. The National Peace Accord (NPA) is an agreement signed in September 1991 by the major political players in the South African arena. In the document, codes of conduct were set up for political parties, the security forces and the police, and mechanisms and structures were set up to monitor and respond to situations of violence in the country. The preamble states that "The NPA signifies common purpose to end political violence and sets out codes of conduct and mechanisms to achieve this."

3. Footnotes 3-10 provide examples from the local press of the use of these terms in newspaper and magazine articles. With regard to a "culture of democracy" we cite the following as typical examples: "We encourage the development of a culture of democracy in the transition to a free South Africa" (Daily Mail 26 June 1990). "Much was also made of the need for a 'culture of democracy', but I soon came to realise that what most speakers and participants really meant was a 'culture of tolerance'" (Nolan 1992:5).

4. "South Africa in transition faces serious problems emanating from the failure to foster a culture of justice and respect for the rule of law" (Jana 1992:11).

5. "On to a peace culture" (ANC 1990:30). "We need to establish a culture of Peace" (ANC 1990:34).

6. "Re-establish culture of learning - Maree" (New Nation 1992b:26). "Ways to re-establish a culture of learning, discipline, [and] rightness of objective standard at schools would have to be found" (New Nation 1992b:26). "Sadtu remains critical of any action...which jeopardises the establishment of a culture of effective learning in schools" (Hindle 1992:24).

7. "In MD Ben Vosloo, the Small Business Development Corp (SBDC) has a chief executive with clear goals: the creation of a thriving small business sector and an entrepreneurial culture in SA" (SBDC 1991:5).

8. Chaskalson (1991:130) suggests that "Years of unemployment produced a culture of recklessness and resistance among the black youth of Vereeniging."

9. The Financial Mail says that within the ANC of 1990 "We detected . . . the residue of a culture of exile" (ANC 1990:3). The quote is interesting as it goes on to describe what it means by this term as "a kind of mind-set formed by the colonial conflicts of the fifties and sixties in which ideas became too fixed in the belligerent stance of too many individuals" (ANC 1990:3).

10. The International Express (7 Jan 1993:8) refers to "A culture of violence [which] then takes hold of a society which is either too frightened or too indifferent to reject it".

11. The introduction of this book, presumably written by the Editor, Clingman, appears without page numbering in the edition cited. Page 1 of the book begins with the first article after the introduction. Hence our notation n.p. (no page number) in this and subsequent references to this Introduction.

12. Sharp (1981:24) reports five factors proposed by Coertze as affecting the acculturation process: "these include (1) the manner of contact, (2) differences in numerical strength between the ethnoses involved, (3) differences in level of civilization, (4) capacity to adopt the culture of another ethnos, (5) racial differences". The school maintains that the acculturation process only leads to a superficial understanding and living out of the norms of an ethnos. For this reason, acculturation can lead to a chaotic situation and weakening of a culture if steps are not taken to preserve the inner harmony of the ethnos.

13. UNISA is the acronym for the University of South Africa: a university based in Pretoria which provides university education largely by correspondence. Apart from one or two departments, it was largely considered to reflect the ethos and culture of Afrikaner Nationalist hegemony, although some steps to move away from this are currently (1992) underway.

14. The summer school formed part of the work of the "Centre for Intergroup studies" of the university whose aim is "to work towards the removal of racial and economic discrimination largely by acting as a mediating body between groups . . ." (Van der Merwe & Schrire 1980:2).

15. The reference comes from an unpublished paper of an address given at the South African Perceptions Forum organised by the Durban Metropolitan Chamber of Commerce 2 August 1989. The paper was supplied by the author.

16. The quote comes from Mbuli (1986:138). It is cited in the reference given in the text.

17. The organisations noted are considered to be linked together in a network reaching out to all areas of life with the aim of safeguarding Afrikaner interests in general and those of Afrikaner Nationalism in particular. The *Afrikaner Broederbond* is seen as the central organising grouping. Its membership is kept secret and entry into the organisation is not open but by cooption. The FAK, *Federasie van Afrikaanse Kultuurverenigings* is a "body for the coordination of all Afrikaans cultural societies . . . based on Christian National principles . . . [whose] object is to organise and combine all available forces into one central Afrikaans cultural organisation to promote the Afrikaans language and to protect Afrikaans culture" (SA Yearbook 1982:735). SABRA, the South African Bureau for Racial Affairs concerns itself with ethnic and interracial studies within the perspective of *Volkekunde*. The AHI, *Afrikaanse Handelsinstituut* is an organisation of Afrikaner businessmen formed in 1942 with the aim of enabling an Afrikaner penetration into the English controlled business sector.

18. The phrase appears, amongst other places, in Masilela 1988:4; Shepperson 1992:48; Tomaselli 1988:36; Tomaselli 1987:3.

19. Tomaselli's approach is essentially similar to that of the American anthropologist, Geertz, in which significance is described in terms of "culture texts" whose relationships one to the other forms the focus of culture studies (Tomaselli 1988:38; Geertz 1973:14, 17, 216; 1983:30-33). Geertz's famous definition of culture runs as follows: "it denotes an historically transmitted pattern of meanings embodied in symbols, a system of inherited

conceptions expressed in symbolic forms by means of which men communicate, perpetuate, and develop their knowledge about and attitudes toward life" (Geertz 1973:89).

20. Kraft quotes Edward Hall's (1959) definition here without the page reference. This understanding of culture will form the main parameter of our own understanding of culture on the epistemological level (9.5.1).

21. The 1983 Vancouver Assembly of the World Council of Churches devoted a considerable amount of time to the relationship between gospel and culture and came up with the following definition of culture:

> Culture is what holds a community together, giving a common framework of meaning. It is preserved in language, thought patterns, ways of life, attitudes, symbols and presuppositions, and is celebrated in art, music, drama, literature and the like. It constitutes the collective memory of the people and the collective heritage which will be handed down to generations still to come.
> [Stockwell 1985:154]

22. See also Tlhagale (1985:33-36) for a development of culture as humanisation from a Habermasian perspective.

23. The simple framework of epistemological, ontological and metaphysical provides a model around which our understanding of culture is presented. Along with Lonergan (1971:21; cf.: 308-309)) we note how the epistemological level is concerned with the coming to understanding and thereby to knowledge and that this process is both leads to and is grounded in a metaphysics. By analogy we affirm a similar relationship between the ontological and the metaphysical.

Notes to Chapter 10

1. The terms "socialisation" and "enculturation" have both been used by anthropologists in describing the process by which children are taught the elements of their culture and the way of behaving in society. Some anthropologists see the terms as equivalent whilst others reserve the former for the process of "adjustment to social living" and the latter to describe the "insertion into one's culture" which "has also, and prominently, aspects which concern the growth of the individual" (Roest Crollius 1978:724 n.12)

2. It seems that in the working papers for the 32nd General Congregation of the Society of Jesus, the term enculturation was translated into the working language of the meeting, Latin, as *inculturatio* since the 'en' prefix is not possible in Latin. During the conference the term took on religious meanings not normal to its anthropological usage and was retranslated back into those languages which allow both 'in' and 'en' prefixes as inculturation presumably to indicate the difference in meaning to enculturation. Note that in romance languages that do not admit an 'en' prefix (e.g. Latin, Italian) inculturation is both the anthropological and theological term (cf. De Napoli 1987:71 n.1; Roest Crollius 1978:725, n.14).

3. Since 1982 the centre "Cultures and Religions" at the Pontifical Gregorian University has published some 15 books in its series of "Working Papers on Living Faith and Cultures" in an attempt to introduce theological reflection on inculturation in widely differing contexts throughout the world.

4. On January 6 1989, Pope John Paul II announced his intention to convoke a Special Assembly for Africa of the Synod of Bishops. In June 1989 a Council of the General Secretariat was given the task of preparing the Special Assembly. In 1990, this Secretariat produce a *Lineamenta* (outline) entitled "The Church in Africa and Her Evangelising Mission Towards the Year 2000 'You Shall be My Witnesses'". This was accompanied by a series of eighty one questions to help Episcopal Conferences in Africa respond to the five areas of concern that the Synod wishes to concern itself with: Proclamation of the Good

News, Inculturation, Dialogue, Justice and Peace and Means of Social Communication. As a result of the responses by episcopal conferences, a working document, *Instrumentum Laboris*, for the Synod was produced and distributed in 1993. The Synod was set to convoke in Rome after Easter 1994.

5. John Paul II's vision of inculturation is spelt out implicitly in some of his earlier encyclicals in terms of his Christian anthropology indicating that through the Incarnation, Christ unites himself with all people in all situations (RH 10, 13, 14). He applies this vision to the working situation in *Laborem Exercens*. More explicit references to inculturation as such are spelt out more clearly particularly in the encyclical *Slavorum Apostoli* which relates to the Pope's own Slavic cultural background. It is here that we find a definition of inculturation as "the incarnation of the Gospel in native cultures" (SA 21). On a more general level we find references to inculturation in *Catechesi Tradendae* (CT 53) and in *Redemptoris Missio* (RM 52). In the latter the same notion of inculturation as "incarnating the Gospel in peoples' cultures" is again emphasised.

6. The citation was first made in an address to the Congress of the "Movimento Ecclesiale di Impegno culturale," January 16, 1982 cf. La Traccia 3, no. 1 (February 15, 1982):55-57. The words are then re-quoted in many different talks and letters (cf. George 1990:87 n. 10).

7. Shorter (1988) includes all approaches and models to inculturation presented so far. George (1990:235) indicates that Pope John Paul II teaches that "not only Christ but also the entire Gospel and the full historical faith of the Catholic Church are to be inculturated everywhere".

8. R.J. Neuhaus indicates the importance of this way of being Church in the "Postmodern World". "Christian unity is inherent in *being* the Church . . . The only unity that is lasting and worth pursuing is a unity rooted in a shared confession of Christ and the Gospel . . . Unity is to be achieved not by ecclesiastical conquest but by reconciled diversity in obedience to the Gospel" (Neuhaus 1987:284). Kalu's (1978) comments are also pertinent in this regard. Speaking from the African perspective he suggests that: "The challenges of our world need the response of a united Church . . . Christ prescribed one-ness as the *esse* of this Church, the people who know and celebrate his task of reconciling the world to his father" (:174). Such a unity is not a mere merger of denominations but "a process of establishing a community in order that a humane future may be developed" (:174).

9. All three terms are found in the document *Ad Gentes*. The relevant paragraphs are as follows:

    Indigenous particular churches 6
    young churches 16, 19, 20, 21, 22
    local church 20, 27.
    particular church 20, 22

10. De Gruchy makes this point in his analysis of theology and ministry in the South African Context.

    > This rediscovery of the local community of faith by Catholic theologians comes at a time when many of us who are Congregationalists by tradition have learnt to stress more strongly the catholicity of the Church. The local community of faith cannot exist except as part of the universal church. And yet, the whole church is present in the local community. [De Gruchy 1986:35]

11. For example, Haleblian 1983, Luzbetak 1981.

12. The term is used in the Pauline sense of those, having been redeemed by Christ, who are living members of the Church. Clearly, such a notion does not negate the necessity for evangelisation *ad intra*, an essential process of renewal and reform which is necessarily part of the Church's ongoing mission. The evangelisers also need to be evangelised (EN15, RM50-54 cf. Saayman 1992:169-170).

13. The methodology of Vela is gleaned both from class notes as well as from the article cited in the bibliography (Cf. ch. 1 n.10.)

14. Clearly the Church finds itself in many contexts and cultures. In our model only the context and cultures within which the local Church is emerging are considered. Area D does not imply a contextless cultureless Church but the Church within the other contexts and cultures which are not indicated in the diagram for the sake of simplicity. Since we are using the mathematical symbolism of Venn diagrams we use the relevant notation E' to refer to all other contexts besides E.

15. The cultural matrix represents the culture(s) within which the local Church is emerging in the sense of culture developed in chapter 9. Again, our diagram does not imply that everything outside areas A,B,F and G is cultureless but rather that these areas reflect the cultural perspectives affected by the process we are examining.

Notes to Chapter 11

1. We have consistently used the word "phenomenon" when referring to the various church Coping-healing practices we have been studying. Clearly the aim of the theological judgement is to ascertain whether or not the practices in this phenomenon are ministries and thus part of the Church's mission to heal. Consequently, we begin to use the words "ministry" and "ministries" with more frequency in this chapter. Since the judgement is itself a process with many facets and steps, these words are not used univocally to indicated a completed judgement but rather in a looser sense as we move to articulate the elements of our judgement.

2. Roest Crollius (1978:733) describes the inculturation process in terms of three moments: Translation, Assimilation and Transformation. See 10.4 for a presentation of these moments within our own understanding.

3. Elements of late twentieth century Western culture used by these churches would include the type of music, the sophisticated use of electronics in sound and visual presentations, the use of decor to create atmosphere, the development of a "consumer stage show approach" in the unfolding of the services, the use of symbols such as suits and ties to reflect success as well as the developments of television ministries, bookshops and other accoutrements of the culture of enterprise. We have also seen, in this regard, how these churches are responding to a culture of alienation being experienced by their members in relation to the existing society (cf. 5.3.1).

4. By unexplained remnant we refer to those healings which have clearly occurred and which cannot be explained within the Western scientific healing paradigm (cf. 8.7.4).

5. See 8.7.3 for more on this point.

6. Ockham's (Occam's) Razor is the name given to a principle stated by William of Ockham (1285-1349?) that *non sunt multiplicanda entia praeter necessitatem;* i.e. entities are not to be multiplied beyond necessity. In our context it shows the lack of a need for direct supernatural explanations of what can be explained through human verified knowledge coming from the human sciences cf. Encyclopaedia Britannica 1992 ed.

7. In its Faith and Order Study Document (Faith and Order Paper No. 151) (WCC 1990b:34-37) the World Council of Churches refers to the "Dimensions and Mission of the Church". In this section the dimensions of Communion (*koinonia*) (:34); Worship (:36); Witness (:36) and Service (:37) are specifically referred to whereas the *kerygma* is implied throughout.

8. cf. WCC 1990b:30. The four marks come originally from the Nicene Creed and have been historically used as criteria for ecclesial authenticity.

Bibliography

AA.VV. 1965. *Our Approach to the Independent Church Movement in South Africa*. Mapumulo, Natal: Lutheran Theological College (Cyclostyle).

AA.VV. 1967. *The Report of the Umpumulo Consultation on the Healing Ministry of the Church*. Mapumulo, Natal: Lutheran Theological College (Cyclostyle).

Alberich, E. 1987. *Catechesi E Prassi Ecclesiale*. Torino: Elle Di Ci.

Alexander, F.G. 1950. *Psychosomatic Medicine*. N.Y.: Norton.

Alland, A. 1977. "Medical Anthropology and the Study of Biological and Cultural

Adaptation." in Landy, D., ed., *Culture Disease and Healing*, pp. 41-47. N.Y.: Macmillan.

Amaladoss, M. 1985. "Culture and Dialogue." *International Review Of Mission* 74:169-177.

ANC 1990. *African National Congress: Financial Mail Survey September 28 1990*. Johannesburg.

Anderson, J.D. 1986. "Faith Healing: A medical perspective." in De Villiers, P., ed., *Healing in the name of God*, pp. 176-181. Pretoria: UNISA.

Arbuthnot, A. 1989. *Christian Prayer and Healing*. Crowborough, Sussex: Highland Books.

Arbuckle, G.A. 1990. *Earthing the Gospel*. London: Geoffrey Chapman.

Asuni, T. 1979. "The Dilemma of Traditional Healing with Special Reference to Nigeria." *Social Science & Medicine* 13B:33-39.

Austin-Broos, D.J., ed. 1987. *Creating culture*. London: Allen & Unwin.

Azevedo, M. 1982. *Inculturation and the Challenges of Modernity*. Rome: Centre "Cultures and Religions" - Pontifical Gregorian University.

Baëta, C.G. 1962. *Prophetism in Ghana*. London: SCM.

Barrett, D.B. 1968. *Schism and Renewal in Africa*. Nairobi: Oxford University Press.

Barrett, D.B. 1982. *World Christian Encyclopedia*. Nairobi: Oxford University Press.

Bate, S.C. 1991. *Evangelisation in the South African Context*. Rome: Centre "Cultures and Religions" - Pontifical Gregorian University.

Becken, H.J. 1967. "On the Holy Mountain." *Journal of Religion in Africa* 1,2:138-149.

Becken, H.J. 1972. "A Healing Church in Zululand: 'The New Church Step to Jesus Christ Zion in South Africa'." *Journal of Religion in Africa* 4:213-231.

Becken, H.J. 1975. "Healing in the African Independent Churches." *Lutheran Quarterly* 27,3:234-243.

Becken, H.J. 1984. "The Church as a Healing Community." *Mission Studies* 1:6-13.

Becken, H.J. 1989. "African Independent Churches as healing communities." in Oosthuizen, G.C., Edwards, S.D., Wessels, W.H.et al, eds., *Afro-Christian Religion and Healing in Southern Africa*, pp. 222-240. N.Y.: Edwin Mellen.

Benor, D.J. 1991. "A Psychiatrist Examines Fears of Healing." *Newsletter: Consciousness Research & Training Project, New York* XV 1:5-15.

Benson, C. 1975. *What about us who are not Healed?* New Jersey: Logos International.

Berger, P. 1966. *The Social Construction of Reality*. Garden City: Doubleday.

Berglund, A.I. 1965. "The Rituals of the Independent Church Movement and our Liturgy." in AA.VV., *Our Approach to the Independent Church Movement in South Africa*, pp. 160-178. Mapumulo, Natal: Lutheran Theological College (Cyclostyle).

Berglund, A.I. 1973. "Crisis in Missions - A Pastoral Liturgical Challenge." *Lutheran Quarterly* 25:22-33.

Berglund, A.I. 1976. *Zulu Thought-Patterns and Symbolism, Studia Missionalia Upsaliensia XXII*. Cape Town: David Philip.

Bevans, S. 1985. "Models of Contextual Theology." *Missiology* 13:185-202.

Boesak, A. 1977. *Farewell to Innocence: A Socio-Ethical Study on Black Theology and Power*. N.Y.: Orbis.

Boff, C. 1987. *Theology and Praxis: Epistemological Foundations*. N.Y.: Orbis.

Bond, J. 1974. "Pentecostalism in the Pentecostal Churches." *Journal of Religion in Southern Africa* 7:10-22.

Bonnke, R. 1989. *Evangelism by Fire*. Eastbourne: Kingsway Publications.

Booth, H. 1987. *Healing is Wholeness*. London: The Methodist Church.

Bosch, D. 1976. "Crosscurrents in Modern Mission." *Missionalia* 4:54-84.

Bosch, D. 1983. "An Emerging Paradigm for Mission." *Missiology* 11:485-510.

Bosch, D. 1984. "Mission and Evangelism: Clarifying the Concepts." *Zeitschrift für Missionswissenschaft und Religionswissenschaft* 68:161-191.

Bosch, D.J. 1988. "Church Growth Missiology." *Missionalia 16:1* 13-24.

Bosch, D. 1991. *Transforming Mission*. Cape Town: David Philip.

Botha, H. 1986. "Faith healing and the physician." in De Villiers, P., ed., *Healing in the name of God*, pp. 182-193. Pretoria: UNISA.

Boucher, F.K. n.d. *The Cadences of Healing: Perceived Benefit from Treatment Among the Clientele of Psychic Healers*. Unpublished Ph.D. Thesis University of California, Davis.

Bradfield, C.D. 1979. "Deprivation and the emergence of neo-Pentecostalism in American Christianity." *The South African Journal of Sociology* 20:36-47.

Brand, P., & Yancey, P. 1983. "A Surgeon's View of Divine Healing." *Christian Today* 27:14-21.

Braud, W.G. 1989. "Using Living Targets in Psi Research." *Parapsychology Review* 20,6:1-4.

Bryant, R. 1975. "Toward a Contextualist Theology in Southern Africa." *Journal of Theology for Southern Africa* 11:11-19.

Bührmann , M.V. 1983. "Community health and traditional healers." *Psychotherapeia* 30:15-18.

Bührmann , M.V. 1986a. *Living in two worlds (communication between a white healer and her black counterparts)*. Illinois: Chiron Publications.

Bührmann, M.V. 1986b. "Some aspects of healing methods among Black South Africans." in Oosthuizen, G.C., ed., *Religion Alive: Studies in the New Movements and Indigenous Churches in Southern Africa*, pp. 105-115. Bergvlei, South Africa: Hodder & Stoughton Southern Africa.

Bührmann , M.V. 1989. "Religion and healing: the African experience." in Oosthuizen, G.C., Edwards, S.D., Wessels, W.H.et al, eds., *Afro-Christian Religion and Healing in Southern Africa*, pp. 25-34. N.Y.: Edwin Mellen.

Bujo, B. 1992. *African Theology In Its Social Context*. N.Y.: Orbis.

Bureau for Information 1990. *This is South Africa*. Pretoria: Bureau for Information.

Cannon, W.B. 1942. "Voodoo Death." *American Anthropologist* 44:169-181.

Cardijn, J. 1955. *Challenge to Action*. London: New Life Publications.

CCH n.d. *In Search of Common Values*. Stellenbosch: Centre for Contextual Hermeneutics.

Chaskalson, M. 1991. "The Road to Sharpeville." in Clingman, S., *Regions and Repertoires: Topics in South African Politics and Culture*, pp. 116-146. Johannesburg: Ravan.

Cheetham, R.W.S., & Griffiths, J.A. 1982. "Sickness and Medicine in an African Paradigm." *South African Medical Journal* 62:954-956.

Cheetham, R.W.S., & Griffiths, J.A. 1989. *Afro-Christian Religion and Healing in Southern Africa*. N.Y.: Edwin Mellen.

Cheetham, R.W.S., & Rzadkowolski, A. 1980. "Cross-cultural Psychiatry and the Concept of Mental Illness." *S.A. Medical Journal* 58:320-325.

Chidester, D. 1989. "Worldview Analysis of African Indigenous Churches." *Journal for the Study of Religion* 2,1:15-30.

Chikane, F. 1985. "The Incarnation in the Life of the People of South Africa." *Journal of Theology for Southern Africa* 51:37-50.

City Press 1990. "Right to Differ is a Blessing." *City Press 2 Sep 1990* . Johannesburg.

Clark, D.L 1984. "An Implicit Theory of Personality, Illness and Cure Found in the Writings of Neo-pentecostal Faith Teachers." *Journal of Psychology and Theology* 12,4:279-285.

Clingman, S., ed. 1991. *Regions and Repertoires: Topics in South African Politics and Culture*. Johannesburg: Ravan.

Cochrane, J.R. 1990. "Christ and Culture: Now and Then." *Journal of Theology for Southern Africa* 71:3-17.

Cochrane, J.R. 1991. *Nation-Building: A Scocio-Theological View*. Paper given to the Institute for Theological Research, Pretoria, September 1991.

Coe, S. 1976. "Contextualising Theology." in Anderson, G.H., & Stransky, T.F., eds., *Mission Trends No.3*, pp. 19-24. N.Y.: Paulist.

Comaroff, J. 1981. "Healing and Cultural Transformation: The Tswana of Southern Africa [1]." *Social Science and Medicine* 15B:367-378.

Comaroff, J. 1985. *Body of Power Spirit of Resistence*. Chicago: University of Chicago Press.

Coplan, D. 1980. "The Emergence of African working-class culture: some research perspectives." *Africa Perspective* 16:10-23.

Costa, R.O., ed. 1988. *One Faith, Many Cultures*. N.Y.: Orbis.

Dale, D. 1989. *In His Hands*. London: Daybreak.

Daneel, M.L. 1971. *Zionism and Faith Healing in Rhodesia*. Mouton: The Hague.

Daneel, M.L. 1974. *Old and New in Southern Shona Independent Churches, Volume 2: Church Growth-Causative Factors and Recruitment Techniques*. Mouton: The Hague.

Daneel, M.L. 1983a. "Communication and liberation in African Independent Churches." *Missionalia* 11,2:57-93.

Daneel, M.L. 1983b. "Charismatic healing in African Independent Churches." *Theologia Evangelica* 16,3:27-44.

Daneel, M.L. 1984. "Towards a *theologia africana?* The contribution of Independent churches to African theology." *Missionalia* 12,2: 64-89.

Daneel, M.L. 1987. *Quest for Belonging: Introduction to a study of African Independent Churches.* Gweru: Mambo.

Daneel, M.L. 1991. "The liberation of creation: African traditional religious and independent church perspectives." *Missionalia* 19,2:99-121.

Dangor, J. 1992. "Violence Against Women." *Challenge* 4: 2-4.

Daynes, G. 1984. "Psychosomatic Disease and Life Style Changes". in *Fourth Interdisciplinary Symposium of the College of Medicine of South Africa 5-6 July 1984.* pp. 89-91.

De Gruchy, J.W. 1979. *The Church Struggle in South Africa.* Grand Rapids: Eerdmans.

De Gruchy, J.W. 1986. *Theology and Ministry in Context and Crisis.* London: Collins.

De Gersigny, C. n.d. *Ministry in the Supernatural: Audio Tape of Talk given by author.* Kloof, Natal: Dove Ministries.

De Haas, M. 1986. "Is Millenarianism Alive and Well in White South Africa?" *Religion in Southern Africa* 7,1:37-45.

De Haas, M. 1989. "Towards a common South African Identity: Myths and Realities about culture in South Africa today." *Unpublished Paper given at the South African Perceptions Forum,Durban Metropolitan Chamber of Commerce, 2nd August 1989.* Durban.

De Napoli, G.A. 1987. "Inculturation as Communication." in Crollius, A.A.R., ed., *Inculturation X: Effective Inculturation and Ethnic Identity*, pp. 69-98. Rome: Centre "Cultures and Religions" - Pontifical Gregorian University.

De Villiers, D.E. 1991. "Liberal Anthropology in the South African Context." *Journal of Theology for Southern Africa* 76:15-24.

De Villiers, P.G.R. ed. 1986. *Healing in the Name of God.* Pretoria: University of South Africa.

De Villiers, S. 1985. "(Consideration of) Illness causation among some Xhosa-speaking people." *South African Journal of Ethnology* 8,2:48-52.

Dearmer, P. 1909. *Body and Soul.* London: Sir Isaac Pitman & Sons.

Degenaar, J. 1980. "Normative Dimensions of Discrimination, Differentiation and Affirmative Action." in Van der Merwe, H.W. & Schrire, R., *Race and Ethnicity: South African and International Perspectives*, pp. 28-55. Cape Town: David Philip.

Diakonia 1991. *Heal, Build Reconcile: Diakonia Theme for 1991.* Durban:Diakonia.

Dollar, H. 1980. *A Cross-Cultural Theology of Healing.* Unpublished D.Min Dissertation, Fuller Theological Seminary.

Douglas, M. 1970a. "The Healing Rite (Review article)." *MAN: Journal of the Royal Anthropological Institute* 5:302-308.

Douglas, M. 1970b. *Natural Symbols: Explorations in Cosmology.* London: Barrie & Rockliff, The Cresset Press.

Dow, J. 1986. "Universal Aspects of Symbolic Healing: A Theoretical Synthesis." *American Anthropologist* 88,1:56-69.

Downs, J. F. 1975. *Cultures in Crisis.* Beverly Hills, Ca.:Glencoe Press.

Du Toit, B.M. 1971. "The Isangoma: An Adaptive Agent Among the Urban Zulu." *Anthropological Quarterly* 44,2:51-65.

Du Toit, B.M. 1980. "Religion, Ritual and Healing among Urban Black South Africans." *Urban Anthropology* 9,1:21-49.

Dube, D. 1989. "A search for abundant life: health, healing and wholeness in Zionist Churches." in Oosthuizen, G.C., Edwards, S.D., Wessels, W.H.et al, eds., *Afro-Christian Religion and Healing in Southern Africa. (African Studies Volume 8)*, pp. 109-136. N.Y.: Edwin Mellen.

Dubos, R. 1977. "Determinants of Health and Disease." in Landy, D., ed., *Culture, Disease and Healing*, pp. 31-41. N.Y.: Macmillan.

Dunbar, F. 1954. *Emotions and Bodily Changes*. N.Y.: Columbia University Press.

Dwane, S. 1988. "Gospel and Culture." *Journal of Black Theology in South Africa* 1,1:18-25.

Eagleson, J., & Scharper, P., eds. 1979. *Puebla and Beyond: Documentation and Commentary*. N.Y.: Orbis.

Easthope, G. 1986. *Healers and Alternative Medicine, A Sociological Examination*. Aldershot, UK: Gower.

Eboussi Boulaga, F. 1984. *Christianity Without Fetishes*. N.Y.: Orbis.

Edwards, F.S. 1989a. "Amafufunyana Spirit Possession: Treatment and Interpretation." in Oosthuizen, G.C., Edwards, S.D., Wessels, W.H.et al, eds., *Afro-Christian Religion and Healing in Southern Africa. (African Studies Volume 8)*, pp. 207-225. N.Y.: Edwin Mellen.

Edwards, F.S. 1989b. "Healing: Xhosa perspective." in Oosthuizen, G.C., Edwards, S.D., Wessels, W.H.et al, eds., *Afro-Christian Religion and Healing in Southern Africa. (African Studies Volume 8)*, pp. 329-345. N.Y.: Edwin Mellen.

Edwards, P. 1967. *The Encyclopedia of Philosophy*. N.Y.: Macmillan.

Edwards, S.D., ed. 1985. *Some Indigenous South African Views on Illness and Healing*. n.p.: University of Zululand.

Edwards, S.D., Cheetham, R.W.S., Majozi, E., & Lasich, A.J. 1982. "Zulu culture bound psychiatric syndromes." *South African Journal of Hospital Medicine* 8:82-87.

Edwards, S.D., Cheetham, R.W.S., Majozi, E., & Makhwanazi (sic), I., 1985. "The Treatment of Umeqo with Hypnotherapy and Cultural Counsellng : A case Study." in Edwards, S.D., ed., *Some Indigenous South African Views on Illness and Healing*, pp. 61-73. University of Zululand.

Eikland, O. 1957. "Does the Christian Church Need to be Divided on the Question of Divine Healing?" *Evangelical Christian (Toronto)* 494,534-535.

Ela, J.M. 1986. *Africa Cry*. N.Y.: Orbis.

Farrand, D. 1986. "Choice and Perception of Healers among Black Psychiatric Patients." in Oosthuizen, G.C., ed., *Religion Alive: Studies in the New Movements and Indigenous Churches in Southern Africa*, pp. 97-104. Bergvlei, South Africa: Hodder & Stoughton Southern Africa.

Feierman, S. 1979. "Change in African Therapeutic Systems." *Social Science and Medicine* 13B:227-284.

Feierman, S. 1985. "Struggles for Control: The Social Roots of Health and Healing in Modern Africa." *African Review Studies* 28,213:73-147.

Ferreira, M. 1987. "Medicinal use of indigenous plants by elderly Coloureds: A sociological study of folk medicine." *South African Journal of Sociology* 18,4:139-143.

Fishman, R.G. 1980. "Transmigration, Liminality and Spiritualist Healing." *Journal of Religion and Health* 19,3:217-225.

Flannery, A., 1984. *Vatican Council II: The Conciliar and Post Conciliar Documents, New Revised Edition*. Grand Rapids: Eerdmans.

Foster, G. 1976. "Disease Etiologies in Non-Western Medical Systems." *American Anthroplogist* 78,4:773-782.

Foucault, M. 1970. *The Order of Things: An Archeology of the Human Sciences*. N.Y.: Random House.

Frank, J. 1961. *Persuasion and Healing*. Baltimore: John Hopkins.

Frank, J. 1975. "Mind-Body Relationships in Illness and Healing." *Journal of the International Academy of Preventative Medicine* 2,3:46-59.

Freidson, E. 1970. *Profession of Medicine: A Study of the Sociology of Applied Knowledge.* N.Y.: Dodd, Mead & Co.

Froise, M. 1992. South African Christan Handbook 1993/1994. Johannesburg: Christian Info

Frost, E. 1940. *Christian Healing: A Consideration of the Place of Spritual Healing in the Church of To-day in the Light of the Doctrine and Practice of the Ante-Nicene Church.* London: A.R. Mowbray & Co.

Fuellenbach, J. 1987. *The Kingdom of God: The central message of Jesus' Teachings in the light of the modern world.* Manila: Divine Word Publications.

Füllenbach, J. 1981. "The Incarnational Aspect of Mission." *Verbum SVD* 22:325-341.

Fuller Torrey, E. 1972. *The Mind Game: Witchdoctors and Psychiatrists.* N.Y.: Emerson Hall.

Gadamer, H-G. 1975. *Truth and Method.* London: Sheed & Ward.

Gardner, R. 1983. "Miracles of healing in Anglo-Celtic Northumbria as recorded by the Venerable Bede and his contemporaries: a reappraisal in the light of twentieth century experience." *British Medical Journal* 287:1927-1933.

Gaybba, B. 1990. "'The People' as a Theological Concept." *Grace & Truth 10,2*:66-74.

Geertz, C. 1973. *The Interpretation of Cultures.* N.Y.: Basic Books.

Geertz, C. 1983. *Local Knowledge.* N.Y.: Basic Books.

George, F.E. 1990. *Inculturation and Ecclesial Communion: Culture and the Church in the Teaching of Pope John Paul II.* Rome: Urbaniana University Press.

Gibbons, D.E., & De Jarnette, J. 1972. "Hypnotic Susceptibility and Religious Experience." *Journal for the Scientific Study of Religion* 11,2:152-156.

Gifford, P. 1987. "Africa Shall be Saved: An Appraisal of Reinhard Bonnke's Pan-African Crusade." *Journal of Religion in Africa* 17,1:63-92.

Gifford, P. 1988. *The Religious Right in Southern Afica.* Zimbabwe: University of Zimbabwe Publications.

Girard, R. 1977. *Violence and the Sacred.* Baltimore: Johns Hopkins University Press.

Glazer, N. 1975. "The universalization of ethnicity." *Encounter (February)*:8.17

Glazer, N. 1980. "Individual Rights Against Group Rights." in Van der Merwe, H.W & Schrire, R., *Race and Ethnicity: South African and International Perspectives*, pp. 10-27. Cape Town: David Philip.

Glennon, J. 1984. *How can I find Healing?* London: Hodder and Stoughton.

Glick, L.B. 1977. "Medicine as an Ethrographic Category." in Landy, D., ed., *Culture Disease and Healing*, pp. 58-70. N.Y.: Macmillan.

Gluckman, M. 1965. *Politics, Law and Ritual in Tribal Society.* London: Oxford University Press.

Goba, B. 1979 "The Role of the Black Church in the Process of Healing Human Brokenness." *Journal of Theology for Southern Africa* 28:7-13.

Goba, B. 1980. "Doing Theology in South Africa: A Black Christian Perspective." *Journal of Theology for Southern Africa* 31:23-35.

Goba, B. 1986. "The Black Consciousness Movement: Its Impact on Black Theology." in Mosala, I.J., & Tlhagale, B., eds., *The Unquestionable Right to be Free*, pp. 57-69. N.Y.: Orbis.

Goba, B. 1988. *An Agenda for Black Theology.* Johannesburg: Skotaville.

Grad, B. 1970. "Healing by the Laying on of Hands: Review of Experiments and Implications." *Pastoral Psychology* 21:19-26.

Gumede, M.V. 1989. "Healers: modern and traditional." in Oosthuizen, G.C., Edwards, S.D., Wessels, W.H.et al, eds., *Afro-Christian Religion and Healing in Southern Africa*, pp. 319-328. N.Y.: Edwin Mellen.

Gutierrez, G. 1973. *A Theology of Liberation*. N.Y.: Orbis.

Haleblian, K. 1983. "The Problem of Contextualisation." *Missiology* 11:91-111.

Hall, E.T. 1959. *The Silent Language*. New York: Doubleday.

Hallowell, A.I. 1977. "The Social Function of Anxiety in a Primitive Society." in Landy, D., ed., *Culture, Disease, and Healing*, pp. 132-138. N.Y.: Macmillan.

Hammond-Tooke, W.D. 1970. "Urbanisation and the Interpretation of Misfortune: A Quantative Analysis." *Africa* 40,1:25-38.

Hammond-Tooke, W.D. 1989. "The aetiology of spirit in Southern Africa." in Oosthuizen, G.C., Edwards, S.D., Wessels, W.H.et al, eds., *Afro-Christian Religion and Healing in Southern Africa*, pp. 43-66. N.Y.: Edwin Mellen.

HAP 1992. *Info 92: Facts and Figures on South Africa*. Cape Town: Human Awareness Programme.

Häring, B. 1984. *Healing and Revealing*. Slough, UK: St Paul Publications.

Haynes, R. 1981. "Faith Healing and Psychic Healing: Are They the Same?" *Journal of Religion and Physical Research* 4,1:22-29.

Herskovits, M.J. 1952. *Man and His Works: The Science of Cultural Anthropology*. New York: Alfred A. Knopf.

Hiebert, P.G. 1983. *Cultural Anthropology*. Grand Rapids: Baker Book House.

Hindle, D. 1992. "Sadtu's plans for education." *New Nation 7 Feb.* Johannesburg, p.24.

Hodgson, J. 1983. "The Faith-Healer of Cancele: Some Problems in Analysing Religious Experience among Black People." *Religion in Southern Africa* 4,1:13-29.

Hodgson, J. 1986. "The Symbolic Entry Point: Removing the Veil of Structure from the Study of Religious Movements." in Oosthuizen, G.C., ed., *Religion Alive: Studies in the New Movements and Indigenous Churches in Southern Africa*, pp. 48-67. Bergvlei, South Africa: Hodder & Stoughton Southern Africa.

Hoedemaker, L.A. 1991. "Local Church." in Lossky, N., et al, *Dictionary Of The Ecumenical Movement*, pp. 626-627. Geneva: WCC Publications.

Holdstock, T.L. 1979. "Indigenous healing in South Africa." *South African Journal of Psychology* 9:118-124.

Hollenweger, W.J. 1972. *The Pentecostals: The Charismatic Movement in the Churches*. Minnesota: Augsburg Publishing House.

Hollenweger, W.J. 1989 "Healing through Prayer: Superstition or Forgotten Christian Tradition?" *Theology* 92:166-174.

Horton, R. 1967. "African Traditional Thought and Western Science." *Africa* 37,1:50-71.

Horton, R. 1971 "African Conversion." *Africa* 41,2:85-108.

Hughes, C.C. 1985. "Culture-Bound or Construct-Bound? The Syndromes and DSM-III" in Simons, R.C., & Hughes, C.C., eds., *The Culture-Bound Syndromes*, pp. 3-24. Dordrecht: Reidel.

Huizer, G. 1987. "Health & Healing in Global Perspective." *Mission Studies* 4,2:75-99.

Hulley, L.D. 1991. "Some Human Values in Society - From a Liberal Perspective." *Journal of Theology for Southern Africa* 76:25-31.

Hyslop, J. 1991. "Food, Authority and Politics: Student Riots in South African Schools." in Clingman, S., ed., *Regions and Repertoires: Topics in South African Politics and Culture*, pp. 84-115. Johannesburg: Ravan.

ICT n.d. *Contextual Theology for Groups: 1st Module*. Braamfontein: Institute for Contextual Theology.

Ikin, G.A. 1955. *New Concepts of Healing: Medical, Psychological and Religious*. London: Hodder & Stoughton.

Illich, I. 1977. *Limits to Medicine. Medical nemesis: The expropriation of health*. Harmondsworth, Middlesex: Penguin.

Inkatha n.d. *Unity: an Inkatha Newsletter* Vol. 1 No. 4.

Jackson, E.N. 1981 *The Role of Faith in the Process of Healing*. London: SCM.

Jana, P. 1992. "Failure of Justice." *New Nation,* Johannesburg 28 February pp.11-12.

Janzen, J.J. 1989. "Health, Religion, and Medicine in Central and Southern African Traditions." in Sullivan, L.E., ed., *Healing and Restoring*, pp. 225-254. N.Y.: Macmillan.

Jelliffe, D.B., & Jelliffe, E.F.P. 1977. "The cultural cul-de-sac of Western medicine: (towards a curvilinear compromise?)." *Transactions of the Royal Society of Tropical Medicine and Hygiene* 71,4:331-334.

Johnson, E.W. 1950. *Everyman's Search*. Wells, Vermont: Merybrook.

Jonas, P.J., & De Beer, F.C. 1988. *Socio-Cultural Anthropology*. Pretoria: UNISA.

Jones, R.K. 1985. *Sickness and Sectarianism*. Aldershot, UK: Gower.

Jules-Rosette, B. 1981. "Faith Healers and Folk Healers." *Religion* 11,127-149.

Jurgens, W.A. 1970. *The Faith of the Early Fathers Volume One*. Collegeville, Minnesota: The Liturgical Press.

Kakar, S. 1985. "Psychoanalysis and Religious Healing: Siblings or Strangers?" *Journal of American Academy of Religion* 53,3:841-853.

Kalu, O.U. 1978. "Church unity and religious change in Africa." in Fashole-Luke, E., et al, *Christianity in Independent Africa*, pp. 164-176. London: Rex Collings.

Karagulla, S. 1968. *Breakthrough to Creativity, The Role of Faith in the Process of Healing*. Los Angeles: De Vorss and Co.

Kayter, E., ed. 1992. *South African Year Book*. Pretoria: S.A. Communications Service.

Kelsey, M. 1973. *Healing and Christianity*. N.Y.: Harper & Row.

Kenyon, E.W. 1966. *The two kinds of Knowledge*. Lynnwood, WA: Kenyon Gospel.

Kenyon, E.W. 1970 *The hidden man*. Lynwood, WA: Kenyon Gospel.

Kew, C.F. 1961. "Understanding Spiritual Healing." *Pastoral Psychology* 12:29-34.

Kibongi, R.B. 1969. "Priesthood." in Dickson, K.A. & Ellingworth, J.H., eds., *Biblical Revelation and African Beliefs*, pp.47-56 . London: Lutterworth.

Kiernan, J.P. 1974. "Where Zionists draw the line: a study of religious exclusiveness in an African township." *African Studies* 33(2): 79-90.

Kiernan, J.P. 1990. *The Production and management of Therapeutic Power in Zionist Churches within a Zulu City*. Lampeter, Wales: Edwin Mellen Press.

Kiernan, J.P. 1991. "Wear 'n' Tear and Repair: The Colour Coding of Mystical Mending in Zulu Zionist Churches." *Africa* 61,1:25-39.

Kiev, A. 1964. *Magic, Faith, and Healing*. London: Collier Macmillan .

Kinghorn, J., Lategan, B., & Van der Merwe, C. 1989. *Into Africa*. Stellenbosch: Centre for Contextual Hermeneutics.

Kleinman, A. 1980. *Patients and Healers in the Context of Culture*. Berkeley: University of California Press.

Kleinman, A., Eisenberg, L., & Good, B. 1978. "Culture, Illness, and Care: Clinical Lessons from Anthropological and Cross-Cultural Research." *Annals of Internal Medicine* 88:251-258.

Kleinman, A., & Sung, L.H. 1979. "Why do Indigenous Practitioners Successfully Heal." *Social Science & Medicine* 13B:7-26.

Knight, J.F. 1982. "Miracles Cures." *The Medical Journal of Australia* 1,3:140.

Kraft, C.H. 1979. *Christianity in Culture: A Study in Dynamic Biblical Theologizing in Cross-Cultural Perspective*. Maryknoll, N.Y.: Orbis.

Krige, J.D. 1954. "Bantu Medical Conceptions." *Theoria,* Charter Commemoration Number: 50-65.

Kritzinger, J.J. 1992. "Mission and the liberation of creation: A critical dialogue with M.L. Daneel." *Missionalia* 20,2: 99-115.

Kroeber, A. & Kluckhohn, C. 1952. *Culture: A Critical Review of Concepts and Definitions*. New York: Vintage.

Kuhlman, K. 1962. *I Believe in Miracles*. Spire Books: New Jersey.

Kuhlman, K. 1969. *God Can Do It Again*. Basingstoke, Hants: Lakeland.

Kuhn, T.S. 1962, 1970. *The Structure of Scientific Revolutions*. Chicago: University of Chicago.

Küng, H. 1967. *The Church*. London: Burns and Oates

Küng, H., and Tracy, D. 1989. *Paradigm Change in Theology: A Symposium for the Future*. Edinburgh: T&T Clark.

Küng, H. 1989. "Paradigm Change in Theology: A proposal for Discussion." in Küng, H., & Tracy, D., eds., *Paradigm Change in Theology*, pp.3-33. Edinburgh: T.& T. Clark.

Lamb, M.L. 1989. "The Dialectics of the Theory and Praxis within Paradigm Analysis." in Küng, H., & Tracy, D., eds., *Paradigm Change in Theology*, pp. 63-109. Edinburgh: T&T Clark.

Landy, D. 1977. *Culture, Disease, and Healing*. N.Y.: Macmillan.

Landman, C. 1991. "The Anthropology of Apartheid According to Official Sources." *Journal of Theology for Southern Africa* 76:32-45.

Lategan, B. 1991. "Socio-religious change in South Africa." *South African Journal of Sociology* 22,1:10-15.

Lategan, B., Kinghorn, J., Du Plessis, L., et al. 1990. *The Option for Inclusive Democracy*. Stellenbosch: Centre for Contextual Hermeneutics.

Lederer, W. 1959. "Primitive Psychotherapy." *Psychiatry* 22:255-265.

Lederle, H.I., 1986. "The Charismatic Movement - The Ambiguous Challenge." *Missionalia* 14:61-75.

Leger, J. 1989. "Key Issues in Safety and Health in South African Mines." *South African Sociological Review* 2,2:1-48.

Lehrman, D. 1970. "Semantic and Conceptual Issues in the Nature-Nurture problem." in Aaronson, L.R. et al. eds., *Development and Evolution of Behaviour*, pp. 65-81 . San Francisco: Freeman.

LeShan, L. 1977. *You Can Fight For Your Life: Emotional Factors in the Causation of Cancer*. N.Y.: Evans.

Lester, D. 1972. "Voodoo Death: Some New Thoughts on an Old Phenomenon." *American Anthropologist* 74:386-390.

Levin, S. 1985. "Faith Cures." *South African Medical Journal* 67:796.

Lewis, G. 1975. *Knowledge of Illnesss in a Sepik Society*. London: Athlone Press.

Lieban, R.W. 1977. "The Field of Medical Anthropology." in Landy, D., ed., *Culture, Disease, and Healing*, pp. 13-31. N.Y.: Macmillan.

Lineamenta 1990. *The Church in Africa and Her Evangelising Mission Towards the Year 2000, "You Shall Be My Witnesses". Lineamenta. Synod of Bishops, Special Assembly for Africa.* Vatican City: Libreria Editrice Vaticana

Linn, M., & Linn, D. 1974. *Healing of Memories*. N.Y.: Paulist.

Linn, M., & Linn, D. 1978. *Healing Life's Hurts*. N.Y.: Paulist.

Linton, R. 1936. *The Study of Man*. New York: Appleton-Century-Crofts.

Lipner, J. 1985. "'Being One, Let Me Be Many': Facets of the Relationship Between the Gospel and Culture." *International Review of Mission* 74:158-168.

Little, K. 1965. *West African Urbanization - a Study of Voluntary Association in Social Change*. Cambridge: Cambridge University.

Livingstone E.A. 1977. *The Concise Oxford Dictionary Of The Christian Church*. London: Oxford University Press.

Lonergan, B.J.F. 1971. *Method in Theology*. London: Darton, Longman & Todd.

Longmore, L. 1958. "Medicine, Magic and Witchcraft Among Urban Africans on the Witwatersrand." *Central African Journal of Medicine* 4,6:242-249.

Lutzbetak, L. 1981. "Signs of Progress in Contextual Methodology." *Verbum SVD* 22:39-57.

Lutzbetak, L. 1988. *The Church and Cultures*. N.Y.: Orbis.

Maake, N.P. 1992. "Multicultural relations in a post-apartheid South Africa." *African Affairs* 91:583-604.

MacDonald, N. 1991. *Jesus the Counsellor.* Video Cassette of the Proceedings of the "Jesus Miracle Crusade" on Thursday 29th August 1991 in Durban.

MacNutt, F. 1974. *Healing*. Notre Dame, Indiana: Ave Maria.

Maddocks, M. 1981. *The Christian Healing Ministry*. London: SPCK. 1990

Maimela, S.S. 1991. "Traditional African Anthropology and Christian Theology." *Journal of Theology for Southern Africa* 76:4-14.

Makhubu, P. 1988. *Who Are The Independent Churches*. Braamfontein: Skotaville.

Manganyi, N.C. 1981. *Looking Through The Keyhole*. Johannesburg: Ravan.

Marks, S. n.d. *Industrialization and Social Change: Some thoughts on Class Formation and Political Consciousness in South Africa, c. 1870-1920*. Paper read to the Boston University African Studies Center. The Walter Rodney Studies Seminar, April 1982.

Marty, M.E., & Vaux, K.L. 1982. *Health/Medicine and the Faith Traditions*. Philadelphia: Fortress.

Masilela, N 1988. "Establishing an Intellectual Bridgehead." in Tomaselli, K., ed., *Rethinking Culture*, pp. 1-5. Bellville: Anthropos.

Matthews, J.R. 1988. *A Practical Theological Analysis of the Essential Elements in the Healing Process*. Unpublished M. Th. Thesis, University of South Africa, Pretoria.

Mbuli, M. 1986. "Culture must be a weapon." in Suttner, R. & Cronin, J., *30 Years of the Freedom Charter*, pp. 138-140. Johannesburg: Ravan.

McAllister, W.R. 1985. "Roman Catholic - Pentecostal Dialogue Rome 1979." *One in Christ* 21,1:43-51.

McCauley, R. 1985. *Our God Reigns*. Basingstoke, Hants: Marshall, Morgan & Scott.

McCauley, R. 1988. *The Gifts of the Holy Spirit*. Randburg: Conquest Publishers.

McConnell, D.R. 1990. *The Promise of Health And Wealth*. London: Hodder & Stoughton.

McDonald, C.A. 1981. "Political-Economic Structures." *Social Science and Medicine* 15A:101-108.

McGilvray, J. 1981. *The Quest for Health and Wholeness*. Tubingen: German Institute for Medical Missions.

Meyendorff, J. 1985. "Christ as Word: Gospel and Culture." *International Review of Mission* 74:246-257.

Milazi, D. 1986. "Social and cultural basis of Mental Illness." *South African Journal of Ethnology* 9:175-180.

Milingo, E. 1986. *The World In Between*. Gweru, Zimbabwe: Mambo.

Mills, J. 1987. "Diviners as social healers within an urban township context." *South African Journal of Sociology* 18:7-13.

Mills, J.J. 1988. "Bridging the gap between theory and practice: A critical perspective of medical sociology within the Southern African context." *South African Journal of Sociology* 19:9-19.

Mkhize, H.B. 1989. "The *umthandazi*-prayer-healer." in Oosthuizen, G.C., Edwards, S.D., Wessels, W,H.et al, eds., *Afro-Christian Religion and Healing in Southern Africa*, pp. 281-294. N.Y.: Edwin Mellen.

Mkhwanazi, I. 1986. *An Investigation of the Therapeutic Method of Zulu Diviners*. Unpublished M.A. Thesis, University of South Africa, Pretoria

Mkhwanazi, I. 1989. "The *iSangoma* as psycho-therapist." in Oosthuizen, G.C., Edwards, S.D., Wessels, W.H.et al, eds., *Afro-Christian Religion and Healing in Southern Africa*, pp. 261-280. N.Y.: Edwin Mellen.

Moerman, D.E.. 1979. "Anthropology of Symbolic Healing." *Current Anthropology* 20,1:59-80.

Mofokeng, T. 1983. *The Crucified among the Crossbearers*. Kampen: J.H. Kok.

Mofokeng, T.A. 1991. "Human Values Beyond the Market Society: A Black Working Class Perspective." *Journal of Theology for Southern Africa* 76:64-70.

Mogoba, M.S. 1985. "Christianity in an African Context." *Journal of Theology for Southern Africa* 52:5-16.

Moltmann, J. 1978. *The Open Church*. London: SCM.

Morley, P. 1978. "Culture and the Cognitive World of Traditional Medical Beliefs: Some Preliminary Considerations." in Morley, P., and Wallis, R., eds., *Culture and Curing*, pp. 1-18. London: Peter Owen.

Morley, P., & Wallis, R. 1978. *Culture and Curing*. London: Peter Owen.

Morran, E.S., & Schlemmer, L. 1984. *Faith for the Fearful?: An investigation into new churches in the greater Durban area*. Durban: Center for Applied Social Sciences, University of Natal.

Mosala, I. 1985. "African Independent churches: a study in socio-theological protest." in Villa-Vicencio, C., & De Gruchy, J.W., eds., *Resistance and Hope*, pp. 103-111. Cape Town: David Philip.

Mosala, I.J. 1986 "The Relevance of African Traditional Religions and Their Challenge to Black Theology." in Mosala, I.J., and Tlhagale, B., eds., *The Unquestionable Right to be free*, pp. 91-100. N.Y.: Orbis.

Mosala, I.J. 1989. *Biblical Hermeneutics and Black Theology in South Africa*. Grand Rapids: Eerdmans.

Motala, M.B. 1989. "The relative influence of participation in Zionist Church services on the emotional state of participants." in Oosthuizen, G.C., Edwards, S.D., Wessels, W.H.et al, eds., *Afro-Christian Religion and Healing in Southern Africa*, pp. 193-206. N.Y.: Edwin Mellen.

Mouton, J., Van Aarde, A.G., Vorster, W.S., eds. 1988. *Paradigms and Progress in Theology*. n.p.: Human Sciences Research Council.

Msomi, V. 1967. "Contemporary Approaches of Healing: The Healing Practices of the African Independent Churches." in AA.VV., *The Report of the Umpumulo Consultation on the Healing Ministry of the Church*, pp. 65-74. Mapumulo, Natal: Lutheran Theological College.

Müller, J. 1974. "Neo-Pentecostalism: a theological evaluation of Glossolalia, with special reference to the Reformed Churches." *Journal of Theology for Southern Africa* 7:41-49

Muller, J. & Tomaselli, K. 1989. "Becoming appropriately modern: Towards a genealogy of cultural studies in South Africa." in Mouton, J., & Joubert, D., eds., *Knowledge and method in the human sciences*, pp. 301-319. Pretoria: HSRC.

Mutiso-Mbinda, J. 1986. "Inculturation: Challenge to the African Local Church." in Waliggo, J.M., et al, *Inculturation Its Meaning and Urgency*, pp. 75-83. Kampala: St. Paul-Africa.

Nair, M.G. 1985. "Update on the Treatment and Outcome of Conversion Disorders." in Carlile, J.B., ed., *Update on Psychiatric Management.* pp. 153-158. Durban: Society of Psychiatrists of South Africa.

Ndebele, N. 1972. "Black Devolpment." in Biko, B.S., ed., *Black Viewpoint*, pp. 13-28. Durban: SPROCAS.

Ness, R.C. 1980. "The impact of indigenous healing activity: an empirical study of two fundamentalist churches." *Social Science and Medicine* 14B:167-180.

Ness, R.C., & Winthrob, R.M. 1980. "The Emotional Impact of Fundamentalist Religious Participation." *American Journal of Orthopsychiatry* 50,2:302-315.

Neuhaus, R.J. 1987. *The Catholic Moment*. San Francisco: Harper & Row.

Newman, M.T. 1977. "Ecology and Nutritional Stress." in Landy, D., ed., *Culture, Disease, and Healing*, pp. 319-326. N.Y.: Macmillan.

New Nation 1992a. "Culture." *Learning Nation: a Supplement to New Nation*. Johannesburg, 7 February , p. 13.

New Nation 1992b. "Re-establish culture of learning - Maree." *New Nation*. Johannesburg, 30 April, p.26.

Ngada, N.H. 1985. *Speaking for Ourselves*. Braamfontein, South Africa: Institute of Contextual Theology.

Ngubane, H. 1977. *Body and Mind in Zulu Medicine*. London: Academic Press.

Ngubane, H. 1981. "Aspects of Clinical Practice and Traditional Organisation of Indigenous Healers in South Africa." *Social Sciences and Medicine* 15B:361-365.

Nida, E.A. 1954. *Customs and Cultures: Anthropology for Christian Missions*. N.Y.: Harper and Brothers.

Niebuhr, H.R. 1951. *Christ and Culture*. N.Y.: Harper and Row.

Nkéramihigo, T. 1986. "Inculturation and the Specificity of Christian Faith." in Waliggo, J.M., Roest Crollius, A., et al, *Inculturation: Its Meaning and Urgency*, pp. 67-74. Kampala: St. Paul-Africa.

Nolan, A. 1988. *God in South Africa: The Challenge of the Gospel*. London: CIIR.

Nolan, A. 1992. "The Search for True Democracy." *Challenge* 3:5.

Nyamiti, C. 1991. "African Christologies Today." in Schreiter, R.J., ed., *Faces of Jesus in Africa*, pp. 3-23. N.Y.: Orbis.

O'Collins, G. 1977. *The Calvary Christ*. London: SCM.

O'Dea, T. 1970. "Religion in Times of Social Distress." in Sadler, W.A. Jr., ed., *Personality and Religion*, pp. 181-190. N.Y.: Harper & Row.

Okure, T. 1990. "Inculturation: biblical/theological bases." in Okure, T., Van Thiel, P., et al, *Inculturation of Christianity in Africa*, pp. 55-88. Eldoret, Kenya: AMECEA Gaba Publications.

Okure, T., Van Theil, P., et al 1990. *Inculturation of Christianity in Africa*. Eldoret, Kenya: AMECEA Gaba Publications.

Olivier, L. 1988. "Family murder as a socio-psychological phenomenon in the Republic of South Africa." *South African Journal of Sociology* 117-119.

Onwubiko, O.A. 1992. *Theory And Practice Of Inculturation (An African Perspective)*. Enugu, Nigeria: Snaap Press.

Oosthuizen, G.C. 1968. *Post Christianity in Africa*. Stellenbosch: T.Wever.

Oosthuizen, G.C. 1975. *Pentecostal Penetration into the Indian Community in Metropolitan Durban, South Africa*. Durban: Human Sciences Research Council.

Oosthuizen, G.C. 1986. "The AIC and the Modernisation Process." in Oosthuizen, G.C., ed., *Religion Alive*, pp. 223-245. JHB: Hodder & Stoughton Southern Africa.

Oosthuizen, G.C., ed. 1986a. *Religion Alive: Studies in the New Movements and Indigenous Churches in Southern Africa*. Bergvlei, South Africa: Hodder & Stoughton Southern Africa.

Oosthuizen, G.C. 1989a. "Indigenous healing within the context of African Independent Churches." in Oosthuizen, G.C., Edwards, S.D., Wessels, W.H.et al, eds., *Afro-Christian Religion and Healing in Southern Africa*, pp. 71-90. N.Y.: Edwin Mellen.

Oosthuizen, G.C. 1989b. "Baptism & healing in African Independent Churches." in Oosthuizen, G.C., Edwards, S.D., Wessels, W.H.et al, eds., *Afro-Christian Religion and Healing in Southern Africa*, pp.137-188 . N.Y.: Edwin Mellen.

Oosthuizen, G.C., Coetzee, J.K., De Gruchy, J.W., 1985. *Religion Intergroup Relations and Social Change in South Africa*. Pretoria: HSRC.

Oosthuizen, G.C., Edwards, S.D., Wessels, W.H. et al, eds. 1989. *Afro-Christian Religion and Healing in Southern Africa*. N.Y.: Edwin Mellen.

Opler, M.E. 1936. "Some Points of Comparison and Contrast between the Treatment of Function Disorders by Apache Shamans and Modern Psychiatric Practice." *American Journal of Psychiatry* 92:1371-1378.

Padilla, C.R. 1978. "The Contextualisation of the Gospel." *Journal of Theology for Southern Africa* 24:12-30.

Parsons, T. 1951. *The Social System*. Glencoe, Ill: Free Press.

Parsons, S. 1986. *The Challenge of Christian Healing*. London: SPCK.

Paulley, J.W. 1975. "Cultural influences on the incidence and pattern of disease." *Psychotherapy and Psychosomatics* 26:2-11.

Peel, J.D.Y. 1968. *Aladura: A Religious Movement Among the Yoruba*. Oxford: Oxford University.

Pénoukou, E.J. 1991. "Christology in the Village." in Schreiter, R.J., ed., *Faces of Jesus in Africa*, pp. 24-51. N.Y.: Orbis.

Photiadis, J., & Schweker, W. 1970. "Attitudes Toward Joining Authoritarian Organizations and Sectarian Churches." *Journal for the Scientific Study of Religion* 9,3:227-234.

Pillay, G.J. 1991. "The Anthropology of Apartheid: The Historical Search." *Journal of Theology for Southern Africa* 76:46-56.

Polgar, S. 1962. "Health and Human Behaviour: Areas of Interest Common to the Social and Medical Sciences." *Current Anthropology* 3,2:159-205.

Pretorius, H. 1987. "The New Jerusalem: Eschatological Perspectives in African Indigenous Churches." *Missionalia* 15:31-41.

Procter, D. 1985. "Miracles as opposed to amazing events." *S.A. Medical Journal* 68:784.

Rahner, K. 1968. *Spirit in the World.* London: Sheed & Ward.

Rappaport, H. & Rappaport, M. 1981. "The Integration of Scientific & Traditional Healing: A Proposed Model." *American Psychologist* 36,7:774-781.

Rayan, S. 1976. "Flesh of India's Flesh." *Jeevadhara* 6,259-267.

Rivers, W.H.R. 1926. *Psychology and Ethnology.* London: Routledge and Kegan Paul.

Robbertze, J.H. 1976. "Psigoterapie. Waarheen is ons op weg?" *Paper presented at the 2nd biennial Congress of the S.A.P.A, Pretoria .*

Roest Crollius, A. 1978. "What is so new about inculturation?" *Gregorianum* 59:721-737.

Roest Crollius, A. 1980. "Inculturation and the Meaning of Culture." *Gregorianum* 61:253-274.

Roest Crollius, A., ed. 1983. *Inculturation II: On Being Church in a Modern Society.* Rome: Centre "Cultures and Religions" - Pontifical Gregorian University.

Roest Crollius, A., ed. 1986. *Inculturation VIII: Creative Inculturation and the Unity of Faith.* Rome: Centre "Cultures and Religions" - Pontifical Gregorian University.

Roest Crollius, A., ed. 1987a. *Inculturation IX: Effective Inculturation and Ethnic Identity.* Rome: Centre "Cultures and Religions" - Pontifical Gregorian University.

Roest Crollius, A., ed. 1987b. *Inculturation X: Cultural Change and Liberation in a Christian Perspective.* Rome: Centre "Cultures and Religions" - Pontifical Gregorian University.

Rose, L. 1968. *Faith Healing.* London: Victor Gollancz.

Rounds, J.C. 1979. *Religious Change and Social Change in South Africa: A Study of Two New Religions among the Zulu.* Unpublished Ph. D. Thesis, New School for Social Research.

Rounds, J.C. 1982. "Curing what ails them: individual circumstances and religious choice among Zulu-speakers in Durban, South Africa." *Africa* 52,2:77-89.

Rubel, A.J. 1979. "Parallel Medical Systems: Papers from a Workshop on the Healing Process." *Social Science and Medicine* 13B:3-6.

Rychlak, J.F. 1973. *Introduction to Personality and Psychotherapy: A Theory-Construction Approach.* Boston: Houghton Mifflin.

SABC 1983. "Born Again". TV Programme in the series *Special Edition* broadcast 30 June 1983

S.A.C.S. 1991. *South Africa at a Glance.* Pretoria: South African Communications Service.

Saayman, W. 1992. "'If you were to die today, do you know for certain that you would go to heaven?' Reflections on conversion as primary aim of mission." *Missionalia* 159-173.

SACBC n.d. *Why Some Catholics Join Evangelical Pentecostal Churches.* Pretoria: Southern African Catholic Bishops' Conference.

Sales, S. 1972. "Economic Threat as a Determinant of Conversion Rates in Authoritarian and Non Authoritarian Churches." *Journal of Personality and Social Psychology* 23,3:420-428.

Sanneh, L. 1985. "Christian Mission in the Pluralist Milieu: The African Experience." *International Review of Mission* 74:199-211.

Sanneh, L. 1989. *Translating the Message*. N.Y.: Orbis.

Sanon, A.T. 1991. "Jesus, Master of Initiation." in Schreiter, R.J., ed., *Faces of Jesus in Africa*, pp. 85-102. N.Y.: Orbis.

Sarpong, P.K. 1988. "Inculturation and the African Church." *Shalom 6(2)* 76-87.

SBDC 1991. *Small Business Development Corporation: Survey Supplement Financial Mail*. Johannesburg: April 19.

Scherer, J.A., & Bevans, S.B., eds. 1992. *New Dimensions In Mission And Evangelization 1: Basic Statements 1974-1991*. N.Y.: Orbis.

Schillebeeckx, E. 1989. "The Role of History in what is called the New Paradigm." in Küng, H., & Tracy, D., eds., *Paradigm Change In Theology*, pp.307-319. Edinburgh: T.& T. Clark.

Schlosser, K. 1967. "Profane Ursachen des Anschlusses an Separatistenkirchen in Sud und Sudwestafrika." in Benz, E., ed., *Messianische Kirchen*, pp. 25-45. .

Schlemmer, L. 1991. "A challenge to political transition in South Africa: majority vs minority rights." *South African Journal of Sociology* 22,1:16-22.

Schoffeleers, M. 1991 "Ritual Healing and Political Acquiescence: The Case of the Zionist Churches in Southern Africa." *Africa* 60,1:1-25.

Schreiter, R.J. 1980. "Issues facing Contextual Theologians Today." *Verbum SVD* 21:267-278.

Schreiter, R.J. 1985. *Constructing Local Theologies*. N.Y.: Orbis.

Schreiter, R.J., ed., 1991. *Faces of Jesus in Africa*. N.Y.: Orbis.

Seago, R.H. n.d. *The Freedom of Forgiveness*. Pinetown, South Africa: City of Life Publications.

Sebahire, M. 1987. "Healing through faith? The Afro-Christian Churches." *Pro Mundi Vita Dossiers* 42:2-26.

Sebidi, L. 1986 "The Dynamics of the Black Struggle and Its Implications for Black Theology." in Mosala, I.J., & Tlhagale, B., eds., *The Unquestionable Right to be Free*, pp. 1-36. N.Y.: Orbis.

Seedat, Y.K., & Meer, F. 1984. "Psycho-Social Hazards of Industrialisation and Urbanisation Among the Racial Groups in Urban South Africans Causing Hypertension." in *Fourth Interdisciplinary Symposium of the College of Medicine of South Africa 5-6 July 1984*, pp. 92-103.

Setiloane, G. 1975. "Confessing Christ Today, from one African Perspective: Man and Community." *Journal of Theology for Southern Africa* 12:29-38.

Setiloane, G. 1978. "How the traditional world view persists in the Christianity of the Sotho-Tswana." in Fashole-Luke, E., Gray, R., Hastings, A., et al, *Christianity in Independent Africa*, pp. 402-412. London: Rex Collings.

Sharp, J.S. 1981. "The Roots and Development of *Volkekunde* in South Africa." *Journal of Southern African Studies* 8:16-36.

Shepperson, A. 1992. "Designating structures: cultural studies, philosophy and semiotics." *Communicatio* 18,1:47-53.

Shorter, A. 1988. *Towards a Theology of Inculturation*. London: Geoffrey Chapman.

Simon, C.M. 1990. "Kinship, illness and therapy management in a rural Transkeian community." *South African Journal of Ethnology* 14,1:11-14.

Simons, H.J. 1957. "Tribal Medicine: Diviners and Herbalists." *African Studies* 16,2:85-92.

Simons, R.C. 1985. "Sorting the Culture-Bound Syndromes." in Simons, R.C., & Hughes, C.C., eds., *The Culture-Bound Syndromes*, pp. 25-38. Dordrecht: Reidel.

Simons, R.C., & Hughes, C.C., eds. 1985. *The Culture Bound Syndromes: Folk Illness of Psychiatric and Anthropological Interest*. Dordrecht: Reidel.

Society for the Propagation of the Faith 1986. *Sects or New Religious Movements: Pastoral Challenge*. Rome: Secretariat for Promoting Christian Unity.

Solle, D. 1987. "'The Moment of Truth'. The Kairos Document from Africa." *Concilium* 192:116-123.

Spiegelberg, H. 1982. *The Phenomenological Movement: A Historical Introduction, 3rd ed. (revised)*. The Hague: Martinus Nijhoff.

Stackhouse, M.L. 1988. "Contextualization, Contextuality, and Contextualism." in Costa, R.O., ed., *One Faith, Many Cultures*. pp. 3-13, N.Y.: Orbis.

Steadman, I. 1988. "Popular Culture and Perfomance." in Tomaselli, K.G., ed., *Rethinking Culture*, pp. 112-136. Bellville: Anthropos.

Stein, H.F. 1979. "The Salience of Ethno-Psychology for Medical Education and Practice." *Social Science and Medicine* 13B:199-210.

Stockwell, E.L. 1985. "Editoral." *International Review of Mission* 74:153-157.

Streek, B. 1990. *Azapo and BCMA September 1990*. Cape Town: a collage of press cuttings.

Stumpf, D. 1985. "Miracles as opposed to amazing events." *S.A. Medical Journal* 67:574.

Stumpf, D. 1986. "A committed doctor's view on healing." in De Villiers, P., ed., *Healing in the name of God*, pp. 215-218. Pretoria: UNISA.

Sullivan, L.E. ed. 1989. *Healing and Restoring: Health and Medicine in the World's Religious Traditions*. N.Y.: Macmillan.

Sundkler, B.G.M. 1948. *Bantu Prophets in South Africa*. London: Lutterworth.

Sundkler, B.G.M. 1961. *Bantu Prophets in South Africa*. London: Oxford University Press. Second Edition.

Sundkler, B. 1976. *Zulu Zion and Some Swazi Zionists*. London: Oxford University Press.

Sunday Times 1991. "Common values begin to emerge." *Sunday Times,* Johannesburg, 18 August p. 20.

Talmon, Y. 1965. "Pursuit of Millenium." in Lessa & Vogt, *Reader in Contemporary Religion*, pp. . N.Y.: Harper & Row.

Theron, J. 1986. "Variation upon variation - a key to a better understanding of the church's ministry of healing. A practical-theological survey." in De Villiers, P.G.R. ed., *Healing in the Name Of God*, pp. 152-174. Pretoria: University of South Africa.

Tlhagale, B. 1983. "Transracial Communication." *Missionalia* 11:113-123.

Tlhagale, B. 1985. "Culture in an Apartheid Society." *Journal of Theology for Southern Africa* 51:27-36.

Tlhagale, B. 1991. "The Anthropology of Liberation." *Journal of Theology for Southern Africa* 76:57-63.

Tomaselli, K.G. 1987. *A Contested Terrain: Struggle Through Culture*. Pietermaritzburg: University of Natal Press.

Tomaselli, K.G. 1988. *Rethinking Culture*. Bellville: Anthropos.

Tomaselli, K. 1992. "The role of the media in promoting intercultural communication in South Africa." *Communicatio* 18,1:60-68.

Tomaselli, K.G. & Shepperson, A. 1991. "Popularising Semiotics." *Communication Research Trends* 11,2:2-20.

Tracy, D. 1989. "Hermeneutical Reflections in the New Paradigm." in Küng, H., & Tracy, D., eds., *Paradigm Change in Theology*, pp. 34-62. Edinburgh: T&T Clark.

Tseng, W., and Mcdermott, J.F. 1981. *Culture, Mind and Therapy: An Introduction to Cultural Psychiatry*. N.Y.: Brunner / Mazel.

Turner, R. 1972, 1980. *The Eye of the Needle*. Johannesburg: Ravan.

Turner, V.W. 1957. *Schism and continuity in an African society: a study of Ndembu religious life*. Manchester: University Press.

Turner, V.W. 1962. *Chihamba, the White Spirit*. Manchester: University Press.

Turner, V.W. 1967. *The forest of symbols: aspects of Ndembu ritual*. New York: Cornell University Press.

Turner, V.W. 1968. *The drums of affliction: a study of religious process among the Ndembu of Zambia*. Oxford: Clarendon Press.

Ukpong, J. 1987. "What is Contextualization." *Neue Zeitschrift für Missionswissenschaft* 43:161-168.

Vail, L. 1989. *The Creation of Tribalism in Southern Africa*. London: James Curry.

Van Der Merwe, H.W., & Schrire, R.A. 1980. *Race and Ethnicity: South African and International Perspectives*. Cape Town: David Philip.

Van Niekerk, A.S. 1985. "Towards a Practical Theology of Healing in the Black Church." *Theologia Viatorum* 13,1:70-82.

Van Rensburg, H.C.J. 1991. "South African health care in change." *South African Journal of Sociology* 22,1:1-9.

Vanderpool, H.Y. 1977. "Is Religion Therapeutically Significant?" *Journal of Religion & Health* 16,4:255-259.

Van Zyl Slabbert, F., & Welsh, D. 1979. *South Africa's options: Strategies for sharing power*. Cape Town: David Philip.

Vela, J.A. 1984. "Un modelo de formación de agentes pastorales en América Latina." *Theologica Xaveriana* 71:141-163.

Verkuyl, J. 1978. *Contemporary Missiology*. Michigan: Eerdmans.

Verryn, T. n.d. *Rich Christian Poor Christian*. Pretoria: The Ecumenical Research Unit.

Villa-Vicencio, C. 1988. *Trapped in Apartheid*. N.Y.: Orbis.

Waite, G. 1975. "The Socio-Political Role of Healing Churches in South Africa." *Ufahamu* 6,3:58-67.

Waliggo, J.M., Roest Crollius, A., et al 1986. *Inculturation: Its Meaning and Urgency*.Kampala: St. Paul-Africa.

Waliggo, J.M. 1986. "Making A Church That Is Truly African." in Waliggo, J.M., et al, *Inculturation Its Meaning And Urgency*, pp. 11-31. Kampala: St. Paul-Africa.

WCC 1982. *Baptism, Eucharist and Ministry: Faith and Order Paper No.111*. Geneva: World Council of Churches.

WCC 1985. "Gospel and Culture: The Working Statement Developed at Riano Consultations." *International Review of Mission* 74: 264-267.

WCC 1986. *Churches' Report on Transnational Corporations*. CCPD Documents No.7. Geneva: World Council of Churches.

WCC 1990a *Joint Working Group Between the Roman Catholic Church and the World Council of Churches, Sixth Report*. Geneva: WCC Publications.

WCC 1990b. *Church and World: Faith and Order Study Document No. 151*. Geneva: WCC Publications.

WCC 1991. *Confessing the One Faith: Faith and Order Paper No. 153*. Geneva: WCC Publications.

Weatherhead, L.D. 1951. *Psychology, Religion and Healing*. London: Hodder & Stoughton.

Welbourn, F.B. 1989. "Healing as a psychosomatic event." In Oosthuizen, G.C., Edwards, S.D., Wessels, W.H.et al, eds., *Afro-Christian Religion and Healing in Southern Africa*, pp. 351-368. N.Y.: Edwin Mellen.

Wellin, E. 1977. "Theoretical Orientations in Medical Anthropology: Continuity and Change Over the Past Half-Century." in Landy, D., ed., *Culture, Disease, and Healing*, pp. 47-58. N.Y.: Macmillan.

Wessels, W.H. 1984. "Transcultural Aspects of Psychiatry." in *Fourth Interdisciplinary Symposium of the College of Medicine of South Africa 5-6 July 1984*, pp. 103-105.

Wessels, W.H. 1985. "Understanding culture-specific syndromes in South Africa - the Western dilemma." *Modern Medicine of South Africa* 9:51-63.

Wessels, W.H. 1989. "Healing Practices in African Independent Churches." in Oosthuizen, G.C., Edwards, S.D., Wessels, W.H.et al, eds., *Afro-Christian Religion and healing in Southern Africa*, pp. 91-108. N.Y.: Edwin Mellen.

West, M. 1974. "People of the Spirit: Charismatic Movement and African Independent Churches." *Journal of Theology for Southern Africa* 7:23-29.

West, M. 1975. *Bishops and Prophets in a Black City*. Cape Town: David Philip.

West, M. 1979. *Social Anthropology in a Divided Society: Inaugural Lecture*. Cape Town: University Press.

Whittaker, J.O. 1966. *Introduction To Psychology*. Philadelphia: W.B. Saunders Company.

Williams, C.S. 1982. *Ritual, Healing, and Holistic Medicine among the Zulu Zionists*. Unpublished Ph.D. Thesis, American University, Washington.

Wimber, J. & Springer, K. 1986. *Power Healing*. London: Hodder & Stoughton.

Wimber, J., & Springer, K. 1987. *Study Guide to Power Healing*. San Fransisco: Harper & Row.

Wise, R.L. 1977. *When There Is No Miracle*. Ventura, Ca: Regal Books.

Wittkower, E.D., & Warnes, H. 1974. "Cultural aspects of psychotherapy." *American Journal of Psychotherapy* 14:566-733.

Wolanin, A. 1987. *Teologia sistematica della missione*. Roma: Editrice Pontificia Università Gregoriana.

Yannoulatos, A. 1985. "Culture and Gospel: Some Observations from the Orthodox Tradition and Experience." *International Review of Mission* 74:185-198.

Yap, P.M. 1977. "The Culture-Bound Reactive Syndromes." in Landy, D., ed., *Culture, Disease, and Healing*, pp. 340-349. N.Y.: Macmillan.

Zola, I. 1972. "Medicine as an institution of social control." *Sociological Review 20*,4: 487-504.

Zulu, P. 1986. "African Indigenous Churches and Relative Deprivation." in Oosthuizen, G.C., ed., *Religion Alive: Studies in the New Movements and Indigenous Churches in Southern Africa*, pp. 151-155. Bergvlei, South Africa: Hodder & Stoughton Southern Africa.

Index

Printed by The Natal Witness Printing and Publishing Company (Pty) Ltd